"Kathy Eldon's memoir is raw, honest, and instantly compelling—an amazing adventure of the heart that enlightens the soul. Thank goodness for this book and for the tremendous source of inspiration that is Kathy Eldon."

—Ricki Lake, television personality

"I couldn't put this book down. It compromised my sleep by keeping me up late at night; it impacted my work by compelling me to put aside things I needed to do so I could 'just read a few pages.' Kathy's story is full of triumph and sorrow, heartbreak, and redemption. A remarkable read."

—Susan Stiffelman, author of *Parenting Without Power Struggles*, therapist, and parenting expert

"The extraordinary memoir of a woman's journey from Iowa to London to Kenya, from all that was safe and predictable to a transformative, dazzling, yet harrowing new life and existence—transforming the depths of pain to the heights of activism."

—Ann Haggart, Annenberg Foundation

"*In the Heart of Life* is not just a memoir, but a journey of the soul looking for the light. Kathy takes us through that journey as if we were right there alongside her—we are taken on a stunning adventure of love, loss, hope, forgiveness, and dreams. A must-read for anyone who has ever loved, lost, and still seeks the answers."

—Elinor Tatum, publisher and editor-in-chief, *Amsterdam News*

"Kathy Eldon shares an extraordinary tale—at times heartbreaking, at times exuberant. Every twist, every turn, every triumph and tragedy reflects a woman facing life's most tender, vulnerable, scary moments and saying . . . YES. Her courage in embracing life inspires me to do the same."

—Lyndon Harris, founder, The Gardens of Forgiveness Project

"Kathy Eldon speaks to the soul of everyone who has endured loss by asking, 'Will I survive?' All of us will face the loss of a loved one in our lifetime—through one means or another. By taking us on her own incredible adventure, Kathy shows us that though we may be wounded, it is indeed possible to survive and to fully love again, but only by keeping our hearts beautifully open to the possibilities of life."

—Dianne Gray, president, Elisabeth Kübler-Ross Foundation

In the Heart of Life

A MEMOIR BY

KATHY ELDON

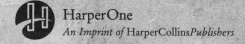

HarperOne
An Imprint of HarperCollins*Publishers*

HarperOne

This is a work of nonfiction. The events and experiences detailed herein are all true and have been faithfully rendered as the author remembered them, to the best of her ability. Some names, identities, and circumstances have been changed in order to protect the privacy and/or anonymity of the various individuals involved.

FIRST EDITION

Designed by Janet M. Evans

Library of Congress Cataloging-in-Publication Data
Eldon, Kathy.
    In the heart of life : a memoir / by Kathy Eldon.—1st ed.
        p. cm.
    ISBN 978–0–06–204862–2
    1. Eldon, Kathy. 2. Eldon, Kathy—Travel—Kenya. 3. Women journalists—Kenya—Biography. 4. Women motion picture producers and directors—United States—Biography. 5. Women philanthropists—United States—Biography. 6. Mothers and sons—Biography. 7. Mothers and daughters—Biography. I. Title.
    PN54499.K42E54 2013
    070.92—dc23
    [B]
    2013000265

13 14 15 16 17   RRD(H)   10 9 8 7 6 5 4 3 2 1

To my beloved Amy and Michael,
who have never, never, never given up on me

You would know the secret of death.

But how shall you find it unless you seek it in the heart of life?

—KAHLIL GIBRAN, *THE PROPHET*

CONTENTS

Prologue

AS A YOUNG WIFE AND MOTHER, I MOVED TO KENYA IN 1969 WITH MY husband Mike and our two small children, Dan and Amy. The wide-open spaces, sparkling sunshine, and brilliant colors of Africa were a rainbow paradise after the gray confines of our London suburb, and almost immediately I felt that I had discovered my roots and my true home—then barely aware that *all* human beings have their origins in East Africa. I came to share the African belief that a spirit exists in each of us and in everything—in the rocks and plants, the trees and animals, the clouds and sky, the stars and sun—though I couldn't accept their belief that those spirits survive death.

But, despite the stimulation of my life as a journalist and an executive in a travel company, like so many others had before me I began to succumb to another aspect of Kenya. Captivated by the concept of life lived as a safari—an exciting journey into the unknown—I became exhilarated by the promise of danger and the seduction of life lived on the edge. Entranced by a new sense of freedom to be and do anything I wanted in a land of far horizons, I lived and loved passionately, even recklessly, soaring higher and higher, as if each day daring death to strike.

And it did—once and nearly twice.

This is the world in which Dan and Amy were growing up, and Dan threw himself into it as wholeheartedly as I did. Still a young boy, he was "adopted" by a Masai family, sharing their brew of fresh cow milk with curdled blood, and tracking wild animals with their young warriors. In his teens, he raised money to lead a team of fellow students from four countries to take funds and supplies to a refugee camp of destitute victims of the civil war in Mozambique. But both he and I tempted fate once too often. I lost my job and my home in Kenya—Dan, much more.

Many years later, in 1993, after I had left behind my life as a wife and writer in Kenya, I was working on a film in Los Angeles. One morning I was awakened by a telephone call telling me that Dan, then covering the Somali civil war as a Reuters photojournalist, had been stoned to death by an angry mob in Mogadishu with three of his colleagues. He was twenty-two.

Numb with grief, Amy and I immediately flew back to Kenya for Dan's memorial service, held on the hills overlooking the vast and glorious expanse of the Great Rift Valley. There our family was joined by hundreds of people from around the world to celebrate the young man who, during his brief life, had become a world-class photographer, global traveler, and passionate crusader for justice. The next day, when we scattered his ashes near the hut of the Masai family who had adopted him as one of their own, I knew I was saying goodbye to our beloved son forever. That night, engulfed by a pain more intense than any I had ever experienced, my brain began swirling with thoughts, memories—and questions. Desperate for release, I yearned to sleep and never awaken again.

Over the next few days, my desperation increased, and only the realization that my daughter—whose loss was as immense as mine—needed my support kept me going. Hoping to find comfort in the company of friends, I flew to London, where I had an apartment; but still I was tortured that Dan's vibrant spirit had been extinguished just as he was beginning to fulfill what he described as his "mission on earth." Even more agonizing was my feeling that I, in some way, bore responsibility for his death. Unable to speak with him, to apologize, ask forgiveness, or seek direction for my shattered life, I knew I would be haunted forever by the incompleteness of our relationship.

But then something very strange happened. One morning the telephone rang and Debbie Gaiger, a young woman I had met at Dan's memorial service in Kenya, asked to speak to me. "I'm sorry to disturb you," she apologized, "but I need to tell you something."

Debbie's voice revealed both hurt and bewilderment as she explained that she had known not only Dan, but also the three others who were killed with him. Finding the tragedy even harder to bear because her private life was a mess, she had searched for help in London, where she was now living. After traditional therapies failed, she had booked an appointment with a highly respected psychic, Mollie Martin, but the visit hadn't gone as she expected.

"I didn't say anything about what had happened in Somalia," Debbie said, "and Mollie didn't know anything about me, but the first thing she said was, 'You're worried about your four friends, the ones who have just died. You can't stop replaying their death over and over in your mind. There's one in particular hovering around you, the charismatic one— young, with the elfin face. It's almost as though he couldn't deal with everything he was seeing and it was time for him to go. He was such a beautiful character, a teacher.'"

"You're really sure you didn't tell her anything?" I asked Debbie, thinking she might have let slip a few clues about the tragedy in Mogadishu.

"Nothing," she vowed. "Absolutely nothing. And I have the tape of the interview to prove it."

Hearing Debbie's story, I decided to go and talk to Mollie Martin myself. If she was claiming my son's spirit was still able to communicate with this world, I wanted proof. Booking under a false name in case she had read anything about Dan, I drove to a quiet street in Chelsea and rang her bell. Over the intercom a woman's voice asked me to let myself in and wait downstairs until she was ready.

While I was turning the pages of a book on the table in the hallway, Mollie Martin called me from the top of the stairs and ushered me into her drawing room, elegant with its old furniture and paintings. She gestured me to one end of a white sofa, while she sat at the other. She seemed a no-nonsense sort of person.

"Don't tell me anything," she commanded, sounding like a strict governess. "I'm afraid I can't guarantee results, but I'll do my best." I pulled out a pad and paper and waited. "You're very angry," she said, her voice softer.

I could feel my mouth tighten. Of course I was angry. I was furious, enraged, heartbroken. But would she know why?

"Your son has died very suddenly," she said. "But although he is no longer here physically, he is very much alive. He is a teacher, and he will continue to teach. In fact, he will encourage and help people he will never meet. He is lovely to work with, a remarkable young man. He was an old soul, and wasn't afraid of death. In fact, he was walking with death and knew that his life would be short."

Amazed at this extraordinarily accurate image of Dan, I felt my innate skepticism battling with my desire, as a grieving mother, to believe that the impossible might be true.

"He's the baby of a group, the hippy," she continued. "He looks about eleven years old—such an open face. You should be very proud. By the way, did you know he used to carry a photo of you?" I nodded. I had found it in his pocket in Nairobi and I had it with me now.

"Now, do you have any special questions about him?" she asked, looking at her watch. Clearly my time was up, so I screwed up my courage to ask the most important of the many questions that had been haunting me.

"Is he okay?"

"He says he's getting settled," she assured me, "but he's still anxious for you to be aware of his presence. Like you, he sometimes feels sad. Because he is physically apart, he misses you, but he can see you."

She sat forward and looked at me intently. "You have tremendous work ahead of you that will be profound and will have an intense creative focus," she said. "You'll be speaking and writing, and you'll be involved in high-profile events around the world, traveling almost constantly. Your son will help you. He had a great purpose, and so do you."

I must have looked shocked, for she added, "Don't be anxious. Just take it one step at a time."

Feeling overwhelmed, I asked one final question: "How will I ever manage to do everything?" Sounding plaintive even to my own ears, I added, "I don't understand why he wants me to take on so much."

There was a pause, and then Mollie beamed.

"Can't you see, Mum?" she said, her voice strong as she relayed his words. "There's so much to do in this world that it's hard to know where to start. But you must understand this: I need help. Most mothers live through their children, but I have to live through you."

It took a moment for all this to sink in. As it did, my natural skepticism came to the fore. "Just a minute," I protested. "Dan never believed in any of this psychic nonsense."

Mollie peered above my left shoulder and seemed to be listening intently. I followed her gaze, but saw nothing. Then she smiled. "He says everyone's entitled to at least one mistake." I had to laugh despite myself. It was typical of Dan to make a joke at an inappropriate moment.

As I was leaving, she stopped me at the door. "There's something else," she said, shaking my hand. "He says that one day you'll write a book."

This is the book. It has taken me a long time to finish, for I have had to make sense not only of my own life, but of Dan's—and Amy's too. Was I responsible for my son's death because of the way I lived my life? Searching for the answer to this question, and to why his terrible death didn't ultimately end his crusade but gave it an astonishing new force, became an exciting journey—a safari as colorful and intriguing as any I had ever made in Kenya or around the world as a journalist in pursuit of gripping stories.

In the Heart of Life is, therefore, an African adventure, a family saga, even a metaphysical mystery, but most of all it's a story about the power of love—and love's ability to heal—even after death. As I began to explore who I was—and what I had done—I felt apprehensive, for in telling the truth I would have to reveal long-held secrets and painful mistakes, as well as bizarre happenings that could best be described as experiences of the spirit. All these broke me, rebirthed me, changed me forever, and made me who I am.

Through writing this book I have learned the truth of Federico Fellini's quote, "There is no ending, no beginning, only the infinite passion of life."

Daylight

HOPE IS A THING WITH FEATHERS
THAT PERCHES IN THE SOUL.

—EMILY DICKINSON

Flying the Nest

RESTLESS, EVEN AS A SMALL CHILD, I OFTEN DREAMED OF FLYING AWAY AND exploring the world, especially in the autumn, when the birds headed south toward Florida, a legendary land of sunshine, beaches, and ever-blooming orange trees. Perched on a stool in our cozy kitchen, I would shut my eyes and imagine that I could leap beyond the long gray days, icy winds, and mounds of dirty snow that were in store for us. But when I jumped, instead of soaring I landed with a thud on the blue linoleum floor of our house in Cedar Rapids, Iowa, a town surrounded by endless cornfields as far as the eye could see.

My family lived in a neat white house set in the middle of a manicured green lawn only two blocks from Grant Wood Elementary School. I had two sisters: beautiful Carolyn, ten years older than I, and saintly Janet, five years my senior. My mischievous brother, John, was sandwiched in between them. I was an afterthought, a clumsy redhead with a permanent grin on my freckled face.

My father, Russell F. Knapp, started in the Depression with absolutely nothing, but over the years he worked in insurance, bought railway cars, and succeeded as a property developer. He eventually became an investment counselor and made lots of money for many people. Sitting on the boards of most of the local community organizations, he always tried to be the first to donate and then convinced those he'd made rich to dip into their pockets too. Dad wore a constant smile and a dashing Borsalino hat to protect his balding head. He was a staunch pillar of our local Methodist church, believing that the fundamentals of a good life were to put God before yourself, value the needs of others, and always be prepared to attempt the impossible. "You can do anything you want," he said, basing his theories on Norman Vincent Peale's book *The Power of Positive Thinking.* "Why, you could even be the president's wife!" In those days it wouldn't have occurred to anyone that a girl could actually be the *president.*

My mother, Louise, had blue eyes, an attractive wide face, rosy cheeks, and long golden hair that she swirled into a bun on the top of her head. Equally idealistic, if not quite so relentlessly upbeat, Mom was my heroine as she raced through her days juggling housework, four active children, myriad charitable works, and my father's busy schedule. Like many women of the day, Mom belonged to lots of women's clubs, but she reserved her passion for the newly formed United Nations organization, which she supported in the only way she knew: at home. Fueled by a desire to unite the world, she enrolled me in German classes at the local college when I was still only in the fifth grade, adding Latin and French tutorials two years later. A creative, quintessential 1950s superwoman with a quick sense of humor, my mother was selfless and rarely complained. She exhibited the stoicism of her mother, a talented musician who tragically went deaf after suffering a case of measles soon after marrying my grandfather.

Sometimes I think my entire family went deaf in the 1950s, when we weren't allowed to discuss anything unpleasant in polite company. Nor, for that matter, were we allowed to argue, swear, or even cry in our household, not to mention say anything that might disrupt the perception that ours was a perfect home.

When I was six years old, this idyllic world collapsed for a time. My mother began to stay upstairs all day with the curtains drawn, and I was not allowed to disturb her; she was "resting," I was told. Then one day she disappeared entirely—my dad took her somewhere in the car—and no one would tell me why. True to my upbringing, I didn't talk about it. Instead, I crept into the kitchen to steal cookies. Somehow, this helped soothe the hurt I felt inside. Looking back at that little girl who was unable to communicate her pain, my heart aches; for that hungry child lived inside of me for decades until something happened that finally set her free.

During my mother's absence, my elder sister was sent off to visit relatives in California. Dad looked after my brother and other sister at home, while I was shipped off to my great-aunt and great-uncle's for what seemed like forever. Much later I learned that my mom had become profoundly depressed and had been hospitalized for six weeks. I recall that even after she returned, and I did too, there was a strange atmosphere lingering in the house.

I often wondered what my mother would have been like had she been able to pursue her love of writing rather than remain just a "housewife." After graduating from college with a degree in journalism, she quickly discovered that it was almost impossible to get a job as a reporter. After my eldest sister was born, she poured her energy into her women's groups and growing brood of children. My mother took me to the library several times a week, and she kept me supplied with journals so I could note everything I saw or heard, including what I ate for breakfast and how my stomach felt when I danced close with Leslie Higgins, the minister's son.

Perhaps my mother's frustrated desire to be a reporter helped nurture my desire to discover what lay beyond the endless cornfields that surrounded our town. Unlike some of my friends, who were content with the peaceful, predictable rhythm of life, I sensed that there was a more complicated reality out there, a place where exciting things *happened*.

Every frigid January I eagerly awaited the annual visit from a group of missionaries who came to speak at St. Paul's Methodist Church, showing home movies of Africa, a dangerous land filled with skinny black children standing by mud huts under blue skies that were too big to fit on the screen. I wanted to be just like Goldie Armstrong, a young missionary from Cedar Rapids whose eyes glowed when she described her work as a teacher in the Congo. After one talk, we children trooped upstairs into the barely heated Sunday school classrooms to create a plaster relief map of Africa, complete with a painted blue line representing the Nile as it snaked its way through countries with exotic names I couldn't pronounce but knew I wanted to explore.

My first chance at overseas travel came in the summer of 1960, when Dad cashed in most of his investments in order to take our family on a galloping "grand tour" through twelve European countries. We even flew to Moscow, the grim, gray center of the Cold War, and finally to Berlin, where the Germans were putting the finishing touches on the ominous wall that divided the city with armed guards and machine gun towers. My German phrases came in handy when I met a young escapee who was exactly my age, fourteen, at a refugee center in West Berlin. Blinking back tears, I watched him try not to cry when describing the friends he had left behind on the other side.

On my return to Iowa I was a different person, for I had discovered that the world was a vast and awesome place and that not everyone was as nice as the folks back home. I couldn't wait to leave again—and learn more. Two years later, inspired by my brother, who had spent a few months in Italy as an American Field Service exchange student, I applied to the program, hoping for a similar assignment.

Thrilled to be one of two students selected from my region, I was a bit stunned when I was assigned to an all-girl, Afrikaans-speaking school run by the Dutch Reformed Church in Bloemfontein, South Africa, a country then best known for its inhumane system of *apartheid*—which means "separateness"—designed to completely separate blacks and "coloreds" (mixed-race people) from the white minority.

My mother bought a "teach yourself Afrikaans" book and in three weeks helped me learn more than three hundred words in a language that made its speakers sound as though they were coughing up phlegm. When I waved goodbye to my family and friends in January 1963, I was beaming. At last I could begin exploring the continent I had dreamed of visiting since I was a little girl.

Unfortunately, there was little to explore in Bloemfontein, a neat little town surrounded by *mealie* (corn) fields that bore an uncanny resemblance to Cedar Rapids. Even more perplexing was the fact that black

Africans seemed to be almost invisible in "Bloem." Unless they were work-ing in white households, black servants had to live in distant townships. When I asked my Boer friends why that was, they patiently explained that God had ordained that blacks and coloreds were inferior and must remain separate from the superior "Europeans" (whites) under apartheid.

After seven months in Bloemfontein, I left South Africa in July 1963, entranced by memories of magnificent landscapes and the friendliness of its diverse peoples, though troubled by the dark cloud of apartheid that wouldn't lift until Nelson Mandela was released from prison almost thirty years later.

A year after my return, at the age of eighteen I enrolled at Wellesley College outside Boston, an institution known for its ivy-covered towers and fiercely intellectual atmosphere. Its motto, *Non ministrari sed minis-trare*, "Not to be ministered unto but to minister," captured the essence of what was traditionally expected of the all-women student body who were being educated to become selfless wives, caring mothers, and wor-thy volunteers, capable not only of changing diapers but of transforming the world around them. But by the time I graduated in 1968, Wellesley superwomen like Hillary Clinton (a year behind me) and Diane Sawyer (a year ahead) would also be expected to leap tall buildings while run-ning multinational corporations or even, for that matter, serving as the president of the United States.

When I first arrived in college, during those tumultuous transition years in the mid-1960s, we were forced to adhere to a strict "no men" rule in the dorms. Actually, that was fairly easy, at least in my case, for at an all-women's college men were difficult to come by. It wasn't until the spring of my sophomore year that I finally managed to snare a Harvard man—a brooding art history major. My friends considered David a "catch."

I readily accepted his invitation to discuss abstract expressionism in his room. I recall the visit through a haze of alcohol, self-administered in an attempt to loosen my Iowa Methodist inhibitions. Intensely self-conscious, I waited several months to take my Playtex girdle off, and even then my slip remained firmly in place.

Aware of my innocence, my friends suggested that one day I was going to need the Pill. I borrowed the dorm engagement ring, a cheap fake diamond from Woolworth's that was circulated as needed, and visited a grimy clinic in South Boston, where I explained that I was engaged to be married, a necessary prerequisite in the state of Massachusetts for getting contraceptives. The doctor, apparently accustomed to the lies of red-faced Wellesley girls, barely looked up as he handed a prescription to me.

When David and I finally managed to "do it," I felt vaguely disappointed and hoped things would improve with practice. But nothing seemed to help, even though every weekend my lover's fingers explored my body, relentlessly searching for something that would give him satisfaction and me pleasure. Too inhibited to discuss with my classmates what was happening with him (or more accurately, *not* happening), and lacking the knowledge or ability to fake an orgasm, much less actually have one, I felt like a complete failure. I was desperate to hang on to this relationship with a man who had all the right qualities to be a fine husband and father, so I pretended everything was great. Still, returning to Wellesley on Sunday nights, I felt sore and unsettled, in need of a bowl of ice cream to make me feel better.

We talked about getting engaged, but instead, just before summer vacation of my junior year, he wrote to tell me that he was marrying a Radcliffe student who, he said, was far less inhibited than I. For several weeks I moped, but by June I realized that life was much more fun without my dark lover, who had always seemed vaguely disappointed with me.

By the time I flew back to Iowa for the summer of 1967 to work as a camp counselor, I was feeling upbeat as I surveyed my charges, a tent full of plump, spotty teenage girls who swatted mosquitoes and gossiped about the Boy Scouts across the river. However, after a week of dealing with their hormonal craziness, I was ready to ditch the wooded confines and readily accepted an invitation for a blind date with Mike Eldon, a dashing twenty-one-year-old Englishman on an internship with Quaker Oats in Cedar Rapids. Having recently graduated from university in England, he would return home in the fall to look for a full-time job.

Over dinner, Mike told me he had been born in Haifa, Israel, of Jewish-Romanian refugees. He and his parents had immigrated to London when he was three, settling in the arty, intellectually stimulating suburb of Hampstead. He had read countless books and plays and was smart, funny, and cultured. With his shock of floppy black hair, Mike reminded me of an English Dustin Hoffman, though more exotic. Despite my determined efforts to forget about men, by the end of the evening I was totally smitten, even more so when he gathered me in his arms under my parents' blazing porch light for a goodnight kiss that left both of us quivering as though we had been electrocuted. Later, feeling positively giddy, I pulled out my journal and wrote that I had finally met a man who made me laugh.

Despite the intense physical attraction, intimacy was difficult to come by, since I was living at home and the local parks were well patrolled. Conversation about art, music, films, and people flowed easily between us, but we found it hard to talk about our feelings. I found this reticence a bit of a relief after David's intense scrutiny of every aspect of me. Even so, as Mike's end-of-summer departure neared, we spoke of our determination to see each other again as soon as possible, and I offered to visit him over the Christmas holiday.

I managed to scrape together three hundred dollars for the ticket to London on Icelandic Airlines. On a rare phone call with him just before my departure, he sheepishly told me that his company was sending him on a training course elsewhere in England and he wouldn't return until four days before I was due to fly back to America. I tried to keep a brave face when he explained that he had made a reservation for me at the Friends International House, a cheap lodging house for students.

It was dark and rainy when I arrived at Heathrow Airport and made my way by Underground—London's subway—to the hostel, where my bleak little room reeked of boiled cabbage from the kitchen downstairs. Despairing at the prospect of a week there, I remembered that a Wellesley friend had stayed with a doctor and his wife in their plush home in Cadogan Square when she was studying in London the previous summer.

They had asked her to pass on their telephone number to other Welles-ley students visiting London. Gathering my courage, I picked up the phone, and the doctor kindly offered a room.

On my arrival, I discovered that Dr. Kahn, a trim, sprightly seventy-year-old with salt-and-pepper hair and quizzical eyes, had just become a widower: his beloved wife had committed suicide in their bedroom. Overruling my protests that I should leave, Dr. Kahn said that having me stay would help him revive his *joie de vivre*. Over the next few days I felt like Eliza Doolittle as he escorted me to elegant hotels.

Five days into my visit I went to bed early with mild cramps. When I heard Dr. Kahn's footsteps in the corridor that evening, I called out and asked if he had any aspirin. His body was silhouetted against the light when he entered my room and sat down on a chair by my bed. "I will just rub your tummy and make it feel better," he said quietly.

I didn't want my stomach rubbed, just an aspirin, but already his well-manicured hand had begun massaging my stomach. I tried to relax under his touch initially, but I froze when his fingers moved lower—then lower still. I wanted to tell him to stop but thought it would be rude, so I feigned sleep as his breath came in gasps and then a great sigh.

After he left, I lay fuming for a long time, furious with myself for not telling him to leave. The next morning I stayed in my room until he had gone out somewhere, then took a cab to the Friends International House. Feeling dirty, I couldn't wait to shower. Afterward I still felt unclean and guilty, as though I were to blame for the incident.

A day later, Mike returned to London, but I was staying on an all-female floor with no men allowed, and he was living at home, so our time together was frustrating.

After four days, I flew back to America, to learn that my high school prom date had been killed in Vietnam, a reality that jolted me out of my ivy-covered tower. Martin Luther King Jr.'s murder in April was another blow. Suddenly, as America was exploding in protests, college seemed irrelevant, and I couldn't wait to graduate and do something that *mat-tered*. In June of 1968, I left Wellesley with a degree in art history. Unlike most of my friends, who were soon to be married or to begin working in publishing in New York, I applied to the Peace Corps, determined to fulfill my long-held dream of returning to Africa.

While waiting, I returned home to Iowa and sent in an application for a short-term job teaching elementary school art, though I didn't mention that my degree had been in art *history* and that the closest I had come to *applied* art was learning to paint frescoes in the manner of Leonardo da Vinci—of questionable use when dealing with nine-year-olds. Somehow, I got the job. Wearing my homemade loopy earrings and long flowing skirts, I entertained my students with songs by Earth, Wind, and Fire and prayed that the youngsters wouldn't destroy the classroom. I hoped that the Peace Corps would rescue me before I had to endure a long Iowa winter.

But by January I was still waiting, and as the days grew colder and the nights seemed longer, I felt that life was passing me by. There was no one as interesting as Mike to date in Cedar Rapids, and yet his letters were so few and far between that I felt out of touch. Things improved when a local CBS television affiliate hired me to demonstrate arts and crafts on air. I invested in stacks of books about how to make tissue-paper flowers, papier-mâché napkin holders, tie-dyed T-shirts, and toothpick sculptures and practiced the techniques that seemed most promising.

Apparently the ratings were terrific for my segment of the show, probably perceived more as a comedy act than an illuminating journey into the arts. Over the next few months I graduated from making wire mobiles to conducting an in-depth interview with an expert on poison ivy. Although still hoping for the Peace Corps assignment, I became intrigued with the idea of working as a broadcast journalist in Chicago or New York and applied to CBS in Chicago for a job. But as summer approached with no offers, I grew increasingly depressed about my chances of ever leaving Cedar Rapids. Every night as I listened to the roars of a lonely lion imprisoned in a cramped cage in Beaver Park I yearned for Mike—and a new life.

Suddenly, to my amazement, in June of 1969 Mike announced that he was coming to Iowa on vacation to see me. Coincidentally, that same week I was offered both a job in the Peace Corps and a position as a trainee television presenter in Chicago. I fully intended to pursue an exciting career, but *after* I took care of item number one—Prince Charming.

My parents, concerned about "what the neighbors would say," insisted that Mike should not stay in my apartment, but remain under the watchful eye of my brother, which meant that again we had little time to be alone. Our conversations were lively and fun, and kissing each other again left us both vibrating with excitement. I knew I was in love with Mike, whose sparkling wit kept me laughing, even though I had no idea how he really felt about me. As his departure approached, I worried that we might be separating forever. Two days before he was to leave, however, coached (I later learned) by my brother's wife, he finally managed to pop the question—just as we emerged from a dip in the unheated swimming pool in my apartment complex. I shivered uncontrollably as he struggled to get the words out. "Will . . . you . . . marry . . . ?"

"*Yes!*" I shouted, grabbing a towel and sprinting for the apartment to call my parents. Mike returned to England that night.

Two months later he flew back to Iowa, just three days before the wedding. There was little time to talk during the frenzied round of parties, but I adored my tall, dark, mysterious fiancé and couldn't wait to begin our new life together. Following the half-Jewish, half-Methodist service in my parents' home, my sister Janet pressed a packet into my hand. Later, when I opened it, I discovered a book entitled *Love Without Fear*, with graphic descriptions of acts I didn't want to even think about between a man and woman, some of which included licking and sucking bits of the anatomy that weren't, in my opinion, edible. Blushing, I stuffed it in my bag before Mike could spot it.

Our first night together, we lay on a damp blanket by the side of a lake in northern Iowa. Relieved to be safely married at last, I wanted more than anything to really know this man. With this in mind, I slid closer to him as we both admired the blanket of stars above. "A penny for your thoughts," I offered. Mike took me in his arms. My whole body began to hum as I felt the strength of his embrace. He put his finger up to my lips. "Enough talk," he whispered, and began to kiss me.

2

Swinging London

IN SEPTEMBER OF 1969 MY NEW HUSBAND AND I ARRIVED IN "SWINGING London," famous for the Beatles, the dueling Mods and Rockers, painter David Hockney, and the delicious Mary Quant. Carnaby Street was at its height then, reflecting a rollicking culture that thumbed its nose at the world. There seemed no limit to the possibilities in such a brave new world. But alas, it was soon clear that for American women, there were few job opportunities. After being rejected by the BBC and a string of publishing companies, I finally accepted a low-paid position stocking shelves in a Primrose Hill gift shop. I wasn't exactly living my dream of changing the world, but we needed the money badly: the rent on our tiny studio apartment cost nearly as much as Mike made as a trainee at International Computers, Ltd., the British equivalent of IBM.

At least we were enjoying married life. Finally away from the embarrassing constraints of my family's scrutiny, we began to relax and get to know each other. With no money to go out, we entertained our equally impoverished friends at home. Our double bed served as the living room sofa, and we sat for hours on it with our friends, talking and telling stories. We had even more fun *in* the bed after they went home.

Every Sunday we ate lunch with Mike's parents, Gaby and Bruno, and his eighteen-year-old sister, Ruth, in their comfortable apartment in the "intellectual" north London suburb of Hampstead, where many East Europeans had found refuge after World War II. His parents had been born in Romania, and I was fascinated by their stories of how they had met and fallen in love against the backdrop of the struggle between Nazi Germany and Communist Russia.

Bruno was a handsome if stern man. In his youth he had worked with Shell in Romania until the persecution of the Jews had forced him to escape the country in a tiny sailboat. Eventually he had managed to reach Palestine, where he met the vivacious Gaby, another Romanian exile, whose family had taken refuge there at the beginning of the war. They were married soon afterward. Gaby's entire family was safely reunited in Israel, as was Bruno's. Together with three-year-old Mike, they immigrated to London in 1946, and Bruno once again found a job with Shell as the head of personnel training. I felt more comfortable with Gaby, who was a fabulous cook.

Mike and I celebrated our first Christmas Eve with his parents, who surprised me with a tree and all the trimmings, with lots of Romanian food and champagne. That was the night Mike and I forgot the foam (a popular, if fallible, alternative contraceptive to the Pill).

After a few weeks, I felt queasy in the morning a couple days in a row, and I suspected I was pregnant. Despite my surprise at conceiving a baby so quickly after marriage, I was ecstatic to think that I would have Mike's child, for we were reveling in each other and in the joy of simply being together. He was pleased too, if a little daunted. My favorite times, during those months of pregnancy, were when we shared a quiet dinner together, talking about his news of the day, then blasted "Proud Mary" by Creedence Clearwater Revival and danced, even when I was hugely pregnant. The evening usually ended when our upstairs neighbor thumped on the floor with her broom, wanting to go to sleep.

I went into labor on September 18, 1970, induced a week early because I got tired of waiting and convinced the doctor that my dates were wrong and the baby was overdue. Mike and I named our firstborn Daniel, which means "beloved of God." It seemed appropriate, as he had been conceived on Christmas Eve.

Once Dan was quietly settled in my arms, I stared into his eyes, feeling a jolt of recognition as he peered back at me. Surely we had known each other before! I whispered his name, marveling at the idea that this small creature was mine. I should have said "ours," of course, but whenever Mike turned up, he seemed like an alien to me, his face too bristly and his voice too loud. It wasn't fair, but just then all my love was focused on my baby.

Dan's arrival meant that we had to move—this time (with Mike making a bit more) to a two-bedroom apartment on the third floor of a large and gracious Victorian house on tree-lined Belsize Avenue. We bought a trendy avocado three-piece suite from Heal's and covered the walls with prints by Toulouse-Lautrec and Modigliani. Determined to stimulate our baby as much as humanly possible, I painted everything—walls, ceiling, and wood parts of the furniture—bright yellow and lined his cradle with an ever-changing selection of greeting cards. Handmade mobiles hovered above him at all times, and Mike and I crafted toys and puzzles, finger puppets, even a climbing frame.

Those efforts seemed to pay off, for Dan turned into a curious little boy with chubby cheeks and alert sparkling eyes that missed nothing. Despite loving him with an intensity that startled me, at twenty-four I yearned for a bit of time on my own, away from the demands of full-time mothering.

When Dan was two and a half, I took a job as an art teacher at the American School in London, where most of the children were the offspring of wealthy expatriates and celebrities such as Julie Andrews, Lauren Bacall, and Jason Robards. I was able to ride my bicycle to the school, so I managed to get in some exercise. Terrified by the rigorous job and my thin résumé, I spent the first week bluffing my way through the classes.

Dan loved visiting my chaotic open-plan classroom, so I supplied him with paint, brushes, crayons, and glue to keep him busy while I did my best to stay one step ahead of my students. It took only three weeks to use up my entire repertoire of arts and crafts projects, at which point I pored over library books for inspiration.

In the fourth week of teaching I discovered I was pregnant again. Meanwhile, Mike had taken a year off to study at the London Business School in Regent's Park, and he was overwhelmed with papers and exams. For the next seven months I battled fatigue and nausea while juggling Dan's schedule, my work, housecleaning, cooking, and helping Mike with his courses. Recalling my mother's seemingly effortless mothering skills, I felt deeply inadequate to the task. Over time, a litany played in my head: do more, don't complain—be Superwoman!

I enrolled Dan at a Rudolf Steiner nursery school just around the corner from our apartment. The school emphasized the role of art and music for youngsters, and I marveled at the tiny students engulfed in blue smocks, swaying gently to classical music as they swirled pastel colors on large pieces of dampened paper.

A week before our new baby was due, I quit teaching and, exhausted and anemic, went to the hospital for a rest. A few days later I went into labor with Mike by my side.

"That's it; you're nearly there! Push!" The voices seemed far away, but everything came into vivid focus when the squirmy body was held up for me to see.

"Amy Louise," I cried, reaching out to gather her into my arms. As with Dan, I felt I had always known our pretty gypsy baby, with her dark wavy hair and rosebud lips. Peaceful and sweet, she looked like a female version of our son, only pinker. Dan was deeply unenthusiastic about Amy's arrival, but at nearly four years of age he was smart enough to torture his GI Joes instead of his baby sister.

Suddenly our third-floor walk-up was inconvenient and too small for our growing family, so we bought a large, remarkably inexpensive house in the frightfully respectable suburb of Mill Hill. We managed to visit the neighborhood only twice before purchasing the house, both times during the day, and thought we were getting a fantastic deal. Mike's commute would be quick on the Underground, I could get involved in the local community, and the children would adore their spacious new backyard. Life would be perfect for all of us.

3

Nightmare in Mill Hill

ONCE WE MOVED INTO OUR NEW HOUSE, WE REALIZED WHY IT HAD BEEN SO cheap; the M-1 Motorway that cut through Mill Hill was so close that during rush hour traffic mornings and evenings we couldn't carry on a conversation in the backyard without shouting. Even worse, after the move Mike's company unexpectedly transferred him. The new location meant that his commute to his job as a computer executive expanded from a mere fifteen minutes on the Underground to a grueling hour and a half by car each way—often in rain, sleet, or darkness. Strung out from his long drive home at the end of the day, he barely had the energy to nod to us before sitting down to dinner.

I was determined to love my new life as a suburban mother. After all, I had everything most women dreamed of: a nice house, a good husband—and a boy and a girl. Who could ask for more? Every morning I dressed up to walk Dan to school, pushing Amy in her fancy pram. Once back home from delivering Dan, I spent my days decorating our new home.

The highlights of our Mill Hill time were dinners with our closest friends, Julie and Kerry Woodward, who had bought our old flat in Belsize

Park. He was a gentle Welsh conductor; she, a fiery singer from New York. Over coffee one evening, Kerry told us about their latest project, producing an opera by a German-Czech composer named Viktor Ullmann. In 1942 the Nazis had deported Ullmann to the concentration camp Terezin, or Theresienstadt, where (because it was a "model" camp—a piece of propaganda window-dressing) the arts were encouraged and he was allowed to continue composing. A group of prisoners there had planned to perform Ullmann's new piece, *The Emperor of Atlantis*—but at the last minute the Germans stopped them and sent Ullmann to Auschwitz and his death in October 1944.

Somehow his fellow musicians had managed to hide and preserve most of the fragile pages of the opera's manuscript score. Now, thirty years later, the protectors of it had asked Kerry if he could arrange for the opera to be produced. But as Kerry studied the pages, he found that certain passages were missing and others didn't make sense. However, he had recently met Rosemary Brown, a medium who had dedicated much of her life to writing down compositions supposedly transmitted or channeled through her by long-dead composers. Kerry had been skeptical of these claims at first, but after hearing that the BBC had produced several programs about Rosemary, he decided to talk to her about the manuscript.

"It was incredible!" he reported to us one evening. He explained that he had told her nothing about the purpose of his visit, but when they had settled down and he had pulled the manuscript from his case, she had asked him to put it back as it was giving off a nauseating smell. Lighting a cigarette to mask the stench of death, she said that an emaciated man with a shaved head was present in the room. With the manuscript still in his briefcase, Kerry began asking Rosemary a list of questions he had prepared about the music. "Change that A-flat to a B" came one suggestion, relayed by Rosemary from the spirit, or "Play that measure with a slower tempo."

Kerry said that when he returned home, he applied Rosemary's various instructions, and to his surprise they resolved virtually all the problems. After he had finished his account to us that evening, I suggested that we invite Rosemary Brown to dinner. I thought it would be easier to spot if she was a fraud at home.

I don't know what I was expecting, but certainly not the woman who looked like a middle-aged Sunday school teacher when she turned up at our door wearing a sensible cardigan, a wool skirt, and thick black stockings. At first, Rosemary seemed hesitant to talk about her invisible contacts, but when pressed, she told us that she had been seven years old when she was first aware of a spirit; he had said his name was Franz Liszt. He remained only briefly but promised to return when she grew up, to "give her music." In fact it was nearly thirty years before he eventually reappeared, suddenly sitting beside her as she was practicing the piano.

It seemed as though his spirit began to animate her hands as if they were a pair of gloves, she said, and she began to play exquisite pieces that she had never heard before and never would have dreamed she could manage. Soon he started to dictate long compositions to her. In the beginning, she made many mistakes, for she knew little about transcription, but as she grew more adept, Liszt brought other composers to work with her. Experts who studied the pieces identified them as being unknown works that closely resembled the styles of Monteverdi, Beethoven, Berlioz, Chopin, Brahms, Debussy, and Rachmaninoff.

Rosemary Brown's story about consulting ghostly composers seemed absurd to me. Iowans don't believe in anything they can't see.

"Are there any spirits in our house tonight?" I asked, trying to keep a straight face.

"Of course there are," Rosemary said calmly. "In fact, this place is filled with an unusually large congestion of visitors. Each of us is surrounded by invisible entities, spirits, guardian angels, guides—call them what you will."

"What about me?" Julie asked, one eyebrow raised. "I'm Jewish. Do I have a guardian angel too?"

"Everyone does," Rosemary said, turning to focus on the far end of our living room, where she said the spirits were gathered. I concentrated hard on the patch she was studying, yet saw nothing but a wall badly in need of cleaning.

"I can't see anything," I said, skeptically.

Rosemary turned to look at me, a smile playing on her face. "As a matter of fact, your grandfather is here."

Good guess, I thought. Most people of my age probably had at least one dead grandfather. But her next remark was more difficult to dismiss. She continued, "Floyd says that he hopes Mamie recovers quickly from her fall."

My mouth dropped open. My grandfather's name, Floyd, wasn't common, nor was Mamie, his pet name for my grandmother—and she had recently broken a hip. Rosemary's knowledge of those details was hard to explain, so I looked around again for signs of a ghostly presence.

"Don't worry if you can't see him," she said. "He says that one day it will all make sense to you. For now, just be open to the existence of spirit guides around you who can channel information to you. You can ask for help at any time, but use them only for good."

Later that night, lying in bed, I reviewed what had happened in our living room. Although I was fascinated by Rosemary's observations and impressed by the BBC connection, I wasn't particularly interested in her music and had absolutely no plans to use my so-called spirit guides, for good or otherwise. My life was far too busy already, without adding conversations with dead people.

Despite the bright spots that were our regular evenings with Julie and Kerry, my spirit was starting to die in Mill Hill. We were too far from central London for me to teach there, and I shared little in common with our very proper neighbors. With nothing to occupy me outside our home, my days seemed long and dreary. The din of the motorway carved a nervous hole in my stomach, and I soon grew to despise the ubiquitous net curtains and isolation of our very respectable suburb. I was bursting to experience more of the world and do something important with my life, not just be a mother. I finally found a job as a home tutor for a young girl with psoriasis, which filled a couple of hours a day, but even that work didn't stimulate my mind or soul. Mike's job grew even more demanding, and most nights he fell asleep in front of the television, leaving me feeling frustrated and alone. I needed more time with him but felt guilty asking for it, aware of the sacrifices he was making for us.

We talked occasionally about the possibility of his changing jobs, but so far nothing promising had come up. Sometimes, on days when we were stuck inside and I couldn't stand the monotony any longer, I would slip out on my own to the pedestrian bridge over the six-lane highway and race to the far side and back, shouting at the top of my lungs. After I returned with a hoarse throat and flushed face, Dan would stare at me as though I had gone crazy. Which, in fact, I suppose I had. After two years in the suburbs I still hated being isolated at home with two small children, however much I adored them.

There may have been another reason for my frustrations. However well my husband and I usually got along, I had never experienced the "climactic sensations" I had read about in the book about marital relations that my sister had so thoughtfully given me after our wedding. Hard as I tried, and passionate as I felt, I couldn't seem to let go. Embarrassed to talk about such things, even with my female friends, I didn't tell Mike about the tensions building inside me. It may sound strange, given the reputation of the 1970s as a time of sexual permissiveness and free-love communes, but Mike was inexperienced when we got married, and I was too inhibited to bring up sex with anyone—not even the nurse at my family planning clinic.

I expended some of my nervous energy by baking, producing cakes and cookies that I distributed to the neighbors so I could bake (and eat) some more. Ever since arriving in Mill Hill, I had been bingeing—in private, of course though I tried not to swallow the food that I chewed.

My emotional state wasn't helped by the fact that the constant roar of the motorway day and night made sleeping difficult, and I was haunted by a recurring nightmare. I would wake up, gasping, trying to rid myself of the memory of a hawk rising on crimson wings into the grainy sky, flying fast toward a distant point of light. Then suddenly it would smash against an invisible barrier and slowly, soundlessly spiral down. Blood-spattered feathers lay scattered around its body, now limp on the ground.

"What's wrong?" Mike mumbled when I woke up one night moaning.

"I'm sorry, darling. It's that dream again." I lay quietly, not wanting to disturb him further. He needed his sleep. In the darkness, the alarm clock glowed beside me: three in the morning. I tried to relax, but my mind was too active. I crept out of bed, padded down the hallway, and opened Amy's door a crack. The glow of the nightlight revealed her tiny shape, half-buried beneath a three-year-old's stash of dolls, books, and toys. I smiled at the sight of her clothes neatly laid out on the floor in the shape of a headless little girl.

In Dan's room I picked my way through his muddle of paint boxes, racing cars, art projects from school, and clothes. He lay on the top bunk, one foot jutting out from under the animal-print bedspread. Stepping back, I nearly tripped over a sketchbook. It was one I had leafed through earlier that day, filled with detailed renderings of people, cars, and airplanes. I had been impressed to see that he had incorporated small details in his sketch of a Land Rover, replicating even the brand name of the tires and the curve of the oversize bumper. A few pages later, the drawings had changed suddenly and I had marveled at illustrations of elaborate cathedrals, mosques, and temples—places we'd never seen—each one created from hundreds of dots like a pointillist painting. The colors were luminous, the images haunting.

I headed out of Dan's room and back down the hallway, trying to ignore the full-length mirror that stood like a sentry on the landing. It reflected an image I had come to hate: a much too well rounded woman with shoulder-length auburn hair wearing rumpled pajamas, a shapeless Norwegian sweater, and mismatched socks. It was too expensive to leave the heat on at night, and it was freezing if I had to get up in the wee hours, so I dressed—or rather, undressed—accordingly.

I frowned, patting my stomach and sucking in my full cheeks. There had to be bones in there somewhere. As I stared at myself I felt hollow, nondescript, vacant. Although I was living what seemed like a perfect life, sometimes I felt strangely apart from the family I adored. It was as though the real me were sitting on my shoulder, watching, while the pretend me acted out the role of happy mother for the benefit of others. The real part of me felt hungry and restless, as though there were something missing. I most certainly did not want to lose what I had, but still I longed for something more—though what it might be or where it might be found I didn't know.

"Stop it," I said out loud, adding silently, Be grateful for what you've got. Shutting down the stirrings of rebellious thought and vowing never to look in the mirror again, I headed back to bed and lay down next to Mike, but my eyes stayed open. It was impossible to deny, even to myself, that after three years in Mill Hill, I was feeling increasingly desperate. Now twenty-nine, I could see my life stretching before me—a monotonous run to senility. Would I ever do anything significant? I sat up suddenly, switched on the reading light, and began to write in my journal:

> After a while you stop hoping, asking, and expecting. You suppress the questions, but always in the back of your mind you are wondering if, and how—and when?

The answer seemed clear: never. Squeezing my eyes shut, I prayed for an imminent transfer for Mike.

It was July of 1977. Sheets of rain drummed the windows of our house, the garden was ankle deep in mud, and our children's shrieks competed with the din of traffic outside and cartoons on television. The telephone rang.

"Darling," Mike said, in a voice that sounded unusually cheerful. "Are you sitting down?"

I lowered myself onto the sagging avocado sofa in the living room.

"Kathy," he continued eagerly, "you won't believe . . ."

I held my breath.

"How would you like to move to Nairobi, Kenya?"

I assured him I'd like nothing better, and we soon signed off, Mike promising to bring full details on his return that evening. Hanging up the phone, I grabbed my bewildered children and twirled them around the room.

My enthusiasm was genuine—not just to leave Mill Hill but to return to Africa. I knew very little about Kenya, but in the coming days I gleaned what I could from reading, among other things, *Out of Africa*, a poignant account by Danish author Karen Blixen (written under the pen name Isak Dinesen) about her struggles to run a coffee farm on the Ngong Hills just outside of Nairobi. Her husband, a brilliant and philandering hunter, is always away "on safari," but she finds a soul mate in his hunting partner, Denys Finch Hatton, a scholarly Englishman who is spellbound by the stories she tells him in the evenings by firelight. I imagined myself flying, as she did, in a small plane over verdant grasslands teeming with game, catching a glimpse of a man-eating lion or gazing up at a starlit African sky. I counted the days until our departure.

We left Mill Hill amidst a frantic blur of packing and goodbyes. We found a family to rent our house and sent a crate of our belongings to Kenya by ship. Our two sets of parents thought we were off on a grand adventure that would be great for the kids, but not everyone shared those sentiments. When we threw a farewell bash, we discovered that most of our friends believed we had taken leave of our senses.

"You can't get a decent education for the children in Kenya," our friend Paula said, her voice rising a notch as she added, "And what about malaria? Not to mention blackwater fever—or the riots in Soweto?"

Aside from being ignorant about African geography, Paula and her husband had always seemed to me old before their time, pursuing stability and security to the exclusion of almost everything else. Now that I was focused on the joy of being four thousand miles from the fumes and roar of the M-1 Motorway, I could answer them blithely, "Don't worry, it won't be long before we're back. Two years will go by in a flash."

But secretly, as we stored our wedding china in the attic, I hoped we would never return.

4

Make Believe You're Brave

"ARE WE OVER KENYA YET?" DAN ASKED, HIS PALE FACE REFLECTING HIS excitement. At seven, he was too restless to sleep and kept opening the airplane shade to peer down as the early light crept across the earth, illuminating the vast expanse of desert below. Looking over his shoulder, I could make out huge craters in a desolate moonscape, then caught sight of a long, thin sliver of water shimmering in the rays of the rising sun; given how close we were to our arrival time, it had to be Lake Turkana. As the sun rose higher, an irregular patchwork of fields appeared, flowing over green hills. The engine tone changed and the plane tilted.

"Fasten your seat belt, Mummy," Dan advised me, sliding back into his seat. "We're landing!"

It was just minutes after dawn, but the sunlight was dazzling when we stepped from the plane. With excitement welling up in me, I could barely restrain myself from letting out a whoop of joy. Although I had never been to Kenya, it was as if I'd come home.

I was not the only one bubbling with energy after the long flight. Dan raced down the ramp, halting wide-eyed at the bottom when confronted by a sea of cheerful black faces. Amy stared suspiciously at the ground crew and gripped my hand as we breathed in the cool, thin air of Nairobi, more than a mile above sea level. Mike, nearly crippled with luggage, brought up the rear.

"*Jambo sana!*" A chorus of hellos greeted us as we pushed our way through the milling crowds into the terminal and were surrounded by a mass of shouting taxi drivers waving placards in the air. One, wearing a grimy baseball cap and flip-flops, grabbed the handle of the battered luggage trolley Mike had nabbed and, ignoring our protests, dragged it straight to his ancient Peugeot. When I tried to open the door of the taxi, the handle fell off in my hand. Mike helped the driver tie our suitcases (stuffed with tropical suits, malaria prophylactics, and jars of peanut butter) onto the roof while I sank into the broken seat and took a deep breath. Our wooden crate of household furnishings was coming later by sea, God willing, if the contents weren't scavenged on arrival in the Kenyan port of Mombasa. I had begun this adventure with such hope, thinking that it would lead us as a family to the best, finest lives we could ever dream of. Now Mike and I had to make that dream come true.

His company put us up during the settling-in phase at the Fairview Hotel on the edge of downtown Nairobi. Though the whitewashed cottages were simple and the furnishings looked as if they might have come from a condemned hospital, the gardens were a lush tangle of bougainvillea and other tropical plants. Towering palms, mauve jacarandas, and soaring trees provided shade for the hotel's children's playground. In the intense sunlight, the colors were luminous, and the fragrances—especially the sensuous scent of roses and gardenias and the night-blooming jasmine outside our cottage—were unlike anything I had ever experienced.

Every morning Mike put on a long-sleeve white shirt, dark suit, and conservative tie, while the children and I dressed in our newly purchased clothes: Dan in Kenya-print shirts and shorts and Amy in pretty dresses fashioned from *kikoy* fabric (normally worn by African women draped around their bodies). I wore one of a collection of brightly colored skirts and tops I had commissioned in a hole-in-the wall Indian tailor's shop on Biashara (Bazaar) Street stacked to the ceiling with bolts of imported silk, satin, and vividly printed African cotton. Seated for breakfast at a table covered with starched white cloths and holding a vase of miniature orchid stems from the garden, we guzzled fresh guava, lime, and watermelon juices, nibbled sweet papaws and mangoes, and bit into hard, wrinkled passion fruit, whose tiny black seeds spurted into our mouths.

Dan and Amy, spoiled by indulgent waiters who at lunch and dinner slipped them extra desserts and called them *memsahib kidogo* and *bwana kidogo* (little mistress and little master), quickly settled into the hotel's delights, leaving Mike and me free to entrust them to a babysitter and explore Nairobi. Every evening there was something exciting to do with the expatriates from Mike's new company and our rapidly growing collection of new friends: concerts and films, opera and ballet performances, diplomatic gatherings, endless dinner parties, Sunday curry parties, and get-togethers to enjoy the infamous "sundowners"—massive cocktails served at dusk. Although I had never worn long dresses in England, there were many opportunities to wear the four formal gowns I had been told to bring for special occasions.

But no matter how late we got home, Mike left for work early each morning, eager to tackle his new job running a firm of nearly fifty employees. Barely thirty-one, Mike was considered very young to be managing director of a regional operation of International Computers. It was clear he had his work cut out for him. A firm believer in equal opportunity for everyone, and committed to an enlightened approach to management, he soon banged heads with the old-fashioned attitude of his boss.

Schools weren't in session yet, so the children and I explored downtown Nairobi, a curious blend of traditional and modern architectural styles. Its tall, glass-fronted skyscrapers dwarfed the old-fashioned two-story colonial arcades packed with all manner of safari gear, tattered lion skins, African drums, ebony sculptures, bizarre masks, and Ethiopian rugs that smelled of charcoal and wet goat fur. Amy loved Uchumi, the only supermarket in town, patrolled by grim *askaris* (guards) who glowered over patrons filling their grimy shopping carts with canned beans, local cooking fat, cardboard boxes of laundry detergent, and cheap Chinese plastic pails.

We marveled at the expansive avenues lined with exotic plants—oleanders, multicolored bougainvillea, purple jacarandas, sweet-smelling gardenias, ruby-red flame trees, and outrageous birds of paradise. Built at the turn of the twentieth century, the streets were wide enough for an ox wagon to turn around in, or so we were told. There were few cars, but the sidewalks were alive with people who reflected the unique blend of the nearly forty-six ethnic groups who were at home here, each with its separate language. I tried not to stare at the charcoal-black African businessmen in tailored suits and carrying briefcases, trailed by their elaborately coiffed and manicured wives in imported silk dresses; almond-eyed Somali women wearing long gowns in vivid prints; and Arabs with café-au-lait skin who were resplendent in turbans and colorful flowing robes.

The first time we explored the vast city market, we were nearly overwhelmed by the crowds who swirled around us, pinching and poking the merchandise. There were pushy traders offering "special prices, just for you"; porters who shuffled about carrying woven *kikapu*s on their heads overflowing with pineapples, mangoes, tiny finger bananas, and fragrant papaws; sunburned missionaries in rugged sandals and straw hats; and haughty expatriate *memsahib*s (ladies of the house) shadowed by their African cooks bearing baskets ready to be filled with the produce their bosses selected.

Across town, tourists in freshly ironed safari gear decanted from zebra-striped minibuses in front of the venerable Norfolk Hotel to mingle with "Kenya cowboys," as some people dubbed the handsome, often extrovert and noisy whites who ran safari camps and resorts. Wearing slouch hats, khaki shirts, dark tans, and tight short shorts, these men seemed to undress every woman in sight. The first time one of them winked at me, I blushed furiously and pretended I hadn't noticed. I had read about the exploits of the Great White Hunters in books by Hemingway and Ruark and had even made a pilgrimage to sit where they had once sat on the "Thorn Tree" veranda of the New Stanley Hotel, but I didn't linger, for I still had to find a house and schools for the children.

It took two months before our real estate agent finally located an appropriate place for us, though he apologized for its location on the Ngong

Road. Having devoured *Out of Africa*, I'd been hoping that we could live as Karen Blixen had, in a low-slung house with deep verandas, sweeping lawns, and a view of the hills. But the Ngong Road turned out to be a wide, empty thoroughfare lined by low-rise apartment buildings and neat stone houses surrounded by high walls. The famous hills were nowhere in sight as we rumbled through a battered gate and down a dusty murram driveway shaded by soaring purple jacarandas in full blossom. A slim gardener wearing an oversize T-shirt and tattered shorts stopped hacking away at a patch of weeds and waved an enthusiastic greeting as the kids and I pulled up with our agent. The simple two-story house surrounded by a half acre of parched grass wasn't quite what I had pictured, but it possessed a certain neglected charm, and after weeks in the hotel I was ready to love just about anything.

The agent banged on the front door, and an African man about my age let us in. Although he was at least three inches shorter than I, and seriously undernourished (we discovered later that he hadn't worked in six months), he appeared dignified, even imposing. He was the color of dark chocolate, with a wide, open face, a broad if slightly ironic smile, and eyes that missed nothing. Dressed in neatly pressed but threadbare clothing and sneakers without laces, he didn't look at us, and he supported his right arm with his left when he shook hands—the traditional African show of respect. I wondered what he was thinking at the sight of the sunburned *mzungu*s (white people) standing before him. Dan gave him a huge smile, but Amy scowled and hid behind my skirt.

"*Jambo, Memsahib,*" he said in a low voice. "My name is William."

Before I could tell him to call me by my first name, he motioned us to follow him on a tour of the house. We had finished inspecting the small guest room off the entrance and the three upstairs bedrooms when there was a sudden shriek and a fierce pounding outside. William broke into a trot and hurried down the stairs. I scooped Amy into my arms and followed to see Dan, already bursting through the front door, watching the gardener run toward something with his knife raised high.

"*Nyoka!* Snake!" the gardener shouted, pointing with his free hand at a slithering blur. Disregarding our pleas to save the creature, he bellowed like a wounded buffalo and brought down the knife, in one stroke neatly slicing the creature in half. Because of all the commotion, I assumed it had been a spitting cobra or black mamba, but when he stood up, he held only the remains of a small and clearly harmless grass snake. Once the excitement was over, I told the agent we would rent the house if he had the grass cut before we moved in—no need to invite further snake trouble. We signed the contract the next day, and Dan took the two halves of the snake to his new school.

At last we could settle in and unpack; or rather, William could, which was the way things were done in Kenya. After meeting William, we had requested that he be included in the house rental, something that seemed to make him very happy, for jobs were few and apparently he had been camping at the house, hoping to be hired. That probably explained how painfully thin he was. It was a huge relief for me to be able to feed him— and have him as my ally, as I had no idea how to run a home with no modern conveniences. From our first day in the house, he took me in hand and taught me how to be a colonial mistress, a true *memsahib*. "Knowledge is better than riches," he intoned, quoting (he said) an old African proverb, one of a seemingly endless supply that he inserted into everyday conversation.

William had entered domestic service at the age of nine. He had started as a servant's servant, standing motionless and silent in a spotless white uniform and fez behind the *memsahib*'s chair, in case anyone needed something from the kitchen. Now he was in charge of the house and all its contents. He explained that his wife, Susanna, and their three children lived far away on a *shamba* (smallholding), where she had a daily struggle to fetch water for cooking and washing, find wood for the fire, and grow the food needed to feed her family. In the past, William had visited his family only once or twice a year, which apparently was normal for servants, a fact that distressed me greatly. It seemed grossly unfair that he should be expected to look after my children when his were deprived of their father for months on end. When I asked him how he felt about the situation, he looked startled. It was clear that no one had ever asked him this before. "My children must eat, madam," he replied with a shrug.

Trying to improve the situation, I paid him at the higher end of the standard scale. Still, I was acutely aware of how much I spent versus how much he made. To assuage my conscience, I slipped him extra money and topped up his monthly rations of tea, sugar, and *posho* (cornmeal porridge), turning a deaf ear to our friends' strict admonitions that we shouldn't pay staff more than the local standard, for fear of "spoiling" them. I'm ashamed to say that it took me no time at all to get used to being a *memsahib*, and I was never sorry to hand over washing dishes, scrubbing floors, changing beds, and cooking—not for a moment, especially since everything had to be done by hand, even the laundry in the bathtub.

William handled our affairs with calm efficiency, always looking impressive in his neatly ironed safari suits and matching socks, beige for everyday and white for important occasions, and reveled in his position as boss, overseeing the night guard and Ephraim, our gardener, who was way down the totem pole as far as William was concerned. I always felt that had William been literate, he could have run a major company, even the country.

As I grew to know him better, I could read what he was thinking about our guests just by watching his eyebrows, which arched in a certain way when he disapproved of someone—which was usually the case. We developed a shorthand communication system, as old married couples do, and William became one of my closest confidants.

Within days of moving in, I was captivated by the excitement and sheer beauty of Kenya, often described as "God's country." In my weekly letters home to my parents and in-laws, I couldn't find enough superlatives to describe the clarity of light, the dazzling effect of the sun glinting off corrugated metal roofs, and the brilliant colors of the bougainvillea beneath the biggest, bluest sky I had ever seen. Even the soil was different in Kenya, ranging in color from coal-black up north near Lake Turkana, where ancient lava flows had left the earth pitted like a moonscape, to bright ocher around Nairobi, where the soil was so rich that a stick stuck in the ground would sprout in two days when the rains came. I felt like I, too, was sprouting in that fertile environment, ready to push back the boundaries and constrictions of my gray old life in England. I was living in a rainbow dream and never wanted to go back to Mill Hill again.

The children were equally enthusiastic, especially after we created a playhouse out of the packing crate that had brought our belongings to Africa. They painted flowers and fanciful animals on its exterior, though within a few weeks fast-growing vines had crept over it, nearly covering their artwork. Dan set up his GI Joes in the backyard, creating elaborate scenarios complete with watchtowers, bridges, tunnels, and turrets, while Amy started ballet and proudly wore her leotard and pink slippers to breakfast, much to the amusement of William.

Because Amy was home so much, she and William had a very special relationship. He nicknamed her Pretty when she was cheerful; otherwise, he called her *Defenzi* (Minister of Defense) in deference to her fiercely independent spirit. When he polished the floor, skating through the house on sheepskin pads, she slid along behind him in her socks, singing. William taught her to use fingers to eat his favorite food, *ugali* (a thick porridge made of white cornmeal), which she rolled into a ball and dipped into stew made with beans, onions, and tomatoes. After helping William cook, she often stayed in the compound with the servants, dancing to Zairean rock music from his tinny transistor radio, wearing her new black doll tied to her back, African style. Around her the adults swayed in time to the beat and the dogs howled. There was always something going on behind the hedge that divided our part of the compound from the servants' quarters, and she was never alone, or bored.

Amy grumbled when we found a half-day nursery school for her a few blocks from our house, which meant she would have to be apart from William a few hours each morning. Every day she left cheerfully enough, but by lunchtime, when she returned, carried on William's shoulders, she was hot, tired, and grouchy—ready for a quick lunch and a nap.

Dan attended Hillcrest Preparatory School, overseen by a crusty British ex-major who kept the boys in line with a shoe applied freely to their bottoms. Dan, who had trouble writing neatly and couldn't spell, hated the place until he was taken under the wing of a white Kenyan class-mate, Lengai Croze, a cheerful, pudgy child with a round, sunburned face only half-visible beneath a mop of pale gold hair. Lengai's shirttail always hung out over his rumpled pants, which usually bore traces of lunch, and his socks wandered down his permanently scratched legs. (Dan, on the other hand, always wore clothes neatly ironed by William—even his underwear!)

Lengai's first name, taken from the Masai language, meant "the Mountain of God," and he and his siblings had to swim across a swollen creek in their underwear to get to school during the rainy season, hold-ing their school clothes and homework over their heads. A car picked them up at the other side. Dan worshipped his new friend, who made sure no one bullied this pale, undersize British newcomer.

When Lengai invited him to spend the weekend at their house in Limuru, some twenty miles outside Nairobi, Dan started packing im-mediately. I had heard that Lengai's mother, Nani, was a talented and eccentric mural and stained-glass artist with an apparently incurable urge to decorate everything in sight. I had seen their battered minibus covered with colorful graffiti and outrageous mythical creatures outside the school gates, and was eager to see more of her work.

However, on Friday morning—the day he was to go with Lengai after school—Dan seemed apprehensive as he filled his backpack with Action Man figures and their gear. "You'll have a wonderful time," I said reassuringly, fastening the straps over his shoulders and hugging him as he headed out the door.

Two days later, Mike, Amy, and I piled into our car to collect Dan. Winding our way toward Limuru, we marveled at the vivid green hills carpeted with tea and coffee plantations. The traffic thinned and little stalls appeared by the side of the road, displaying corn, hard red toma-toes the size of plums, and heavy, green-tipped pineapples. Young boys held out baby rabbits by their ears, waving them in the air as we drove by, much to the horror of Amy and me, who wanted to rescue them all. We stopped to buy a sheepskin for the living room, and Mike haggled cheer-fully with an elderly Kikuyu woman, whose hunched shoulders and scarred bare feet betrayed a lifetime of hauling water and sticks. After a good-natured negotiation, she burst into a toothless grin when she saw Amy curl up on the fleece on the backseat of the car.

As we drove on, Mike swept a film of dust off the windshield with the wipers and I glimpsed my first tea plantation, a sea of impossibly green fields. Ahead of us, huge white clouds lay on the horizon like feather pillows. The clarity of the light and purity of the air meant we could see for miles. When we finally spotted a sign marked CROZE, we parked beneath the sparse shade of an acacia tree and made our way into a clearing among spiky thornbushes. Lengai's mother, Nani, greeted us with a smile that lit up her face. She was barefoot and wore a long blue skirt and flowing white blouse that revealed her voluptuous curves.

"Watch out for the vulture," she said nonchalantly with a slight German accent, while tucking a strand of long fair hair back into her bun. I pulled Amy behind me and Mike stepped to one side as a large, fierce-looking bird headed straight for us. It attacked my watch, leaving a deep scratch on the crystal, before heading off. Trying to look unconcerned, I extended my hand to Nani, who ignored it and gave us all warm hugs.

Lengai soon appeared, running toward us with a wave. Wearing a tattered shirt, oversize khaki shorts, and flip-flops, he looked even more disheveled than usual, though he had a new haircut, apparently accomplished at home with a bowl and a hacksaw. Dan ran up too, a cluster of half-grown Jack Russell puppies nipping at his feet. He was sunburned and shirtless, his dark hair sticking out every which way, and he had fresh scratches on both knees. He looked happier than ever. Grabbing my hand, he led us on a tour of the Croze home, a series of mud-walled rondavels under a thatched roof. The children's quarters turned out to be an aging double-decker London bus, decorated with Nani's whimsical paintings.

"Mummy, check out the colobus monkeys!" Dan cried, pointing out a troop of black-and-white creatures that lived in the trees, keeping watch over the bizarre menagerie below, which included a motley collection of frogs, lizards, birds, rats, and kittens, not to mention an evil-tempered crown-crested crane and a porcupine that fancied itself a house cat.

We sat down around a rough wooden table piled with homemade sugar cookies, slabs of ginger cake, and brown bread and butter, and drank tea served with milk, fresh from their cow. Mozart was playing in the background on an antiquated tape recorder as Nani's husband, Harvey, opened one bottle of wine after another and kept us laughing with stories about his wild life in the bush, where he studied, of all things, crows. Anselm, Lengai's older brother, and his little sister, a waiflike child named Katrinika, slathered marmalade onto a thick slice of bread for Amy. Normally fussy, my daughter devoured every bite before politely asking for more, all the time gazing in admiration at her new friends.

As I took in everything around me, I vowed to start living like my new heroine, Nani, who was without a doubt the most original person I had ever met. She appeared to do exactly what she wanted to do, no matter what anyone said or thought. I had been taught always to be polite and not upset anyone, which had resulted in some very uncomfortable situations. It was time to be less afraid of "what the neighbors might say." I resolved to paint murals on our walls, tame a pig, and stop wearing shoes as soon as I got home. I wasn't sure what Mike would think, but just then I didn't care.

The sun was low when we finally said goodbye and made our way back to Nairobi, listening to the whir of cicadas echo across the hills. The air was sweet and cool, and a soft breeze rustled the leaves of the banana palms and rippled the grasses. Stripes of purple appeared against the darkening sky, and the sun, a great orange orb, balanced for an instant on the rim of the earth, then disappeared. The temperature dropped quickly, and I used my sweater to cover the children sleeping on the backseat as we sped home.

That night, when I put Dan to bed, I saw how tanned his face was and how his eyes gleamed, radiating a new sense of confidence.

"I went skinny-dipping in a river!" he announced proudly, watching to see how I would react. "There was an enormous snake," he added. It was hard not to look horrified as he described the creature, thick as a man's thigh, that had swum alongside the boys until it disappeared in the murky water. Apparently boa constrictors aren't interested in eating little boys.

Dan beamed as he described how the pair had walked cross-country across dusty plains to visit a Masai *boma* (compound), where young warriors-in-training a little older than they were, wearing only beaded jewelry and red *shuka*s (pieces of cloth tossed carelessly over their shoulders like Greek togas), had shown the visitors their scars from hunting expeditions while their bright-eyed sisters greeted the boys with dazzling smiles. "They promised to take me giraffe hunting," he exclaimed.

Suddenly he grew quiet and his forehead furrowed.

"What's up?" I asked.

"Lengai jumped off a cliff straight into the river."

"So?"

"I was too scared."

"I would have been terrified," I said, meaning it.

"Really?" he asked, his eyes wide.

"Even grown-ups get scared sometimes," I assured him. It occurred to me (though I didn't say it out loud) that it felt as though I, too, were diving into water way over my head. As excited as I was about Kenya, it was definitely scary for a newcomer. Casting about for something that would comfort him—and me—I recalled a few lines from *The King and I* that had always cheered me up as a child if I was feeling frightened.

"I have a secret you can remember all your life," I said. I watched a smile creep across Dan's face as I began singing:

Make believe you're brave and the trick will take you far;
you may be as brave as you make believe you are!

That night I needed to hear those words as much as my son did. Faced with the realities of our new life in Africa, I would require every trick possible to face the challenges that lay ahead.

5

Lions in the Garden

BURSTING WITH A NEW SENSE OF WHAT MIGHT BE POSSIBLE, I BEGAN TO envision a new *me*, unbounded by the constraints of my past and present life; I imagined an existence that embraced all possibilities. Now I wanted a *real* job, but I quickly found that it was almost impossible for an expatriate wife to get a work permit in Kenya. Most wives, or "two-year wonders" (short-term residents), spent their days in a lively round of bridge parties, Swahili classes, tennis dates, and, as I began to discover, clandestine affairs. Given the fact that servants cost almost nothing, any form of housekeeping or child-tending was not included on the list of activities.

I tried to fit in and joined a Swahili course, sitting alongside rosy-cheeked missionaries, earnest Peace Corps workers, and corporate wives with dark tans, but I bailed out after a few sessions and bought a teach-yourself phrase book. It took only one embarrassing rubber before I quit bridge as well, and I made only a half-hearted attempt at sunbathing and tennis at the Nairobi Club. After a few weeks I joined the American Women's Association but met only more bored wives like me.

That left the long hot afternoons for an affair, but I certainly didn't want one. What was wrong with me? Surely there was *something* I could do. Finally, I discovered an outlet for my restless curiosity contained in a most unlikely place—the staid Nairobi Club. The club's classy downstairs lounge was reserved for men, who were served tepid drinks by creaky Kenyan waiters, while women were allowed only in a dreary upstairs room where they could read tattered copies of *Field & Stream* or week-old copies of British newspapers strung up on long poles so no one would walk off with them. Downstairs, the musty chintz chairs might as well have had nameplates on them, for their occupants, ancient British colonialists with handlebar mustaches and rumpled khakis, rarely budged and only grunted if spoken to. Grumpy and chauvinistic, they were definitely not amused when a bouncy American woman inadvertently took one of their places.

I hid myself in the club's library, where I devoured old books about Kenyan wildlife and people. One of the most intriguing was a rare first edition of Beryl Markham's autobiography, *West with the Night*, which told the story of Beryl's unconventional childhood in Kenya, growing up wild as the daughter of a horse trainer. I was glued to descriptions of her adventures as a bush pilot in the 1930s and her nearly disastrous flight from England to Nova Scotia, where she crashed in 1937. She returned to Kenya after the war, and her reputed lovers included Karen Blixen's beau, Denys Finch Hatton, the celebrated conductor Leopold Stokowski, and, at the same time, both the Prince of Wales and his brother, Henry. Yet another was Lord Erroll, the mystery of whose murder was the subject of *White Mischief*, a book later made into a film dramatizing the lives of a notorious set of wife-swapping expatriates dealing with the effects of Kenya's "three A's": altitude, alcohol, and adultery. To me, Beryl Markham represented the fatal combination of three other elements that made Kenya so irresistible: beauty, sex, and danger.

I was also fascinated by another lively book, *Among the Elephants*—then newly published—written by a dashing, aristocratic Scottish scientist, Iain Douglas-Hamilton, and his half-French, half-Italian wife, Oria, a raven-haired beauty who had abandoned a career in film to join her lover in the bush, where he studied elephant behavior. The couple was raising two little girls, Saba and Dudu, in a hut without running water or electricity. I wanted to be like her, living a life unbounded by middle-class expectations and limitations.

Day after day, tucked away in the Nairobi Club library, I pored over books, curious to know how so many women living in Kenya managed to lead such creative, passionate, and exciting lives. Apparently unbounded by convention and tradition, they tackled challenges with a *joie de vivre* that I found extraordinary after living in the suburbs, where my neighbors had been cautious about everything. With few movie theaters and no television except for the stultifying state-owned Voice of Kenya, which broadcast a steady diet of badly shot political rallies, we had to make our own entertainment for the children. A houseguest drew a large map of the world on Dan's bedroom wall and the children spent hours adding lions, elephants, and wildebeests to the continent of Africa. Every day we set off on "adventures," walking safaris around the neighborhood.

"Where are we going?" Dan would ask.

"As far as the eye can see," I said once, waving my hands in the air as I explained that it wasn't the destination that mattered, but what we saw—or even better, imagined—along the way. I spun stories about outrageous animals I spotted on the path, describing miniature giraffes and buffaloes that made them giggle.

On Sundays I dropped the children at a Christian Science Sunday school class, where they were the only white children in a sea of black faces. I chose it because a friend of mine was the teacher; they dropped out when she left a year or so later. Much later I learned that the brief exposure to Christian Science teachings triggered Dan's lifetime aversion to all forms of medicine—and an equally powerful belief in the power of positive thinking. In an attempt to educate Dan and Amy about his religious roots, Mike took the children to the Nairobi synagogue a few times, but neither of us felt committed to a specific spiritual tradition, and after a while we concentrated less on formal religious studies than teaching the children to treat others kindly. We emphasized the Golden Rule, common to all traditions: "Do unto others as you would have them do unto you."

Mike taught the children geography by creating elaborate stamp albums and brought history alive by reading them stories about Napoleon, Lord Nelson, and Roman emperors. We took Dan and Amy to the National Museum of Kenya to learn about snakes, African anthropology, and paleontology. Located on a gentle rise above the city, it had been founded by the world-famous paleontologist Louis Leakey, whose statue stood outside one of the newer buildings. Together with his skull-hunting, cigar-smoking, straight-talking wife, Mary, Louis had discovered the remains of some of humankind's earliest ancestors at Olduvai Gorge in Tanzania.

Intrigued by stories of the Leakeys and their three adult sons, I was eager to meet members of this famous family who had made so many contributions to Kenya. Surprisingly, it was Amy who led to our meeting them. Her best friend at school was another three-year-old named Lara, who turned out to be the daughter of Valerie, a dark-eyed and beautiful Scottish intellectual who had left her husband, a professor, to run away with Philip, the youngest Leakey son. But before we got to know them well, the lives of everyone in Kenya came to a standstill.

Suddenly an even more famous Kenyan figure dominated the news. One morning, as usual, William's bare feet sounded on the wooden steps. He usually entered our room carrying a tray piled high with homemade bread, scrambled eggs, and smoked bacon, along with pots of strong Kenyan tea and freshly brewed coffee. Ephraim, our teenage gardener, or *shamba* boy, would totter behind him bearing cups and saucers, fresh butter, honey, and marmalade. Our dogs Snowy (named after the snow on Mt. Kilimanjaro) and Delly (short for Lord Delamere, one of Kenya's early settlers) always skittered up the steps behind them.

But this day, as Mike and I lay in bed chatting, both children having joined us for a morning cuddle, William burst into our room alone and without a tray. "*Bwana, Memsahib,*" he said, his voice up a notch, "something very bad has happened."

My heart skipped a beat as I gathered the children to me. However friendly the Kenyans were by day and however much we enjoyed the beauty of the landscape, there was always a sense that danger was lurking just around the corner. Every expatriate gathering provided an opportunity to share the latest horror stories about carjacking, armed robbery, or—worse still—gang rape, which had just befallen two sixteen-year-olds we knew. Our *askari*, a fierce Masai warrior, patrolled our compound every night from sunset until dawn, which meant that now—daytime—there was no one on duty to protect us.

Fortunately, the situation in Kenya was relatively peaceful under the leadership of President Jomo Kenyatta, who had led his country to independence fifteen years before, in 1963.

William leaned in close and looked over his shoulder, as though worried someone might be listening. I whispered, "What happened?"

"They say that Mzee is dead," he intoned, lowering his head in respect. In Swahili *mzee* means "old man," and it was the name most Kenyans gave to their president, then eighty-nine years of age. When he was a young man, he had changed his last name to Kenyatta, which means "burning spear" in Swahili.

"Who killed him?" Dan asked, suddenly all ears. Even our children knew that most African leaders met violent ends. I shot a warning look at William to keep quiet, hoping he would realize we didn't need all the gory details. Dan's imagination was powerful enough as it was. As it turned out, though, William didn't know yet what had happened, so we had to wait for news.

The prospect of a coup in Kenya was chilling. There was always the chance that a prominent political leader might be assassinated like the controversial Tom Mboya, who had been mysteriously murdered in 1969. To the north, in Ethiopia, Marxist revolutionaries had first imprisoned, and then suffocated, the emperor, Haile Selassie. In neighboring Uganda, Idi Amin was conducting a reign of terror that had left nearly half a million people dead and had expelled eighty thousand Asians from the country virtually overnight. Amy had frequent nightmares that Amin was going to cut off her head and put it in his refrigerator, a fate that had befallen several of his victims, though heaven knows who would have told that to a three-year-old. I suspected it was Dan.

Around midday, we heard the news on the radio that the country's beloved president had apparently died peacefully in his bed. We breathed a sigh of relief, though we wondered whether there would be a peaceful transition of power or the country would erupt in chaos. That afternoon we locked the gate for the first time during the day, and by midafternoon armed guards patrolled the streets in heavy trucks.

Over the next few days I stocked the larder with essentials and bought jerry cans of gasoline, sharing the latest gossip with other expat wives who were convinced that the end of their idyllic life in paradise was nigh. Some packed their bags and were ready to leave the country, but I thought they were crazy. Although I wouldn't have said it out loud, I savored the sense of danger in the air and couldn't wait to see what would happen next. I found the power struggles in my adopted country fascinating, even if they were potentially life-threatening.

The skies were gray and overcast on the day of Kenyatta's funeral. We had been invited to join a BBC friend at the Intercontinental Hotel, where his team would be reporting on the historic event, and we decided to take Dan along to witness the departure of the dignitaries from the hotel on their way to the service. Police barricades cordoned off the route, and we passed lines of armed soldiers in sunglasses, somber officials in dark suits, and Red Cross women in neatly pressed bright red uniforms. After all the dire warnings, we were relieved to see that the crowds packing the streets were dressed in their Sunday best and remained perfectly calm.

Stationing ourselves along the red carpet in the hotel lobby, we watched the leaders of many African nations making their way toward a fleet of new black Mercedes limousines that would take them to the ceremony. Some wore Nehru jackets, while others sported long, flowing robes, beaded caps, and animal-skin capes. They swept ahead of their plump wives, whose heads were covered with yards of brilliantly colored fabric that made them appear like exotic birds of paradise.

Mike pointed to a cameraman about our age, snapping photos of the dignitaries. "That's Mohamed Amin," he whispered. "He spoke last week at the Rotary Club." The man looked up and gave my husband, a photography buff, a conspiratorial wink.

Mo, as he was known, was an energetic, round-faced man in his early thirties with a black goatee and dark, mischievous eyes that appeared to take in everything. Born in Tanzania of Pakistani parents, he was already a legendary news photographer, having covered nearly every conflict and famine on the African continent. Mo seemed to know everyone, and even the various presidents smiled when he aimed his camera at them over the rope barrier.

"Come here," he said, gesturing to Dan. My son edged his way closer, and Mo showed him how to look through the eyepiece of his camera and even let him snap some photos. We joined the correspondents later while they monitored the broadcast of the service from an upstairs suite. The men were tanned and rugged in their khaki safari suits, and the women—attractive and (by reputation) fearless—appeared unscathed by years spent reporting horrors I didn't want to even think about. Impulsively I invited all of them home for dinner, for I wanted to get to know these extraordinary people better.

We drove back under dark clouds and a torrential downpour to find a despondent William huddled in the kitchen. "The sky is weeping for the president," he said, and confessed that he was worried about what would happen to the country now that Mzee was dead.

That evening we let Dan stay up late as the correspondents, inspired by our best Scotch, recounted their adventures with earthquakes and famines, revolutions and wars. The BBC correspondent, Brian Barron, spoke of harrowing events in the Vietnam and Cambodia wars, but Mo Amin topped them with stories of his multiple car crashes, confinement in horrific prisons, narrow escapes, and spectacular scoops. His tales that evening enthralled both Dan and me, and I'm sure that the day had a lasting effect on my son's life—and mine. Dan would later trace his fascination with photography to that encounter with Mo Amin, while at the same time something in me that had lain dormant since I was a young girl in Iowa, a lifetime away, was starting to awaken. It was impossible to identify it at that moment, nor even guess at its magnitude, but it's probably true that what happened to me is the story of every woman who has ever gone in search of herself. I was beginning a journey that would transform me utterly, indelibly, horribly—gloriously—taking me places far beyond my wildest imaginings.

For a few weeks after Mzee's death, Nairobi and the rest of Kenya were tense, but things settled down when the succession of Kenya's president and cabinet turned out to be peaceful. Happily, we were quickly able to return to normal life, which included our growing friendship with Amy's friend Lara Leakey and her family, who turned out to be just as exotic as the Crozes.

When Philip Leakey had met Valerie years earlier, he was living in a tent fashioned from a large plastic sheet on the edge of the Nairobi National Park, but as soon as Valerie was free to join him, Philip built her a two-story mud house where the tent had stood, and Lara arrived soon afterward. Philip, a fourth-generation Kenyan, prided himself on speaking several African languages, including Masai. Committed to social change in Kenya, he was running for office as a member of Parliament. If elected, he would be the only white MP in Kenya.

Valerie was serving as his campaign manager. She reminded me of Ma in Laura Ingalls Wilder's *Little House on the Prairie,* with the difference that a warthog named Bonaparte rooted through her vegetable patch, and lions and rhinos strolled across the surrounding plains. Practical, outspoken, and fiercely independent, she ran the house, the servants, and Philip with total efficiency. She had to transport everything over fourteen miles of rough roads—gas canisters for the stove and water pump, wood for the fireplaces, drinking water, gasoline, and, because the antiquated icebox was only big enough to contain a few packets of milk, daily rations of fresh fruit, vegetables, and meat.

Whenever Amy visited the Leakeys, she returned with wide-eyed tales of roofs made of tin and thatch, a giant, round bed swathed in mosquito netting, and a sunken bathtub filled with water that had been pumped up from a muddy river that cut a gorge through the game park bordering their house. The girls' favorite outing was a swim in the slow-moving waters, where buffaloes, tiny dik-diks, and giraffes came to drink. Otherwise, they had the run of the garden, an untamed space dotted with spiky euphorbia bushes, droopy willows, and the rusty hulk of an abandoned Volkswagen. All this took place under the watchful eye of Harry, Lara's dog, and her *ayah* (nanny), Wanjiru.

Lara, a serious, pixie-faced child, was as dark and slim as Amy was fair and round, and preferred puppies and kittens, while Amy loved dolls. Fortunately, they sorted out their differences by dressing up the animals and pushing them in doll buggies along the gorge.

One afternoon Amy came home with a story that made my hair curl. She and Lara had been playing on the veranda when Harry began to bark furiously. When Wanjiru stepped outside to investigate, she spotted three full-grown lions stalking him. Brandishing her broom and shouting, she tried to keep the beasts at bay, but one grabbed poor Harry by the neck and dragged him into the bushes. Undaunted, Wanjiru ran shrieking after the lion until he dropped the dog and loped away. Val bundled the girls and the dog, spurting blood from his jugular vein, into her pickup truck and raced to the vet. Against all odds, Harry survived, unlike some of the Leakeys' less lucky pets, who were poisoned, snared, or carried off by hawks, baboons, and leopards, never to be seen again. The *ayah* never let Lara and Amy out of her sight again, as they would have been equally easy prey for all kinds of predators.

Getting to know the Leakeys and the Crozes introduced us to an Africa that we might otherwise never have known. Their friends included Africans from neighboring countries, indigenous Kenyans, and Kenyan Asians (the label given to the local population of people from India or Pakistan). The *mzungus*, also described as "Europeans" by locals—although many had never left Kenya—represented a wide array of professions: wildlife experts, paleontologists, anthropologists, politicians, environmentalists, writers, and artists. Many seemed larger than life, which wasn't surprising, as most of them, or their parents or even grandparents, had abandoned a safe and predictable life elsewhere to enjoy the excitement and pleasures of this challenging continent. Their pioneer spirit captivated me. For these intrepid people there were frontiers everywhere, new horizons, a sense of confidence, and a passionate belief in the future of Africa.

Nothing seemed impossible for such adventurous pioneers. No one told them what they couldn't—or shouldn't—do. If they wanted to build a house, they slapped up walls and a roof. If they had an idea for a new business, they launched it. If it failed, too bad; they'd think of something else. And they did, over and over again, seemingly undaunted by failure. Fascinated by their endless creativity, inventiveness, and active spirits, I wanted to meet more of them.

I didn't have long to wait. It happened through another of Dan's classmates—Pierre Burton, a tall, sensitive child with platinum hair and the enormous blue eyes of his mother, an elegant ex-model from France. Her husband, Miles, was ruggedly handsome, with a full beard and thick brown hair. He had a warm greeting for everyone when he picked up Pierre and his little brother, Luc, at the Hillcrest School gates, and I began speaking with him one day while we waited for our children.

To my joy he invited our family to join him on a safari in the Masai Mara National Reserve. Dan asked what it meant to "go on safari." He knew that in Swahili the word meant "journey," but to me it seemed more than that—it was an exciting trek into the unknown. I told him about old-fashioned safaris led by intrepid hunters wearing pith helmets and spine protectors, who ventured deep into the wilds of Africa to hunt game, trailed by a train of bearers carrying guns, ammunition, bathtubs, and steamer trunks on their heads. I explained that we wouldn't have bearers, but we would definitely take a bath in the bush. I don't know who was more excited, Dan or I.

Miles gave us a date well in the future, for this wasn't to be any ordinary safari. It was going to be the subject of a BBC wildlife documentary, and our family would be featured in it as typical tourists, except that we would be on foot and as close to the animals as possible. I made a special trip to Biashara Street for safari gear, including a smart khaki vest for Mike that would hold all his film and camera gear. Then we made sure everything was well washed and suitably rumpled, so we wouldn't look like newcomers in brand-new, freshly ironed outfits. Now all we had to do was be brave in the face of whatever lay ahead.

6

Safari

THE SIX-HOUR DRIVE FROM NAIROBI TO THE MASAI MARA GAME RESERVE
seemed interminable. With Mike at the wheel, we lurched over dusty,
corrugated roads under the blazing sun with the children quibbling in
the back of the car the entire time. Mike was having some management
troubles at work and was talking them over in detail, while I tried to read
a guidebook on Kenya.

"I wish to God that Derek would just get out of the picture," Mike
said. Engrossed in a passage about indigenous peoples, I forced myself to
pay attention.

Noticing that he was hunched over the steering wheel and his knuck-
les were white, I tried to be encouraging. "Relax, darling—you're doing
a great job," I said, reaching for his hand.

"Derek is constantly trying to bring me down. He actually canceled
a project when he found out that my Kenyan manager was working so
closely with me on it."

"That's just insane," I said, genuinely indignant. "How on earth does
he expect your company to make it in the future without any Africans
involved?"

The superior attitude of many expatriates upset me, for the eager, enthusiastic, well-educated young Africans Mike and I were meeting were the future of this country, not the short-term residents from England and other European countries, or the sometimes hidebound white Kenyans who still controlled much of Nairobi's infrastructure.

"I know how frustrating it is, darling," I began, wishing he would forget the office and enjoy the moment. Taking in the incredible view unfolding before us, I exclaimed, "I can't believe how lucky we are to be here!"

My positive mental attitude and tendency to break into camp songs was often anathema to my much more reserved and realistic husband, who tended to be preoccupied with his own very real challenges. Noticing his face grow even tenser at my exclamation, I took a deep breath. He was the reason we were in Kenya, after all. I needed to be supportive. I massaged his neck with one hand as we discussed strategy. Neither of us wanted to endanger his position at the office, but at the same time, he had to keep pushing if anything was to change.

By late afternoon we reached our destination: Fig Tree Camp, nestled beside the Talek River, which meandered through the rolling plains. A beaming steward in a neatly pressed shirt and khaki shorts greeted us each with a glass of chilled lime juice and escorted us to our tent, mounted on a wooden platform with an unobstructed view of the reserve. Dan and Amy giggled when they saw that instead of a tub there was a rusty showerhead attached to a canvas bucket, and that discreetly tucked behind a canvas sheet a wooden toilet seat and frame stood atop a shallow hole. A roll of gray toilet paper, nearly as coarse as sandpaper, lay nearby, adjacent to a pail of dirt and an ancient spade.

Dan and Amy followed a young Masai warrior in a red *shuka* down to the river, now just a slow trickle of muddy water during the dry season. Barely able to contain my excitement, I passed the time sketching the children in the journal I had started on our arrival in Kenya. Later we donned our specially bought safari gear and stiff new Bata boots to join Miles and the BBC crew for sundowners in the mess tent. Dan was all ears, but Amy fell asleep in her chair during the five-course dinner that followed, complete with crusty brown rolls, roast impala, and a perfect papaya tart baked on white-hot coals in an old tin trunk.

I put the children to bed in the tent and returned to sip brandies with the film crew around a crackling fire. The director, wearing an impressive khaki vest lined with rows of pockets, all of which seemed to be empty, ran through the protocol for the next day's shoot. His message was simple. "Don't look at the camera," he barked, "and get as close to the animals as humanly possible." It sounded easy enough. Miles explained that we would set off just before dawn, hoping to film the "Big Five"—lion, leopard, buffalo, rhino, and elephant.

"Naturally, we'll want a bit of drama in the show," the director interjected. "Ideally a confrontation with a charging elephant or an encounter with a buffalo. Makes great television."

That didn't sound good to me. To be honest, I hadn't really thought about what it would mean to make the safari on foot, but after seeing notices at the park entrance requiring tourists to remain in their cars at all times, it seemed that what he expected us to do for the cameras was irregular and probably insane. I tried not to worry as Mike and I strolled back to our tent, accompanied by a Masai *askari*, an ancient rifle tucked into the crook of his arm and a spear in his hand. We paused for a moment outside, enjoying the soft breeze that fluttered the leaves above us and the smell of wood smoke mingled with the scent of fresh grass. Millions of stars and the haze of the Milky Way shimmered in the dome of the inky black sky.

As Mike unzipped the flap, I could hear the low hiss of a hurricane lamp inside. In the flickering light we could see that someone had turned down the rough blanket that covered our bed, and when we crawled between the sheets, we found two hot water bottles tucked inside. Never had I experienced anything so romantic.

"Don't you just love this, darling? I feel so alive," I said. There was silence. My husband, exhausted from the long drive, had already fallen asleep.

I nudged him with my foot. He stirred, and I nestled close to him, hoping for a response. Realizing how selfish I was being, I lay still until his breathing slowed again. He needed his sleep; besides, we had another night at Fig Tree to be together. But I was restless, so I switched on my flashlight and pulled out my journal to capture the noises I was hearing—the haunting cough of a distant leopard, the gentle rustle of branches against the tent, and a sudden sharp cry that made my heart stop. As the beam began to dim I finally dropped off, awakening to a chorus of chirping birds.

A low voice called, "*Chai tiyari*" (Tea is ready). Outside the tent, tea and a plate of cookies awaited us, along with hot water in a canvas basin. There was just time to splash our faces, pull on our clothes, and down a quick cup of sweet milky tea before we were off, driving with Miles in his Land Rover deep into the heart of the Mara reserve, followed by the film crew. Paradise opened before us, vast undulating plains stretching to the far-off horizon. The air smelled like sweet grass, and foamy, flat-bottomed clouds raced across the impossibly blue sky. A herd of zebras surveyed us from a distance, prancing away on dainty hoofs when we came too close.

Cresting a hill, we stopped to take in the sight of three elegant giraffes, which seemed to study us before they, too, wheeled and loped off.

Even after they were gone, Miles held his binoculars to his eyes, explaining that he was searching for circling vultures, the movement of hyenas, or darkened trails in the dewy grass, clues that might lead us to a recent lion kill. After a moment he handed the glasses to me. In the dappled shade of the spreading branches of an acacia tree, a lioness lay panting, her mouth half-open, muzzle smeared dark brown with drying blood.

"She's had a tough time, that one," Miles said. Sure enough, I could see her ribs, clearly visible beneath her tawny, scarred coat. I handed the binoculars to Dan, who scanned the landscape for a long time, teasing Amy, who poked him impatiently for her turn. But when he finally passed them to her, she took one look and said, "That's yucky. Mumma, can we go home now?"

I shushed her as Miles turned off the engine and we sat motionless in our seats watching the lioness. It was wondrously quiet in the bush: there was the buzz of an insect, a quiet breeze on my cheek, otherwise nothing.

Then we noticed two half-grown cubs ripping into the haunch of a newly killed zebra not far from the lioness. Mike pulled himself through the sunroof on top of the vehicle, hoisted Dan up to join him, and showed him how to frame photos of the bloody scene. Amy climbed onto my lap and buried her face in my jacket.

"You know how lions kill?" Miles called up to Dan. "After they bring their prey down, they smother it by covering the snout with their mouths. It takes a long time, but lions are patient."

Dan put Mike's camera to his eye and stared at the dead zebra. "Does the animal cry out?"

"No, it doesn't make a sound," Miles said.

Amy stiffened, and I shuddered at the thought of such a slow, silent, horrible death. I understood the laws of nature and all that, but surely there had to be a better way. Normally, Dan was squeamish at the sight of blood, but he kept looking through the camera lens and didn't seem to mind the gore. Perhaps the camera created an emotional barrier between him and his subjects. Whatever had happened, I was pleased to see his calm determination as he carefully framed shot after shot.

Amy had fallen asleep, and I slid her onto the backseat and covered her with my jacket while Miles started the engine and Mike and Dan returned to their seats. As we drove on, ten or twelve impala took off, leaping in unison through the tall grass like members of a fluttery *corps de ballet*. Cresting a nearby hill, he slowed again and gestured toward a lone buffalo standing by the side of the road. Flies clustered around a raw, open sore on his massive rump, and his hide was ripped and torn, as though he had survived many fierce battles. Lowering his head, he tossed his horns in our direction, appearing as malevolent as any creature I had ever seen.

Miles gave him a wide berth, turning off the track onto the grass to avoid coming too close. "Here we call those buggers Black Death," he said. "They're the most dangerous animals in Africa."

A few minutes later, as we bounced along the road again, I caught my reflection in the rearview mirror. My tanned face, gleaming with perspiration, had grown leaner in Africa and was lightly sprinkled with freckles.

My hair, redder than ever before, was wind-tousled and wild. As I tried to tame it with my fingers, I realized that Miles was watching me in the mirror. Blushing, I turned away. Like Dan, I was in awe of him and felt awkward in his presence.

The gears ground as Miles downshifted and we headed off the road toward a stand of trees. In front of them there was a line of gray bumps, like boulders. Coming closer, I realized they were elephants—at least thirty of them—ranging from babies to a great matriarch standing apart from the others. She flapped her ears threateningly when she saw us and trumpeted a loud warning, tossing her slender tusks in our direction. My heart beat faster and I drew Dan toward me as Miles drove closer to the herd. About forty feet from the nearest animal, he slowed and cut the engine, while the cameraman in the neighboring vehicle began to film us watching the animals. I tried to look nonchalant, as if I did this sort of thing every day.

Growing accustomed to our presence, five or six of the young females glided steadily forward again, twirling grass in their trunks and popping it into their mouths, occasionally calling to one another. We were so close that I could see their soft pink tongues and the occasional trail of liquid from their eyes—liquid that looked for all the world like tears. Hiding behind their elders were three babies, lighter in color than the adults, the smallest lurching unsteadily on stiff legs like a human toddler. He kept stopping to seek reassurance from his sisters, who constantly reached out to touch him or entwine trunks. Just then, an enormous bull elephant emerged from the cover of the trees and ambled toward the herd. Much larger than even the oldest female, he had a hide like ancient tree bark, a massive head, and thick stained tusks that curved halfway to the ground.

"Perfect!" Miles exclaimed under his breath. "Time to get out now." Rifle slung over his shoulder, he stepped down from the Land Rover and beckoned us to follow him. The cameramen were sensibly keeping their distance from the animals, focusing their lenses on our movements. Feeling uncertain, I paused for a moment, and then noticed Dan watching my hesitation.

"Stay here, Amy; stay with Daddy," I said. Gritting my teeth, I jumped out—onto an impressive mound of elephant dung that made my feet slide out from under me.

Just then, the matriarch wheeled to face us and raised her trunk, trumpeting so loudly that the ground shook. I was ready to climb back into the safety of the Land Rover, but Miles beckoned us closer. There was another bellow from the female as she started toward us, stamping and blowing dust from her massive trunk. Miles, waving and shouting, stood his ground. To my amazement, so did I, with Dan at my side.

After what seemed an eternity, the elephant tossed her head and shuffled away as though nothing had happened, followed by the rest of the herd, which slowly broke into a run until the ground shook with their thundering feet.

Miles and Mike went over to talk with the delighted film crew, joined by Dan and Amy, while I collapsed onto the prickly grass. I could feel my heart pounding wildly, and my breath came in gasps as I realized what could have happened if the elephant hadn't turned away at the last minute. Adrenaline pumping through my veins, I sprang up and brushed the grass from my pants, ready, even eager, for another confrontation that would make me feel this alive again.

That evening the film crew packed up and left for Nairobi. At the end of dinner, with the children tucked in bed, Mike and I sat with Miles beside a flickering campfire enjoying drinks brought by the camp steward. Night birds called to one another in the trees above us as Mike grilled Miles about his life in the bush. Then Miles questioned Mike about his job. My husband grumbled about his obstructive boss, Kenya's erratic electricity supply (which was wrecking his computers), and the rampant corruption that made it difficult to do a "straight" deal with his suppliers or customers. When he finished, Miles shook his head.

"Man, I find it completely baffling that you can remain at a desk for ten hours at a crack."

Mike chuckled. "Not at all. To me, the challenges of setting up this business and training Africans in a high-tech company are fascinating. There isn't anything else I'd rather be doing."

Miles snorted.

"In fact," Mike added, "I find it incredible that you don't get bored being out in the bush all day."

As I watched their exchange, I couldn't help comparing them. Mike, with neatly trimmed hair and spotless khakis, seemed out of place in the simple surroundings. Miles, big and bearded in shorts, with a well-worn bush jacket and sandals, couldn't have been more at home.

They were silent for a while and then my husband dozed off, his head resting against the back of the safari chair. When the fire blazed up for a moment, I could see Miles's eyes glowing in its light, looking at me.

"Now it's my turn to ask *you* some questions," he said quietly. I liked his voice, with its East African intonation somewhere between British and Australian. I looked over to see if Mike might wake up, but he was gone.

"Tell me," he continued, "how do you feel about your new life in Kenya?"

"It's like I've come home," I said, speaking quickly. "In fact, Mike and I never want to leave." As I told him how happy the children were and how much we were all learning about his fascinating country, I struggled to find the right words to articulate the intensity of the experiences I'd had.

Miles fetched a bottle from a camp steward and offered me another brandy. I sipped it slowly, swirling the amber liquid in the wide glass.

"So why do you think you're here?" he asked, pouring himself another.

"We thought we'd make a new start in life," I began.

"No, I mean why are you *here*—on earth?" he interrupted. "What's your purpose?"

"Oh," I said. No one had ever asked me that before, and I wasn't sure how to answer. Feeling tipsy, though I wasn't sure if it was the brandy or perhaps Miles himself, I stared into the flames, which seemed to burn brighter and release golden sparks as he prodded the embers with a long stick. "Ah, I . . . I don't know," I stuttered, uncertain about putting into words an old dream that had come to life again when I met the foreign correspondents following the death of President Kenyatta.

"Well, then, what do you need to do before you die?"

"I know it sounds silly, but I've always wanted to make a difference in the world. I feel like I'm supposed to communicate something important, perhaps as a broadcaster or journalist."

Miles leaned forward in his chair, and his eyes captured mine. "So what do you think is important for you to communicate, then?"

I had to confess that I had no idea—and what's more, without a work permit, there didn't seem any point in trying to communicate anything at all. But as soon as I said this, I realized that I was always finding some reason not to do what I really wanted to. And I wondered why.

Miles chuckled. "*Hakuna matata.* One day you'll figure out what matters to you, and then you'll be able to do anything you desire. You just have to be clear about what you want, and then go for it with all your might. You can do it."

After years of being a housewife I couldn't imagine why he, or I for that matter, believed in my ability to do anything great, but his encouragement stirred something in me.

"What about you?" I asked, relieved to be changing the subject. He stoked the fire and began to talk about a place called Kitich, a remote tented camp he had leased for long-term use in an ancient forest, high in the Mathews Range of northern Kenya. Mesmerized by the shimmering flames, I listened as he described tracking the last of the rhinos that had taken refuge in the forest there, watching the fish eagles circling over the stream, and seeing the old leopard that sometimes haunted his camp at dusk. Then he cupped his hands and mimicked the eagle's cry and the cough of the leopard.

His dream was to create a haven in that forest where animals were safe from poaching and visitors could watch the game on foot instead of from a minibus. "Kitich is the place where I feel happiest and most peaceful in the world," he said, staring into the embers, now white around the edges. Looking up again, he spoke in a low voice that made me lean forward to hear him. "Maybe the real purpose of life is simply to be calm with where you are and at peace with who you are."

I nodded, though I wasn't at all sure what he meant. I'd get really bored hanging around a forest all day, unchallenged. On the other hand, staying at home was equally boring. It was time to pack my life with adventures.

As the flames died down and the air grew cold, my teeth began to chatter. Miles got up and gently wrapped his jacket around my shoulders. I felt his warmth surround me. His hands rested on my shoulders for a moment and I sat still, electrified by his touch.

"One day I'll invite you to Kitich," he said, turning to stamp out the remains of the fire, "and if you think what I'm doing matters, perhaps you'll write about it."

I nodded. I wanted to go there more than anything. Just then, Mike stirred in his chair. As he opened his eyes, I stood quickly and the bush jacket fell off my shoulders to lie in a heap on the ground. Miles shook hands with Mike and kissed me on both cheeks, his beard grazing my skin. As the *askari* appeared from the darkness to take Mike and me to our tent, Miles sat down again and reached for his pipe. When I looked back, all I could see was a lone ember glowing in the darkness.

That night I lay awake, trying to deal with the unaccustomed feelings surging through me. I pulled out my flashlight and journal and began to write:

> After thirty years, someone has taken the time to look for my identity, and I am discovering that I have one—somewhere. I am finding a soul tucked away deep inside me where I never thought to look before. Now I truly want to achieve great things in the world. But what do I do with this new person I am carrying around within me?

I wanted so badly for Mike to ask questions as Miles had done—to really want to know me, not just trudge through life together. And I wanted to get inside his mind and emotions too. A long time ago, when we were first married, I had glimpsed a treasure inside him and loved the rare moments when we talked about our feelings about each other and our dreams for the future. But after the children were born, and Mike's job took over our lives, my efforts to penetrate his head and heart were thwarted; it was like trying to open a jammed locket. We still hadn't found the keys to one another, and it seemed we had both stopped trying. Suddenly overcome with feelings of guilt for even thinking such thoughts, I added more lines to my journal:

> Shall I smother this newly born creature, aware as I am of its potential power? Do I release my soul to grow and develop, shedding another in the process? Or can I bring him along with me, sharing what I am learning?

Lying next to my sleeping husband, I tried to make sense of the thoughts racing through my head. Could I fully explore my nature without endangering my relationship with my husband? Was it possible to reconcile the two? There was a grumbling roar in the darkness, and in that instant I recalled the moan of the lion locked in a cramped cage in Cedar Rapids.

Suddenly ravenous, as hungry as I had ever been, unable to go another moment without devouring something, anything, I unwrapped a bar of chocolate that I had tucked in my bag under the bed and bit it in half, swallowing almost without chewing. I tore open another one, but this time spat it, half-eaten, into a Kleenex. I took a third, chewing and spitting until my tongue hurt. Ashamed, I pulled the pillow over my head and tried to go to sleep.

7

Carpe Diem

INSPIRED BY MY CONVERSATION WITH MILES, I DECIDED THAT IF NO ONE would employ me without a work permit, I would simply have to employ myself. After exploring a number of ideas, I decided to collaborate with two members of the American Women's Association in assembling a newcomer's guide to Nairobi.

We had no idea how to start but plunged in anyway, collecting information for newly arrived expats from embassies and corporations. Once we finalized the content, we realized we would have to sell advertising space to pay for our printing costs. Fortunately, I knew how to promote just about anything, thanks to a lesson my dad had shared with me when I was six years old. After dressing me up in my Blue Bird uniform, complete with a little billed cap, he had taught me how to sell brooms made by blind people for the local Lions Club charity drive. Before we went out, he had me practice my pitch.

"Smile!" he urged, adjusting the broom in my hand. "Smile like you mean it." (Dad always urged us kids to smile, no matter how we felt inside.) I grinned broadly and launched into my well-rehearsed speech.

Dad's coaching continued. "If they say no once, don't take any notice," he said. He went on to explain, as if to a customer, the qualities of the broom, the fine dust-gathering characteristics of the straw, the neat twine plaiting, and the sturdy wooden handle.

"If they say no twice," he interjected, "you still ignore them." Beaming, he demonstrated the smooth, graceful flow of the broom over a wooden or concrete surface, even a carpet. "But if they say no a third time, you thank them and say goodbye."

Twenty-five years later, true to my father's teaching, I was still smiling broadly as I hawked ad space through the streets of Nairobi. I wore brightly colored skirts and tops from the tailor in Biashara Street and accented them with hand-woven African belts, beaded bracelets, earrings, and necklaces that I had fashioned myself from trade beads. Every day became an adventure—sharing Assam tea with an Austrian taxidermist who was stitching the hide of a wildebeest, sipping Turkish coffee with a belly dancer who taught me how to shimmy, and drinking warm Cokes while pitching to a deported Ugandan ex–government minister turned doughnut-maker. A smarmy Indian acupuncturist sent my blood pressure plummeting with his needles, while the Czech ambassador sent it up again, plying me with slivovitz at ten in the morning. He misinterpreted my giggly, overly enthusiastic response and invited me back, so I took Dan along in his Cub Scout uniform and taught him to smile too. Many years later, when my son became a persuasive salesman, able to convince just about anyone to do just about anything, he attributed his successful techniques to early childhood training.

Not *everyone* bought ads from me, of course, but I heard lots of amazing stories, and our zebra-striped guidebook had loads of advertisements and sold out its first print run of five thousand copies in just a few weeks, with all proceeds going to charity.

I was glad for a brief respite at Christmastime. There were no evergreen trees in Nairobi back then, so the children and I draped bougainvillea blossoms on a palm frond and threaded popcorn onto strings to make garlands. I baked my grandmother's traditional cinnamon rolls, though they refused to rise in Nairobi's mile-high altitude. Instead of turkey and all the trimmings, we feasted on curry and condiments served by William, resplendent in a red-paper hat. He and Ephraim danced an impromptu jig when we gave them new uniforms, extra rations of tea, sugar, and *posho*, and, as a special treat, a live goat.

I couldn't wait for New Year's Eve, because the Leakeys had invited us to a party. Uncertain about what to wear, I debated for days and finally chose a low-cut lime-green evening gown with dyed-to-match shoes that I had brought from London. While I was in the final stages of putting on my makeup, Mike walked into the room.

"Kathy, why do we have to go?" he complained. "Val's lovely, but I really could live without the rest of that crowd."

I knew that Mike didn't feel at ease with the macho Kenyan men and their fondness for safaris, beer, and flirting, but I continued brushing my hair and said nothing.

"The British Embassy is having a wonderful gathering tonight," he said. "Why don't we attend that instead?"

Two different temperaments, two different perspectives. "I'd rather not, darling," I said, my heart sinking at the thought of spending yet another night with the uptight expatriate crowd. "You'll have fun at Val and Philip's. Your boss is going to be at that other party. I don't want to bring in the new year with him. Do you?"

There was no more discussion, and Mike and I set off after dark in our new red MGB with a bottle of champagne for our hosts. When we turned off the main highway onto the narrow road leading to the Leakeys', we realized how foolish we had been to head into the bush at night in an open sports car with an undercarriage so low that it scraped over the corrugated track, littered with rocks and gouged with deep potholes. Bouncing along slowly, we were forced to a sudden halt as a pair of giraffes seemed to float across the road in front of us, their knobby knees level with our startled eyes.

We were the last guests to arrive and tucked our frivolous little car behind a tree, far from a line of rugged Land Rovers and pickups. A Masai *askari* in a knitted balaclava, long black overcoat, and tire sandals handed

Mike a flashlight and went before us down the steep slope of the gorge beside the Leakeys' house. I did my best to keep up, digging my heels into the hillside while grabbing at branches with one hand and clinging to the bottle with the other. Mike followed, cursing quietly. From somewhere far below, I could make out the faint sound of music.

My tights were ripped and I was panting when we arrived in a small clearing dimly lit by lanterns hung from low branches. The party was in full swing, with a dozen people dancing on the trodden earth. Val, her shoulder-length black hair striking against a simple white cotton dress, hugged Mike, while the boyish Philip surveyed me with a cheeky grin, one eyebrow raised.

"Woman, you look as if you've been dragged through a bush backward," he drawled, before introducing us to Giles, a horn-rimmed British ecologist who wore a tuxedo jacket over a faded-blue *kikoy*.

Tor, a smiling Norwegian safari guide, and his wife, Susie, whom I liked instantly, came over and asked us about our safari with their friend Miles. Surrounded by so many beautiful and confident people, I felt out of place until a man who claimed to be a hyena researcher led me onto the dirt dance floor while his companion, a wild-eyed brunette in a flowing blue dress, dragged Mike off to get a drink.

The party was unlike any I had ever been to. The smell of juicy steaks and corn grilled over a charcoal fire mingled with the sweet scent of marijuana. The conversation was noisy against the thumping bass, which grew louder as the evening wore on, blending with the din of the cicadas, the racket of frogs, and the roar of the river below. Someone offered me a joint, and I took one puff, then another. Flinging off my shoes and tights, I danced barefoot. Mike seemed to be enjoying himself too, swirling one woman after another with elegant ease.

Later, he pulled me into his arms and we started to dance, but someone cut in, and then another, and everything grew hazier until I heard shouts that it was midnight. As I was looking around for Mike, a man grabbed my arm and pulled me through the bushes to a small clearing where we collapsed on the ground.

"You've been driving me crazy all night," he murmured urgently, his hands moving aggressively over my body. Pinning me down, he kissed me, and I could smell cigarettes and beer on his breath. Not sure whether to be offended or flattered, I froze, breathless from his vigorous investigation of the inside of my mouth. I heard people nearby and pushed him away, feeling like an adolescent girl afraid to be caught by her parents after the prom. Reluctantly he rolled off me, leaving me sprawled on the ground, suddenly aware of the prick of thorns against my back.

"Happy New Year!" he called out over his shoulder. My head was whirling as I pulled myself together and staggered out to see Mike staring at me.

"What's going on?" he asked, his voice flat. I felt my stomach knot as I searched for some plausible explanation.

"Call of nature," I muttered, struggling to keep my balance as I straightened my clothes and ran my fingers through my tousled hair. We left soon afterward, driving in silence while I relived what had happened, wondering what I might have done to avoid it—and also what could have occurred had I been more receptive. For days afterward I felt unsettled by my first experience with the free-and-easy lifestyle so long prevalent in our adopted country.

"Are you married or do you live in Kenya?" was an old tag associated with the residents of "Happy Valley" (as the European enclave in Kenya came to be known) in the 1940s: it seemed to be just as appropriate now. I wondered why this "white mischief" had stuck. Was it the altitude? Or could it be the lack of clothes worn by people in the tropics? Could it be explained by a moral code that originally allowed a man to have a wife as well as a string of mistresses because as a colonial settler he was free of censorious relatives to gossip or blacken his reputation? Whatever the explanation, I was suddenly confronted with the reality of a society that would have shocked my friends in Mill Hill or Cedar Rapids. I was shocked as well, by the chance of freedom that now beckoned.

I discovered quickly that there was a certain twinkle in the eyes of many people, regardless of their race, as men assessed women and women sized up men, knowing full well that anything was possible, and indeed fairly likely. Unaccustomed to being flirted with—and even less used to compliments—I found it exciting to be appreciated.

Our telephone rang very early one morning, and I recognized the voice of Mary Anne Fitzgerald, a new journalist friend of Mike's and mine. She struggled to remain composed as she told me that Miles Burton and several members of a film crew had been taking off from Nairobi's Wilson Airport on a routine flight in a small aircraft when it caught a wing on the perimeter fence and crashed. Everyone on board had been burned alive.

Shaking uncontrollably, I dropped the phone and staggered down the hall to tell Mike what had happened. I found it difficult to believe what I had just heard. The only dead person that I had known well was my grandfather, who had died in his sleep at eighty-three; his death was sad but expected. It wasn't possible that someone like Miles could have died so young—but then another friend called to confirm the news.

Despite my father's admonition to keep smiling no matter what, that day I couldn't stop crying. Miles had given me the greatest gift possible— asking me to articulate my purpose in life and inspiring me to believe I could achieve it. He had seen and heard me, recognized and known me—long before I ever knew myself.

Later in the day, Mike and I went to visit Miles's wife, Evelyn. Her friends had already gathered around her, each bringing food or drink, as is the tradition in Kenya. She sat, pale and motionless, on a sofa in a room filled with the treasures Miles had brought back from his safaris: animal skins, interesting rocks, crystals, Masai beads, and Tanzanian carvings. Seated on the sofa next to his mother, their son Pierre was solemn and unmoving, while his little brother, Luc, ran in and out of the house, not yet understanding that his father would never come home again. I held myself together during the visit, but once outside I broke down again.

That night, Mike and I told Dan and Amy about Miles's death.

"What will happen to Pierre and Luc without a daddy?" Amy asked, one hand tightly clutching mine.

We explained that Pierre's mummy would look after the children.

"Could you die?" Dan asked, his face contorted as he stared at Mike. I struggled to remain composed. Although I couldn't say it out loud, I felt as though a part of me had perished, a part visible only to Miles. Now no one would know who I really was.

As our family struggled to come to terms with our loss, suddenly our lives didn't feel so secure anymore.

In the weeks after Miles's death, I discovered that nearly everyone I knew in Kenya had a tragic story to tell. One acquaintance had lost her seventeen-year-old son from snakebite, another had watched her husband die in a freak hunting accident, and a hippo had killed the twenty-two-year-old son of a third during a fishing trip with his father. To my surprise, people seemed to accept their loved ones' death.

"Africa is cruel," someone said. "And Africa always wins."

Eventually I began to understand why *mzungu*s lived so hard and fast in Kenya. Most seemed to drink too much, drive too fast, and take absurd risks, as though they didn't care whether they lived or died. In Africa, death was in your face. Victims of car crashes could lie uncovered by the side of the road for hours, awaiting transport to the morgue. Children routinely starved, fell into cooking fires, or perished from simple diarrhea. Every year hundreds of thousands of Africans died from malaria, cholera, tuberculosis, riots, and war. People were shot to death in robberies, and light planes crashed when they hit animals on the runway or birds flew into their engines. Each morning, the newspapers were filled with gory photographs, leaving nothing to the imagination. The consequence of so much dying seemed to be a reckless, devil-may-care attitude. Precious as it is, life came with no guarantees. Many *mzungu*s celebrated it, living on the edge, as though each day they dared death to seize them.

Something changed in me when I realized that I might not die in my bed as my elderly grandfather had. I could go at any moment. And if I did, what would I have accomplished? This new, intimate understanding of my mortality transformed my life. *Carpe diem*—seize the day—became my motto, and I resolved to live each day as if there would be no tomorrow. I didn't want to miss a thing.

8

Cradle of Mankind

AS I SAT CURLED UP IN MY FAVORITE SPOT BENEATH THE BOUGAINVILLEA bushes in the back garden, an idea took shape in my mind. I began to dream of gathering Kenya's most creative spirits—artists and writers, musicians and actors, photographers and filmmakers—for a grand celebration of their arts and crafts.

I would need a venue and thought of the National Museum, run by Richard Leakey, the second son of Louis and Mary, and brother of our friend Philip. Richard had a reputation for being brilliant but difficult. Lacking a university degree, he adopted a defensive stance, keeping people at bay while he did what he pleased. Powerful, fiercely intelligent, and determined, he was nonetheless highly effective. I resolved to speak with him.

Within a week I was sitting in the great man's office, feeling daunted. "I want to run an arts festival," I blurted, aware of my naïveté. Though Richard and I were exactly the same age, the rakishly handsome, charming man had a presence that made him seem much older, and his raised eyebrow made me feel foolish. But I was determined to be brave—so I kept going. Happily so, because coincidentally he was looking for an idea to celebrate the fiftieth anniversary of the founding of the museum, and my idea turned out to be just what he had been searching for. When I walked out, I had an office, a typewriter, and a job: I was to produce a three-day arts festival in six months' time. Oh, and there was another challenge: it was up to me to raise all the money.

With Richard's support, I was able to obtain seed funding of two thousand dollars from the managing director of Cadbury Schweppes Kenya. Mike helped me approach other corporations while I began to commission original plays, organize art exhibits, and schedule films. It didn't seem to matter that I didn't know what I was doing, as long as the money flowed, but I had to make sure that our range of places, activities, and cultures fully represented the peoples of Kenya.

Richard invited Mike and me to travel around the country to experience it firsthand. Our first visit would be to Koobi Fora, Richard's camp on the shores of Lake Turkana some five hundred miles north of Nairobi. I'd read a lot about the wild place where he and his wife, Meave, had unearthed many remarkable anthropoid and humanoid fossils that they believed were directly related to humans. Some experts disputed Richard's theory, though the remote site's label as "the cradle of mankind" had stuck.

I was accustomed to traveling with Mike, but he was busy at the office and encouraged me to go on my own. I was disappointed by his decision, and a little frightened by the prospect of traveling with someone as daunting as Richard. My palms were sweaty as I joined him and a pair of earnest young research students in his little Cessna and we strapped ourselves in. When we roared down the runway and took off, easily clearing the perimeter fence, I glanced down and spotted the blackened wreckage of Miles's airplane still lying there. Sickened by the thought of my friend's last moments, I tried to put the image out of my mind and think instead of our conversation on safari that had indirectly led to this adventure with Richard. It meant that a remnant of his spirit would survive in me, a phoenix rising from the ashes into a new existence.

As we skimmed the undulating crest of the Ngong Hills, the plane's shadow scattered goats tended by Masai boys who waved at us, their crimson *shuka*s bright against the dry grass. Suddenly the land dropped away into a deep gorge, becoming the vast crack in the earth called the Great Rift Valley, which runs over four thousand miles, beginning in Lebanon and cutting south through Africa to Mozambique. The massive fault originally occurred when the earth's crust heated, then bent, thus creating some of the most beautiful scenery on earth.

After flying over Lake Naivasha and then Lake Nakuru, home to millions of pink flamingos, we spotted the expanse of water that I had seen as we flew into Kenya for the first time. It now shimmered like pale-green silk under an ominous gray sky. A sudden flash of lightning nearly took my breath away, and I could feel bile in my throat. Richard, at the controls, appeared to ignore the thunderclap that followed as he headed for the far end of the lake through a tunnel of billowing clouds. The plane bucked, and rain streaked the windows.

"Hang on, we're going down," Richard shouted a few minutes later. With that, he spiraled rapidly toward a rough airstrip barely visible in the distance and soon glided to a stop in the middle of what appeared to be absolutely nowhere. With the propellers still whirling, I jumped out heaving and dashed for the nearest bush. When I returned, Richard had already been whisked away in a Land Rover, leaving his other passengers by the plane. The squall had vanished and high clouds sailed slowly above us, tiny wisps in a vast blue sky. The colors around me seemed faded—old lavender, pale green, dusty ocher, and beige, as though bleached out by too much sun. The temperature of Koobi Fora often hovers well over one hundred degrees during the daytime, and I was wilting in the heat by the time one of Richard's staff picked us up in another Land Rover and dropped us off at our huts.

That evening, we all gathered in a large thatched enclosure lit by flickering hurricane lamps. Over fried Nile perch and white wine, Richard, pipe in hand, held court, speculating on the origins of mankind—and of God. Did God invent man, he asked, or—more likely—was God simply the projection of our imagination and desires? Just as the discussion was getting lively, he sent us all to bed, cautioning us to watch out for scorpions in our shoes in the morning. On the way back to my hut I stopped for a moment, aware of all the lava beds that blanketed the ancient fossils and forests of petrified wood, so close to the rippling waters of the lake that stretched into the darkness. As I gazed up at the myriad stars glittering overhead, I realized that I was standing where hundreds of thousands—no, millions—of years ago, one of man's earliest ancestors must also have stared in wonder at that dazzling sky. What did he (or she) think he was doing here? For that matter, what was I doing here?

With the wail of the wind across the lake and the stifling heat inside the hut, it was hard to sleep, so eventually I gave up, lit the lantern, and pulled out my journal.

As I began to write notes about the day, I felt a twitch in my fingers and held the pen more firmly, then watched in astonishment as my hand moved across the page as though propelled by a force that had nothing to do with me. The pen seemed to take off, producing peculiar squiggles and loops that turned into letters after a few lines; then the letters became words. The first word was "love," then "power," and finally "energy." The words kept forming, over and over again, until my hand slowed, then stopped. Heart thumping, I thought, Who, or what, is guiding me to write these words?

I waited for an answer but nothing happened, so I asked out loud, "What do the words mean?" I was hoping for a response from my unconscious, or from whatever was communicating through me, but there was no answer. I extinguished the lantern and lay on my narrow bed with my eyes wide open as I tried to figure out what was going on. It would be many years before the questions of this night would find voice or resolution.

After a restless night, it was a relief when Richard invited us all for a swim before breakfast. As we paddled in the warm alkaline water, I noticed what seemed to be a giant log floating my way. I soon realized it was a huge crocodile. Shrieking, I splashed toward the shore but halted when I saw Richard standing nearby with a smirk on his face.

"They're Nile crocs, and there are lots more of them here," he explained. He pointed to three massive creatures less than twenty feet away. "Don't worry. They have plenty of fish and aren't remotely interested in eating you." Gritting my teeth, I waded back in.

The next day, on the flight back to Nairobi, I asked Richard why I seemed to feel more at home in Kenya than I ever had in London, or even Iowa. Over the roar of the engine he explained that it's a common reaction in people who come out to East Africa, perhaps because it triggers a "genetic memory"—a subconscious awareness that this is the home of the first human beings. Whatever the explanation, I never wanted to live anywhere else again. Landing at Wilson Airport, I felt different from the person who had taken off two days earlier. No longer afraid of Richard Leakey, little planes, or traveling by myself, I finally felt I belonged in Africa; and I felt ready, and maybe even able, to meet the challenges of the festival I had conceived.

Every week the newspapers ran stories on our museum event, and it was clear that excitement was building throughout the country. Hundreds of schoolchildren, including Dan and Amy, mailed in entries for the drawing contest. Regional theater groups submitted ideas for plays, while traditional dance groups offered their services and people inundated us with samples of artwork from every district.

As my life shifted into second, third, and fourth gear, I became aware of a remarkable phenomenon. Once I had fully committed to the project, whatever I needed or wanted seemed to materialize—exactly on time. I noticed with delight that people, money, ideas, and help turned up at just the right moment. Doors and windows opened, bringing opportunities I'd never imagined possible, as if I were being swept along on a fast-moving current that carried me effortlessly in the right direction.

Although I was not conscious of the process, this was my first experience of synchronicity. Years later I would read Deepak Chopra's description of "synchrodestiny," which argues that when we are in the flow of being, with our heart open and our focus intentional, seemingly random events occur that are actually gifts from the universe—or responses from the universe to our intent. Events don't function separately on a timeline, he says, but occur simultaneously. As we begin to recognize the meaning and pattern behind the coincidences, we become aware of ourselves as part of a divine flow of existence, living in a world where "miracles" are a daily occurrence.

That said, I was in too much of a hurry in those prefestival days to notice the deeper meaning that may have been behind many of the things that happened that year. I hurried backward and forward between home, the children's schools, and the museum, speeding around Nairobi in my red MGB, leaving clouds of dust in my wake. It wasn't the best way to endear myself to the members of the staid Museum Society, a group of mostly white Kenyan traditionalists and conservatives who weren't interested in helping a young American woman with strange multicultural ideas that disturbed the status quo of their thinking. In fact, they strongly disapproved of me and weren't shy about expressing their feelings. Their idea of Kenya was a colonial culture that kept "Africa" at a distance. My determination to showcase the diverse ethnic groups and their traditions, and the amazing pool of talent that existed in this multiracial society, angered the more conventional ladies whose remarks so hurt and troubled me that I finally gathered the courage to ask Richard what to do.

"Ignore them," he said firmly. "Remember that when you raise your head above the parapet, someone will shoot. To the best of your ability, do what you believe is right. If those people want to help, they can. If they don't, it's their loss. You can't be ruled by other people's views of what you should and shouldn't do." It was a lesson I would never forget, though I didn't always manage to follow it. Do what you must. Be who you are. You can't please everyone.

As I got to know Richard better, I discovered that although he and Philip Leakey were brothers, they definitely weren't friends. Philip, some eight years Richard's junior, was his polar opposite. Whereas Richard was orderly and precise, Philip was all over the place, chaotic and creative. Both brothers were extremely charismatic, however, qualities on which they relied to achieve many things in life.

One day when I was meeting with Richard, I noticed that a blood vessel had burst in his eye. He dismissed it lightly, saying he had a small problem with blood pressure. The next time I saw him he appeared yellow and exhausted. I picked up the rumor that he was dying of kidney failure. As a child, he had developed a kidney infection after a sore throat. That infection had left both kidneys weakened, and over time they had become useless. His staff tried hiring a *mganga*, a medicine man, to ease his suffering and remove evil spirits that might be exacerbating the condition, but it was already too late: only a new kidney would save him.

When Philip was told this, he volunteered to donate one of his kidneys to his brother, assuming they were a match—and they were. The only problem was that Philip was determined to see through his imminent parliamentary election first. As he waited for the operation, Richard kept working, though as the day of the museum festival approached, he had grown so much weaker and more jaundiced that I wondered if he could survive until after the election.

Despite his precarious state of health, Richard remained deeply involved in the upcoming event, and he encouraged me to extend the festival into all the regional museums. He even organized a visit for me to the Fort Jesus Museum in Mombasa so I could help with festival preparations there. It was the perfect excuse for me to get Mike and the kids away for a long weekend. This time, Mike could make it.

The four of us boarded the famous old train that left Nairobi every night at dusk for the three-hundred-mile journey to the coast. After settling into our compartment, we made our way down the carriages to the dining car, where ancient waiters decked out in neat safari suits and impeccable white gloves greeted us like old friends. I wondered if they had once served Karen Blixen and her lover, perhaps even using the same silverware they had laid before us on a starched white linen cloth. Perched on a worn leather banquette, I felt time slip away as I peered out at the ink-black night. From a distance I heard Mike's voice.

"What do you have planned for us in Mombasa, Kathy?" Mike had left the organizing to me since this was a family vacation of sorts.

"Well," I said, reluctantly dismissing the image of Karen and her lover, "tomorrow we're going to meet the director of the Fort Jesus Museum. I'm hoping he'll give us a tour. I want to explore bringing the festival there when it travels. What do you think?"

"Good idea," Mike said, though I could see he wasn't excited about the idea of taking time off from his much-needed vacation. We ate in silence after that until the kids started getting rambunctious and we left for our compartment. Then Mike began reading aloud from a travel guide that described the history of Kenya. Amy and Dan listened wide-eyed as he described how seafarers—Romans, Arabs, Portuguese, and British—had traded with the locals in ports along East Africa for more than two thousand years, attempting to colonize them. However, it was only in the twentieth century that the British had managed to open up the region by building a railway from Mombasa across Kenya, to Lake Victoria in Uganda. It took thirty thousand imported Indian laborers more than six years to build the tracks! Painfully hacked out of the bush, desert, and forest, the railway claimed more than two thousand lives, most lost to malaria, blackwater fever, and other diseases.

With the railway finished, thousands of settlers poured in from England, determined to exploit Nairobi's natural resources and wide-open spaces. Many died in the process, but their offspring, captivated by the perfect weather, the free-and-easy lifestyle, and the seemingly limitless opportunities, stayed on and tried to tame the wilderness—and the people who lived in it.

As Mike read on, he became fully animated, enjoying the chance to relax with the children. I listened too, but my mind was wandering again. What a glorious trip this could have been at a different time in our lives. Mike and I had begun our life together with such promise, sharing so many of the same dreams, values, and tastes. Now a distance seemed to separate us, and I sometimes felt as if I barely knew him. We were running in different directions. His life revolved around the office, where he was doing what he loved best—building a company, creating innovations, and developing the talents of those around him—while I was completely taken up by the children and the festival from morning until late at night.

But that night I forgot my concerns and vowed to have a carefree family holiday. We slept soundly on our narrow bunks, gently rocked by the train as it rumbled through the darkness to the coast. Within minutes of our dawn arrival in Mombasa we were dripping with perspiration in the humid air and swatting furiously at the flies swarming around the raffia baskets of mangoes and bananas on the platform. A porter nonchalantly picked up two suitcases in each hand, balanced another on his head, and led us to an antiquated taxi that drove us to our hotel, the driver leaning on his horn all the way to the sea.

We dropped the bags in our room, barely able to focus in the dimly lit interior, then squinted in the dazzling sunlight when Dan threw open the shutters to a view of gleaming white sand and the turquoise sheen of the Indian Ocean, blending seamlessly with a brilliant blue sky. We all changed into swimming gear and headed toward the water, Dan racing outside, his skinny arms flapping to scare off the falcons that divebombed the hotel veranda for scraps. Then he climbed onto the low wall that bounded the beach. I stood a few feet away, with Amy by my side.

"Come on, Amy," he shouted, spreading his arms out. Hesitantly, she climbed onto the ledge, paused for a moment, and then thrust her arms out in perfect imitation of her brother.

"Fly!" I cried. Dan leaped as far as he could onto the sand below. A moment of indecision. Then Amy jumped too, landing in a heap of giggles beside her brother.

We wandered along the deserted beach sprinkled with tiny shells, tangles of seaweed, and colonies of busy sea crabs that glided across the beach like translucent sand dancers. Mike and Dan rented goggles and flippers to explore the coral reef on a boat for hire, while Amy and I settled on *kikoys* under a cluster of palms. Since our arrival in Kenya, she had begun to emerge as a brave child with an adventurous streak. Shaded under a large umbrella, I buried myself in my journal while she shaped a sandcastle. As the heat intensified, we dozed off.

"*Bella.*" I heard the word from far off, as though in a dream. Opening one eye, I squinted against the sun at a bronze-faced man, almost too handsome, his eyes concealed by expensive dark glasses. His jet-black hair was slicked back, and he wore nothing but a small pair of swimming trunks with a striped *kikoy* draped around his neck. Embarrassed by the frank gaze that slowly moved over my body, I grabbed my own *kikoy* and covered myself.

He lifted his Ray-Bans and his eyes pierced mine. "The sandcastle, I mean," he said, with a trace of irony. I detected an Italian accent. I could feel my face redden and wished I weren't so absurdly pale and freckled, then blushed even more. What did it matter? I was a married woman and shouldn't care what any other man thought of me. I was trying to think of something to say, preferably witty and urbane, when I heard the putt-putt of Mike's boat approaching the shore and sensed Amy stirring beside me. "Mummy," she said, looking quizzically at me, and then at the man. Heart pounding, I sat up as the stranger turned, without a backward glance, and strode away. A few minutes later, Dan and Mike scrambled out of the boat, both looking four shades darker than when they had set off.

"Who was that guy?" Mike asked, pulling off his sunglasses.

Amy frowned. "I didn't like him," she said, crinkling her nose.

To my relief Dan interrupted before she had a chance to go further. "You'll never guess what we saw!" His words tumbled out of him. "Lots of brilliant fish, a sea urchin, tons of coral, a starfish, two jellyfish, and ten groupers." I breathed easily again, determined to forget the man whose look and words had so unsettled me.

Late in the afternoon, I took the family with me when I went into Mombasa to interview Omar Bwana, the director of the museum at Fort Jesus. The children listened intently as he told us stories about the original fort, built by the Portuguese in the sixteenth century to protect Mombasa from Turkish invaders. It had been the scene of many bloody battles and escapes, attacks and executions, starvations and bombardments that had left it scarred but surprisingly intact. Locally built *dhow*s had docked there since Roman times, long before the fort was built, carrying exotic cargoes from the Indian state of Goa, from the Persian Gulf via the Horn of Africa, and from as far south as Mozambique. Setting out with swords, brass, precious textiles, and delicious dates, traders returned with mangrove poles for building, as well as spices, gold, ivory, and slaves.

On the map Omar showed us, Dan and Amy were able to trace the route the *dhow*s took to their final destination, the romantic island of Zanzibar, famous for cloves, ginger, and cinnamon, but infamous as the center of the brutal East African slave trade, conducted for centuries by the Arabs.

Omar directed us to the streets of old Mombasa, thronged with locals, vendors, and sunburned tourists like ourselves. The delicious smell of lamb kebabs mingled with the stench of rotting vegetables from the piles of rubbish in the back alleys. Women, hidden in their houses behind lavishly carved doors during the day, now paraded through town in clusters, nearly all veiled from head to toe in black *bui-bui*s that left nothing but their kohl-rimmed eyes exposed. I wondered about their lives, lived in the shadows.

As we made our way back to the hotel, glimpsing high minarets that loomed above the narrow streets and thatched roofs, suddenly the air was filled with the call of many *muezzin*s broadcast from loudspeakers jutting out of the towers. While Mike and Amy wandered on ahead, Dan and I slowed to glance inside a mosque, marked by a neat row of sandals on a mat outside.

Men and boys sat on Persian rugs on the floor, casually reading the paper and chatting quietly. Watching with fascination, I lost track of the time, and when I looked around Dan had vanished. It took a few anxious minutes to find him, deep in conversation with an old man at a hole-in-the-wall shop lined with shelves of miniature *dhow*s, complete with tiny masts, sails, and ropes. After I joined him, Dan selected a finely carved boat to purchase, and then pointed to a collection of small painted medallions tacked to the wall. Each one had a white star and crescent moon carved into its red center.

"What are those?" he asked.

"They are for good luck," said the shopkeeper, pulling one from the wall to show Dan. "Sailors call them the eye of the *dhow*. They nail them on the prow of their boat to guide them home if they lose their bearings."

The man wrapped the medallion in a scrap of an old *Nation* newspaper and fastened it with a string. "This one is yours," he said to Dan.

Bowing slightly, he added, "When you are lost, this will always protect you."

Over the years that medallion was to assume an almost mystical significance for Dan, perhaps symbolizing his desire to return home safely from the dangers and excitement that life offered those who willingly set off from safe harbors toward uncertain danger.

When we reached the hotel, where we again met up with Mike and Amy, a perfect crescent moon hung low over the horizon. The buzz of disco music and cheerful voices drifted out from the hotel's beachside bar. A man appeared in the open door and lifted his hand in a casual wave. I recognized him instantly and involuntarily raised my arm, only to let it drop, hoping Mike hadn't noticed. But he had.

"It's that guy from the beach," he said, looking at me.

"Who?" I asked, trying not to sound defensive. "I don't even know his name," I said, perhaps too quickly. But an idea had crossed my mind.

"Come on, my love," I said. "Let's get the kids to bed and go for a drink." It would give us a chance to relax, maybe even to dance.

"You won't find anyone interesting in that bar," he said disdainfully as we headed for our room. "It's just a bunch of Italian tourists and boring KCs," using the derogatory nickname for Kenya cowboys.

Although I fumed as we tucked in the children, I tried not to show my irritation. All I wanted to do was have fun and dance like we used to. Inside our room, mosquito netting hung over our bed like a wedding veil. The shutters were tightly closed, and the smell of frangipani and a trace of insect repellent hung in the air. Torn between staying and going, I opened the door, letting in a soft wind off the ocean.

"Go if you want to," Mike said, pulling off his clothes. "But we have a lot planned for the morning, and it's really more sensible to have an early night." He was right, of course, so I undressed and crawled into bed, and we read for a while before he switched off the light.

A large fan revolved slowly overhead as I lay awake listening to Mike's deep breathing and the whine of a mosquito searching for a way through the netting that hung over us. When a sudden draft carried in faint strains of music from the bar, I covered my head with a pillow and tried to go to sleep. But in my heart I wanted to dance.

Back in Nairobi I added Fort Jesus to the growing number of regional museums participating in the festival. During the final run-up to the event, scores of volunteers turned up to create a sculpture garden and hang an exhibit of children's art that filled the main hall. Costumed actors from around the country practiced their lines in the theater, cheered on by plumed dancers in lion masks and ankle rattles and fierce drummers with painted faces. Dan mimicked their accents and Amy copied their intricate movements, soon learning them by heart. During the dress rehearsal, Mike and the children joined me on stage and we all helped coach the performers. Never before had I been so completely stretched, nor so fulfilled.

On the day of the festival it began to rain, and Museum Hill grew soggy in the downpour; but the dreary weather didn't keep scores of school buses from bringing excited children in from outlying areas, and by midmorning hundreds of people of all races were milling about the museum grounds. Carrying a shovel in one hand, Richard Leakey, his eyes bloodshot and his face yellow with jaundice, directed teams of men tamping down the sodden earth. Mercifully, the sun came out in the afternoon. By nightfall, thousands of Kenyans of all races had toured the art and sculpture exhibitions, applauded the continuous program of plays, concerts, and films, and gazed in fascination at the craftspeople weaving carpets and mats, sculpting, carving, knitting, and sewing in large tents erected for the occasion.

The final tally after the weekend was thirty thousand visitors to the National Museum and countless more across the country. From Mombasa to Lake Victoria, there were joyous celebrations in the local museums reflecting the energetic, creative, unified spirit of the young nation.

The next day I was totally exhausted, but I had never been happier. Back under the bougainvillea bushes, notepad in hand, I was already plotting my next project.

9

Warnings

THE WEEK AFTER THE FESTIVAL, MIKE CAME HOME WITH SHOCKING NEWS. His boss's deepening displeasure with his attempts to develop his African managers had reached a crisis point. We were being reassigned to America. I burst into tears at the news. How could I leave behind my work, my friends, the sky, the sun, William and Ephraim, our dogs, and, most of all, my newly found self? I all but refused to go. Mike felt the same way, but we had no choice.

The company organized a farewell party for us in the garden. Five-year-old Amy and Dan, almost nine, wore their traditional African costumes and watched solemnly as Mike received a traditional elder's colobus monkey–skin robe and headdress, while a Kikuyu woman presented me with a hand-woven *kikapu* bag. Later, I hid behind a jacaranda tree and tried not to cry. I managed to hold off until William slaughtered a tethered goat for the feast to follow, and then I couldn't stop. Reluctantly we packed, gave away our dogs and Amy's cat, Scary, and said goodbye to our friends. As the day of our departure approached, I grew even more depressed, feeling like a caged bird that had somehow escaped but had quickly been recaptured.

Forty-eight hours before our departure, Mike received an unexpected call from a Kenyan Asian who asked him to set up a new company in Nairobi that would represent the Wang computer company. We were saved, just in time! William put a tea cozy on his head and danced when Mike announced that we weren't leaving.

Setting up a new company took all of Mike's time: some nights he wouldn't return home until three or four in the morning, ashen with fatigue. His new boss had no concept of time or family life and drove himself as hard as he worked his staff. As always, I was up at dawn, leaving Mike sleeping, which meant we saw very little of each other except at our frequent social events—dinners, barbecues, national days, Rotary Club functions, and American Women's Club dinners.

During the day I was busy volunteering for every organization that would have me, along with working on a new children's book about music in Kenya, co-written with the region's leading musicologist, Professor George Senoga-Zake. Always I juggled my time playing the Superwoman act. Dan was a Cub Scout, frequently needing a ride to meetings or events, and Amy required transport to ballet and visits with friends. We transferred her from her nursery class to Hardy Manor School in Langata to be close to Lara Leakey. It meant a long bus commute every morning and afternoon, but she loved the ride, which took her past the Nairobi National Park, meaning that she was likely to spot rhinos, buffaloes, and gazelles along the way.

At nine, Dan was socially and academically adept, although he had difficulty writing neatly, which embarrassed him. Fortunately, he had an inquiring mind well above his years and a Monty Python–inspired wit that surprised those who took the time to listen. William was teaching him Swahili, the first of five new languages he would try to speak in his life. An avid reader, Dan devoured books my mother mailed him from Iowa, including the *Whole Earth Catalog*, which he found particularly intriguing.

When a new headmaster welcomed my desire to start a Parent Teacher Association, Dan helped me launch a school library in an old bus that we lined with shelves and filled with magazines, journals, and books donated by other parents. He took particular delight in sifting through piles of Kenyan newspapers, often illustrated with blurry pictures of two-headed pigs, man-eating snakes, and crashed *matatu*s (minibuses designed to hold nine passengers that were frequently packed with more than twenty). He cut out his favorites and glued them in his scrapbooks.

Dan tried to spend every weekend with Lengai, whose family had moved to a cluster of thatched mud huts and an old caravan set high above the same narrow gorge that cut through the Leakeys' property by the game park. The Crozes' menagerie had expanded to include a pair of vicious ostriches, a flock of boisterous geese, and two irritable camels. The two boys explored the surrounding area like their great heroes, the explorers Burton and Speke, swinging from vines across the gorge, and befriending the Masai children living nearby. Whenever Dan returned from Lengai's, his backpack held some new trophy: a bird's nest, a fossil from the riverbed, a beaded bracelet, a Masai knife, once a monkey's skull. Another time he returned with deep scratches on his wrist following a scary, though triumphant, encounter with a determined baboon that had tried to snatch his bowl of chocolate mousse.

If Lengai came to us, the boys had to invent their own fun. One sultry afternoon in February (the seasons were upside down in Kenya, which lies on the equator), I suggested they build a tree house. As a child, I had always wanted one, but the trees in my parents' yard were too tall and straight. Luckily we had the perfect tree in our back garden now, with low, heavy branches that spread outward like the spines of an umbrella. The boys nailed wooden planks onto the trunk leading up to a rough wooden platform big enough to seat thirteen for lunch. Over time, it became a playhouse for Amy and her friends, or a command center, spaceship, and hideaway for Dan and Lengai, who preferred to camp there when we had visitors. The tree house also became a haven for Dan when it was time to go to school, which he now claimed gave him terrible stomachaches. Normally upbeat and positive, he was becoming increasingly negative and depressed, so I took him to Nairobi's only child therapist, who couldn't figure out what was troubling him.

I did my best to cheer him up and pasted signs proclaiming THIS TOO SHALL PASS where he would be sure to see them—even in the bathroom.

But Dan's anxiety worsened; it was a daily battle to get him to leave the house. In despair, we called his beloved pediatrician, who pried the cause out of him: his school's grumpy headmaster's use of corporal punishment. The doctor suggested we transfer Dan to the International School in Kenya.

It proved a wise prescription, one that was to transform both his life and Amy's, since she joined him in the move. Founded by the American and Canadian embassies and set fifteen miles from downtown Nairobi, ISK had grown into a lively school for nearly a thousand youngsters from forty-six countries. A lush coffee plantation surrounded the grounds, and classes were held in neat round *banda*s (huts) dotted across the campus. The teachers were young and adventurous; many had worked in other international schools, bringing with them exciting new approaches to education and a genuine commitment to the educational and emotional well-being of their students. In striking contrast to his previous Dickensian school, ISK's dynamic atmosphere encouraged curiosity, creativity, and compassion for others.

We were relieved when an observant school counselor advised us that Dan suffered from dyslexia, a common learning disorder that explained his difficulties with spelling, his messy handwriting, and his problems with math. Once the condition had been diagnosed, he seemed like a different child and quickly taught himself to write legibly, albeit in a strangely stilted Victorian script that never seemed to match his very modern spirit.

Every morning Mike and I walked the children to the school bus. As we waited, I sometimes plucked blossoms from the jacaranda trees and bougainvillea bushes to weave into Amy's hair ribbons. At lunchtime, Amy reported, large and greedy kites, similar to falcons, sometimes swooped down to try to snatch the brightly colored ribbons, which they mistook for food. She would shriek with delight and a bit of fright as she and her friends dove for cover under the picnic tables on the grassy lawn.

Now that the kids were settled in school, I was eager to work again. Mike encouraged me to get out of the house and managed to get me an interview with fellow Rotarian Joe Rodrigues, editor-in-chief of the largest English-language newspaper in Kenya, the *Nation*. Somehow I convinced Joe to let me write a weekly recipe column. It wasn't exactly covering breaking news for the *New York Times*, but at least it was a foot in the door.

Few white Kenyans wanted to set foot in the *Nation*'s building, located as it was at the wrong end of a very bad road. But for me it was heaven. Panting up the grimy steps with a sheaf of recipes, I wound my way through the crush of reporters who sweltered under fans hanging from the corrugated metal roof. Their desks were almost as ancient as their typewriters, which, like the battered chairs and dented tables, were chained to the floor with huge steel links. I was always surprised that the reporters didn't have shackles around their ankles to keep them in place too. A haze of cigarette smoke hung over the room, alive with clattering typewriters and ringing telephones.

Dan loved going to the newspaper office with me and always headed straight for the photography lab, where the film developer, Wilson, a shriveled man, old before his years, lived in a netherworld of darkness and revolting fumes. After watching Wilson develop some horrific pictures of a car crash on the road to Mombasa, Dan announced that he wanted to be a photographer.

It took a few months, but the editor suggested that I attempt the paper's first restaurant column. I was thrilled, though in a matter of weeks I had run through all the decent eating establishments in Nairobi. In desperation, I dragged my family along to backstreet dives to sample such delicacies as sheep intestines, curried testicles, and sautéed sweetbreads. Following one of these meals, the whites of Mike's and Amy's eyes turned a hideous shade of yellow, a sure symptom of hepatitis. Amy recovered quickly, but Mike was bedridden for a month and couldn't drink alcohol for several years. When he was finally back on his feet, he was a good sport as I researched an eating-out guide to more than three hundred Kenyan restaurants.

In my spare time, I was editing a book project called *Tastes of Kenya* with Eamon Mullan, the executive chef of the Norfolk Hotel. I haunted his kitchens and drove his staff crazy as I stood over their shoulders taking down recipes. Dubbed "the Iron Stomach" by a bemused journalist colleague, I had managed to turn my lifelong obsession with food into a credible profession.

Over time I began writing investigative pieces for the *Nation*, including an article that questioned Colgate's importation of fluoride toothpaste into a country where hundreds of thousands were suffering from fluorosis, a condition characterized by brown, mottled teeth that results from naturally overfluoridated water. Fearful of alienating the managing director of another multinational company, Mike suggested, and I agreed, that I adopt two pen names—one African and the other Asian—for my articles, which often averaged more than three a week.

My boss at the newspaper was Rashid Mughal, a small, wiry man with endless energy and a ready wit. He was a Kenyan Asian, one of more than 130 thousand Indians and Pakistanis in a country of 15 million. Many were descendants of the Indian laborers who had built the Kenya-Uganda railway. Sometimes the black Kenyans resented the hardworking and resourceful Asians for their relative prosperity and because they were often in charge of African laborers.

Rashid asked me to write about people but ordered me to stay away from politics. Since Kenyatta's death in 1978, it was unwise, even dangerous, for a foreigner to get involved in internal affairs. Under President Daniel arap Moi's government, expatriates could be denied work permits or deported overnight. The danger was much worse for the locals, however. The *Nation*'s editor, Joe Rodrigues, had been tossed in jail more than once after the paper published articles critical of the government. Most Kenyans looked over their shoulders when discussing politics in any public place, wary of the Special Branch, the notorious secret police.

Rashid pushed me to interview authors, composers, actors, aid workers, diplomats, religious leaders, and environmentalists—anyone with an interesting story to tell. I shot most of my own pictures, which Rashid blew up and accompanied with lively graphics to draw more attention to them. Never having trained as a photographer or journalist, I often felt like a fraud. My most humiliating moment came after turning in my first feature about a Kenyan political leader. A few hours later, Rashid phoned me and announced, with a voice like thunder, "The editor stopped the presses because of your article!"

My stomach knotted as he continued: "You didn't fact-check your piece and you got the man's title wrong. The editor is furious and wants to see you right away!"

Over the next few years, I made many more mistakes but somehow managed to keep my job as I wrote hundreds of articles on people, projects, and issues that I thought were important. My favorite subjects were visionaries of all races who were contributing to a positive future for their interracial country, then a model for the rest of Africa. I was inspired by Sir Michael Wood, founder of East Africa's first Flying Doctors Service, and moved by the quiet courage of Michael Werikhe, dubbed "Rhino Man" for his marathon walks to create awareness of Kenya's endangered rhinoceros population. Our family adopted, as honorary grandparents, India-born John Karmali and his English wife, Joan, both of whom faced enormous opposition when launching Hospital Hill School, Kenya's first mixed-race school. They, and many others, helped shape my belief, and our children's, in the power of creative and courageous individuals to transform the world around them.

I often dragged the kids along while researching my stories, and Dan began shooting photographs to accompany my articles. Later he even submitted his own articles for the paper, several of which were published. Meanwhile, Mike and Amy acted as our clipping service, gluing Dan's and my stories into a series of scrapbooks.

Dan joined me on one of my most memorable assignments, the opening by Mother Teresa of a health center in the Nairobi slum of Kibera. As the speeches commemorating the event droned on, I studied the diminutive figure hunched on a wooden chair, aware that her darting eyes took in everything around her. We swapped many smiles, and I noticed that the more she beamed, the brighter she seemed to glow. I had never seen an aura before—and have not since—and only wish I had been able to capture hers on camera.

Of all the personalities that Rashid ever asked me to interview, the most colorful and unusual was the American psychic Sylvia Browne. Her gifts were said to be so exceptional that she had been enlisted by several police departments and hospitals in California to help locate missing persons and to diagnose mysterious illnesses. Rashid, like me, was always inclined to be skeptical.

"It may be a scam," he said, "but check her out and let me know what you think."

Although I had been impressed by Rosemary Brown's sincerity when describing her interaction with the spirits of dead composers, I hadn't thought much about the psychic world since meeting her some ten years before—until arriving in Kenya, that is. There, I learned that Africans traditionally believed that everyone and everything has a spirit—not only people and animals, but also rocks and trees, rivers and lakes, stars and even the sun. This philosophy, called *animism*, a word that derives from the Latin word for "soul," is the oldest form of religious belief on earth. Animists think that it's possible to communicate with the ancestors of those who have died and with the spirits of objects, like trees. Some animists create shrines in their homes to honor their dead relatives, and keep those relatives happy with offerings of food or drink placed there. However unfamiliar the whole idea was to me, I was careful not to offend local traditions.

I was nervous as I knocked on Sylvia Browne's door at the Norfolk Hotel. Although I had interviewed many locals, this was my first "international" assignment. Sylvia Browne turned out to be a striking figure, with tinted blond hair, brown eyes lined in blue eye shadow, and a voice so husky that it sounded like she smoked three packs of cigarettes a day. Motioning me to an easy chair, she barely looked at me as she launched into a disturbingly exact account of a trip I had planned only the previous day, speaking accurately about a book I had just decided to write, and then mentioning a minor medical complaint that I was experiencing. I sat quietly, careful to offer no clues when she pinpointed an incident a year before which had led to my present job. Sylvia used words about me that only a friend could have chosen, and I wondered how she knew so much about me. Even if she had tried to research my life, no one but me would have known most of what she was saying.

"You have two children, a boy and a girl," she said, without waiting for me to confirm or deny the truth. No big deal, I thought. That would be easy to find out.

"And you have a husband." Obviously: I was wearing a wedding ring. But then I realized I wasn't. It had given me a rash and I had stopped wearing it a few months before.

"But," she added, staring at me intently, "you're looking around."

"You're mistaken, Sylvia!" I protested, perhaps too emphatically. "I'm very happy."

"I'm only saying what I am told to say," she said, leaving me to wonder who was telling her.

I moved on to safer subjects—like how she was getting all this information.

Sylvia explained that when she was five years old she'd had a friend she called Francine who often told her what was going to happen in the future. Sylvia loved her and was surprised when she realized that only she could see her. When Sylvia asked her why this was so, Francine said that she was Sylvia's spirit guide, there to provide her with information to pass on to those who needed it. I had heard that concept before—from Rosemary Brown, no relation to Sylvia.

Sylvia looked at me intently. "You're angry," she said.

"What do you mean?" I was genuinely confused. After all, I tried to smile all the time.

"No one knows about your anger but you," she continued. "And of course your spirit guide, who knows everything."

Her words made me feel invaded, watched. I wondered if the invisible entity could see me when I stalked down to the kitchen late at night and sometimes even plundering the larder, eating food I didn't want or need, as though swallowing my frustration and anger. I was curious whether it knew how sad I felt that the husband I loved so much seemed to be growing further apart from me, separated by a gaping void caused by his fatigue and overwork and my own determination to squeeze more into each day than it could possibly hold.

"Anger is a form of depression," Sylvia continued, "in this case caused because you can't be who you really are."

Even if I didn't want to admit it, I understood what she was saying. Despite all my activities and the many people and projects in my life, I felt there had to be more to me than I had yet discovered. Too often I felt shallow, fragmented, and without true purpose. Sometimes it felt, as it had in long-ago London, as though I were carrying an invisible observer on my shoulder. There was the good Kathy whom everyone saw, the ever-smiling one, and then there was the other Kathy, who wanted to lead me places I didn't think I should be going. I had to be on guard all the time to make sure that the bad Kathy stayed in line.

"Tell me," Sylvia said, her eyes capturing mine, "who do you admire most in life?"

My mind darted around. Churchill maybe? Mahatma Gandhi? I was about to speak when she continued, "You look up to the person who knows who he or she is and does what he or she believes is right."

I wasn't sure what she was trying to tell me.

"You don't say what you'd like to say," she said with feeling. "Remember, you hurt a person only if you *don't* tell the truth, not if you *do*."

I found Sylvia's words very disturbing. I often wanted to open up to Mike, to understand who he really was and to let him into my inner world, for after thirteen years of marriage there was a lot that had been left unsaid. I loved him dearly, but more as a brother than a lover, though I couldn't tell him such a hurtful thing.

I was relieved when she changed the subject. "There will be major political problems in Kenya very soon," she said, lowering her voice. "Someone will try to take over the country."

"Will he succeed?" I asked, although if I reported a prediction like this, and if the rumor came true, I could be accused of being an instigator, arrested for treason, and thrown into jail without trial. That was how President Moi's regime ensured its survival without opposition.

"I can't see everything," she said, "but I know there will be an uprising in late July or early August of this year." I scribbled notes furiously, deciding to hide them as soon as I got home. Shaking off my feelings of unrest, I turned in a feature about Sylvia a few days later, leaving out her political forecast and her disturbingly perceptive remark about my restless spirit.

The piece was published on Tuesday, and from Wednesday to Friday the *Nation*'s switchboard was jammed with calls. Rashid asked me to do a follow-up article on Sylvia, so I spent the following Saturday afternoon with her, asking more questions. I found myself increasingly intrigued.

Eager to learn more about Sylvia—and maybe get more insight into myself—I invited her to stay with us for the rest of her holiday. Although I was impressed by my new friend's psychic skills, Dan thought she was more than a bit strange. Amy refused to be alone with her, worried that Sylvia could read her thoughts and would know that she found her dyed hair too blond and her eye shadow too bright.

While Sylvia was with us, the telephone never stopped ringing. Examples of her various gifts, most of which I could describe only as psychic, were so numerous that eventually I had to believe she really did possess something out of the ordinary.

She had never previously met any of the people she was treating and had no way of gathering information on them. What's more, she actively discouraged people from telling her anything about themselves, and often impatiently cut them off when they tried, so she wouldn't be biased.

As a journalist, I wanted to test Sylvia's psychic abilities in a controlled experiment, so I contacted Dr. Mark Horton, a visiting Oxford University archaeologist who had spent several summers digging among the ancient ruins on Pate, an island north of Lamu. Although skeptical of the outcome, he had agreed to bring a collection of coins and potsherds to the Norfolk Hotel for her to evaluate, assuring me that only an expert would be able pinpoint their age and origin.

Mark set up a video camera on the Norfolk Hotel's veranda to film the proceedings. Once we were all settled, he opened a map of East Africa on the table in front of Sylvia and pulled out the first coin from his bag. Knowing his reservations about the whole exercise, I hoped it wouldn't be too embarrassing for her if she performed badly on camera. She looked totally unconcerned as Mark held up the silver coin.

"Where is this from?" he asked.

"There," she said, pointing without hesitation to the island of Pate on the map. "Minted around 1320." Mark watched without reacting.

"What about this one?" His fingers gripped a small copper coin.

"Over here . . . and there," she said firmly, moving her red-polished nail from one point on the map to another. "It's from the 1630s."

"Correct," said Mark, raising an eyebrow at me. "The coin was originally found in a hoard at the first location, but it was moved to the other some years later. And yes, the date is right too."

He plucked one coin after another out of the bag, carefully noting Sylvia's answers on a pad. To my surprise, he confirmed that not only did she accurately describe the places where the coins had been found, but also dated them to within twenty years, even though some were more than six hundred years old. After that, Mark repeated the experiment using potsherds, also dug up in East Africa. The first he handed Sylvia was thick, with a lovely blue glaze. It looked just like some pottery my mother had bought in the 1930s.

"Chinese, from 1190," Sylvia said, barely glancing at it.

After the session Mark told me that as a professional archaeologist, he found it difficult to understand how a layperson could know so much. In a controlled, filmed experiment, Sylvia had demonstrated that she could relay information that she had never consciously acquired. Even though I couldn't understand how she did it, it seemed clear that she wasn't a fraud.

Just before Sylvia left Kenya, we met in her room at the Norfolk Hotel for tea and I told her about the mysterious communication I had experienced while visiting Lake Turkana, when the words "love," "power," and "energy" had been transmitted through my fingers. Sylvia said this could have been a form of "automatic writing," which she described as the process of communicating thoughts that don't seem to come from the conscious mind of the writer. She said that whatever its origin, whether from an outside source or from the subconscious, the words were important. One day I would undoubtedly be able to make sense of them.

She looked at my face and added slowly, "I understand you'll have help. There will be someone, a messenger, who will teach you what you need to know, and then you'll communicate the truth you have learned."

I felt a shiver down my back. Although Sylvia's room wasn't air-conditioned, I was chilled, and a bit afraid.

That night I wrote another article on Sylvia, delving more deeply into the concepts she had explained to me. I wrote about the nature of spirit guides, talked about how we can use energy to heal ourselves (and others), and said that Sylvia didn't believe death was an ending, but rather the beginning of a new kind of life. As I finished the article, I realized that I hadn't included the most important thing Sylvia had said just as I was going out the door.

"In many cases people haven't finished their work on earth and have more they want to accomplish," she said. "Then they have to use those of us who are still living to help them. And you will be one of those people."

I shook my head and decided not to add that part. It was too unbelievable, even for the most gullible of readers.

10

Temptations

ALTHOUGH I DIDN'T WANT TO ADMIT IT, SYLVIA WAS RIGHT ABOUT ME "looking around." Mike and I were rarely home together. We found it difficult to relax when it was just us: as I became more confident he seemed to withdraw, becoming increasingly abrupt with me in ways that reminded me of his father. We rarely made love, and when we did, it felt as though I were observing myself from outside my body.

One evening I attended a glittering dinner party in the home of a diplomat, where I was seated next to a tall, round-faced West African named Robert. He made me feel like an important journalist when he invited me to meet with him soon to discuss an article on tourism that I had written for the *Nation*. Flattered by his interest, I agreed to have lunch with him at the Kentmere Country Club.

Mike was pleased when I told him about the meeting. "He's an important customer. Use this opportunity to spread the word about Wang."

Top down, I drove my MGB the eighteen miles through lush green coffee plantations to the quaint "olde English" establishment set amidst tropical gardens cascading down a steep hill to the fast-flowing river below. Robert was waiting for me on a sofa in the darkened lounge. I sat on another sofa opposite him and began asking questions about his company. Eyes gleaming, he jumped up and nestled close to me. Blushing furiously, I made a dash over to the opposite sofa. He followed, creating a bizarre musical chairs routine to the obvious amusement of the waiter, who appeared used to such antics. Indeed, Robert had not only organized lunch but had also booked a room for the afternoon.

"So sorry, R-r-r-robert," I stuttered. "I would love to stay, but I h-h-h-have to pick up my children from school." Not cool, certainly not sophisticated, and probably very bad for Mike's business.

Another time, a white Kenyan safari guide invited me to discuss public relations for his company over lunch. When I arrived neatly turned out in a straight skirt, high heels, and stockings, carrying a briefcase for the anticipated business lunch, he drove me instead to the game park, where he unfolded a blanket and pulled a basket of food and a bottle of wine from his cooler. It was clear that he had an entirely different kind of relations in mind.

Nothing dire had happened so far, though to be honest I was strangely excited by the possibility that one day something might. After thirteen years of marriage I yearned for a deeper intimacy and greater passion than now existed between Mike and me. Once, when he and I were arguing, I jokingly suggested that we each take a sabbatical.

Mike wasn't amused. "Kathy, you want to have your cake and eat it too," he said with a stern look.

"I'm just kidding, darling," I said, laughing. But I wasn't really. I never would have admitted it out loud, but I would have liked a little time out from our marriage to see what it was like to be free. I had married young and now wished I could have experienced the guilt-free attitudes toward sex that some of my contemporaries enjoyed. The loose view of many Kenyans about monogamy in that pre-AIDS era was shocking to me, but also intriguing, for not only the men but also many "respectable" married women had their dalliances. They were like some French or Italian spouses in their attitudes, embracing the concept of the *cinq à sept*, the interval between five and seven in the evening when husbands and wives did as they wished and no one talked about it. Of course such morals didn't mesh with my upbringing, but sometimes my mind went places it shouldn't.

Mike seemed to relax only when he played tennis with Mary Anne Fitzgerald, the East Africa correspondent for the London *Sunday Times*. Drop-dead gorgeous, she glided through rooms like a leopard, the envy of other women, in a tight T-shirt and skimpy shorts, her slim arms covered in silver bangles. She had been born in South Africa and was responsible for the welfare of five Kenyan boys, as well as the divorced mother of two lively fair-haired daughters, Tara and Petra, who were the same age as Dan and Amy. Mary Anne unnerved us with her stories of encounters with Ethiopian bandits, the atrocities she had witnessed in Liberia, and what it felt like to walk through mounds of corpses slaughtered by the Lord's Resistance Army in Uganda. Utterly intrepid, she became my heroine, for she was everything I wanted to be. Whenever I listened to her, I wished that I, too, could travel all over Africa, covering life-and-death crises.

My chance came when Royal Air Swazi, the national airline of Swaziland, a tiny country nicknamed "the Switzerland of Africa," invited me to write a piece for the *Nation* about their burgeoning tourist business. It wouldn't be an important news story, but it would be fun to review the country's new lodges and restaurants, meet the people, learn about their arts and crafts, and enjoy the glorious landscape.

Seated in Royal Air Swazi's first-class section, I lay back and anticipated four hours of fine wines and elegant food. Suddenly, the sky darkened and our small Fokker Friendship began to buck and roll in a most alarming way. After that initial jolt, the plane struggled on through the night as rain sheeted the windows and lightning pierced the sky. Alone with my thoughts and suddenly aware of my mortality, I grappled with the realization that despite my determined efforts after Miles's death, I still hadn't achieved anything of merit. The plane dove suddenly and I gasped as my stomach turned over. I pulled out a notepad from my bag and started writing frantically. There was so much more to do, to be, to experience; so much more to feel, to achieve, to *love*. My thoughts were as tumultuous as the storm that swirled around us. After five anxious hours—we had been slowed down considerably by the storm—we began our descent, the aircraft creaking like an old ship, and bounced to a stop on a sodden, rutted runway littered with branches. The pilot then announced that this had been no ordinary storm; we had passed through the eye of a hurricane, the first in Swaziland's history.

Later that day, instead of visiting tourist attractions, I interviewed bewildered survivors of the hurricane and photographed ruined homes, collapsed bridges, and devastated farms. That night I returned to the hotel, exhausted and troubled by all the destruction and despair I had seen, and headed to the bar. I hoped that being around other people would make me feel better. But it was so packed and noisy that I was ready to leave without a drink when a tall man with shaggy brown hair, horn-rimmed glasses, and a two-day growth of beard, wearing a khaki photographer's vest, stopped me. He seemed vaguely familiar.

"Buy you a drink?" he asked, introducing himself. I recognized him then as an on-air correspondent whom I had seen on television when we lived in London. Flattered that he had asked me, I joined the press of other journalists and downed one glass of wine and, too quickly, another. When he asked me what newspaper I represented, I casually announced that I was a reporter for the *Nation*. I didn't specify which *Nation*, nor did I mention that the only disasters I had previously covered were in restaurant kitchens. My companion's arm crept around my waist as he asked me to join him upstairs in his room for a nightcap.

Feeling light-headed, I heard myself accepting his invitation. As I lurched down the hallway, I hazily recognized that it was a bad idea, but I followed him anyway. After all, I had nearly died. It was time to experience all that life had to offer. I watched what happened next as though standing above myself, detached from my body. He peeled off his clothes, then mine, while I tried not to think about what was happening. The two Kathys were back again—one watching and telling the other, who wanted to feel awakened and appreciated, that what she was doing was wrong. They merged again afterward when I slipped out, leaving the snoring stranger behind.

Mortified by what I had done, I crept back to my room, where I lay awake until dawn. As soon as I could, I caught a plane back to Nairobi. Settled in my seat, I realized to my horror that I couldn't even remember my partner's last name. Whatever I had been hoping for, this certainly wasn't the love I was seeking to experience—nor the kind of intimacy that I yearned for.

When Mike picked me up at the airport, I found it hard to look him in the eye as he said how much he had missed me. But he didn't seem to notice my distance and quickly launched into an animated description of the new crises he faced at the office. Once we were inside the house, though, William looked at me as though I had abandoned my children for three months, not three days. Or perhaps he was seeing something new in my eyes and understood what it meant. Racked by guilt, I tried to forget about the encounter in Swaziland and concentrate on being a better wife.

That determination lasted only until an American tour operator offered me a job promoting Kenya by hosting dinner parties for zoo and museum directors in the United States. It was ironic that food was literally my meal ticket to a more exciting life.

My first assignment was to host a lavish "Tastes of Kenya" dinner—based on recipes from Eamon's and my book—in Arizona for a group of zoo directors, to encourage them to bring groups to Africa. Afterward, a few of them invited me to share the joys of the Jacuzzi, and I discovered that they were an uninhibited bunch, especially at three o'clock in the morning after a few rounds of margaritas. I returned to my room alone that night, but on my next trip I stayed up a little longer, and on the third I didn't go back to my room at all.

Far from Mike and the children, it was exciting to toss off my inhibitions and be free. I rationalized my behavior, explaining to myself that having a reasonable outlet for my frustrations made my marriage stronger—and besides, no one could be hurt by my behavior in a foreign country. However, when I returned to Nairobi, there was a constant dialogue between the two Kathys in my head—one urging me to stop my irresponsible behavior, the other eager for more.

11

Death at Midnight

OVER TIME, DAN AND AMY BECAME LONG-DISTANCE TRAVELERS THEM-
selves. They loved the stopovers Mike and I planned in faraway places
like Brazil, South Africa, Israel, Mexico, or Egypt every year, en route to
visit my family in Iowa. We encouraged our children, as my mother had
done with me, to keep scrapbooks filled with itineraries, ticket stubs,
playbills, photographs, and other artifacts from their adventures.

Every year, we sent them away for the long vacation in July and August. Mike's parents would pick them up in London and take them on
ambitious expeditions to Paris, Berlin, Copenhagen, or Rome, chronicling
the children's adventures in a series of small, black-bound artist notebooks.
Dan and Amy also grew very fond of their uncle "Gugu" and his wife,
who took them to museums, concerts, and art galleries in London.

After that London-based visit, the children flew on to Cedar Rapids,
where they spent two weeks at Camp Wapsi learning "good values" and
the "gratitude attitude," as well as canoeing and riding horses with their
many Iowa cousins. At the end of their stay, I generally joined the children for a week in Cedar Rapids, but during the summer of 1982 I was
too busy completing another cookbook and decided to remain at home

with Mike, who was far too busy to travel. It was a tense time in Kenya, with talk of shifting political alliances and tribal rivalries in rural areas, but we were too preoccupied to notice. We barely had time to speak.

On Saturday, July 30, one day before Dan and Amy were due home, returning via London, we received a call from Gaby to say that the final flight of the children's trip was overbooked and that they would arrive a few days later. We planned to sleep in on Sunday but were awakened early by William.

Outside, there were popping noises like distant fireworks, and as we ran to the window to see what was going on, the telephone rang. It was a journalist friend who lived in an apartment at the edge of downtown Nairobi.

"There's been a coup!" he shouted over the crackling line.

Throughout the morning, the phone rang constantly as friends passed on the latest rumors that were flying around Nairobi like wildfire. Piecing together the news, we concluded that a handful of junior air force officers who were angry with the Moi regime had taken over the airport and the government-run Voice of Kenya television and radio station, across from the Norfolk Hotel. People meeting planes in the early hours of the morning had been run off the road, their cars hijacked and possessions stolen. If the children had arrived when they were meant to, we would have run straight into the fierce gunfight between the rebels and the security forces, which apparently had left hundreds dead. We phoned Gaby and told her not to put the children on their rescheduled flight; we would let her know when it was safe for them to return.

As the day wore on, air force jets screamed across the sky, leaving the ground, and me, shaking. We worried about the safety of the tourists in the downtown hotels and the plight of our friends marooned in the distant suburbs of Karen, Langata, and Muthaiga. I was concerned about our own safety too, of course—but, strangely, I felt more exhilaration than fear as I fielded constant calls from people seeking information.

At one point an announcer, identifying himself as a member of the newly formed rebel People's Redemption Council, interrupted the reggae music playing on the radio and condemned "the corrupt and intolerable government and the crazy and irresponsible bandits . . . indulging in rampant corruption making life unbearable for the *wananchi* [Kenyans]. After the revolution," the voice continued, "the people of Kenya will be able to breathe a sigh of relief."

We felt anything but relief at the news, especially hearing that a large mob was spilling out of the overcrowded slums of Mathare Valley, looting the downtown area, and rampaging through the nearby Asian neighborhoods. Concerned that looters might also burst out of Kibera, a sprawling slum less than half a mile from our house, we buried our passports and a few valuables in the garden, pausing only to snap surreptitious pictures as truckloads of drunken soldiers, wearing mirrored sunglasses and waving guns, thundered past our gate, shouting *"Pambana!"* (Struggle) and "Power to the People!"

Suddenly, the martial music on the radio stopped, and a new announcer declared that the attempted coup had been suppressed. The president was on his way back to Nairobi, a curfew was in effect, and everyone should remain calm.

Surprisingly, that night turned out to be one of the best in our lives. Mike and I had no place to go and no one was able to come to us, so the two of us ate dinner alone on the veranda, hearing only the chirp of crickets instead of the usual roar of traffic on the Ngong Road. Holding hands across the table, we talked in a way we hadn't managed to for years, and resolved to take a vacation together, just the two of us. We went to bed early and fell asleep in each other's arms, savoring the unaccustomed intimacy. Afterward, I thought about why it is that people seem to fall in love during war and other crises. Perhaps they realize that small disputes don't matter and every moment is precious.

The next day was gray and rainy when Mike drove us into town, using my *Nation* press card to get through the many roadblocks. The Ngong Road was littered with abandoned cars, and the area around the mortuary was filled with distraught people. Downtown looked as though a bomb had hit it. Nearly every security grill was mangled and most shop windows were shattered, with television, furniture, and food stores robbed of anything valuable. Bullet-riddled cars lay abandoned on the streets, some with bodies still inside.

Military snipers stood silhouetted on the roofs of government buildings, and we heard sporadic gunshots as we drove through town. With all the soldiers patrolling the streets, we felt safe; but we later learned that a tourist who had been leaning out of a window at the Hilton Hotel was killed at almost the same moment we had passed, picked off by a sharpshooter who mistook him for a rebel.

The usually bustling street outside the *Nation* office was deserted as we pulled up, and inside only a skeleton staff manned the phones. Wade Huie, a young reporter from Atlanta, stopped me in the hallway. Normally brash and funny, that day he was tense as he pointed to Rashid's empty chair.

"He's disappeared," Wade said, "and there's no trace of his family."

"We've got to find him," I urged, heading for the door with Wade.

Mike returned home in case his parents called with news about how our concerned children were doing, while Wade and I took his old Toyota and set off in the direction of Rashid's house. The Mathare Valley mob had poured into a nearby middle-class Asian neighborhood, which was now taking the full force of their looting rampage. Long angered by the Asians' wealth and status, the insurgents had finally taken their revenge. There was chaos throughout the Asian section of town, where many citizens were wandering the streets, wide-eyed, seemingly too traumatized to speak. Any exhilaration I may have felt the day before at the prospect of danger evaporated when we pushed open the door at Rashid's house and found that the interior had been ransacked. The family was nowhere to be seen. The neighbors directed us to another house across town, where we found him, several miles away, hiding with his wife and children behind drawn curtains in his cousin's home.

"Hell is better than this," Rashid lamented, pointing to the slashes on his arms and bruises on the children's bodies. His wife, Sadiqa, wearing a long tunic over her trousers, sat hunched on the far end of the sofa, her slender arms cradling their youngest child, five-year-old Imrana. She wouldn't look at me as Rashid described how he'd held the crowd at bay in their courtyard until a group of looters crashed through the gate, screaming. I wanted to vomit as he told how the young men had stripped his little girl, then tore off Sadiqa's trousers and threw her on the ground.

Rashid's voice quivered as he spoke of how friends had managed to rescue them from the mob. It was a miracle that his gentle wife and child hadn't been raped or killed.

"It seemed better to die running." Rashid's face darkened as he described how they raced barefoot through deserted side streets and across open fields to his wife's family home.

"I want to get out of this country," Rashid said with an anger I hadn't before seen in him. "I hate them all."

He and his wife had lost everything, and I grieved for them—not only for the stolen possessions, but also for the loss of trust in their fellow humans. Rashid was a fourth-generation Kenyan Asian and had always described himself as a proud son of Africa. The mob's brutality had transformed him into a person I didn't recognize.

Sadly, the Mughals were just one of many families whose hopes of a good life in Kenya were dashed that day. Only twenty years earlier, the newly independent nation had exhibited an inspiring spirit of unity and collective enterprise. Now, under President Moi, the specter of tribalism was raising its ugly head as people began to fragment into disparate elements, protecting only their tribal members. The attempted coup had shattered the facade of Kenyan society, revealing a glimpse of seething anger beneath.

Many Africans were equally upset by the turn of events. William was desolate. "There is no medicine to cure hatred," he said, quoting another of his African proverbs.

A message was waiting for me when I got home. Sylvia Browne had telephoned from America and asked me to check the notes of our February interview. When I found them, hidden in my filing cabinet, I was shaken to see that not only had she been accurate in her description of this uprising—which not even the sagest political pundits had predicted—but had pinpointed its date almost exactly. Once again, I was reminded that there were invisible forces at work that I couldn't explain. I knew that one day I should pay attention to what was being revealed to me, but right then I had other things on my mind.

The children returned a few days after the coup, and we picked them up at the airport. First into the arrivals hall was Dan, nearly twelve, pulling two suitcases behind him, his eyes scanning the crowd anxiously until he saw us. He turned back to shepherd eight-year-old Amy, clutching her doll with one hand and one of my mother's alligator purses in her other. When they came through the gate, I fell to my knees, wrapped both arms around my daughter's small, firm body, and began to rock her.

When she stepped back and saw the tears streaming down my cheeks, she smiled and said, "Don't cry, Mummy. Everything's all right now."

Driving home from the airport, we passed many burned-out cars and considerable twisted wreckage from the recent violence. Seize the day, I thought yet again. Live for the moment: it may be all we've got.

Our friends and relatives abroad urged us to pack up and leave Kenya. "It's the tip of the iceberg," they warned. "Get out while you have a chance."

We ignored them. We were shaken by what had happened but remained committed to Kenya. The government cracked down on the air force, public confidence was restored, and over several months life returned to normal. However, the memory of Rashid's face that awful day has never left me.

Sylvia Browne returned often to Kenya. Gruff, gutsy, and unflappable, she told it like it was, no matter what. She didn't care whom she offended, for, according to her, the information came from a "higher source" and she simply relayed it as best she could. In May of 1985, Sylvia stood on the veranda and surveyed our garden, taking in the overhanging trees and crimson bougainvillea climbing over the roof.

"I'm sorry I won't be coming back to this house again," she said. "You'll be moving soon," she added.

"No way!" I retorted. "Our lease isn't up for three years." I never wanted to leave my beautiful home.

"Don't worry. Everything will be changing soon," she answered with certainty. "But you'll love the new place."

Dusk

THINGS FALL APART;
THE CENTER CANNOT HOLD.

—WILLIAM BUTLER YEATS

12

Children of Africa

EXACTLY A WEEK AFTER SYLVIA BROWNE TOLD ME WE WERE MOVING, OUR Kenyan landlord knocked on our door. Mr. Kamau, a local politician, was crammed into a shiny, too-tight suit and sporting a Rolex watch and highly polished shoes. Over a cup of sweet milky tea, he broke the news.

"I'm sorry," he said, as he picked an invisible speck off his trousers, "but I have to ask you to leave the house. I'm selling it this year."

There was no discussion. We had to go. We were desolate.

For days, the real estate agent and I trekked across Nairobi, looking at ticky-tack ultramodern houses perched on hilltops, rambling old hulks in Karen and Langata, and cheaply built Spanish mansions in the new suburb of Gigiri on the outskirts of town. When only a month of our lease remained, I was desperate and called Sylvia Browne in America.

"Stop panicking," she commanded. "Go north a few blocks. The house is within a half mile of your place. It's huge, sprawling, with a turret, and has what looks like an airplane hangar in the garden." Now that was really absurd—so much so that I ignored her advice.

A day later, the agent called again. "I have a place just up the road from you, but it's a bit strange. It used to be four missionary houses and heaven knows how many rooms there are, but I think you should have a look at it."

When I drove up to the house, exactly half a mile north of us, I couldn't help smiling. On one side was a round water tower that, from a distance (or perhaps through a psychic's eye), could be mistaken for a turret. The house itself was an impossible maze of twenty-three rooms and a separate guesthouse. Perched in the garden was a corrugated metal Quonset hut that could have held a Cessna. We signed the lease the next day and moved in a few weeks later.

Dan claimed the guesthouse, complete with its own kitchen, which he turned into a darkroom. William approved of the new servants' quarters, and our latest gardener, Benjamin, took on the neglected garden. The hardest part was finding enough furniture to fill all the rooms. When we ventured into the hut, we discovered that it contained hundreds of prosthetic legs and arms stored there by the missionaries. Dan and Amy used them to terrify unsuspecting guests. Once cleared, the hut became a perfect party place for the kids. Nicknamed by Dan the *mkebe*, which means "tin can" in Swahili, it also became an ideal venue for the monthly tourist gatherings I laid on with William's help for an American tour operator. Sadly, we never built another tree house. As Sylvia had predicted, one era had ended and another was about to begin.

Dan still spent many happy weekends at Lengai's, exploring the gorge or racing mopeds around the perimeter of the game park. At fourteen, Lengai was a few inches taller than Dan and strikingly handsome, though his blond hair was still cut in the shape of a pudding bowl by his mother.

Things were going very well for the boys until one Sunday afternoon a tearful Nani announced that she and her husband were separating. I was stunned. No one in my family had ever divorced. As challenging as it sometimes was to be married, and as much as I sometimes dreamed of a sabbatical, I couldn't imagine facing life on my own.

I tried to discuss Nani's situation with Mike. In one of our rare private moments, as we sped to a social engagement at the Nairobi Club, I broached the subject.

"You know, Mike, the whole thing is unbearably sad. Nani and Harvey are both great people—and they're such loving parents."

"It's shocking," Mike said, his voice impassioned. "What were they *thinking*, anyway, to get into this situation?" He swerved suddenly around an enormous pothole. "We must make sure that kind of thing doesn't happen to us," he added grimly.

Not only were Nani and Harvey getting divorced, but they had decided to send Lengai to boarding school in England. Dan was devastated to lose his best friend and their life together in the bush, though at last he was flourishing at his new school. The principal told me that he was pleased with Dan's friendliness toward everyone on campus, starting with the cleaners and lunch ladies. Perhaps that's why he had tolerantly accepted Dan's transformation of the school newspaper into a lively, graffiti-covered flyer that poked fun at the administration and local politics. His group of diverse school companions included the half-Nigerian, half-American twins Kwame and Twumasi Wiesel, the gorgeous Laurie Diaz from the Philippines, and Long Westerlund, a Chinese American youth with a challenging stutter that had kept him isolated from the other students until Dan revealed his extraordinary artistic talent and made him his sidekick. I described them as members of the ISK "global tribe."

Because of the cost and the American curriculum, there were few Kenyans at the school. Dan befriended one of them, Atieno, a scholarship student who lived in her father's bakery in Kibera. In this sprawling slum, only a few blocks from our old house on the Ngong Road, hundreds had to share a single water tap, and children played near open drains flowing with raw sewage. Dan was concerned by her family's poverty and suggested that I write an article in my Eating Out column for the *Nation* about the bakery to bring in more customers. We decided to drive over so that I could see the place firsthand.

I always ventured into the shantytown carefully, aware that there was more than a hint of danger in a place where crowds could become instant mobs and mobs could kill if incited. Just shouting "Thief!" was enough to attract a frenzied group ready to stone a suspect to death. Naturally, I felt anxious when our open car was engulfed by a mass of people packed into the narrow road on their way to a political rally.

"Hey, *mzungu* [white boy], what are you doing?" A drunken young man poked at Dan from beside the car. I smiled and tapped the horn, hoping the crowd would part so we could get by, but an elderly woman turned to shout at me and stood her ground in front of us. Behind us, another woman swore. Goosebumps rose on my arms as the mood of the crowd shifted quickly from good humor to hostility.

I tried to inch the car forward, but there was no way out through the crowd and I could feel the vehicle swaying slightly. Sensing my fear, Dan muttered, "Don't worry, Mum." Reaching under the seat, he pulled out a bag and groped for something inside. Before I could stop him, he covered his face with a latex mask, transforming himself into an old man with a bulbous red nose and tufts of gray hair sprouting from his bald skull. Leaning out of the car, he shook his fist in the air and started to berate the crowd in high-pitched Swahili. At first there were angry looks, then raised eyebrows, and then the same people who had been ready to beat us were laughing at the absurd sight of the old man.

I was proud of Dan for taking control of the situation but aware that the outcome could have been disastrous. I breathed a sigh of relief as we turned off the main track and headed down a side road toward the bakery, an unpainted wooden shack with a corrugated tin roof. Out front, goats picked through an overflowing mound of rubbish on which half-naked children were playing, and a mangy dog lapped at a puddle. Atieno was standing at the door watching for us. She was petite, with charcoal-colored skin, delicate features, and haunting dark eyes. Her hair was neatly braided into rows, and she wore a bright yellow dress on her slender frame. She beamed when she saw Dan and invited us to sit on benches at a long wooden table opposite her seventeen-year-old sister, Beatrice, who passed us cups of thick *chai*—milky tea boiled with sugar, cinnamon, cardamom, and ginger.

Their mother was dead, so it was their father, Elias, who pulled off a floury apron tied around his ample belly and handed us plates piled with warm banana cake topped with lemon-butter icing. His cheerful demeanor changed as he explained how Beatrice, like the majority of young people in Kenya, was jobless and had few prospects for the future. The family's future rested on Atieno, with her opportunity for an advanced education. If she did well at the International School, she could find a good job, not only to pay for school fees for her brothers and sisters, but also to take care of Elias in his old age. When Atieno left the room, her father confided that doctors had recently discovered that she had a faulty valve in her heart, which left her weak and permanently breathless. If she didn't have an operation, she was certain to die within a few years.

On the drive home, Dan asked many questions about Atieno's condition. Though I didn't know much about her specific condition, I did know something about health care in Kenya, having researched it for various articles. I explained that due to mismanagement and dishonesty, the state-run hospitals were overcrowded and had limited medical resources. To survive the complex operation Elias had said she needed, Atieno would require expensive private care. Funds were hard to raise where there were so many needy causes, but I promised to do what I could. Back home, Dan filled a bag with books and art supplies to help Atieno pass the time when she felt too ill to go to school, but I must confess that I forgot about my promise in the flurry of other commitments.

It didn't surprise me that he was concerned about Atieno's well-being. Far from our real families in the States and England, we had found an extended family of friends and neighbors in Kenya who made us feel completely at home, and we tried to give back to these people who had been so welcoming and generous to us.

Another of our special friends was Kipenget, a Masai woman who lived out in the Ngong Hills. Mary Anne Fitzgerald had first taken us to her simple hut on the knuckle-shaped ridge of the hills that the Kikuyu believed were molded by the hand of God as he shaped the earth in the beginning of time.

Like many traditional Masai women, Kipenget wore a red *shuka* tied over one shoulder, tightly cinched with a heavy leather belt around her waist. Her slender arms were covered with colorful bracelets, long bead earrings hung from loops in her ears, and she wore rough sandals cut from an old tire. Kipenget supported her eight children, as well as her husband's younger wives and their many offspring. A hard life had etched deep lines on her face, but she always beamed when she greeted me, planting moist kisses on both my cheeks and embracing me. I always looked forward to visiting her smoke-filled wooden hut, where she ladled out sweet milky tea boiled with water carried on her head from a distant spring, and passed around chunks of white bread we had brought her, as though serving champagne and caviar.

Kipenget called Dan her *mzungu* son and nicknamed him Lesharo (Laughing One) because, she said, he always seemed to have a smile on his face. It was no wonder, for the Ngong Hills was his favorite place on earth. Every time he visited, he brought home bags of Kipenget's jewelry to sell to our tourist visitors, fellow students, and teachers at school. No one was safe from his determined efforts, and as often as possible he hitched rides back to Kipenget's *boma* to give her the profits, along with extra beads, wire, and packets of tea and sugar. Kipenget needed the extra income and came to rely on Dan, who took his job very seriously.

As Lesharo, Dan took a new personality, more carefree than his Western persona. Adopting the loose walk of the Masai, he could stride for miles without growing tired. He loved to chase giraffes with the young *morani*, the handsome young warriors-in-training with intricately plaited hair. Sometimes Dan slept in the mud-and-wattle huts used by the *morani* on beds made of woven twigs and shared a mixture of curdled milk and blood taken from the jugular veins of their cows, stored in charred gourds that left the brew tasting smoky and strange.

The *morani* staged mock battles so that Dan could learn to fight and defend himself with knives and long staves. One afternoon, they dressed him as a young warrior in an elaborate headdress and *shuka*. He set up a camera and the boys—Dan included—took pictures of themselves solemnly balanced on one leg, holding spears. Afterward, they collapsed on the ground, laughing. The best photo found its way into his latest scrapbook, along with many other images and stories of his Masai experiences. I was grateful for the time Dan spent with Kipenget and her family, who taught him how to endure hunger and pain without complaining and how to be patient while dealing with extraordinary hardships.

Back when Dan was little, I had started a collection of poems for him, and we had always created scrapbooks of our travels, but he began his first real journal as a school assignment at the age of fourteen, when he returned from an outing to the Loita Hills in northern Kenya, his pockets filled with feathers, ostrich eggshell fragments, old coins, beads, jewelry, leather thongs, and other treasures. Most of the other students wrote essays, but Dan chose an option that allowed for pictorial representation: his journal was illustrated with carefully drawn studies of Masai jewelry, tools, and weapons. His teacher gave him an A for his work, which encouraged him to start a second, more elaborate book—and then another and another.

Each journal became more ambitious than the last, expressing Dan's maturing response to the world. Before long, intricate illustrations of Land Rovers were interspersed with pinups of beautiful women and images of war, the normal obsessions of an adolescent boy. Dan cut the photos into pieces, then rearranged them with his drawings, trimmed feathers, and clippings, sometimes adding beaded jewelry to create whimsical frames. Some pages were overlaid with watercolor, markers, or ink, even smudges of blood. The effects were dazzling, as though his spirit had been released through these pages.

He drew cartoons on a range of controversial issues, lightheartedly showing his irritation at our constant stream of houseguests and, more seriously, at the exploitation of the Masai. Once, he surprised me with his eloquent description of a visit to an elder he had met on one of his adventures in Masai land:

I am wearing the earth. My jacket is so stiff with dust that to touch it with closed eyes feels like stroking a patch of earth. I slap one of my arms, setting off a volcano of red African dust to hang above me. The dust smells old. It is old, older than the forest that clings to the base of this hill and older than the old man who stands before me, draped in a blanket. All old Masai have strong hands. When the hands become weak and soft, they die.

Dan was shy about showing his journals to visitors, but he would sometimes whisper to Amy to bring out the books for a special guest. "My brother made these," she would say proudly. "Would you like to see them?" She would patiently turn the pages while Dan watched from a distance, eventually allowing himself to be dragged over to explain a particular collage or one of his special techniques. Once, when someone asked what Amy could do, Dan said with equal admiration, "Amy can dance a hole in the floor," and urged her to prove it.

Despite a stormy relationship as youngsters, the two children grew fiercely protective of each other as they grew older. Dan could also be very possessive and bossy, which irritated Amy, though he always stretched her mind, challenging her fears. When she was eleven, he taught her to drive, forcing her to maneuver our red Fiat Uno—successor to our MGB—backward around the garden three times while he shouted out instructions. Sobbing in frustration she finally screamed, "I hate you, Dan Eldon!"

"Never say anything you don't mean, Amy," he said severely, then made her do it again.

During a trip to India, Dan taught Amy the *Namaste* greeting—both hands together, palms touching, usually at the chest, or below the chin or nose. He had learned that Hindus, Muslims, and Sikhs all accepted the salute that means, "I honor the spirit in you that is also in me," or "Your spirit and my spirit are *one*." However, he would also use the salute mockingly if she reacted crossly to his overprotectiveness.

Amy was still quite close to William. He'd had three children when we moved to Kenya. Nine months after his first home visit he had four, and so on, until he had seven—the last two, twins named Dan and Amy, usually dressed in hand-me-downs from their namesakes.

William watched over Amy like a second father and spoiled her outrageously. I would plead with him to let her make her own after-school snacks, recalling my Iowa upbringing, which stressed self-reliance.

"She is only small, *Memsahib*," he would answer, calmly stirring cocoa powder into a glass of milk or cooking her macaroni. Fortunately, even though Amy didn't have to make a bed or wash dishes, she was poised and polite. Our friends found her unusually considerate, perhaps because William demanded that she and Dan show respect for elders. He had taught them how to shake hands properly in the African way and warned that if they were ever rude, toads would pop out of their mouths.

One day, William brought home a distinguished gentleman in a dark suit and striped tie held in place with a gold pin, and introduced him as President Kenyatta's former *mganga* (traditional healer). William suffered from terrible gout and had unsuccessfully tried every medical treatment for his malady, including imported antibiotics we had purchased, but after the *mganga* rubbed herbs into a series of tiny nicks that he cut in William's ankles, the pain disappeared and never returned.

Another time, William was anxious about a dispute he was having with someone outside the house and called in the *mganga* again, who insisted that we bury a headless chicken in our garden to placate any bad spirits. We did this, and sure enough, things settled down. Amy took the *mganga* aside for a private consultation. He handed her a packet of finely ground silver-gray powder with instructions to use it sparingly. When Dan discovered that it was a love potion, he teased her unmercifully, but she continued to dab it behind her ears for special occasions.

One such special occasion occurred for all of us when Hollywood film director Sydney Pollack flew in to film *Out of Africa*, the story of Danish writer Karen Blixen that had inspired me before we left London. Judith Thurman, author of a book on Blixen, describes her life as a "story of loss." After six years in Kenya, I now knew what she meant. Loss was a recurring theme in ways that most Westerners rarely experience.

Journalists were banned from the set, but as a public relations gesture I was allowed to write a special report for the *Nation*, a project that gained me repeated access. A local contractor, Charlie Simpson, a transplanted Scotsman, had painstakingly reconstructed the Nairobi of 1913 from old photographs and diaries of the era, creating an elaborate movie set that was an accurate representation of the frontier town. Charlie took me through the streets, showing me shop windows filled with perfect replicas of old tins, bottles, and dry goods. There was even a graveyard with inscribed tombstones, incongruously set in the midst of the African plains.

Enthralled by the complexity and creativity of film production, I soon realized that nothing is more powerful than a major motion picture to move the hearts and minds of millions of people around the world. Used effectively, film is the most potent means of communication ever invented. If I had my life to live over, I thought, I would go to Hollywood and make movies that mattered. It was just another crazy dream, born of the strange frustration that kept nudging me, calling me to do more, be more, experience more, and create more. Always dissatisfied, I was never content with where I was, or with whom.

My interest in movie production grew when Sydney Pollack's assistant called to invite the children to work as extras in the film. A week later, dressed in high-button shoes and an embroidered period dress, Amy spent an afternoon frolicking on a hill while Dan, wearing a slouch hat, rough shirt, and homespun trousers, was assigned to a night shoot at the Nairobi Railway Station. Dan's job was to bump into Meryl Streep— fifteen times, as it turned out—before Sydney called, "Cut!" Afterward, Dan asked the star, who was carrying her infant daughter, Mamie, on her hip, for her autograph, which found its way into a spread in his journal.

Dan was clearly on a mission one hot afternoon early in 1986, when he strode into my office, trailed by his new dog Murdoch, a feisty Jack Russell given to him by Nani Croze. I was frantically trying to meet a deadline and barely looked up.

"Mum," he said sternly. "You have to pay attention."

I pushed my chair back and studied the young man standing before me. Now sixteen years old, at five feet ten he was already two inches taller than I, stalk thin, with dark-brown hair brushed straight back from a narrow face. Tiny laugh lines radiated from his eyes, but this time he was serious.

"We have to do something about Atieno," he continued, pulling up a chair and scooping Murdoch onto his lap. Dan's friend was growing weaker all the time, he said, and now could barely stand. She hadn't attended school in more than a year.

"We can't wait for someone else to help," he said adamantly. "We've got to find the money for an operation ourselves."

I immediately called our friend Dr. David Silverstein, President Moi's cardiologist, who generously agreed to operate for free if we could find five thousand dollars to pay for Atieno's hospital expenses. It was a huge amount, and we had to find it quickly. Mike and I pledged to help, but it was Dan who really went into action, setting up a "Save a Girl's Heart" committee, which mobilized the entire school. He tapped the local Rotary and Lions Clubs, organized teams to sell T-shirts he designed, set up bake sales, and—together with Amy—organized parties in the *mkebe*.

Various teenage musicians, most of whom had more enthusiasm than talent, provided live music for these fund-raisers, and rather than charging entrance at the door, Dan cleverly sold his artful invitations in advance so that even those who didn't attend could make a contribution. Although the neighbors hated Saturday nights when the music was cranked up and the kids danced their hearts out, Mike and I weren't allowed to complain about the noise because it was all for a "good cause."

After three months, the money was in place. Before Dan and Amy set off for their summer break in England with Gaby, after which they would go on to America, I drove Dan to Atieno's house to deliver a bag of gifts he had assembled for her. His face was glowing in anticipation of the visit as we bounced along the corrugated track. We made our way past the squawking chickens and entered the dimly lit bakery to greet Beatrice, who called her sister. Atieno took a long time to reach us: every step was a major effort. In the past year, she had lost even more weight, though she was more beautiful than ever, her dark eyes luminous.

Dan slipped around her narrow wrist a bracelet that he had made from trade beads and silver wire and handed her a sketchbook.

"This is for you to fill up in the hospital," he said. Before we left, he ripped a page from the book and drew a picture of Atieno standing on top of a hill in a long swirly dress with the moon and stars above her. Handing it to her, he said, "See you in September, and then we'll go dancing!"

She smiled at the prospect, hiding her mouth with her slender fingers. Dan helped her outside, and she leaned against the door, waving as we drove away.

After undergoing a successful operation at Nairobi Hospital, Atieno began to feel better and was moved to the Kenyatta National Hospital, also in Nairobi, where the care would be free. I didn't visit her right away, though I was concerned about how she would fare in the overly crowded wards. I drove to the nearby bakery the following week, thinking she would have been sent home already, to see how she was progressing. When I arrived, Beatrice looked more tired and drawn than I had seen her before. Thinner, she was wearing a white kerchief and white dress, and when I hugged her, I felt tension in her body.

"Where's Atieno?" I asked, looking past her into the kitchen.

"She passed away last week," Beatrice said, with no expression in her voice.

Elias appeared in the doorway, shoulders stooped and looking much older, with dark shadows beneath his eyes. He related an all-too-typical story. The operation itself had gone well, but when her family moved Atieno to the government hospital for her recuperation, she entered a packed, badly managed institution, stripped of most medications due to the corruption and incompetence of hospital authorities. Unable to access more painkillers or antibiotics to fight infection, she contracted malaria and died almost immediately.

"Why didn't you tell me?" I demanded, my throat tightening.

"There was no time." Beatrice's face was contorted.

"It was God's will," Elias added, pinching the bridge of his nose with his floury fingers.

I fled to my car, scattering chickens and goats in the rubbish outside, and drove home, sobbing in rage and despair at the idea of sweet Atieno, alone and in pain.

The children were due back in Nairobi soon, and I dreaded their return. How could I tell them what had happened to their young friend?

On their arrival at the airport, Dan was first through customs, with Amy at his heels. Both seemed to have grown another inch over the summer holiday. Dan's first words were, "How is Atieno, Mum?" as he dropped his suitcase onto a trolley and opened his arms to hug me. When I didn't answer, he withdrew. I was unable to look him in the eye.

After I explained what had happened, Amy burst into tears. "No, Mumma," she said, her face crumpling.

"It's not fair," Dan cried, voice breaking. I tried to hold him, but he pulled away, striding as fast as he could into the sunlight outside.

Afterward, it was too hard to talk about Atieno, and we each dealt with the hurt in different ways. I kept writing articles in the newspaper about the bakery. Amy sent clothes to Beatrice, while Dan turned to his journals. I noticed that his collages took on a darker tone as he struggled to express his anger and make sense of the tragedy.

A couple of years earlier, in January of 1983, my journalist friend Mary Anne had invited me to share her office at the new Press Center in Chester House, a modern building in downtown Nairobi, with polished marble floors and gleaming yellow walls. As a freelance writer, I felt honored to have my name inscribed on a large brass plate in the reception area, along with that of Mo Amin and the correspondents for the Voice of America, the *Washington Post, Time* magazine, and other news agencies. There was also a stringer representing an unknown twenty-four-hour network called CNN, financed by someone named Ted Turner. Everyone seemed skeptical about the future of such a risky venture.

After Dan helped me carry my computer and an Ethiopian carpet into our new office on move-in day, we wandered down the hall to say hello to Mo in his expansive corner suite filled with photographs from his many assignments across Africa. Several phones rang intermittently, and a Teletype buzzed in one corner, slowly unrolling a long strip of paper onto the floor. In 1984, Mo would make headlines with his film of the horrific famine in Ethiopia, alerting the world to the massive scale of the human disaster there. This film inspired Bob Geldof's production of Live Aid, the largest charity concert of its kind ever given.

Dan pored over a pile of lavishly illustrated coffee-table books, many Mo's, and asked him technical questions about how he had captured the images in a recent copy of *Selamta*, the Ethiopian Airlines magazine that he published. For Dan's twelfth birthday, I had purchased darkroom equipment advertised in the American Women's Association newsletter and set it up in the bathroom for him to use, though he would eventually shift his operation to the guesthouse.

Just as we were leaving Mo's office, Dan pointed to a newspaper article pinned up on a corkboard on which Mo had highlighted the words, "I don't need to rest in this life. I can rest when I die. Then nobody's going to bother me."

"I think he's got a point there," I said.

"Me too," he replied with a grin.

After two years with the *Nation*, I had become a reasonably proficient freelance journalist, though I had never thought of myself as a full-fledged professional like Mary Anne, who covered African wars, famines, and other world crises. On her return from covering breaking news in exotic cities like Monrovia, Marrakesh, and Timbuktu, I loved to watch her fingers dancing over the keys and then read her stories fresh from the printer. I always wondered how frontline journalists seemed so normal despite the horrors they had witnessed, realizing later that they only *appear* normal. Nightmares, failed marriages, and secret drinking are often the price these people pay for witnessing so much death and destruction.

The Press Center was a gateway to a new way of life, offering me the freedom to shake off the constraints imposed on conventional wives and mothers and the ability to explore a darker, more dangerous side of Africa. Of course, this freedom was an illusion, and as I ventured further into the less savory parts of Kenya—and of myself—the contradictions began to give me nightmares.

Each day it seemed I was having greater difficulty keeping track of who I was—the cheerful businesswoman, journalist, mother, and wife, or the guilty, sleepless me who kept secrets. Never feeling good enough, I ran faster and faster without stopping to ask why. If I had stood still I might have wondered what I was doing with my life. Although I looked happy and well adjusted, underneath I was confused and distracted. Somehow I managed to keep my risky life under control so that my family and friends weren't aware of what was going on.

In May of 1987 Dan graduated from ISK. Not only had he received both the Class Service Award and the International Relations Award—the highest honor the school offered—but he had also been voted the most outstanding student by his classmates and, along with the valedictorian, was chosen to be the principal student speaker.

At the graduation ceremony, William sat with us, dressed in one of Mike's old suits and a striped tie and looking very much like a bank president. We swayed and clapped as an exuberant African choir sang a hymn of celebration. When Dan stood up to speak, I was amazed to see how grown-up he looked, now nearly six feet tall, with his hair brushed neatly back from his forehead. Taking a breath, he scanned the room and, settling his gaze on the principal, began his speech.

"The International School of Kenya has been a destructive experience."

There was a gasp from someone in the audience, and the principal pursed his lips. Dan paused, smiled mischievously, and continued. "ISK has been destructive of ignorance, prejudice, and racism," he said. The principal caught my glance and smiled as Dan went on.

"A student who comes to the International School of Kenya will encounter an impressive cross-section of the people of the world. I have seen sports teams that resemble United Nations meetings and have heard a Norwegian explain to a Japanese student the Masai way of starting a fire. I have felt the excitement as Israelis and Arabs worked together to find a settlement for the price of chocolate at the student store. After every year, when friends disperse to every continent, if you have kept in touch, the world practically becomes your school."

As Dan spoke, I gripped Mike's hand, proud of our son, who had made such a powerful, positive impact on his teachers and fellow students. Dan continued:

"ISK has given us the chance to venture north to Turkana with the vast desert and the Samburu tribe. We can travel east to Lamu, with mosques, *dhows*, and the Swahili people. We have gone west to visit the people of Lake Victoria in their homes and schools. We even go up to the top of Mt. Kenya with rugged mountain guides and a case or two of frostbite. On these trips, it is always interesting to see which aspects of culture rub off on whom. It is just as funny seeing a boy who has lived his whole life in Ohio gulping down a jug of blood with the Masai as it is seeing the warrior standing next to him brandishing a spear while wearing an ISK baseball hat."

Dan described the community of friends who had become like family to him:

"I recently read a book by Kurt Vonnegut in which he describes a group of people—for example, a class, a religion, or even a country—as being a *granfalloon*. This is a group of people joined together by a common characteristic or by chance, but not necessarily by choice. When people are together because of friendship or love alone, Vonnegut calls their relationship a *karass*. I see many members of my *karass* here today: students in the senior class, other friends, and my family."

When Dan sat down, he looked up and smiled at Mike and me as thunderous applause from his *karass* rippled across the auditorium.

13

Merry-Go-Round

HOWEVER WELL DAN'S LIFE WAS GOING, MINE WAS NOT SO HAPPY. FOR YEARS I had been troubled by occasional food binges during times of emotional turmoil. Now, though, those binges were starting to get out of hand. No one knew about my obsessive secret gorging but me.

Late one night, I pushed open the kitchen door and switched on the light, then paced back and forth across the floor like a leopard in a cage, pulling boxes of cereal and cookies out of the cupboard. The refrigerator was filled with containers of leftovers, which I lined up by the sink. Standing over it, I stuffed myself with cold tuna and congealed macaroni. I finished off a bowl of Corn Flakes and milk before attacking the cookie jar. After that I devoured a pint of ice cream.

I dumped the empty containers in the sink and filled it with bubbles, cringing as my fingers reacted to the detergent. I had recently been diagnosed with acute contact dermatitis, which resisted all creams, medicines, and the power of my positive thinking. I wore plastic, cotton, or suede gloves to cover my hands, which were etched with tiny slits and cuts. The condition was so painful I couldn't dial a telephone or thread a needle.

Few people in Kenya knew about mind-body connections then, and how, if we repress our feelings, they can manifest themselves in physical illnesses. No one explained to me that many conditions, including allergies and asthma, could be triggered by stress or a feeling of being out of control of one's life. Since then, scientific research has confirmed the role of emotions in the weakening of the immune system, which can lead to a variety of illnesses.

Breathing deeply, I recalled a poem I had taped above my desk in an attempt to remind myself to slow down:

> Go placidly amidst the noise and haste
> and remember what peace there can be in silence.

I laughed out loud. I couldn't remember the last time I had felt peaceful in the self-created chaos of my life. Just then, I heard a sharp rap on the kitchen window and looked up to see the concerned face of our guard, Joshua, peering at me from beneath his knitted cap. He looked a bit taken aback. After all, it was three in the morning!

"*Hakuna matata*. No problem," I mouthed, stuffing the few bits of remaining food back into the fridge.

He smiled tentatively and turned away, the beam from his flashlight bobbing through the darkness.

My face felt hot and my mouth was dry as I clicked off the light and tiptoed upstairs. That night I scrawled a desperate entry in my journal, one of several books I filled that year. Barely legible, the entry reflected my attempt to come to terms with the mysterious black hole that was growing inside me:

> What took hold of me to make me chew scraps and crumbs? Why did I consume foolish things? I feel soft today, rounded and undefined, seeking form, sharp lines, and direction . . . a cluttered mind, anxious to please, creating chaos from order.

I often wonder what might have happened if, instead of secretly bingeing, I had sat down with Mike and told him what I was feeling, how empty and sad I was behind my smiling mask. We both had trouble communicating our emotions, which, given our cultural backgrounds, was not surprising. His Romanian Jewish family and my Iowa Methodist relatives had identical inhibitions. Neither of our mothers knew how to speak about their innermost thoughts and would have deemed it a weakness to try. And I'm not sure it occurred to their husbands to ask. Mike's father almost never praised him; and he used not-so-subtle put-downs to keep his wife in line—not that she would ever have defied him.

Determined to spend some time together alone, we sent the children to their grandmother in London during the Christmas vacation and flew to India and Sri Lanka. It would have been the perfect opportunity for us to talk, but instead we sat for days, lost in our own thoughts in a battered taxi that hooted its way over narrow, winding, hilly roads to some new tourist venue where we gloomily snapped pictures for one of my endless articles. We stopped for curry and rice in a mountain cafe one afternoon outside Kandy. Brilliant green fields of tea stretched to the horizon beneath a cloudless sky. Mike was writing a poem—he'd recently taken to capturing his feelings and experiences in poetry— while I was catching up with my journal. I looked at Mike's face, aware, yet again, of how long it had been since we had truly connected. Suddenly I felt homesick, but for a place I had never visited, but only suspected might exist.

Perhaps sensing my gaze, he looked up. His eyes probed mine as if he, too, were searching for an answer deep inside me. I reached for his hand.

"What are you thinking?" I asked.

"What rhymes with flowing?" he replied, scratching his nose with his pen.

I think we were both contemplating the chasm between us. Though I still loved Mike, I didn't always like him and I'm sure that conflicted feeling was mutual. Every marriage goes through challenging times; but in Sri Lanka I began to feel that we were on two separate trajectories, and it was hard to see how we could ever find each other again.

On our last afternoon in Sri Lanka, I spotted a wise-eyed brass sun god hidden behind bundles of spices and rolls of silk in a crowded street market. I carried him home in my hand luggage and hung him on the wall above my desk. I polished that mask regularly and, late at night, shared secrets with it that I dared tell no one else.

I wasn't the only person having problems. Mary Anne was due to fly to London on assignment for the *Sunday Times.* I hugged her goodbye the night before she was to leave Kenya, but the next morning when I arrived in the office, I received a call from William.

"*Memsahib,*" he shouted down the line, so excited he could barely get the words out. "Something bad has happened to Mary Anne. She is at the police station at the airport. You must go right away."

I jumped in my car and sped toward the airport, frantic about what might be happening to her. Kenyan police stations were notoriously ruthless. Detainees were often beaten, and political prisoners were sometimes locked for weeks in underground cells filled with up to eight inches of water in which they had to sit, sleep, and excrete. As a foreign correspondent who was sometimes critical of the government, Mary Anne might be considered a political risk.

There was a row of dilapidated cars in front of the simple concrete police headquarters, marked by a faded Kenyan flag hanging from a rusty pole. When I asked for Mary Anne in the bleak reception area, a beefy policeman made a quick phone call and then motioned me to follow him down a dark corridor lined with well-used riot shields, helmets, and nightsticks. The smell of urine and disinfectant hung in the air, and so did a distinct feeling of fear. He knocked on an unmarked door with his club and gestured me inside, where a uniformed officer sat behind a wooden table opposite Mary Anne. She looked up, her face pale, and explained that she had been arrested and would be tried, but for now she was free to leave if she paid bail. I offered my car as security and signed the necessary papers.

"*Asante sana*—thank you, Corporal," Mary Anne said, extending her hand with a smile. Her silver bracelets jangled. "I'm sorry for the trouble." The officer beamed. "Come and visit us again," he said with a crisp salute.

"What a relief that's all over," I said as we headed to the car, though a few days later we learned that it wasn't entirely true. Mary Anne was in serious trouble, and her problems had just begun.

In those days, Kenya had strict currency controls: people traveling abroad were not allowed to carry any money—whether a foreign currency or Kenyan shillings—out of the country. So everyone hid their money in their shoes or underwear until they were on the plane. But Mary Anne had forgotten to remove her traveler's checks and cash from her purse, and when she was asked if she had anything to declare, she had pulled out a few hundred dollars in traveler's checks, hoping she would be allowed through with them. The official had demanded a bribe to ignore her crime, but she was annoyed and had torn up the checks rather than hand them over. Immediately she had been hauled off to the police station and warned that the penalty for her crime could be up to ten years in jail.

While out on bail, Mary Anne received word of her trial date. At the specified day and time, Mike and I drove her to the Central Court, where she joined the other prisoners waiting their turn in the notorious underground holding cells. When hours passed and her case hadn't come up, I began to worry that she might have to spend the night in jail. The day dragged on and I sat watching the gaunt faces of the manacled prisoners in filthy clothes being led in and out of the courtroom. Finally, just before five, Mary Anne's lawyer appeared with a sheaf of papers in his hand. "They'll let her out," he said, adding grimly, "But you have to bring her back at eight tomorrow morning."

Pushing my way through a milling crush of people, I headed down the stone steps. At the bottom, a guard waved me along a narrow passage lined with open cells. These were packed with half-starved male inmates, nearly all with shaved heads and many sporting nasty bruises and open wounds. The smell was nauseating, and I held a handkerchief to my nose. At the end of the corridor I could hear women's voices and hurried toward them. The stench got worse. A scowling female guard with a plaited leather whip hanging from her belt stopped me.

"What do you want?" she barked.

Behind her, Mary Anne pulled herself up from the concrete floor, her turquoise skirt wrinkled and white shirt smudged, but she smiled warmly as she turned back to hug several of the women in the cell.

"*Kwaheri, rafiki*—goodbye, my friends. See you tomorrow." She smiled, but outside the cell, her face collapsed. "I'll never make it, Kathy," she said, trembling as she described the building where many of the women were kept before their trial: a drafty, smelly shed filled with several hundred prisoners seated on the floor, existing on a meager diet of gruel and tea. Despite the cold Nairobi nights, each one had only a cotton dress and a single blanket. Many of them were being detained for minor offenses, and most were the victims of men. Few, if any, had legal representation. If Mary Anne were convicted, that was where she would go, and she wouldn't get out until her sentence was served. I wondered how a white woman would fare in prison. It was bad enough for the African women, who were used to more spartan conditions.

"Don't worry," I said, taking her hand. "The lawyer will take care of everything."

And he did. Despite our worst fears, thanks to his efforts the judge fined her a thousand dollars and released her the next day. But from then on, Mary Anne was a marked woman, and although she tried to conceal her fears with the old bravado, she was different inside. She would wake up in the middle of the night, terrified that she was locked in a cell and that no one could find the key.

Meanwhile, my own nightmares were getting worse. I often stumbled out of bed in the middle of the night, sweating and trembling. The downward-spiraling hawk of London days was gone. Now I dreamed of being whirled around on a merry-go-round as I rode astride a galloping stallion. Deafening music I couldn't shut off engulfed me. Desperately, I stretched my hand toward the gold ring suspended above me, trying to slow down my runaway horse—but my fingers could never quite reach it. On several occasions I touched our panic button instead of that gold ring, summoning security guards who poured over our walls with clubs and dogs. Wearing a bathrobe, Mike turned them back, explaining that I had set off the alarm by mistake.

I started to tempt fate: I drove recklessly to increasingly dangerous sexual liaisons, high on fear-induced adrenaline. I hated my dishonesty but couldn't seem to stop putting myself in risky situations, as though almost wanting to get caught. I jammed my days with endless people and projects, and filled every nook and cranny of our big house with guests, perhaps to avoid ever having to find myself alone with Mike.

We also had a constant stream of dinner guests—including, on one memorable occasion, the outspoken New York politician with the trademark hat, Bella Abzug, and Betty Friedan, the equally assertive founder of feminism. Although Mike enjoyed the interesting conversation over dinner, he was definitely not amused when he had to chauffeur the formidable duo to their hotel and they treated him like a limo driver—except they didn't tip him.

Dan found many of the travelers stimulating, especially the photographers and filmmakers who passed through our house on *National Geographic* assignments, but he was less than excited about a tousle-headed young English visitor named Thomas who turned up one day, claiming to be a writer.

"So write," I said, tossing Thomas some ideas for articles for the *Nation*. When nothing emerged from his typewriter, I asked him what his problem was.

"I write books," he replied defiantly, diving into our refrigerator for another beer.

"Okay, you have time, I have ideas. Let's do a book together." In fact, I had begun working on an outline for a steamy novel, *An African Affair*, but had never found the time to develop it. Thomas and I worked on it for the next few weeks, and after he flew back to London, we exchanged pages of the manuscript by mail. Finally, after months of work, we sent it to an agent in London who said she thought she could place it.

It was hard to concentrate on writing, for we continued to be deluged by visitors. Having signed on with a tour operator, I was entertaining American tourists almost nonstop in the *mkebe*, which could seat sixty for dinner.

One night, after lining up behind a group of blue-rinsed retirees, Dan took refuge on the roof and threatened to stay there for the night, much to the distress of William, who lured him down with a bowl of chocolate mousse. The family asked that I cut back on the guests; but with so many interesting people around, it was hard for me to hold down the numbers.

In October 1986, an Australian photographer named Angela Fisher arrived in Nairobi to promote her spectacular new illustrated book, *Africa Adorned*, and I invited her to spend a weekend with us. A sudden storm left our driveway a sea of mud, and she had to wade to our doorstep barefoot. Tall, blond, and resplendent in a turban and clinking silver jewelry, she hugged us all and over dinner regaled us with stories of her travels across Africa. It was very late when Mike offered her a brandy.

"No, thank you. I don't feel very well," she replied. Her face was flushed, her eyes bright, so I sent her to bed with two aspirin. The next morning she felt even worse and her eyeballs were an alarming shade of yellow. The doctor confirmed my suspicion that she had hepatitis and she couldn't possibly travel back to London for at least six weeks. We asked her to stay with us until she recovered, and she moved in that day.

As she grew stronger, Angela looked through Dan's journals. She studied every page, offering photographic tips and helping him plan a safari to northern Kenya. It was Angela who first alerted me to the unusual talent Dan showed as a budding photographer and artist. She loved his grit, energy, and style.

Angela also spent hours with Amy, by now a willowy twelve-year-old, and the two became quite close. Both Amy and her best friend, Marilyn, adored Angela, especially when she draped them in silver and bead necklaces and coached them on how to apply makeup.

When Angela was well enough to return to London, we threw her a farewell dinner party. At the last moment she asked if she could invite a friend. "His name is Jeremy. Interesting guy—born in Rhodesia, lives in London, and works in publishing. Who knows," she said hopefully, "he might be able to help sell the rights to your novel."

As it turned out, he was to do something far more fundamental than that.

14

A Dangerous Man

WHEN THE DOORBELL RANG FOR THE LAST TIME THAT NIGHT, ANGELA opened the door. It was Jeremy. Nearly six feet tall with a high forehead, wide face, and neatly trimmed brown beard, he bore a startling resemblance to Steve McQueen in his "angry young man" stage. He said hello in a soft voice that bore a trace of a South African accent and looked at me with intense, gray-green eyes as he shook my hand. I turned away, unsettled by his gaze. I felt I knew him from somewhere but couldn't quite remember where. Our eyes met again.

"Come in," I said quickly.

Dinner was a comedy of errors. The mismatched guests included a white Kenyan balloon pilot and his wife, a Ghanaian businessman, a visiting professor from Cambridge, and an earnest young aid worker. Racing from one appointment to another, I hadn't had time to shop for food, so we served a range of leftovers and an undercooked chicken with dried-out rice. I tried to make up for the fiasco with a babble of cheery conversation, interrupted by frequent exits to help Amy with her homework. Dan made a brief appearance before escaping to his room. Throughout the meal I was aware that Jeremy was watching me. By dessert I'd had enough of everyone and drifted away without saying goodbye. I curled up on Amy's bed, quickly falling asleep.

The next afternoon, I was typing away in my home office when I heard William call me. "*Memsahib*, there's a *bwana* at the door for you."

I went to the entryway and found Jeremy standing at the threshold with an envelope in his hand. I opened the handwritten letter, at once a thank-you note and a witty review of the dinner, with its ludicrous mix of guests and unappetizing food. Jeremy knew about my job as Kenya's only restaurant critic and parodied my style as he described a series of imaginary women who had briefly appeared at the table. I was surprised to see how accurately each represented a different aspect of me, but his last line was a stunner: "Someone named Kathy was there too, but she left early."

I felt hugely embarrassed. This stranger had seen the fragments of my personality I had been hiding from everyone else.

As I was struggling to come up with a decent response, he said, "Would you meet me tomorrow for tea at the Norfolk Hotel?"

The next day when I turned up on the hotel's veranda, I saw him, beer in hand, in deep discussion with a cluster of young Africans. Immediately, he pulled me into a lively conversation about Kenyan literature and politics and bought another round for everyone present. After the others had wandered off, Jeremy explained that after leaving Rhodesia, he'd been an antiapartheid student leader at the University of Natal in South Africa and had fled the country to avoid being drafted into national service. After spending a few years in the Sudan teaching English, he had relocated to London, where he was now working as a publisher's representative. "Really more like a traveling salesman," he said, describing his job to me. He sounded regretful, and it seemed clear that what he wanted more than anything was to be a writer.

I sank into my seat and listened, feeling strangely tongue-tied.

"Angela told me you wrote a book," he said. "I'd love to read it. Maybe I could help you find a publisher."

Before I had a chance to reply, he kissed me on both cheeks. "Must go. Heading to the airport," he said, his words clipped and without ceremony. His beard felt soft against my skin, which flushed as he touched it. "But send me your book and we can talk about it when you're next in England. Angela has my address."

A week later, it was Angela's turn to leave Kenya. Now tanned and radiant, she was heading back to London to resume her long-delayed book tour. I gave her my manuscript for Jeremy and asked for her address. She wrote it down on an envelope.

"Incidentally," she said, jotting down something else. "I know Jeremy would love to see you. Here's his London number. He lives only a block away from me. Do be careful, though," she added. "All my friends fall for him, but he's a real cowboy—and dangerous!"

After the car had disappeared down the driveway I read what she had written. It wasn't possible. There were ten million people in London and she lived in the exact house that Mike and I had left in 1974! And, coincidentally, Jeremy lived just down the road.

Something had shifted inside of me the night Angela brought Jeremy home for dinner. Although I tried to put him out of my mind, I kept his telephone number, and when we flew to London for Christmas, I took his address with me. Within minutes of arriving at the house of Mike's mother, I found myself dialing his number. I was about to hang up, second thoughts having gotten the best of me, when he answered.

"Come to tea," he suggested, sounding as though we had parted only hours earlier. "I'm only a few blocks away."

Gaby had plans for the children, and Mike was busy running errands, so I excused myself and hurried up the hill, enjoying, for a change, London's moody sky and slick pavements, so different from the brilliant sunlight and parched red soil that I was now used to seeing. Jeremy's address was halfway down a street lined with imposing townhouses, all painted white. There were a number of bells by the door, and I hesitated before pressing the one with his name on it. Before I had time to reconsider this rendezvous, Jeremy's face appeared in the bay window.

His apartment was warm and welcoming and smelled of freshly brewed coffee. Filled with books, paintings, and unframed photographs, it was barely large enough to hold everything jammed in it—a sofa, a mismatched armchair, an old oak table piled high with newspapers, and a baby grand piano wedged into a corner. A straggly Christmas tree with tiny white lights sat on top of his television set. The resounding chords of a Brahms piano concerto engulfed us from his stereo as I settled onto the sagging sofa covered with an old bedspread and a few ratty pillows.

Jeremy was wearing blue jeans and a cable-knit Irish sweater. He was even more handsome than I remembered, his face lightly tanned even though it was midwinter, and his hair tousled. He poured us tea and sat down opposite me.

"I read your manuscript," he said. "Stayed up all night to finish it, in fact. It's good trash. I especially enjoyed the love scenes."

I felt my face redden. Again tongue-tied with him, I found it difficult to answer his subsequent questions—about Angela, about Nairobi, about the book. After a few minutes, I looked at my watch and said I had to go.

"Come again," he said. Then he leaned forward and kissed me, his lips barely touching mine. Startled, I hurried out the door.

That night I couldn't stop thinking about our encounter; I lay awake for hours, reliving every moment of it. The next morning, although I knew it was wrong, I slipped out of the house and called him from a telephone box down the road.

"Come," he said, his voice low and urgent. "Now."

As I ran up the hill, I nearly turned back. Inside his apartment, I followed him into the living room and stood there awkwardly, not sure what to say. He reached out for me and I allowed myself to be held. Slowly I relaxed in his arms.

Without another word he drew the curtains, shutting out the gray December afternoon, then turned on a haunting track of South African jazz that made my insides ache. I stood in the center of the room, watching his every move. In theory we were two strangers with little time to spare, but for once nothing distracted me as I looked into the eyes of a man I had just met, but who felt strangely familiar. I followed him into the tiny bedroom and undressed, carefully folding my clothes and placing them on a chair. I watched him as he stripped off his shirt and jeans and dropped them on the floor before sliding beneath the duvet.

"Come to bed," he said. And I obeyed him. We made love over and over, and each time I was more desperate than before with a desire that came from deep within, from a place I didn't know existed. I couldn't get enough of him, nor he me, until we were both too exhausted to continue. Later, he peeled back the duvet and studied my body.

"No, please," I begged, trying to cover myself with my hands.

"You're beautiful," he whispered, peeling them away. "Why are you hiding?"

Looking beyond him to the window, I noticed darkness around the *kikoy* that served as a partial curtain. Suddenly aware that I was going to be very late for dinner, I grabbed my clothes. Jeremy walked me to the door. "See you tomorrow," he whispered. A light rain brought me back to reality as I jogged down the hill with Jeremy's last words flickering through my mind. Why did he think I would ever come back? Surely I had learned my lesson.

With my hair plastered to my head from the damp run, I was met by curious stares from the family gathered around the table. I caught a glimpse of Mike's stern face and smiled brightly while muttering something about losing track of time in a bookshop. I felt Amy's hand reach beneath the tablecloth to touch mine, but Dan's face mirrored Mike's. Much later, I crept into bed after Mike was asleep, fearful that he would sense the change in me, the awakening of a part of me I had lost track of, or perhaps had never known.

That night I resolved never to see Jeremy again. It would be too dangerous, and already I felt something greater than regret. But the next morning I changed my mind and told everyone that I was going shopping. Instead, I ran up the hill and fell into his arms again, drawn by a force I chose not to resist. Wanting to be out in the world, we walked to a dark Italian restaurant he favored, careful not to hold hands in the crowded street. We hid out there for hours, drinking wine and talking, our feet touching beneath the table. Totally absorbed, I suddenly noticed that the daylight had gone and I was late again. As I gathered my things together, he stopped me.

"Why are you always running, Kathy? Is it to—or from—something?" He paused for a moment, staring at me intently. "Or . . . from *someone*?"

I avoided his gaze. "Don't be ridiculous," I muttered, burrowing in my purse for a tissue to stop the tears welling in my eyes. I had no answers to questions I didn't want to hear.

"I have to go," I said firmly. "I shouldn't be here." I had a family, after all. This was so wrong. But I didn't mean it: I never wanted to leave him. With Jeremy, my feelings no longer felt detached, as if I were watching myself from afar. Instead, I was totally absorbed and engaged with someone I felt I had known forever.

"Who says *should* or *shouldn't*?" Jeremy demanded. "Life's in the living, for God's sake! Be peaceful, Kathy," he said. "And remember the quiet moments, for in them we find ourselves, if only a glimpse."

He was right, of course, but part of me wondered whether there was anyone worth finding inside me.

Once back in Nairobi after the Christmas holidays, I tried to forget about Jeremy and busied myself with my work and Dan and Amy. I kept telling myself that things were fine as they were. I loved Mike and my children. I was the luckiest person in the world. Everything was perfect. Determined to move on, I wrote Jeremy a brief letter that ended, "You strolled into my life and blew my mind out of my body. What we had was quite mad and irresponsible, but now it must be over."

Out of the blue in February, however, British Airways offered me a trip to London to visit their kitchens at Heathrow Airport. As soon as I landed just after dawn, I called Jeremy. By the time I arrived at my hotel, he was waiting impatiently in the lobby. Once in my room, I sank into his arms as though returning home. Again, we devoured each other. I allowed his fingers to explore my body, groaning in pleasure and exquisite pain at his touch. I loved his smell, the taste of him, his voice, the softness of his beard, and his sense of entitlement over me. All too aware of my body's imperfections, for the first time in my life I felt unselfconscious, submerged in him, liberated from anything that constricted my mind or spirit. It was dark when we finally left the room.

The next day, after my Heathrow tour, he cooked dinner for me at his place. There were candles and bottles of wine everywhere, and we danced as the room blurred into shimmering flames. We collapsed onto the bed and made love again—and again. In the middle of the night Jeremy woke me up. "We mustn't waste a minute," he whispered urgently, pulling me to him. And we didn't.

As I flew back to Kenya the next day, I realized that by racing through life at breakneck speed, I had failed to experience what it was to be truly engaged in every single aspect of it, except my children. Now, with Jeremy, I felt connected to a deeper part of myself; I was discovering what it was to be fulfilled, not simply as a wife, or mother, but as a woman. I couldn't imagine my life without Jeremy, yet at the same time, I couldn't bear the thought of hurting Mike.

Again back in Nairobi, I found it difficult to focus. One weekday morning I padded into Amy's room to wake her. When I leaned down to kiss her, her eyes opened instantly.

"Mumma, I've just had the most terrible dream."

Distracted by a looming deadline, I answered, "Darling, how terrible for you," and turned to leave.

"Mumma, *listen*," she begged. "You didn't hear me. In my dream you were riding away from us on the back of a bicycle pedaled by a man with a brown beard. Daddy's heart fell out of his body onto the ground, and it broke. I called to you but you didn't stop."

It was as if someone had punched me in the stomach. The guilt was overwhelming. I held her. "There is no way I would ever leave you, my darling," I said, stroking her hair gently, regretting my initial casual response to her confession. It was time to stop being so unaware of those around me, those whom I loved so much.

Then, again without my seeking the assignment, in April I was sent to England for another story.

I thought about not letting Jeremy know, I *tried* to not let Jeremy know, but then a few days before my trip I phoned him. He picked me up at the airport and drove me home. His flat had been transformed; the sofa, piled with cushions, had been recovered, and there were new paintings on the wall. Light streamed in through newly washed windows. "Look what you've done," Jeremy said, pointing out the new additions. "I've even started writing again."

Our time together over the next few days intensified my feelings, leading to a relaxed intimacy between us that released words that shouldn't have been spoken by a married woman to a man not her spouse. I asked myself what it was about him that I loved so much. It wasn't his money, for he had none; nor his prospects, which were uncertain. No, I loved him for the intensity of his emotions, for his passion about life, books and politics, music and painting. I loved him for his mind. And for his body, too, which was awakening mine. But most of all—I loved him because of how he made me feel when I was with him. I felt not only desired, but *heard*.

Now Jeremy wanted to understand me, to know me inside and out, and I him. Still, after a lifetime of keeping secrets, I was afraid to reveal too much to him.

"You've been skating on the surface of your life for too long," Jeremy said over an intimate dinner at his flat that night. Between us, a candle flickered next to a bottle of wine and two half-empty glasses.

"There's so much that's hidden inside you; talking to you is like going on an archaeological dig. What are you so worried about?"

For the first time I found myself ready to tell him. With tears streaming down my face, I revealed the truth about my double life, my guilt, my shame and self-hatred for who I had become. I spoke of my emotional numbness, the constant activity that masked a dark emptiness inside, which, despite my obsessive eating, I found it impossible to fill. I described my two selves, the good Kathy and the bad part of me, the latter keeping secrets and doing things that would devastate my parents and Mike, if they knew. Jeremy listened quietly until I was done. Steering me tenderly onto the sofa, Jeremy retrieved a book from his shelf.

"We have to peel away the debris to find bedrock," he said, opening a well-worn book to read a poem by Conrad Aiken:

And this alone awaits you, when you dare
To that sheer verge where horror hangs, and tremble
Against the falling rock: and, looking down,
Search the dark kingdom.
It is to self you come.

Terrified by the idea of that "dark kingdom," I stood up to leave, but this time he wouldn't let me.

"Don't be afraid," he said, with a gentleness that startled me. "Finding yourself is like casting off into the unknown. That's the way people make themselves into who they finally are, for good or for bad."

"Please don't ask me to go there," I begged. Things were fine the way they were. Why did he have to complicate my life?

"Go back to Mike," he said. "Or marry me. But stop living a lie. You'll kill yourself."

My mind raced, the merry-go-round music growing louder. Although I desperately wanted to be with Jeremy, it was impossible: I *couldn't* leave Mike and my children. Never had I felt so confused, so lost, or so completely incapable of making a decision. However, when Jeremy said goodbye to me at Heathrow, I promised to return.

The flight back to Nairobi was nine hours of hell. During it I could barely breathe as I wrote a long letter to Mike, trying to express on paper everything that had been unspoken between us for so long.

Mike met me at the airport, but I couldn't look into his eyes when we kissed hello. He sensed my distance as we drove home, talking banalities. Later, inside our bedroom, with the door shut, I handed him a piece of the marble cake that his mother had sent him. As he bit into it, I handed him the letter and watched him read it:

My love, to tell you what has been happening will be difficult for me, so I shall try to write it all down and let you read about the desperate journey I have been on for the past few months. My feelings of dissatisfaction about our relationship have existed for

many years, and I feel we may have gone in such different directions that coming together may be difficult. Now I would like to
live a positive life, utilizing my energy in nondestructive ways.

I could see his hand quiver as he began to comprehend my words. My
stomach knotted as he continued reading:

Because of my need for intimacy, for friendship and love, men
have been attracted to me. I thought they were harmless, which is
generally the way I managed to keep them. I shouldn't have required the ego boost, or those close friendships, if love was suffi-
cient. I tried very hard not to be affected by Jeremy. I didn't want
to be, tried not to be, and found myself terrified by the implica-
tions of my feelings. Saying these things makes me incredibly sad,
but I realize that the only way I can now exist is to be totally honest with you, so we can decide what we want to do for ourselves,
and for each other.

There was a knock on the door and William came in, carrying my
suitcase. Mike, his face frozen, told him to leave it by the bed. William
shuffled out as Mike turned back to the letter and read it to the end:

By now you must feel as though a sledgehammer has hit you. Although this letter must be extremely difficult for you, I suspect it
comes as a bit of a relief as well. This is where I am, what I feel. I love
you, always have, but haven't loved you constructively or well for a
very long time, if ever. It is only in receiving a different kind of love
that I realize how very far we were from where we should have been.
    There, I have put on paper what has been haunting me for
weeks. And now I must await your reaction, aware that I am hurting the person I love so deeply.

The piece of cake in Mike's hand had crumbled by the time he had
finished reading. Weeping, we clung together.

15

Journey to Delphi

MIKE FOUGHT DESPERATELY TO KEEP ME. HE DIDN'T WANT TO LOSE ME, OUR family, or the life we had built together. My letter made him aware of how distant we had become. For years he had focused on his job, his Rotary Club responsibilities, and our frenzied social life. I had been equally consumed by the children, our friends, and my career. Now we made time for each other. In May we took a trip, just the two of us, to Bangkok and Hong Kong. When we returned, Mike scheduled family walks and long weekends in the country. For the first time in many years, we played, made love, and talked to each other about how we felt. We appreciated one another, cherished and loved each other in ways we had never imagined possible.

It was a golden time, those months with Mike—a sunshine period for the two of us. Yet there was a bittersweet dimension to every moment, for as much as I loved Mike, I knew I was deeply *in* love with Jeremy. The shift had already occurred.

Fortunately, the children were unaware of what was happening. This was back before the graduation ceremony I described earlier. Another school year had just started. Dan, now a senior at ISK, was excited about taking baccalaureate art, and Amy, thirteen, had enrolled in a theater course. Both were involved in many extracurricular activities, and I returned with great relief to my role as chauffeur, mother, and wife. I even tried not to think about Jeremy. For a little while, everything was fine. Mike and I treated each other kindly, like survivors of some indefinable wreckage.

After three weeks of this, Jeremy called.

"What are you doing?" he demanded, his voice cutting through me. "How soon can I see you? You said you'd be coming back to London."

I felt sick. My entire being yearned for him. "I'll come," I whispered and put down the phone.

I walked through the house and into our bedroom, where Mike was reading. "I have to go," I said.

He looked up. "What are you talking about?"

"I have to go to London." At this point even I was dazed, not believing what I had just said.

He jumped to his feet and held my shoulders firmly. "What are you talking about? Are you crazy?"

I shook my head.

He strode over to the telephone and dialed my parents' number, then brought them up to date on my marital shortcomings. That began an entire afternoon of phone calls between my parents and us. They urged me to return to my senses, and advised Mike to get psychiatric help for me. Mike also called my sister Carolyn. I still distinctly remember her words: "You know, Kathy, don't you, that Amy will become a juvenile delinquent and Dan will go off the rails if you leave Mike?" The implication was clear: I was a bad mother for considering such a thing. I knew she was right.

My sister Janet, a marriage counselor, explained that the "catalyst" for a separation between a couple is rarely the person one ends up with. So why bother to leave Mike if I wasn't going to end up with Jeremy? Everyone in my family had the same question for me: "Do you know what you're doing?"

Suddenly I heard a terrible thumping in the study next to our bedroom. Glad of a distraction, I hurried to check it out. To my horror, I found Amy banging her head against the wall. She had apparently been doing homework there and had heard us on the phone, going over the whole situation with my family. Convulsed with guilt, I begged her to stop. She fled to her room.

That night we held a family conference. "Mum, you can't leave us," Dan said emphatically as he sat, head bowed, in the corner of the room. "We are complete, the four of us together. If we're at the table without you, it's like the yin and the yang aren't balanced. It isn't *right* if you aren't there." Amy didn't say much, but she had made her feelings pretty clear earlier.

I didn't go to London right then, but neither did I settle in at home. The nights were awful, filled with endless confrontations and arguments with Mike, who tried to use logic to make sense of my decision; in truth, though, my choices made no sense to anyone other than me. How could anyone in her right mind leave the security and joy of what looked like a perfect family? I couldn't be reasoned with. I loved my children, my husband, but felt detached from them all, lost in myself, selfish and alone.

Finally, Mike said that although he didn't want me to go, he wouldn't stop me if this was what I truly wanted. In November 1987 I moved into a guest room at the far end of the house. It was a temporary separation, I explained to my close friends, who knew how distraught both Mike and I had been, but in my heart I sensed it would be permanent. At first I reveled in the peace I felt, finally relieved of the pressures of our nightly "discussions," and began to breathe more easily.

The separation came at a terrible cost, however: although I still shopped for the food and organized the meals that William cooked, Mike and the children ate in the dining room while I sat on my bed in another part of the house, listening to their voices and the clink of silverware through the thin wall that divided the guest room from the kitchen. William didn't make jokes anymore and asked me to return to the *bwana* so that the house would be happy again. I heard him—but not really. I had carved a path for my life, and I was going to follow it.

Shredded by guilt and indecision, I slept much of the time when I wasn't working, and could barely eat. Every night I collapsed in my single bed, drained and exhausted by the effort of surviving the pain for one more day. When I awakened, often in the middle of the night, feeling empty and hollow, I was troubled by dreams of being lost in long, dark tunnels. Overcome by despair, I longed for the hurting to stop and for a glimmer of light to appear. After a lifetime of rarely crying, now it seemed I couldn't stop; my eyes were permanently red and aching. My journal reflected my anguish:

> Time of transition, time of tears, time of wondering which way to go, if any. Feelings of despair, sadness, pain, and anger, knowing that so much lies inside me and I just haven't found it yet.

I lived for Jeremy's letters and infrequent phone calls, which promised a new beginning for me, with Amy and him in London, after Dan had gone to college. He agreed to wait until the time was right for us to be together.

Later that month, Olympic Airlines commissioned me to write an article on Greek tourism for *Diners Club Magazine*. While planning my trip, I chose not to mention to the family that I would be meeting Jeremy in Athens and that we would spend four days in a village near Delphi, where he had rented a little house.

Once in Arachova, tucked on the slopes of a mountain, where I had anticipated feeling loved and supported, I discovered that Jeremy could veer quickly between tenderness and emotional distance or even verbal abuse, leaving us both exhausted.

And yet the old Jeremy, the charming Jeremy, was still present. In a moment of calm he told me that he imagined how we might grow old together, still in love with one another. Walking through the streets of Arachova, he pointed out the patchwork of crisscrossed lines on the faces of elderly Greek women.

"Those women are beautiful, for they have truly lived," he said, tracing the tiny new lines that had appeared on my own face. "Think of the passion in their hearts."

Most of the time we stayed inside, making love under a white crocheted bedspread. At night we slept fitfully, both haunted by unsettling dreams. He would cry out, and I would hold him until he fell asleep. Then I would awaken, rigid with fear, and he would draw me to him while I pulled the pillow over my head, trying to shut out the thoughts that scrambled my brain.

In his happy moments, Jeremy cared for me in ways I had never before experienced. He washed my hair in the outdoor shower, toweling it dry by the fire. With great tenderness, he prepared a spread of olives and rough bread, goat cheese, and sausage. During his kinder moments, I fantasized that we would stay forever in the village, far from the demands of my real life. But after too many glasses of *retsina*, or if he noticed another man looking at me over dinner, he would fly off the handle and we would spiral into arguments. More than once we had to leave a restaurant before the end of our meal because the violence of our discussion was disturbing the other diners.

Once, in a rage about something I had done, he slammed his hand through a window while railing about my behavior. With Jeremy, I allowed myself to become diminished, my horizons dictated by his expectations. I almost wanted to go back to the life I was now trying to escape. But how could I return to my family when I had shattered the trust of everyone I loved? In any case, I couldn't imagine life without the man who knew all my secrets and yet still said he loved me, with whom lovemaking seemed like salvation. Each night before we fell asleep we promised to make a new start the next morning, but we were barely out of bed before we would begin to fight.

On our last day in the village, we explored the haunting ruins of Delphi with its crumbling temples, sanctuaries, and shattered treasuries rising along gentle terraces up the side of the mountain. The atmosphere on that crisp autumn day was magical, allowing panoramic views of the pale valleys and the summit where criminals were once hurled to their death. Jeremy read aloud from a guidebook as we followed the well-worn pathways to the temple of Apollo—paths that had been trodden, over the centuries, by pilgrims seeking wisdom from a succession of priestesses whose words were considered the Oracle of Delphi.

More than five hundred aphorisms had been engraved on the porch of the sanctuary by those who had consulted the Oracle, including NOTHING IN EXCESS and KNOW THYSELF.

Suddenly, the words "Know thyself" started echoing in my mind, transported through centuries as though they had been uttered for me alone. And although Jeremy continued reading, I was far away, lost in my thoughts. Until this point in my life I hadn't had a clue, but now I knew I didn't want to be dishonest anymore. I wanted to be true—to myself—even though I wasn't sure what that really meant.

That night, Jeremy and I argued violently again. We never came to actual blows, but sometimes words can wreak more long-term damage than a physical beating. He was tired of waiting and wanted me to go immediately to London with him.

We screamed at each other, then made love and wept, before starting all over again. In all our years of marriage, never had I shouted at my husband nor he at me. But now a black hole had been opened within me, and all my buried rage poured out from my newly found soul like molten lava.

On our last night in Greece, neither of us knew if we would see each other again. Our frenzied desperation led to lovemaking unlike anything I had known before. Losing and finding ourselves, merging over and over, together we traveled to heights neither of us had ever experienced. I was suddenly overwhelmed by a rippling sensation of bliss. Waves of ecstasy rolled through me, moving up my body, slowly at first, then faster, currents surging higher and higher, barriers straining until they broke as the power of our passion enraptured me. Hurled into a state of oblivion, I felt suspended in space, as though my whole being had been released into the realm of spirit with Jeremy. I wanted to remain in that place with him forever.

When the moment passed, I wept uncontrollably. It seemed that the age-old message of the Oracle had released me from a lifetime of frustra-

The family in front of our house
on the Ngong Road.

Amy had a deep
bond with William,
who taught her to
speak kindly at
all times or toads
would come out of
her mouth.

When he was 16,
Dan's Masai
friends dressed
him as a *moran*,
a warrior-in-
training.

No helmets or safety belts for Amy or Dan on
a bicycle ride with Mike in Mill Hill.

We looked like the perfect family,
but in truth, my heart was breaking.

In his journals Dan included many images
of Amy and our friend's pet cheetah.

7 JUN 1992

While working on *Lost in Africa*, Dan posed
with an imported Hollywood lion that later
broke three of the stuntman's ribs.

A rare quiet moment with Dan and Geoffrey on the set of *Lost in Africa*.

Dan with a chimp on one of his many safaris with Deziree. (Note the "eye of the dhow" above the driver's seat.)

Dan at the wheel of Deziree.

Dan and STA members with their Landrovers,
Deziree and Arabella. Lengai Croze is second
from the left.

Amy joined Dan's
Student Transport
Aid expedition
to bring aid to a
refugee camp in
Malawi when she
was 16.

After Operation
Restore Hope
brought much-
needed aid into
Somalia, Dan
hoped that the
situation there
would improve.

Dan's haunting
photo of a marine
standing guard
before a stone
wall blasted by a
mortar shell into
a crater that
eerily resembled
a human face.

This photo of Dan surrounded by Somali
children appeared on the front page of
newspapers around the world.

Dan put on a
brave face
just before
his return to
Somalia. This
is the last
photograph I
took of him.

I put on an
equally brave
face. This is
the last photo
he took of me.

We found several versions of *Murder of the Messenger*
after Dan's death, including this one where the image
repeats and intensifies the fervor of the mob.

It seemed only
Dan could
control Deziree,
who refused
to start when
it was time
to go to Dan's
Celebration
of Life.

Dan's friends
and cousins
around the
blazing fire at
the celebration.

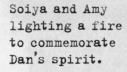

Soiya and Amy
lighting a fire
to commemorate
Dan's spirit.

Amy and me with our Somali bodyguard on the roof of the Al Sahafi Hotel in Somalia.

Visiting the ruined villa where Dan was killed was a powerful experience for both Amy and me.

Amy interviewed Christiane Amanpour for our film about frontline journalists, *Dying to Tell the Story*, and later, together with Julia Roberts, Hillary Clinton, and Rosie O'Donnell for *Extraordinary Moms*.

It was an honor to present Muhammad Ali and his daughter with a copy of Dan's book at the Blazer Education Center in Los Angeles.

Amy and I had the honor of meeting Kenyan Nobel Laureate, Wangari Mathai, whom I had first interviewed as a young journalist.

Meeting Michael Bedner and Sammy transformed my life yet again.

Amy, Jack, and me on our way to my wedding on Topanga Beach.

Amy and me at home (and at peace)
in Malibu.

tion and questing to become an awakened, orgasmic, sexual being. Jeremy was overwhelmed too, but I even more so, and I couldn't stop thanking him. Both shocked, we wept together.

As I lay awake next to Jeremy, who had fallen asleep soon after we lost ourselves in that wild, hitherto unknown place, I understood why the term *petite mort* (little death) describes so accurately the state I had just experienced. It seemed that by finally expressing my deepest emotions—acknowledging the anger and frustration within me, and then letting it out—the old Kathy had died. In dropping the mask that protected me from others—and myself—I had finally been able to escape from my imprisonment. At the age of forty-two I was beginning to know myself.

The next day, Jeremy taught me how to find that wild place by myself, a liberating discovery that left me feeling joyous, then incredibly sad when I realized how long the liberation from the inhibiting constraints of my past had taken. After years of desperately seeking release through a man, it seemed that I alone held the key to my freedom.

Strangely enough, from that day on, my eating disorders disappeared completely. Within a few weeks, I had lost ten pounds and was never again interested in writing about food. I wanted to speak for the Oracle myself, to shout from the mountaintop, Say what you feel, and *feel* what's going on inside you; communicate even though it hurts—speak the truth, and it will set you free.

Back home again, over the next few weeks I had to face the damage I had caused—and was still causing—and the kind of example I was setting for my children. Amy was particularly vulnerable. While Dan would leave for college in the fall, Amy was just starting her teenage years, when girls need their mothers, even if they don't admit to it.

Outwardly poised and in control of herself, Amy now had trouble sleeping and had developed a facial tic.

"I'm fine, Mumma," she protested when I began to fuss over her. "Just get better yourself."

Constantly anxious about me, she became ultra-responsible, making lists meant to keep me from forgetting things and choosing my clothes for me in the morning before she left for school. Often she left notes in my room to cheer me up. One in particular, written in a seventh-grader's loopy handwriting, particularly touched me: "Mummy, I love you, don't be sad, it breaks my heart. But if you are sad, don't hide it!"

On the surface, Dan seemed less affected, but I knew he too was disturbed. Since our family conference, his collages had grown darker and angrier. Not only was he suffering internally, but he was acutely aware of the pain I was causing his father, and he resented me for it. He tried to get Mike to stop working so much and to enjoy life more, but, like me, Mike dealt with unpleasant issues by working even harder. Both Dan and Amy told me that Mike broke down at times, though (ever the diplomat) he always kept a stiff upper lip in public.

Much as I wanted to explain myself to Dan, I felt he was too young to understand what lay behind my self-destructive behavior. Wanting him to deal with his complex feelings as he tried to support both Mike and me, I decided to use the art-therapy techniques I had learned as a teacher.

"Draw how you feel," I suggested late one night when he seemed especially tense. I had joined him in his room, cluttered with his personal artifacts and treasures. Three Masai masks decorated with ostrich feathers hung on the wall, interspersed with printed African cloths, posters, spears, and knives. Primitive clay figures and small bronze sculptures lay on his desk, piled with mounds of clippings, film containers, tiny bottles of ink, brushes, and pens.

Sketching emotions with crayons was a game we had often played when he was little, but this time he reached for a thick black Magic Marker and drew a bleeding antelope caught in a barbed-wire fence. Its anguished face reflected bewilderment, fear, and pain. He added the words "Distrust" and "Betrayal" to the margin and then stopped, staring at the page.

"I'm so sorry," I said, my throat tightening. "Please go on."

He hunched closer to his journal, inking in another drawing with pen, then smudging it carefully with his fingers. I watched him closely, wishing he were ten and that everything was as it had been a long time ago. His forehead was furrowed when he looked up again, handing me his pen and a sheet of ivory writing paper.

"Now you draw, Mum," he said. "Show me what you're feeling."

As I began to sketch, I told Dan about the Oracle in Delphi and the command "Know thyself." I added the Shakespearean admonition, "This above all: to thine own self be true."

Dan wouldn't look at me. His gaze was riveted to a spot on the floor.

"It's what I'm trying to do," I insisted.

Still no response from my son.

"I want to live with integrity," I said, struggling to find words to describe my attempt. I took a deep breath and tried again, "To be integrated, one person." Maybe that's what being true really meant. I wasn't sure.

As I spoke, a picture emerged from my pen: the figure of a woman, her arms outstretched, rising from the ground, taking flight, heading toward a destination known only to her.

Dan studied the sketch, then looked at me, as though seeing me for the first time. His face relaxed. "It's okay, Mum. I understand and I'm proud of you."

The transparent sincerity of his words, such torture for him to say when he loved Mike so much, almost made me feel worse. "It takes courage to do what you're doing," he added. "Don't worry, we'll be all right."

After that, on the surface he appeared to be doing well, distancing himself from our family problems and organizing weekend safaris with his friends. He had recently discovered girls, or rather they had discovered him, and he seemed comfortable in the new mixed-gender grouping. His journals reflected the carefree trips they took together, setting off in my red Fiat Uno with William's carefully packed sandwiches, often visiting his adopted mother, Kipenget, at her *boma* on the side of the Ngong Hills. I was envious of these adventures, for I was finding it increasingly difficult to relax.

In my dreams at night, the merry-go-round swirled ever faster, and I finally accepted my need for professional help. With therapists hard to find in Kenya, I decided to go to weekly counseling sessions with Sister Leone, a Catholic nun who proved to be a welcome beacon of light. Her office was in a crowded shopping center, reached through a maze of cars parked every which way and a jumble of fruit and flower vendors' stalls. Once arrived safely in Sister Leone's spartan space, I settled into a chair next to the box of tissues—so rough they could cause nosebleeds.

As I poured out my heart, I wondered how a celibate nun could fathom my wild double life and the recent discovery of my sexuality. Always accepting and embracing, she didn't judge, but rather encouraged me to find my own voice, to take responsibility for my own life, and to know that I didn't have to tell anyone everything. "Humankind cannot bear too much reality," she warned, quoting T. S. Eliot. She added, "Be gentle with yourself."

Sister Leone helped me understand that taking on so many things had prevented me from thinking about my actions. I had deliberately never stopped long enough to observe, understand, or deal with the consequences of my behavior.

First of all, she told me, I had to stop working in my office at home, located in a corridor connecting the various parts of the house. It was a bit like Grand Central Station—chaotic and not at all private. She insisted that I have a space of my own in which to create. "You must have boundaries and a clearly defined sense of who you are."

Although I knew she wanted to see our family reunited, she never asked me to decide one way or the other. When I quoted Jeremy saying that I had to find "bedrock" inside me, she advised me to go more deeply still, in search of the wellspring of love and energy.

"There's more inside you," she kept repeating. "Dig deeper. Pray. Open your heart to the source of all life. Let your spirit be free." To find peace and quiet in the midst of my chaos, she encouraged me to learn to meditate. Burdened with shame, guilt, and the awareness that I was about to lose everything I loved on earth, I found meditation impossible.

My living in the guest room, so close to the rest of the family, hurt everyone. Mike and I avoided each other whenever possible. He parked at the front of the building and I at the back. We used separate entrances and communicated by passing notes through William. The arrangement meant unrelenting pain for all of us, but I couldn't bear to be apart from the children.

Jeremy called frequently from London, and we talked about what we would do when we were finally together. He begged me to come to London for Christmas and to bring Amy along so I wouldn't miss her so much. Unable to stand being away from home on Christmas Day itself, I booked a flight for the two of us for December 26, 1987.

Determined to create a positive memory for our family's last Christmas together, I bought presents for everyone, filled the stockings, decorated the tree, and baked cinnamon rolls, just as I had for the past eighteen years. We all pretended we were happy, but no one was convincing and I kept retreating to my room to pull myself together, aware that I was on the verge of losing everything I treasured in the world. Dan's gift to me was a tape of Cat Stevens's recordings.

"This is for you, Mum," he said, as he played his favorite track. Snatches of one verse hauntingly stuck in my head:

You're only dancing on this earth for a short while.

16

Crossroads

AS SOON AS AMY AND I ARRIVED IN LONDON, AMY WENT TO WEST HAMP-stead with her grandmother, while Jeremy and I locked ourselves away in his flat. At first I blurred my feelings with wine and passion and tried to forget the world outside. There was no tomorrow. I had no children, no husband, no worries. There was only the power of our love that would engulf me forever.

Except the next day *did* come, and Jeremy, angered by my indecision about moving to London, began a relentless verbal attack on me. For the first time in years I had nothing to hide, but he wouldn't believe me. Our conversations deteriorated into accusations and defense as we seesawed back and forth in a battle for control. Jeremy claimed that he was being hard on me for my sake, and I knew he was right in one sense: I deserved punishment for all the terrible things I had done to my family—and to him.

Though I saw Amy several times at her grandmother's during that visit, one day she spent the night with us, sleeping on Jeremy's sofa. Un-like Dan, who had a complex relationship with Jeremy, admiring his macho qualities but also hating him for taking me away from Mike, Amy was, as always, a peacemaker and accepted Jeremy, although she was increasingly aware of his erratic mood swings and worried about me. I tried not to talk about why I had left her father, feeling that neither she nor Dan could understand the deeper issues surrounding my breakup with Mike.

As I lay on the sofa next to Amy that night, saying goodnight to her, I was troubled that she had been forced to grow up so quickly, robbed at thirteen of the innocence of her childhood. I talked quietly with her for an hour, and before she went to sleep she reached out to touch my hand.

"Don't feel sad, Mummy," she said, gently stroking my fingers. Her brown eyes fixed on mine. "I'm okay, and Dan's fine. Please be safe." She was quiet for a moment, and then added, "I hate it when Daddy cries, but he's getting better. We all want you to be happy."

That was the incredible thing: angry and hurt as he was, Mike tried not to condemn me or speak badly about me to the children. The shock of my announcement the previous summer had awakened in him a new awareness of himself and the world around him. A rational Jewish businessman, Mike had started attending seminars espousing the teachings of an Indian mystic named Guru Mai who urged acceptance and forgiveness, which Mike was trying to achieve in a situation where most ordinary men would have condemned me.

However, Mike's tolerance finally reached its limit. When Amy and I returned to Nairobi, he announced with an anguished look that he wanted me to move out of our house altogether. I knew I couldn't refuse, given my atrocious behavior. It wouldn't be easy, though: I walked for hours from room to room, touching the baskets of feathers, the brass bowls, our paintings and books—all the treasures accumulated in nearly two decades of marriage.

To start making the break, I decided to organize a sale of anything we no longer needed. Mike was just as eager to let go of the past and helped Amy and Dan sort through their unwanted possessions. William and I collected old furniture, bedclothes, toys, and ornaments from the sprawling house and piled them on the lawn. We strung clotheslines from tree to tree, draped them with clothes, and then opened the gates to our neighbors and passers-by, Kenyans, mostly house servants, who bought these remnants of our lives for a few shillings each. I watched, dry-eyed and numb, as our history disappeared in plastic bags or wrapped in yellowed newspaper. I wanted everything to go.

But after the sale Mike said I could stay in the guest room a little longer. He was aware of how hard it would be for me to be away from the children. Although I was relieved at the time, I realize now that it was much harder on everyone to have me around under those painful circumstances.

In April 1988, Sabena Airlines commissioned me to write an article about Lake Turkana, the place I had visited with Richard Leakey almost a decade earlier. Jeremy offered to travel there with me, so he flew to Nairobi and we rented a Land Rover for the rigorous seven-day safari. We were barely outside city limits when we began to argue. As we drove north, an ominous thunderhead hung over the Great Rift Valley. It was an omen, for when we reached Lake Turkana, the petrified logs, pitted roads, and charred black lava fields seemed to reflect our despair.

Jeremy's jealousy and possessiveness were growing inexplicably, like cancer. While he was in the throes of his rages, he harped on one idea only: I was guilty of making him angry by my actions. His attacks left me drained and depressed. Despite that, I couldn't separate from him. It was clear that we had no idea how to love each other and instead were killing what we'd most cherished.

On our last evening at Turkana we slept outside, sharing a narrow camp bed beneath a canopy of glittering stars. With the sound of the waves washing the shore and a gentle breeze on our faces, it could have been a moment of reconciliation. Instead, it was the beginning of the end. We were clinging together like drowning swimmers in an ocean of despair, but it was becoming clearer to me that the only life I could save was my own.

We barely spoke on the journey back to Nairobi, and Jeremy returned to London angry. Concerned that I wouldn't join him there, he launched a barrage of calls and letters designed to keep me on track.

My only confidante was Mary Anne, who loved me and also cared deeply about Mike. "What do you want to do?" she asked, repeating the question like a mantra. I answered that I knew I had more to learn about myself, and I didn't think I could do it with Mike in Kenya. On the other hand, Jeremy had opened me up and forced me to examine myself. Therefore, I had to be with him in London.

Mike still surprised me with his compassionate approach to my dilemma. "Think carefully about your decision," he urged. "What might look like utopia from a distance may be only half-good. There are no fights in *our* house," he said quietly. "No rage, only enormous love and the possibility of a celebration if you stay."

Deeply moved by who Mike had become, I decided I had to close my heart and turn my back on the love that was destroying me—and my family. I told Mike that I had finally and irrevocably made up my mind to stay with him, and I wrote Jeremy a letter to try to explain why.

The children rejoiced. It was the end of Dan's last semester at ISK, and my decision meant we could all go to his graduation ceremony as a united family. After that event we took William out for dinner—a family again, united in love: the yin and yang finally in balance.

Mike was naturally cautious about my change of mind and guided me through the transition the only way he could. "Try hard to focus on today and tomorrow, and try not to worry about yesterday," he told me one morning in an effort to be encouraging.

I sipped my tea, desperately hoping for more strength than I seemed to possess. "I'm trying," I said, swallowing hard.

"I hope so, Kathy, for the sake of us all."

The anguished look on his face shredded my soul. I never wanted to hurt my husband again, yet it would have felt strange to move back to our bedroom; so on my return I moved into the guest room. One night I crept into Mike's bed. Though he welcomed me joyfully, I still felt uncomfortable in his arms. He had changed a lot in the previous year. Thinner and less frantic, he seemed to be much kinder, more open and aware. For a while I felt hopeful and wrote:

Slowly, very slowly, I'm healing inside, while outside, scar tissue grows over ragged edges—smooth skin, strong flesh binding me together again.

Dan's postgraduation plans were uncertain. Instead of setting his sights on a traditional college in the States, he had applied to the Otis Art Institute of Parsons School of Design in Los Angeles and had been accepted. Now he just had to make up his mind. While he waited, he continued experimenting with many of the new photographic techniques he had picked up in his baccalaureate art class at ISK. Each print was different, some mirroring aspects of Picasso, van Gogh, Matisse, and other artists he had studied. One spread featured Mike, Amy, and me. But since we had rarely been photographed together during the past year, he had glued in a collage of separate pictures of each one of us to create a family group. Leafing through his latest journal, I noticed that he had pasted several pages together and had obliterated others with ink or paint. Presumably he had tried to blot out images of our trauma.

Hoping the hard times were now at an end, we planned a family holiday in Turkey for late June. I had to travel to Zurich for an article on Swissair but would join the others in Istanbul and return with them to London and then Kenya. Before the split with Jeremy, I had planned to meet him in Switzerland, but now I would make the trip on my own. The whole family came to see me off at the airport.

"See you in two weeks, Mumma," Amy whispered, giving me an extra hug before I went through customs.

Dan wrapped his arms around me. "I love you, Mum," he said. As the children and I said our goodbyes, I could feel Mike's eyes following me. The hurt was still there. I squeezed his hand as I left, hating my inability to do more.

Switzerland was agony. Staying in luxury hotels and eating by myself, I sank into a deep depression. Night after night I couldn't get to sleep, managing to drop off only as the sun was rising. Then I didn't want to wake up. Leaving the room was difficult: I shut myself away, spending hours working on my journal, trying to understand what had happened to the dynamic woman I had once seemed to be.

After four days I checked out of the hotel and bought a ticket to London, where I stayed with our friend Antonia Carr, a hypnotherapist and former actress who had visited us several times in Kenya. Strikingly attractive, with sapphire eyes and a ready smile, Antonia greeted me warmly after I unpacked and came downstairs, where she had tea waiting.

"You look terrible," she said, mincing no words. "Tell me what's happening."

I told her the whole story. "I can't stop thinking about Jeremy," I concluded. "I can't live with him, but I can't seem to get over him."

Antonia shook her head. "You've merged with another person, entirely giving away your identity. You talk about being true to yourself, but you've completely forgotten who you are."

She was right. I had to stop thinking about Jeremy. I yearned to hear his voice, but I knew the risks of calling him, and I wouldn't do such a thing. Yet after hours of trying not to pick up the phone, at midnight I dialed his number. No one answered and I hung up, relieved. I had made a mistake and wouldn't repeat it. Ten minutes later I tried again, slamming down the phone in frustration when he didn't answer. Over and over I called, each time growing more agitated. In the end, I dialed and lay the handset on the pillow next to me, letting it ring and ring. An hour later, Jeremy picked it up.

"Hello," I whispered. "It's me. I'm sorry." Within minutes we were screaming again, venting our frustration at a love that had nearly destroyed us both. As the sun began to creep around the edges of the curtains, he agreed to come and get me.

Late that night, he dropped me at Antonia's flat, where she was waiting for me. I lay down on her sofa, completely spent.

"Have you ever thought that maybe neither Mike nor Jeremy is right for you?" she asked gently. "Perhaps you've grown in a direction that means you can't be with either of them, at least for the time being. Maybe your purpose in this life can't be achieved with *any* man, no matter how much he loves you—or you him. Can you accept that your job now is to find out who you are? Once you discover that, you'll know what to do. Take time to find out who's inside you," she advised.

Mike called the next day from Nairobi. "I can't wait to see you, my darling," he said, and I could hear his excitement. "We'll meet you in Istanbul on Friday," he confirmed. I took a deep breath, hating myself for what I was about to do.

"I'm sorry, Mike," I said, twisting the phone cord, "but I don't feel very well right now and can't make it to Turkey. I'll see you in London when you get here." There was a long silence. I knew he sensed the uncertainty in my voice and I heard it reflected in his.

"Fly to Istanbul, please," he said gently. "And come home to Kenya with us. We love you. *I* love you."

"I love you too," I said, meaning it, but unable to add more.

The night before Mike and the children were due in London, I went to bed early, my head a muddle of contradictions. Antonia sat beside me and tried to calm me.

"Allow yourself to remain quiet and listen inside," she said, smoothing the blanket as I lay propped up on pillows like an invalid. "You may be really surprised by what you hear. You will know what's right, if you can only be still enough to listen."

She turned out the light, leaving me alone. The ceiling came alive with flickering shadows caused by the streetlight outside. I closed my eyes and tried to breathe myself through the anxiety that churned my stomach and muddled my brain. Slowly I grew calmer as I thought about what I really wanted to do, not what I should do—or what Mike or even what my parents and my children wanted me to do.

By the time dawn approached, I had made up my mind.

When I arrived at my mother-in-law's house, I found a noticeably downhearted family. I smiled when Amy presented me with a leather handbag she had chosen for me in Turkey, but she didn't smile back. Dan was gloomy because his latest journal had been lost when his suitcase had disappeared on the flight to London. Though he tried to make light of it, I knew how upset he must have felt to lose this precious record of his emotions during the past agonizing months.

Mike said apprehensively, "Now let Mummy and me be together for a moment." Alone for the first time in two weeks, he sat beside me and touched my cheek.

"How are you—really?" he asked. This was the moment I had been dreading.

"I'm sorry, Mike, but staying together just won't work." I knew the pain I was inflicting on him—and regretted it deeply. "I've changed too much. I love you, but I can't come home, at least not now. It isn't about you, or Jeremy, or anything else," I added helplessly. "I've lost *me*, and I've got to find myself again." I realized at that moment that I had come to the end of a long and agonizing road. This time there could be no turning back.

Months later, I wept when I read a poem Mike wrote that night.

I saw the sky fall in that day
As darkness spread.
I saw my love,
My wife,
Fade into night.

17

Veil of Illusion

IT WAS MID-JULY, BUT ICY RAIN STREAMED DOWN MY BACK AS I STOOD outside the front door of my new apartment building and struggled with the key. After hauling my suitcases up three flights of stairs, I crumpled onto the floor in the middle of the small, empty living room. For nineteen years I had been a wife, living in a safe, comfortable family home. Now I was on my own in London—with very little money, no job, and no prospects. Wrapping myself in a blanket, I curled up on my only piece of furniture—a bed.

Home. I repeated the word over and over again. Home. Home. Home. Would I ever feel at home again?

My new world consisted of four small rooms in a tired red-brick building on Elgin Avenue, in the politely called "transitional" area of Maida Vale. Mike and I had bought the flat years earlier as an investment, figuring the at some point we might want to be close to his parents. The neighbors were a mixed lot of Irish gypsies who siphoned gas from any car they found in the street and fought much of the night, cheeky Rastafarians with pretty babies, stolid British matrons in hand-knit cardigans, a sprinkling of students, and the local drunks who philosophized on street benches.

In the next few weeks I rarely left the apartment except to visit the little Indian shop on the corner, where I bought tea, cereal, and milk. I avoided the eyes of the man at the cash register, who always looked at me like I was a crazy person, which was true. I had no energy; I sleepwalked through the days, engulfed in a gray haze. I bumped into walls and couldn't stop weeping, desperately missing my family and my home in Africa, painfully aware of the damage I was causing everyone I loved.

Having embraced my life in Kenya so fully, I was trying now to reject it, as one would an old lover, desperate to be free of its grasp. But I was discovering that I was suffering from *mal d'Afrique*, the homesickness for Africa so eloquently described by Karen Blixen when she was forced to leave Kenya—a longing for the sunlight, the earth, the people, and the incredible opportunities I had so much enjoyed. Like malaria, Africa lingers in your bloodstream, causing unexpected aches and pains as you yearn for the spirit of adventure and far horizons that beckon you. You long for more life, more love, and more joy, only to discover that those blessings all too often result in more pain, more loss, and sometimes even death.

I decided to use my old art-therapy techniques to help me through my anxieties. My first drawing was that of a floating woman, weightless and hovering in space, a notion that unnerved me. Try as I might, I couldn't make her stand up. The second was equally upsetting—a figure, eyes tightly shut, curled up in a fetal position.

Although Jeremy and I had agreed not to speak with one another or to see each other, neither of us could resist going without contact for more than a few days. I wrote in my journal:

It's hard getting someone out of your heart and bones. It's like being addicted to heroin. It's much easier to stay with it, even though it poisons you.

My money was rapidly disappearing, and I had to find a job. One day, I took a survey of my wardrobe and realized that my colorful Kenyan dresses were totally unsuitable for a professional person in London. I had only one respectable outfit, and it had a large spot on it. Dabbing at it with cleaning solution only made it worse, so I took it to the dry cleaner, but when I picked it up I could see that it was ruined. I asked for the manager. After showing her the damage, I burst into tears.

"There, there," she said, coming around the counter, obviously concerned about my mental state. "We'll pay for it. Please don't cry." Within minutes I found myself pouring out my heart to a complete stranger. I explained to her that it wasn't the dress that was ruined; it was my life.

Zarina, a handsome Indian woman with sparkling nut-brown eyes and a smile that could melt ice, was completely unfazed as she invited me into her office for a cup of coffee. Seated across from her, I poured out all the bad things I had done, explaining how I was determined to find myself but was hurting my family and didn't know what to do.

"It's all part of a journey," she said. "It's not your destination; it's just something you have to go through to get where you need to be."

"I have a book I want you to read," she said, "but if you do, just know that everything will change in your life." She handed me a tissue. "Are you ready?"

I nodded. Zarina opened a drawer and pulled out a bright orange book titled *Living in the Light*, by Shakti Gawain. By page three I was hooked by the author's description of a place that "all of us must pass through at one time or another—what mystics call the 'piercing of the veil of illusion.'"

I read on:

It's the point where we truly realize that our physical world is not the ultimate reality, and begin to turn inward to discover the true nature of existence. The moment may coincide with a sense of reaching rock bottom but then we may fall through a trapdoor into a bright new world, the realm of spiritual truth. Only by moving fully into the darkness can we move through it into the light.

I had certainly reached rock bottom emotionally—or so I hoped—and desperately wanted to find the trapdoor. I wondered if it was the same place that Sister Leone had talked about when she described the source of energy beyond the bedrock. And if so, how could I move toward it?

Over the next few weeks I met frequently with Zarina, who told me about the power of dreams and explained that in hers, she was often a hawk, who saw things that the earthbound Zarina couldn't. In many cultures, she said, hawks and eagles represent mysterious, magical links between the spiritual realm and the material world. Through her experiences as a powerful bird Zarina had come into a new sense of her own power and vision. I had always longed for the ability to see beyond the confines of my existence but still felt earthbound, caged by my own fears.

Zarina encouraged me to start a dream book. Before I was fully awake I had to write down the strands of any remembered dream, because those images could provide clues about my unconscious thoughts.

In my first dream I was sweeping a huge empty room over and over again, until it was perfectly clean. Was I reaching the bedrock that Shakti Gawain had described—the foundation on which I could begin building my life again? Could I find the trapdoor? The dreams continued to flow, night after night, and every morning I awakened with what seemed to be pieces of a puzzle, but I couldn't put them together to make any sense.

"Be patient, Kathy. Everything happens in its own time," Zarina urged. "When the student is ready, the teacher appears. Just follow your own intuition. You have all the answers inside you." Always she urged me to watch for coincidences in my life, explaining that moments of synchronicity should be acknowledged and explored. She explained that we all carry within us a deeper sense that can best be described as a psychic gift. Too often we ignore it, and like an unused muscle it atrophies over time; we then lose the art of seeing clearly, listening inside, and receiving the deep knowing that lies within us. In a world filled with busyness, too often our senses are overloaded and our minds are fragmented, focused on anything but the present and the miracles unfolding around us. Zarina encouraged me to be silent, receptive to whatever might come.

Despite her admonitions to be peaceful, it seemed impossible to battle the jumble of emotions inside me. Worst was the shame I felt about myself, which made me reluctant to get in touch with Mike's sister and mother, who were living a few blocks away from me in Hampstead. I was also aware that my own family in Iowa disapproved of what I had done, believing that married couples should "ride the lows" for the sake of their children. They felt I had rejected their values, and they worried—as did I—about Dan and Amy. I didn't heed suggestions that I go back to Mike and be a good wife, aware that I still had a long way to go before I could return home without repeating old patterns.

Amy arrived in mid-July for a brief stay on her way to camp in Iowa. On our first day together, I watched her closely as she walked up the steps from the Underground. Barely fourteen years old, she was slim and her face had a guarded look and I could tell she was trying to figure out how I was faring. No child should have to worry about a mother. It was my job to care for her.

She chose the bedroom overlooking the street for her room during visits. It was bright and airy, with three tall windows and a pretty Victorian fireplace that we filled with a blue vase of dried flowers. Amy arranged her antique dolls in the corner and placed a pot of daisies on her windowsill. She helped me pick out a kitchen table and four chairs at a rummage sale and hang a few posters on the bare walls. The only thing I had brought from Kenya was the brass sun god that Mike and I had found in a Sri Lankan flea market. Amy hung it in the bathroom above the tub.

"He'll watch over your new beginning, Mumma," she said hopefully.

Despite my attempts at positive thinking, I seemed incapable of getting entirely organized, and Amy knew it.

"We'll make a list," she said calmly, pulling out a notepad. "And don't worry about Daddy and Dan. When I get back, I'll look after them and you can just get better."

Several weeks later, after Amy had been to camp and had returned to Nairobi, a curious incident occurred that convinced me that although Amy and I were separated by thousands of miles, we were still connected in a profound way. That morning I had awakened feeling anxious about her, and as the day wore on I became increasingly agitated. Finally, at three in the afternoon, I called Nairobi.

William answered. "She's not well, *Memsahib*," he said, disappearing before I had a chance to ask why. I was left gripping the phone with apprehension and fear until Amy came to the phone. In a tired voice she explained that she had been overcome by a terrible migraine headache at ten in the morning, almost exactly the time when I had begun feeling so worried about her. She had lain in agony, calling out, "Mumma, Mumma, help me," over and over again. I struggled to maintain my composure at this news, horrified that I was so far away when my child needed me, yet grateful that I had been able to pick up on her distress. I wished that I could be with her but knew that I wasn't ready to return to Kenya. Lately, I was beginning to accept an intuitive conviction that I couldn't return to my old life but must leave my past behind. I must face the practical difficulties of starting a new life.

As my first step, I bought a twelve-year-old yellow Citroën Deux Chevaux that I nicknamed Crabby. Daunted by London traffic, I was lost most of the time, driving around in circles or heading in the opposite direction from what I had intended. Antonia knew how close to the edge I was and recommended a spiritual bookshop in Camden Town where I might pick up some reading to help me find a new direction in my life. Restlessly searching its counters, I tossed several books into a basket, barely looking at the titles.

That night I stacked them by the bed and dipped into one or two before I tried to sleep. At first my head whirled with the events of the day, but as I tried to relax, I became aware of a peculiar sensation; my mouth opened and closed and my tongue began probing its roof. I felt shivers run down my spine as a surge of powerful energy forced my head hard into the pillow and I heard a strange voice emerging from deep inside me.

"We have been waiting such a long time for you," it said calmly. "We have so much work for you to do. Remember that everything that has happened, good and bad, has been part of your learning."

Who was speaking? I was terrified. I had read about people who heard voices: Joan of Arc had heard voices, crazy people hear voices, but why should I? Of course, I must be crazy—especially since the voice I heard was speaking through me!

"You have all that you need in order to do what you know you must do. Just begin it now. For a very long time, you have been walking backward," the voice continued. "Now it's time to turn around, face forward, and keep walking. Today you are to start on a new path."

With effort, I shut my mouth and slid out of bed, turning on the light to search the room. No one was there. Anxiously I called Antonia to tell her what had happened.

"Don't worry," she said calmly. "You're probably channeling."

Channeling? I remembered vaguely that Sylvia Browne had said she channeled a spirit guide called Francine, who seemed to know more than she did, but I didn't want any unseen visitors popping into me. Creeping back to bed, I reached for one of the books on the nightstand, figuring I would read for a while before trying to sleep.

To my amazement, I saw that the book was called *Opening to Channel*! Intrigued by both the topic and the coincidence, I read it from cover to cover in two hours. Written by Sanaya Roman and Duane Packer, it described exactly what had just happened to me. I recalled my friend Zarina's instruction about synchronicity—that there are no real coincidences, but rather, "when the student is ready, the teacher appears"—and started to read the book all over again.

The next day Antonia stopped by and explained her views. "Most of us deny even the possibility of getting help or energy from outside sources, but we can access this energy at any time—it's just a question of learning how. You don't have to call it channeling. Inspiration can come in many forms, such as listening to our intuition, acting on hunches, tuning in to our 'sixth sense,' and noticing coincidences." She explained that most of us deny the possibility of receiving information from other sources, from a wiser part of ourselves (our "higher self," if you will), or even from God, the Creator, the Universe, the Force—call it what you wish. "*Everyone* can channel," she said. "In fact we're doing it all the time."

On her suggestion I began carrying a tape recorder and pad with me at all times to catch whatever wisdom, from whatever source, might come to me. One night I awakened from a deep sleep and managed to turn on the machine as more channeling began. In the morning I listened, startled at what had come out of my mouth:

"Your world is sick and requires assistance from each and every individual if it is to survive," a voice like mine said. "There will be a time when the air is not breathable and the cities are not habitable. Human beings can change that future, if each person realizes that his or her actions affect every other person. We in the spirit world can help, but we need human voices, hands, and feet. You, and many others, will have a role to play in communicating the fact that we do indeed exist. Right now you do not believe it yourself, but one day you will understand much more and will be in a position to communicate this reality to an audience that will encircle the planet. The message is one of harmony with man and earth, man and spirit."

Absurd, I thought. How could I travel the world speaking for the so-called spirit world? I couldn't even find my way to the supermarket! But there *was* some advice that made sense to me: "Remember," the voice cautioned, "that when you are ruled purely by emotion, forgetting your own true self, it is almost impossible for us to help."

I wondered why the channeling, or whatever it was, was happening to *me*. Was it possible that in making a decision not to return to Jeremy or Mike right now I had reclaimed myself? And in reclaiming that sense of self, was it possible that I was being given additional power?

In search of further guidance in spiritual matters, I decided to read *Creative Visualization* by Shakti Gawain, the author who had originally launched me on a path of inner exploration. In that latest book, she wrote that it's possible to use the power of imagination to create or attract what we most want in our lives—whether it's inner peace and harmony, better health, a job, prosperity, or a new relationship. She outlined the basis of her theory:

> Our physical universe is not really composed of matter at all; its basic component is a kind of force that we call energy; everything

within us and around us is made up of one great energy field. The energy vibrates at different rates of speed, with thought a relatively light, fine form of energy, quick and easy to change, while matter is more dense and compact, slower to move and change.

She described how energy of a certain vibration tends to attract energy of a similar quality and vibration. With focused thought, you create energy that can attract form on the material plane. In other words, what you put out into the universe will be reflected back to you. When we are negative and fearful, insecure or anxious, we attract the experiences, situations, and people that we are seeking to avoid. The converse is also true. Life, therefore, offers a perfect mirror of where we are at any point in time. Gawain herself used the term "law of attraction."

I recalled how my life had been when I felt happy and focused, doing what I believed I was here to do: life flowed, sometimes more smoothly than others, but always moving in a positive direction. In the past few years, when I'd been lost in emotion and dishonest with others and myself, nothing good seemed to happen.

Now I wondered if I could consciously create a flow that would attract the ideas, things, people, and spiritual awareness that I so badly needed. I experimented with the concept at a purely practical level, visualizing a chest of drawers for my clothes, another for the guest room, two bookshelves for the living room, and cupboards for the bedroom. I focused on how they looked and imagined them in my flat. It's probably a lot of nonsense, I thought, as I tucked the mental list away. But to my delight Angela called out of the blue a few hours later. "I'm going to be giving away some furniture," she said, "maybe you could use it?"

It took three trips to bring everything over: three chests of drawers, two bookshelves, and a neat white bathroom stand.

Over and over I tested the technique, intrigued as I managed to materialize a dishwasher, more furniture, and clothes. As I experimented with energy, I noticed that when I was fully focused, a shiver often ran down my spine, an intimation that some intuitive power was at work.

One morning I woke up blinking in unaccustomed sunlight that poured through my windows, which were still without curtains after three months. Feeling a shiver, I grabbed my journal to write down the dream that had awakened me. It was a vivid scenario in which I was given the blueprint of a company that I would one day create, a multimedia organization dealing in film, television, and books. It would be housed in an airy penthouse office that would include an art gallery and center that supported young artists, writers, and cinematographers. In my vision I even heard the name of the organization: Creative Visions.

I watched my fingers form the words "a multimedia company dedicated to helping individuals achieve their potential, both for themselves and for the world." Intriguing, I thought, tucking the journal away, but right now I just needed a job. My funds had nearly run out and I had a mortgage to pay. Still, I knew that it was important to listen to my dreams and decided to register Creative Visions as a limited company, only to discover that the name had already been taken. It was a relief, really, for it was a much too ambitious idea.

I would have to make do with whatever turned up and in late August accepted a part-time job promoting a charity concert. The money was bad, but at least it was a start. I would give it everything I had and see where it led me.

I still saw Jeremy occasionally. He and I were like lost souls, unable or unwilling to stay permanently away from each other. We talked sporadically about starting over again, but neither trusted the other enough to try. Maddened by memories, I was almost glad when he said he was flying to San Francisco to visit friends for a few weeks. It meant temporary relief from my obsessive dilemma about whether to meet him or not.

Then suddenly everything changed. Angela called me to say that Jeremy was marrying an American woman who lived in San Francisco and that she had come over to spend a week in London with him. I refused to believe what I was hearing; he had never mentioned that he was dating anyone. Angela assured me that the story was true. He simply hadn't screwed up the courage to tell me yet.

I hung up quickly, went to the bathroom, and threw up. My stomach aching, enveloped in a haze of depression, I wasn't sure that I could ever feel happy again.

Later that week I agreed, as a distraction, to meet a friend for an afternoon drink in a pub I'd never been to on the other side of London. It was a beautiful day. The sun glinted off the beveled edges of the pub's cut-glass windows, flowers tumbled from its window boxes, and I felt that there was hope for life after love. Feeling a tap on my back, I turned around. There stood Jeremy! He had shaved off his beard and looked different—smaller somehow. Behind him was a woman who looked at me curiously. I jumped up to greet his fiancée. We stood eye to eye. Her hair was short and auburn, cut like mine, and we were wearing almost the same outfit. I hugged her.

"What a coincidence," our voices echoed.

After we'd chatted for a few minutes, I wished her luck. Jeremy quickly pecked me on the cheek, and I watched them disappear down the street.

Before he left England in September, we met one final time. I had a present to give him, a piece of crystal to add to his collection. It was cold and drizzling as I pressed his bell and, just like the old days, glimpsed his face, pale now, in the window before he opened the door. Inside, empty wine bottles and dirty coffee cups stood on the floor amidst furniture and packing cases; the bookshelves were nearly empty, and the flat was between lived-in and deserted. Neither of us could look at the other, and we could barely speak, perhaps unwilling to accept that it was really over.

As I was leaving, a bee flew in through an open window, buzzed through the flat, and stung my ankle. By the time I reached home, an angry welt had appeared, and before long the wound became infected, leaving a scar that remains to this day.

18

Bleeding

ANTONIA TAUGHT ME THAT IF SOMETHING DOESN'T HAPPEN EXACTLY AS you want it to, it's probably because you haven't thought it through carefully enough or your desired outcome wouldn't work toward your highest good. In much the same way, Sister Leone had always encouraged me not to battle too hard to change things—people and circumstances—but rather to change *me*.

This was the perfect moment to test her theory. Although I was haunted by the memory of my time with Jeremy, the haze began to lift from my mind, the pain in my stomach began to disappear, and slowly it became easier to breathe normally again. Although I felt exhausted much of the time, my journal entries grew more positive:

I am free of the long ache of unresolved love. With relief and excitement I am at last in control of my life. I am. I am.

Next to this one I added some words from the French novelist André Gide, who had traveled in the Congo:

To free oneself is nothing. The really arduous task is to know what
to do with one's freedom.

I still hadn't figured out what to do with my freedom, but at least I felt
more optimistic. I booked myself on an inexpensive ski trip that I hoped
would leave me clearer and stronger—ready to tackle the bright future I
knew was just around the corner. However, once on the slopes, I found
that I was too tired to ski well, and after innumerable tumbles, somer-
saults, and facedown dives, my entire body was covered with angry purple bruises.

When I returned home, I felt a familiar wetness. Damn, my period, I
thought. But two weeks early? By the next day I was bleeding heavily.
Even worse, the September bee sting still throbbed, and a nasty cold that
wouldn't go away had left my voice hoarse. Over the next week a cut on
my finger filled with pus and the nail dropped off, the skiing bruises
multiplied, and my gums began to bleed: some days I was barely able to
walk to the corner shop without feeling worn out. Still, conscious that
happiness can be a choice, I tried to be upbeat, covering my purple
blotches with long sleeves, tights, and makeup.

Finally the day came when it was impossible to ignore the bloody
patches that kept appearing on the back of my skirt. I booked an appointment with my doctor at the Cromwell Hospital.

"Where did you get these bruises?" he asked, peering over his glasses
as he peeled back the drape to study my legs and torso, covered, like my
arms, with colorful bruises. "What have you done?"

"I fell a lot when I was skiing," I offered weakly.

I watched his expression grow somber as he noted all my other symp-
toms, including the infected scar on my ankle from the bee sting.

"First thing Monday morning I want you in for a bone marrow test,"
he said. "Over the weekend, I don't want you to move out of your flat.
You should be deeply concerned."

Outside the hospital, I breathed in the polluted air of Cromwell Road,
glad to be alive and upright, but when I arrived at my building, I climbed
the steps slowly, one at a time, in case I might trip and bleed to death.

On Monday I arrived, as instructed, at the Cancer Unit of the Cromwell Hospital, where the waiting room was packed with pale, hollow-eyed people. A few were bald, many wore wigs, and others had moonlike faces. There was an air of great weariness in the room. An emaciated man with a tube curling out of his arm limped past me, pushing a trolley before him. I didn't know whether to say hello or pretend not to notice.

I swallowed hard when my name was called, then followed an aide as she led me to a cubicle. After another anxious wait, a Filipino nurse pulled back the flowery curtain that enclosed the cubicle and beamed at me. "Hello, my love. Bone marrow tests are nasty," she said sympathetically, explaining that the technician would jam a thick needle deep into my hip bone to draw out living marrow. Despite a local anesthetic, the procedure would be uncomfortable, she said. Closing the curtain again, she settled me on the bed and called for the technician. When he was done, I stood up unsteadily and walked slowly through to the reception area. A man looked up from his paper, revealing a face that must have been very handsome before his cheeks disappeared, revealing how his skeleton would look without skin.

A couple days later, in his office, the doctor fiddled with his glasses while he studied the reports. "Your blood isn't clotting," he said. "If you had fallen on your head while skiing, you could have had a brain hemorrhage and bled to death. No one would have known what caused it, or how to treat you."

"Do I have leukemia?" I asked, dreading his answer.

He shook his head. "The good news is that it isn't cancer. The bad news is that your immune system seems to have broken down. Your platelets are at 17,000 when they should be above 150,000. I don't know what triggered this condition—but you have what's called *thrombocytopenia*, an autoimmune disease that makes it difficult for your blood to clot. You are very ill, indeed."

Armed with medication and a strict admonition to do absolutely nothing, I went home, determined to *will* myself better. But I continued to bleed. Blood poured out of me, it seemed, splashing in the toilet, dripping down my legs, puddling on the floor, staining the carpet and my clothes. I felt my energy, and gradually my will to live, draining away. After years of shame surrounding my sexuality, perhaps I shouldn't have been surprised. It seemed that my womb was mortally wounded. Besides, I knew that part of me wanted to escape from my life. However hard I was trying to embrace an uncertain new future, there were moments when dying felt much easier than living.

Every day I fought to stay out of bed, but after an hour or two had to crawl back under the covers. Whenever Amy called, I tried to sound upbeat. I didn't want her to be aware of how ill I really was, although I let Mike know, in case something happened. Neither his encouragement nor the antibiotics seemed to work, and no amount of makeup could conceal the dark bags under my eyes, my lank hair, or my pale skin. My bones ached, my stomach hurt, and I shuffled around, hunched over like an old lady. Every day I felt weaker. In despair I wrote in my journal:

Barely alive today,
cold fingers limp
to no touch,
soft body hollowed
beneath no gaze

Late one night that winter, there was a terrible storm and I lay without moving, listening to the roar of the wind as it smashed huge trees against each other, hurling branches to the ground outside my flat. As I watched the driving rain swirl patterns across the window, I decided that if I were going to die, I needed to make my peace with those I loved. I began with a letter to the children but couldn't find the right words to say goodbye.

It was then that I realized I absolutely had to live—if not for my sake, then for theirs. Unable to muster the strength on my own, I closed my eyes and bargained with God, promising that if I got well, I would devote my life to serving others. Then I prayed for a miracle to heal my body, my mind, and my broken spirit.

As if in answer to my prayers, my friend Allegra Taylor telephoned the next day. Strikingly beautiful and charismatic, the mother of six children, three of whom were adopted from Africa, she was the author of many books, including *I Fly Out with Bright Feathers*, a book about healers around the world. Now she was working on a BBC documentary about healers, a subject that was particularly intriguing to me after my experience with traditional *mganga*s in Kenya.

"How are you doing?" she asked.

I said that things could be better.

"I'm coming over now." Click.

An hour later Allegra was at my door. She was the kind of person who made you feel better just by being there and seemed to glow like some sort of celestial being.

"Why did you come?"

"I had a feeling you needed me," she said, smiling like she knew something that I didn't. "We'll get you well in no time."

I chose a patch of sunshine in the middle of the room and, at Allegra's instruction, lay down on the floor, painfully aware that my hipbones, usually well camouflaged under ample flesh, were clearly visible under two layers of sweaters.

"Just close your eyes and breathe," Allegra said. "Concentrate on letting energy flow through you."

As her hands hovered over me, shimmering colors appeared before my eyes, glorious hues that flowed into velvety blackness, then into swirling mixtures of violet and blue. Tears flowed down my cheeks, and I brushed them away unselfconsciously, hovering in a state of pure love and peace for several minutes. When I felt Allegra lean back, I opened my eyes and saw that she, too, had been crying.

"What happened?"

"It had nothing to do with me," she said and shook her head.

When I sat up, a new energy surged through me, and I knew without a shadow of doubt that I was going to be well. It felt as though I had bled away all the pain, humiliation, and shame of my recent life and that in this moment of healing I had received a second chance.

After that, every day I meditated and prayed, focusing on healing and light, and every day I grew stronger and more hopeful.

A week after Allegra's visit, I made it down three flights of steps and to the corner shop without having to stop for a rest. When I returned to my flat, I pulled out a sheet of bright yellow paper and wrote:

I opened the windows of my soul today
unlocked the tight shut
impenetrable barrier,
flung up the sash,
and in the light
found a self
waiting to see out.

Over the next few weeks, I drew in my journal constantly, watching with delight as my figures began to stand upright, then walk, stride, and run. I even managed to sketch a man and woman who were standing apart from one another—separate entities, linked by a ring. Curious about its significance, I showed the drawing to Antonia, who explained that in order to achieve wholeness as a human being, both the male and female aspects of an individual have to come together. The ring, she said, was a symbol of the uniting of the two parts of myself, often described as the *animus* and the *anima*. This image, which had arisen from my subconscious—or, as the philosopher Carl Jung might have said, from the "collective consciousness"—is apparently universal to all cultures and traditions. Angela suggested that it represented a symbolic marriage between the two parts of me, resulting in a new sense of unity and harmony.

Soon afterward there was a startling new development: a baby appeared in many of the drawings. Antonia interpreted it for me: "Babies represent hope, rebirth, new ideas, and new projects. A baby usually means something good's coming your way." It couldn't come quickly enough for me.

I was delighted when, in the midst of all my health challenges, Mary Anne asked if she could come and share my flat until she found one of her own.

She moved into my tiny third bedroom, providing company that I sorely needed.

Things hadn't gone well for Mary Anne in Kenya after her trial. She had grown increasingly angry with Moi's corrupt government, and after she wrote a mildly critical article about the president, she was declared *persona non grata* by the head of immigration and given twenty-four hours to pack her suitcase and leave—never to return. Luckily her two daughters, Tara and Petra, were already out of the country in boarding school, and Mike agreed to take in one of her Masai foster sons, Peter Lekarian, who at nineteen was close to Dan's age. The remaining four foster sons were taken in by other friends in Nairobi.

Now Mary Anne was struggling to pull the strands of her life together; but it was difficult for such an experienced and adventurous foreign correspondent, whose beat was Africa, to adapt to a boring desk job covering local news in London. Many nights she would awaken weeping and I'd sit by her bed, listening to her nightmares. On other nights, she would listen to mine. I couldn't have made it through the long winter without her. We had both left our homes and friends in Africa. I chose to leave, while she had to, but neither of us was emotionally or financially equipped to take on the challenges we faced.

My favorite times were when Tara and Petra, who were the same ages as Dan and Amy, joined us for long weekends, camping out in Amy's room and on the sofa. When they were around, the house was filled with their music and laughter, and life seemed positive again. After they left, I missed my own children even more, though I tried not to let them know how unhappy I was without them. Since my arrival in London, I had been writing them often, and lately I had been decorating the letters with cheerful drawings. Dan's favorite was a tiny cartwheeling figure whose exuberant ups and downs reminded him, he said, of my life's tumultuous journey.

It was Amy, though, who was most often on my mind. Every day in London when I saw young girls on the street, I longed to be with my daughter. When I'd left her in July, it was only to be for a short time, but the days had stretched to weeks, and now months. She was a busy ninth-grader, immersed in student council activities and rehearsals for a leading role in a musical, *Bugsy Malone*.

But one day in the spring of 1989, Amy called with the most wonderful news. "I've made a decision, Mumma," she announced. "I'm coming to London to live with you next year."

Holding my breath, I asked with trepidation, "What does Daddy say?" I had made a number of entreaties to Mike to let Amy live with me, but he had been insistent that he would keep her at home in Nairobi for as long as he thought she needed it.

"He wants me to be happy, and he knows that right now I need to be with you." The long, agonizing separation would finally be over. Mike and I had never had a war over the children, nor had we used lawyers for our recent separation agreement, which was written in humane terms and had put their welfare first. Under it, the funds to look after the children's educational needs provided by my parents were set aside, after which we split the rest of what remained—which meant I had almost nothing to live on.

My friends told me that Mike was slowly beginning to heal. His informal adoption of Peter Lekarian, a wise and caring young man, had helped fill the gap left after my departure, and that of Dan when he left for the United States. I knew that Mike had taken up meditation, and I admired the man he was becoming.

Every day I journeyed farther into myself, trying to be fully alive in the moment, not rushing ahead nor lagging behind; simply experiencing my emotions—whether they were happy or sad, angry or hurt. I had learned the hard way that to be truly alive is to *feel*, although after a lifetime of insulating myself from my emotions, I wondered at times if I would be able to survive *feeling* so much.

Amy arrived in London in late August 1989 and quickly settled into the American School. She had changed radically since I had last seen her. Always poised, even as a little girl, she had developed a nurturing, compassionate, adventurous, and fun spirit as well. She quickly attracted a wide variety of friends of many races, all of whom seemed fascinated by her tales of life in Africa. Like her classmates at ISK, the students at the

American School had also grown up in a number of countries and cultures. However, unlike most of those other students, who were the sons and daughters of wealthy expatriate bankers, businessmen, and diplomats, Amy was the offspring of a mother who was barely scraping by. Despite that, our little flat, with its makeshift furniture and nearly empty refrigerator, soon became a popular gathering place for her new friends.

Amy quickly became streetwise in London, but one evening she arrived in the apartment looking shaken. She explained that a pack of teenage thugs were beating up a boy on the street outside the restaurant where she and some friends had been dining. She marched outside and right into the center of the action, demanding that the young men stop—which, to her friends' amazement, they did.

After the near-perfect weather all year round in Kenya, Amy found the cold wetness of England hard to take, especially when she was bicycling on her long, uphill ride to school. Guitar strapped to her back, book bag in the basket, and umbrella in hand, she would cycle past the young guardsmen of the queen's Household Cavalry as they trotted down Elgin Avenue exercising their horses. I watched from my window as they swiveled in their saddles when she rode by, her back straight, looking for all the world like Mary Poppins.

Despite her quick adjustment to school and a new circle of friends, she found our little London flat a major culture shock. She had been the *memsahib kidogo*, or little *memsahib*, of Mike's house ever since I left Nairobi. This involved overseeing the meals bought and cooked by William. Now she had to shop, master a vacuum cleaner, do the dishes, help Mary Anne and me clean and cook, and fold laundry. Her skills at these things were lackluster at best, and housecleaning became the number-one issue of contention between us. But after our long separation we were getting to know each other again, and for the first time since I left Nairobi, I felt that not only my body but also my soul was beginning to heal.

19

A Dancing Star

WHILE AMY SETTLED INTO LIFE IN LONDON, DAN WAS MAKING HIS WAY IN the world on his own. He had convinced Mike, me, and my parents, who were funding his education, that he could gain more from a hands-on job and traveling than from going to art school. When I called him to try to change his mind, he protested.

"It's my life, Mum." He wanted to take what he called "a year *on*," not off, which would begin with a three-month stint at *Mademoiselle* magazine. The previous summer the art director had become fascinated with his journals and invited him to work as a paid intern in New York. After that, he would finally take his place at the Parsons School of Design in Los Angeles. Mike and I agreed with his decision.

As I had anticipated, New York proved to be a challenge for him. Although he loved his job at *Mademoiselle*, he was barely eighteen years old and the other employees were at least five or six years older than he. Constantly battling feelings of fear and isolation, he wrote that he "flirted with insanity, shouted in the streets, and pounded his fist against the walls of his apartment." He liked to hang out in the rougher parts of town, where he said he felt comfortable with homeless kids, street people, and gang members, with whom he had an immediate rapport.

Images he sent from New York seemed to reflect not only his fascination with the underbelly of the city, and his sense of alienation there, but also his ongoing confusion at our family's dissolution and his resulting distrust of women. His collages had become hard-edged, cold, and industrial, bustling and cynical, though often nostalgically overlaid with lyrical silhouettes of dancing African figures, buffaloes, and wildebeests. Slowly, though, over the three months he spent in New York, he began to rise from the depths of pain and darkness, and I hoped that he and I would be able to find a way to reconnect.

In December, Dan flew back to Kenya. I was amused to hear that as part of his "year on" he was using my father's sales techniques to convince my parents to let him spend some of the funds they had put aside for his college to buy a Land Rover, arguing that he could learn about history, geography, and social studies far more effectively by taking a trip across Africa than by reading books. He knew that some people might find his approach to learning difficult to understand, but he reasoned that his method would open up to him "a different education and angle on life."

Once again, his wise grandparents respected his well-planned arguments: his new vehicle turned out to be a decrepit seventeen-year-old Land Rover that he named Deziree after a wild Italian friend. He and his longtime best friend, Lengai, made the most of their newfound freedom by plotting a grand adventure in the vehicle—a five-thousand-mile safari from Nairobi to Cape Town. Few people at any age attempt such an ambitious expedition, much less teenagers. Mike and I had always encouraged both our children to set their sights high and follow their hearts, so once Dan showed us his detailed plans, we felt it would be wrong to stop him. Besides, several of his friends had embarked on similar adventures, and both young Dan and Lengai were the African equivalent of streetwise, so we figured, as did Nani, that they would be safe.

After overhauling Deziree, they attached a buffalo skull to the roof above the driver's seat, along with the "eye of the *dhow*" medallion that Dan had been given in Mombasa. The boys painted "Fight the Power" in bright yellow letters on the center of the steering wheel and loaded the car with sleeping bags, a boom box, extra cans for gasoline, and plenty of tradable objects to sweeten the border guards along the way. In test runs, they discovered that Deziree had a way of breaking down in awkward places, which made their planned safari a challenge, to say the least.

Setting off one July afternoon in 1989, Lengai and Dan crossed the border into Uganda without too much trouble, then headed into the wilds of neighboring Burundi, where they photographed themselves with a tribe of pygmies before turning south through Tanzania and down the three-hundred-mile length of Lake Malawi.

At first Dan and Lengai cheerfully faced the everyday hazards of African travel—flat tires, breakdowns, and petty officials eager for bribes. But when they reached the border of Mozambique, they came up against the effects of a civil war as vicious as any in Africa. Dan's postcards and infrequent phone calls mentioned little about their race through this dangerous war zone.

Deziree's axle cracked in Harare, the capital city of Zimbabwe. Unfortunately, Lengai had to fly home at that point to get ready for his first term as an architecture student at Sussex University in England. Always engaging and often lucky, Dan was fortunate enough to meet a young woman, Nancy Todd, whose family invited him to stay with them for two weeks while a mechanic worked on his damaged vehicle.

Since the repairs dragged on longer than expected, he decided to hitch a ride to South Africa. In a journal entry he noted that he carried only a backpack stuffed with a few clothes, a camera, two journals, his old man and gorilla masks, George Orwell's *1984*, and *The Prince* by Machiavelli.

Traveling alone in Africa is always hazardous, but Dan had a knack for making friends along the way. One night he found himself stranded in Soweto, a vast, squalid township outside Johannesburg. He had no place to sleep and little money. Recalling advice that Jeremy had once given him, he turned up at a local police station and asked for shelter, somehow convincing the amused warden to lock him into a cell for the night. The guard awakened him at dawn with a steaming cup of tea and a chunk of bread before sending him on his way. Dan's journal entry put the experience in a nutshell:

> September 10: Very large room, thirty square feet. High barred ceiling open to the night. Spotlights from above throw shadows of bars artistically below, enveloping me in a spider's web. I remember students in 1976 in cells in Soweto. The buzz in my head was from Carlsberg; theirs was from clubs or tear gas.

He concluded his entry with a quote from Machiavelli: "There is no avoiding war. It can only be postponed to the advantage of others."

Dan hitched on down to Cape Town, where he was swept up in a surging crowd of thousands of demonstrators cheering Bishop Desmond Tutu, who demanded the release of Nelson Mandela from prison, declaring, "Today, Cape Town belongs to the people; tomorrow South Africa will belong to the people."

Dan's adventure filled him with an incurable wanderlust that he described in a letter to my parents: "The most utopian feeling I have found is the excitement and freedom of exploration, of 'Safari as a Way of Life.' This is what makes me happy now."

He was still happier when, on his return to Harare, he found that Deziree was fully repaired and ready to take him back to Kenya. He left Zimbabwe on his own, but within a few hours had to cross the frontier into Mozambique, where he would have to follow a notorious route across the war-torn country to reach Malawi, en route for Tanzania and, finally, Kenya. That stretch of Mozambique was known as the Tete corridor, and such was its danger—it had to be cleared of land mines once a week and was frequently blasted by shells—that the Zimbabwean army insisted vehicles should cross it only in convoys that they regulated and escorted. Not unreasonably, Dan headed his diary account of the passage with the words "Convoy of Death through Marxist Utopia."

When I asked to join the night before [the next convoy] was to take off, the sergeant objected to my taking photographs, but before my camera was inspected, I managed to smuggle my roll of shot film into the trunk. Later, when a group of soldiers turned surly, I put on my gorilla mask and charged them. Some fled, some laughed, and the sergeant insisted on wearing it himself to perform a Gure dance.

The convoy left at five that morning for the Malawi border. Over one hundred trucks set off, going absolutely flat out. The convoy is like a deadly Grand Prix race, as huge lorries jostle and fight for front positions. Drivers overtake recklessly and many accidents occur, ranging from wing mirrors being sheared off to trailers jackknifing and rolling off the road in flames in true Mad Max road warrior style. Zimbabwe armored personnel vehicles bristling with weapons drive up and down the convoy attempting to monitor this anarchy. Sometimes when they see a driver getting too far out of line, they stop his truck and beat him with a stick before sending him on his way.

Dan had allowed a New Zealand hitchhiker to take the wheel of Deziree for the end of the convoy run. He must have been a savvy driver, given Dan's report:

We were doing well in my Land Rover in second position. In front of us was the company commander, whose vehicle was generally accepted as the pace car, and behind him a huge Afrikaner from the Transvaal. We could see his enormous pink face and handlebar mustache looking back from time to time in the rearview mirror of his Mercedes 240. He was a ruthless driver, so we came in second.

The company commander had been watching the whole rally. He sent his sergeant over to us with a message: "The boss says that he doesn't want to see you guys in Mozambique again." He smiled. "You make the country dangerous to live in."

Fortunately, Dan made it home to Kenya without further incident—grimy and exhausted, but also inspired.

After spending time in Nairobi with Mike, Dan announced, to my great joy, that the next step of his utopian safari would be a visit to London.

Too insecure to drive to the airport to pick him up, I left Crabby at a parking meter in Central London and jumped on an Underground train to Heathrow Airport. I paced nervously as I waited for him in the lounge but had to smile when I saw him emerge from the immigration hall flanked by two pretty girls. Weighed down with two battered suitcases, an overloaded backpack, a boom box, a tin box, and a burlap bag bulging with mangoes from William, he looked like a refugee from the Third World, except that, incongruously, he wore a suit and tie (which he later confessed probably spared him from too careful scrutiny by overzealous customs officials).

Smiling his crooked smile, he gathered me in a huge hug and then stood back eyeing me. It was clear that he was concerned about my state of mind, and I wondered what Amy had been saying in her letters to him. He was right to be worried, for I couldn't remember where Crabby was parked and we had to drag Dan's belongings through the streets for an hour before locating her. He roared with laughter when we finally spotted my derelict vehicle. Stuffing her with his bags, we cruised home, music blaring, the roof rolled back like a sardine tin to dilute the noxious fumes that spewed from a hole in the floor.

Our simple flat and barren fridge clearly upset Dan, who was accustomed to Mike's more luxurious lifestyle. If my cooking disappointed Dan, at least he appreciated the inspirational quotations that covered the refrigerator door. I tended to rely on the wisdom of others to keep me going and had a growing supply of quotes to cover all needs. Dan quickly jotted down several in his notebook, including one of my favorites: *Let me not be afraid of endings or beginnings. Teach me to embrace all of life with joy.*

"Who wrote this one?" he asked, pointing to a line scrawled in my handwriting: *You need chaos in your soul to give birth to a dancing star.*

"Nietzsche," I answered.

"If he's right," Dan said dryly, "then you should be the mother of a galaxy."

He rummaged in his jacket pocket, pulling out a carved wooden disc with a star and a crescent moon. I smiled in recognition. It was the medallion he had been given as a young boy in Mombasa.

"I brought this to protect you, Mum," he said. "It will help you find your way." I hoped he was right. My eyes welled with tears when he hung it on my bedroom door. Inside my room, he looked questioningly at a new drawing I had taped to the wall above my desk: a woman standing upright instead of floating in space.

"I'm fine," I said firmly. It was time for me to worry about him, not the other way round.

That evening, after dinner, he called Amy and me into his room, where he was seated cross-legged on the floor, surrounded by journals. Amy and I pored over various volumes, turning the pages one at a time, marveling at what lay within the battered covers. Layered like an archaeological dig, the collages recorded his experiences in detail, bringing them alive with photographs, ticket stubs, visa applications, clippings from magazines and newspapers, feathers, bits of cloth, coins, bills, and cartoons. Bizarre in places, they were colorful relics of a multifaceted inner civilization—one that, though intensely personal, seemed to be inhabited by many different people. Each journal began with an analysis of his external surroundings and moved inexorably to an internal evaluation of his role as both observer and creator. To make it difficult to read his words, he sometimes wrote in black ink on black paper, or glued sheets of paper over great chunks of writing.

Several pages featured the hair-raising drive across Mozambique along the so-called Tete corridor that I had already heard about from him. Dan grew grim when he told Amy and me about a tragedy that he and Lengai had come upon on their southbound trip in a camp at Mwanza, just inside Malawi, before they crossed into Mozambique. It was a crude sanctuary for twenty-three thousand refugees from Mozambique, a fraction of the more than five million civilians who had been displaced from their homes by the civil war that had been raging there since 1977. The ruling party, Front for Liberation of Mozambique (FRELIMO), was violently opposed by the Mozambique Resistance Movement (RENAMO), funded by Rhodesia (as well as its later incarnation, Zimbabwe) and South Africa. Almost nine hundred thousand people had died during that war.

"You can't imagine the rapes and mass killings those refugees survived," he said, describing some of the many mutilated people he had seen (including babies), whose limbs, fingers, ears, even lips had been amputated by force. The refugees lived with little food or water, always on the brink of starvation.

"I'm determined to do something," Dan said, his eyes shining with a light I remembered from his fund-raising attempts for Atieno. I asked him how. "Not just with money, which can be dehumanizing, but with tools, seeds, and resources that will help the people help themselves," he said. Despite the challenges ahead, clearly he had made up his mind and nothing would stop him, a fact that made me very proud.

Almost every page of the journals Amy and I perused held a new revelation of the raw reality of Africa's endless capacity for danger and violence, but thankfully, neither he, Amy, nor I could imagine the relevance of his description of his visit to a secret dance society during his visit in Zimbabwe:

> I see guys with horrible masks. Devil baby face, pink monster, red devil, bangles on feet. . . . They ask me to dance, I give it like crazy. . . . I see them gather up stones. I am led to the center of a crowd and thrown to the ground; . . . dust, moon, and fire drums reach frenzy. Volvo lights shine on me. Devil dancer comes out and beckons me. Kisses me by rubbing the mask against my face. The old man is holding me down and the woman is screaming.

It was clear, from our conversation after I read that entry, that the experience of being symbolically stoned to death by a frenzied mob had left a powerful impression on Dan. He carried on talking for hours that night. At some point Amy, too sleepy to keep her eyes open, excused herself, but I stayed on. When I finally stood up to say goodnight, he pulled me back.

"Don't go, Mum," he implored, holding my hand tightly as he had when he was a little boy. "We have so much more to talk about."

I felt slightly uneasy as I sat down by his side. For the past year we had tiptoed around certainly potentially explosive subjects that might hurt us both, but it was a relief to know that he wanted me close by. Dan described the big family he wanted to have one day, with many children and grandchildren. He wanted to create a relationship with a partner that would allow them to serve as "pillars for the group," as his grandparents had. It was difficult to look him in the eye when he said that he wanted to avoid the traps and mistakes he had seen his parents experience.

When I began to apologize for my behavior, he said, "It's okay, Mum. You mustn't worry." His forehead furrowed like a monkey's. "When you're old, I'll build you a little house at the end of my compound so that you can tend your goats and look after my ten children."

I laughed but somehow felt safer. Another hour passed talking about family and friends before we finally went to bed, grateful for our peaceful time together.

After that evening, our conversations were livelier and more direct, for the same restless energy that fueled me was obviously part of him too; and whatever we discussed, we seemed to challenge each other, waving our hands in the air as we debated. He still thought my interest in psychic matters was ridiculous and pooh-poohed the whole idea of spiritual guides, healing, and creative visualization. I explained my curiosity by stating that scientific research had begun to prove a convergence between physics and metaphysics, a fact that he mockingly questioned.

Dan could feel my sadness and anxiety as the time for him to leave drew close, so he suggested that I join him on "an adventure." As when he was a youngster, he loved to make everything an exciting safari, sometimes dressing up in a crazy hat or mask to go to the supermarket. That day we wandered through Covent Garden, glimmering with festive lights and packed with people. We shared a slice of pizza; then I joined him on the merry-go-round in Leicester Square, laughing in a way I hadn't done for years. My nightmares of being whirled around and around, music blaring and lights flashing, were just a faint memory now.

Later, we were racing through the Piccadilly tube station when he grabbed my elbow and hurried me down the escalator toward a young Jamaican musician strumming on a guitar. He was tall and skinny with a hand-knit black cap crowning a tangle of dreadlocks and with battered tire sandals on his feet. When Dan tossed a few coins in his guitar case, the young man looked up and winked at me, then played a little more loudly. "No woman, no cry," he sang, "everything's gonna be all right."

This was a Bob Marley song that I had heard only once before, in Dan's room, in the horrible days when I was about to leave home. Since then, Dan had written the phrase "Everything's gonna be all right" over and over in his journals. It must have meant as much to him as it did to me.

"Hey man, that's great music!" Dan exclaimed, managing a quick high five with the musician before guiding me back up the escalator. At the top, he turned and said, "Don't worry, Mum, it *is* going to be all right. Just watch: you will be happy one day."

In the morning, Dan flew back to Kenya. I drove him to the airport, and this time I found my way home without losing my car. The next day, I gave in to an urge to go to an art shop and buy new paints and brushes to console myself. An hour later I was standing in my bathroom gazing at the wall where my brass sun god hung. Removing it, I outlined the shapes of five women. Grabbing one of my new brushes, I seized a tube of Matisse blue paint.

Filling in the figures took all day, but by evening the mural was finished and I stood back to survey my work. There, swirling before me in vibrant energy, were five nearly life-size women; three of them danced joyously, reaching out to one another in a circle, and at the top a young woman held aloft a small child, the hope for the future.

20

Do What You Love

I KNEW IT WAS TIME TO DANCE AGAIN. BUT BEFORE I COULD, I NEEDED A real job, not just part-time. I wanted to use my experience in journalism, public relations, and marketing. What's more, it had to bring in at least three thousand dollars a month, and it needed to start yesterday.

The problem was that I would require a new wardrobe, for I had only summer clothes from my life in Nairobi and the secondhand warm clothes I'd bought when the weather first got cool in London. Now another winter was fast approaching. But there was only three hundred dollars left in my account—exactly enough for one month's mortgage payment. Should I buy clothes or pay the mortgage?

Taking a deep breath, I decided to spend my last savings on two suits and a pair of decent shoes so that I would be ready for the job I was sure I was going to attract. A few tense days later, I received a call out of the blue from a friend who had noticed an advertisement seeking a publicist for a three-month position promoting the *Daily Express* newspaper's *Lifestyles 2000* exhibition, which was to be a futuristic exhibit of the world in the new millennium. Donning one of my new outfits and my brand-new shoes, I turned up for the interview and, despite competition from better-qualified candidates, I got the position. Delighted to be participating in such a visionary project, I was equally delighted to deposit my first month's paycheck of three thousand dollars—just as my account hit zero.

After the *Lifestyles 2000* exhibition closed, I was ready to set the world on fire, but instead became a public relations consultant promoting Brite-Shield Glass. It meant a one-hour commute each way to a window-less shed on an industrial estate in north London—where I suffered from a permanent headache made worse by the overpowering smell of chemicals pouring out of the adjacent factory.

At least I had plenty of company when I got back home in the evenings. It was great fun, especially during the school holidays when Mary Anne and I had all four of our children staying. Tara and Petra slept on the old sofa in the living room, and Dan, if he happened to be there, camped on Amy's floor, usually buried under his art supplies and laundry. With everyone's books and clothes pouring out of suitcases piled in the narrow hallway, the flat resembled a school dormitory. The walls were plastered with posters, and an old cardboard box covered with a *kikoy* served as the coffee table. We lined up to brush our teeth and, due to a tiny immersion water heater, always had to share the bathwater.

We spent most of our time in the crowded kitchen at the back of the flat, with its view of a vacant lot below and a skyline crowded with chimney pots. Money was still scarce so we lived on cereal, stir-fried rice, and yogurt, with chicken for special occasions. But there was lots of laughter in the house, and we nurtured one another, sitting up late into the night over hot cups of spicy *chai*, listening to each other's stories, all aching for Kenya. "New beginnings" became a house motto, along with "Knock 'em dead!" shouted at anyone heading out the door.

Pleased as I was to receive a paycheck each month, I desperately wanted to do something that would make a difference in the world. But what could that be?

When I had time alone I tried to analyze and jot down my objectives: I wanted to travel, to research and produce films that would encourage people to become more involved in positively changing the world. I also thought that my novel, *An African Affair*—which I hadn't yet managed to get published—could be turned into a movie that might inspire women to be true to themselves. Yet as soon as the ideas were out on the page, I grew frightened. It was all too much for me to manage by myself. I needed someone who could teach me about the world of film and communication. I added that request to the list as well. Mary Anne took a look at what I had written.

"Get a grip, girl," she said, trying not to smile at my grandiose ideas. "Stop daydreaming and focus on the job you have."

I told her about the latest self-help book I was reading, Marsha Sinetar's *Do What You Love, the Money Will Follow*, which suggested that if you follow your passion, you will eventually find a way to make it your profession. It sounded far-fetched, but at that point I was prepared to give it a try. To help focus my intention, I peeled my favorite Goethe quote off the fridge and carried it around in my purse:

> The minute one definitely commits oneself, then Providence moves too. A whole stream of events issues from the decision, raising in one's favor all manner of unforeseen incidents and meetings and material assistance, which no man could have dreamed would have come his way. Whatever you can do or dream you can, begin it. Boldness has genius, power and magic in it. Begin it now!

It seems that when Providence moves, it moves quickly: two days later I received an unexpected call from Charlie Simpson, the contractor who had overseen the sets for *Out of Africa*.

"Come for lunch at the Ritz," he boomed in his Scottish brogue. "I have a film producer you should meet, and he might have just the job for you."

Crossing my fingers, I put on one of my good outfits and turned up a few hours later. Charlie was standing in the hotel lobby talking to a round, silver-haired man with a thin mustache who looked a bit like Santa Claus (or maybe Clark Gable, if he had lived to be sixty-five). Over lunch, Geoff Dudman, a charming Englishman, entertained us with stories of his life. His eyes twinkled as he described his days as business manager for Terence Young, director of the first three James Bond films, when he had rubbed shoulders with celebrities such as David Niven, Liv Ullman, and Sophia Loren. Over coffee he turned to me and said, "I've got some development money for a film on ivory poaching in Kenya. Perhaps you'd like to help us with the project?"

Thanking Providence, I said goodbye to the glass factory and the next day instead turned up for work with Geoff and his young partner, Charlie Mayhew, at their office in his mews flat near Sloane Square. I again felt like Eliza Doolittle as I entered a new world of fine restaurants, expensive shops, and the possibility of making a film about an important issue in Kenya, my favorite place on earth.

As much as I enjoyed working with Geoff, I was surprised when he suggested that I spend Christmas with him in Gibraltar. Raw from my experience with Jeremy, I was definitely not ready for a new relationship, especially with a man who was twenty-six years older than I. But he wouldn't give up.

"The rest will do you good," he said, urging me to take a break. I wasn't convinced, but as December approached and Amy made plans to fly to Nairobi to spend Christmas with Mike and Dan, I dreaded being left alone in London. Finally I agreed to join Geoff in Gibraltar.

Once there, I literally collapsed into Geoff's care, sleeping almost continuously for three days. When I revived, we sat together in a little café on the top of the Rock as he outlined his vision of our future. We would travel the world producing movies, eventually earning enough money to finance what I really wanted to do—write, speak, and make films that could inspire positive change in the world. Touched by his kindness and also lured by the promise of what sounded like an exciting life, I agreed, though I was terrified by the thought of anyone trying to control or possess me again. I wrote him a letter that clearly defined my boundaries. I wanted to remain free and independent, answerable to no man.

As soon as we were back in London, Geoff set about "improving my image." Surveying my paltry wardrobe, he organized expeditions to some of London's more elegant shops to fit me with a beautiful coat, silk scarves, perfume, and jewelry.

"You're a woman," he said firmly, eyeing my scruffy fingernails and booking a hair appointment. "Not a college girl."

Next he attacked my flat, tossing out the *kikoy*-covered cardboard-box "coffee table" and replacing it with a glass-topped wicker table. Ripping down our posters, he hung neatly framed paintings and covered my shabby sofabed with a woven tapestry.

He started on my business affairs next. "You must register Creative Visions as a company," he said firmly. I explained that I had once tried, but the name had already been taken. "Let's try again," he said. When he called the registration office, the clerk was discouraging, but a week later he called us back.

"Quite a bizarre coincidence," he said. "The day you called, the previous Creative Visions company deregistered, and your application was in before anyone had a chance. You were jolly lucky, you know."

Recalling my friend Zarina's comment that there is no such thing as a coincidence, I thanked whoever—or whatever—was helping me out. I hadn't told Geoff about my belief in spirit guides. After all, I didn't want him to think I was crazy.

Although Amy was grateful that Geoff was taking such good care of me, she was wary. The young are sometimes more intuitive than their elders, and at sixteen she was wiser than her years. Like many of her contemporaries at the American School in London, she had watched her parents separate, but, unlike most of her friends, she had also seen her mother lose herself in another relationship.

"Mumma," she cautioned, during one of our late-night talks, "be careful. I don't want a man to build a cage around you ever again like Jeremy did. Promise me you won't let that happen."

Confident that there was no possibility of that, I agreed.

21

Deziree and Big Blue

DAN, NOW AT PASADENA COMMUNITY COLLEGE IN CALIFORNIA, HAD started off living with his old ISK friends, twins Kwame and Twumasi Wiesel. After a few weeks with them, he moved into a small apartment near campus with two Japanese students, who introduced him to Akiko, a striking young woman who soon became his girlfriend.

When I told Dan that I was going to make a film, he replied with a letter decorated with whimsical drawings of his new life, and I could see that he was feeling better about himself—and also about me. Still, he seemed uncertain about his direction. In one of his letters he confided,

> These transition periods always make me start wondering and worrying about everything as I try to work out what I want from this life. Although I don't like to admit it, sometimes I feel confused, as I'm sure everyone does at my age, and maybe at any age.

During one of our phone calls, I reassured Dan that his emotions were normal. Change is always difficult, which is why we humans tend to follow the path of least resistance.

I was proud of his desire to leave the familiar behind and challenge himself, though when he called to tell me about an ambitious idea he wanted to pursue, I questioned whether Mike and I should support it. Still haunted by memories of the refugees in the camp at Mwanza, Malawi, and desperately homesick for Africa, he had begun plotting a mission he and his friends called Student Transport Aid, STA for short. After some preliminary fund-raising, they would fly to Nairobi, drive from there to Mwanza, and then use their funds and energy in whatever ways seemed most useful once they were on site.

Dan's calls grew more frequent as he described his growing team of helpers, which now included both Lengai and Amy at long distance, and their wild (but successful) schemes to raise funds for the expedition. I was skeptical when I called Mike to discuss Dan's far-fetched plan. As always, my throat tightened when I heard Mike's voice on the other end of the telephone and felt how it turned cooler when he heard it was me. Neither of us knew how to *be* with the other, even at a distance.

I tried to be upbeat. "Do you think any parents in their right minds would allow their kids to go on such a risky journey organized by a nineteen-year-old?"

"It's amazing, isn't it?" he said, the hint of a smile creeping into his voice.

"They really do seem to be joining up, Mike," I said. "And on top of all the expenses, each and every person has made a contribution to the refugee fund. It's just that there are so many things that could go wrong. Do you think Dan is fully prepared?"

"He's perfectly capable, Kathy," Mike said. "Stop worrying. I'm sure that by now he's sorted out all the angles."

After months of hard work Dan and his friends had seventeen thousand dollars that they would spend in Kenya on a Land Cruiser, along with tools and equipment for the refugees, with money left over for a discretionary fund. In London, Amy, a student council member at the American School, managed to cajole the school's staff into donating the proceeds from the sales of the school Coke machine to the cause.

In early July Dan spent a few days in London on his way to Nairobi and designated our apartment for the rendezvous for seven of his team members. Watching them unroll their sleeping bags on the living room floor, I wondered how such a disparate group could ever make it to Malawi and back without getting killed—or killing each other. There were fourteen STA members altogether, ranging from our Amy, the youngest at just sixteen, to twenty-one-year-old Hayden Bixby, a teacher in training and the "wise elder" of the group. Perhaps rashly, Dan invited not only a former girlfriend, Akiko, but also another, earlier girlfriend, Marte, a stunning Norwegian.

Once in Kenya, the group stayed with Mike. The night before they left for Mwanza in Deziree—still running!—and the new Land Cruiser, dubbed Arabella, Mike sat Dan down to discuss everything that might go wrong along the way and how each issue might be addressed. The list was daunting: traffic accident, illness, mugging or theft, border problems, lost passport, danger near Mozambique, random arguments, jilted lovers, bad food, breakdowns. By the end of their deliberations Dan, the eternal optimist, felt that whatever happened, they would manage.

"Just tickle them along," Mike finally said with a smile.

Before they set off, Dan composed a mission statement for the group, now nicknamed Team Deziree:

Team Deziree: Free at Last Voyages

The search for clean water in a swamp

Energy, sincerity, clarity of vision, creativity

"Safari as a Way of Life"

To explore the unknown and familiar, distant and near,
and to record in detail, with the eyes of a child, any beauty
(of the flesh or otherwise), horror, irony, traces of utopia or hell

In the margins he penned a few more observations, including *Look for solutions, not problems* and *There is little difference between exploring and being lost.*

From the first, Dan and Lengai made a good partnership as joint leaders, negotiating their way past hostile border guards and somehow charming suspicious mercenaries manning checkpoints. They quickly learned how to become even more effective at leadership, coaxing the best out of the twelve other strong-willed young people, who often grew irritated with one another by the end of long hot days in the dusty vehicles.

The STA team was received with open arms when they reached the Mwanza Camp. Although the refugees possessed little more than the clothes on their backs, their lives were rich in ways the young people had never seen before. Existing in a tight-knit community, they supported one another; elders guided their clans and childrearing was shared, with babies passed from lap to lap. There was a sense of joy and community in the camps that astonished the students, who had expected a dreary environment filled with hopeless people.

For the next few days, Dan and his friends divided up into pairs to gather information about the camp and its needs. After interviewing each of the aid organizations involved, they assembled to figure out how their funds should be spent. Following a lively discussion, Dan called for a vote. Clean drinking water won, with a decision that the money would go to the Norwegian Refugee Council to build two wells and to a children's orphanage for blankets. They also decided to donate Arabella— somewhat the worse for wear after the arduous journey—to the Save the Children organization for self-help agricultural projects.

Following a farewell dinner, most of the group dispersed the next day. Dan, Lengai, and a few others planned to drive back to Nairobi while Amy would fly to London. Before she climbed onto a bus headed for the Blantyre Airport, she and Dan had time for a last hug.

"Goodbye, Dan," Amy said, wrapping her arms around him.

"Never say that, Mutz," Dan demanded, using his private pet name for his little sister. "Always say, '*Kwaheri ya kuonana*' . . . goodbye until we meet again."

The STA safari was a transforming experience for its members. Several of the group changed their planned careers to include some form of service through international diplomacy, journalism, teaching, or politics. Team Deziree alumni include Oscar-winning director Chris Nolan (*Batman Begins, The Dark Knight*, and *The Dark Knight Rises*), Oscar-nominated director Roko Belic (*Genghis Blues*), Pulitzer Prize–winning *New York Times* East Africa bureau chief Jeffrey Gettleman (who survived a 2004 abduction in Fallujah), and Elinor Tatum, publisher and managing editor of the *Amsterdam News* (America's largest African American newspaper), as well as two teachers, an architect, several high-powered international businesspeople, and a flight attendant for an international airline.

Long afterward, I received a letter from Hayden Bixby talking about what the Deziree trip had meant to her: "Dan reminded me that challenging myself and having fun along the way was not only what a safari is all about, but what life is all about."

Amy returned to London for her last year at the American School, while Dan drove back to Nairobi, where he moved in with Mike and updated his old darkroom. He found work shooting for the Kenya Airways magazine and the *Nation* newspaper, as well as for advertising agencies and other Kenyan magazines.

He seemed at peace with himself and the world when he wrote me a letter on his twentieth birthday:

> It is September 18th and I am twenty years old. Well, it's been quite a life so far, and I want to thank you for all the energy and input that you gave, for things like getting me the camera and making me excited about making things and building things and drawing things and writing things. I think these are some of the things I enjoy most about my mission on earth.

After Christmas Dan flew to England and enrolled at Richmond College, an American college just outside London. At first he camped in Mary Anne's little room—she was away writing *Nomad*, a memoir of her adventures as a reporter in Africa. Within hours of his arrival, her desk was buried beneath his art supplies and her floor was piled with mounds of dirty clothes. I peeked around the door to say goodnight one day and saw him sitting cross-logged on the floor, surrounded by journals.

"Sit down for a while, Mum," he said, clearing a space for me. Honored that he wanted to share his work, I planted myself beside him as he jammed a tape into his boom box and opened a bulging black-bound book. Barely held together with a sturdy leather belt when not in use, the latest journal weighed at least three pounds and was startlingly diverse, reflecting his interest in the nature of life and death.

Thanks to his stint at *Mademoiselle*, his artwork was better than ever, and I asked if he would create a piece that I could hang on my wall. He frowned at the thought. "These pages are just for me," he said. "One day I'll try to make you something, but I'm just not good enough yet."

Nonetheless, he turned up later at our flat carrying a long tube. "It's for your wall," Dan announced, unrolling a large sheet of paper swirling with a mass of images and words. His eyes gleamed when he reminded me of the story it illustrated. While still a senior in high school, he had gone for a walk in the bush with a friend's dog, a feisty Jack Russell named Obelix. To Dan's horror Obelix ran ahead of him, yapping, straight into a lone buffalo, the most dangerous animal in Africa, half-hidden in the undergrowth. Angered, the massive animal lowered its head and charged at Obelix and Dan, quickly narrowing the gap between them. Running for his life, Dan crashed through spiky thorn-bushes, badly lacerating his arms and legs. Worse still, he lost his flip-flops in the long grass, leaving his feet bleeding and torn.

"I knew the buffalo might kill me," Dan said, "but later, with the sight and smell of it behind me, I felt as though a lifelong veil had been lifted from my senses." That day, he said, he had seen every tree as an escape ladder, and felt in every wind-change a betrayal. His destination "lay at the end of the labyrinth of bush, guarded by invisible Minotaurs," as he put it.

After telling me the story behind the painting, which I had heard in only the barest details when it happened, Dan confessed with a wry smile that, although there had been many women in his life, that day he had been chased by the buffalo was the first time he had made love. He went on to say that during his darkest hours, when he was tormented about the breakup of our family, it was she who had urged him to forgive me, explaining that each soul has its own journey to make, and when we love someone, as she knew Dan loved me, we have to offer them support even if we don't approve of their decisions.

Dan's intense experience of passion, danger, and first love perhaps explains why buffaloes appeared so frequently in his journals. Above the image of one sinister-looking beast, he wrote: "Buffalo, the original face of death." On another page marked "good versus evil," he juxtaposed two photos: one of himself, labeled "good," and another of a buffalo, marked "evil." For him, buffaloes had become symbols not only of danger or death, but of evil too—three forces which from then on he never avoided facing. While I savored my memories of life lived on the edge and never wanted to live a boring existence, there was always a middle ground. I knew how addictive danger could be. And I worried for Dan.

With the approach of summer, Dan began planning his next adventure, a grand safari to Morocco with Lengai and Amy. He bought another old Land Cruiser, complete with green checked curtains, and dubbed the vehicle Big Blue because her color reminded him of an African sky. She had plenty of space for camping equipment and the crates of silver and brass jewelry and leather goods he planned to buy in Morocco. His ultimate objective was to ship the merchandise back to America in the vehicle, which he planned to convert into a mobile shop, perfect for selling his wares on college campuses. He would donate the proceeds to his next STA project.

After crossing the English Channel, Dan, Lengai, and Amy meandered south through Spain and caught a boat to Tangiers, bargaining their way through Morocco, picking up leather belts and vests, as well as silver bracelets and other jewelry, in backstreet markets along the way. Just before they were due to leave, Big Blue broke down. Dan was left on his own in Casablanca to wait for parts while Lengai and Amy returned to London, laden with gunnysacks filled with jewelry and what turned out to be badly tanned, very smelly leather goods.

Bored, lonely, and broke, Dan explored the city on foot, both intrigued and disgusted by what he found. His journal for that period, packed with bizarre, often sinister collages, reflects his fascination with the dangerous underworld of Casablanca:

A labyrinth of sewers where a melange of low-life swirls and collides. The very scum of the earth, thieves, whores, pimps, victims, and carriers of every loathsome disease known to man, pickpockets, rapists, serial killers, child molesters, con men, prisoners, practitioners of voodoo and witchcraft. Who is at the center of this kaleidoscope of depravation? I am. L'Etranger. The Stranger.

After driving back to London alone, Dan was in a hurry to get on with life. Having had enough of Richmond College, he decided to return to America. Much to my neighbors' annoyance, he left Big Blue, dented and rain-streaked, on the street outside my apartment building when he flew off. Concerned about his lack of direction, I encouraged him to go back to college—*any* college—but he still seemed uncertain. On the plane from London to Los Angeles he wrote a letter to his new friend Soiya Gecaga, a beautiful granddaughter of President Jomo Kenyatta and friend of Amy's, who was headed back to university in Scotland.

I want to do great things in my life—I want the plane to land, so I can start. The only problem is where do I start? What do I do when I get off the plane to do great things? Is university the best place for me? Should I take off with my camera to El Salvador? Listen to what your heart tells you, you say. Well, I'd like to rip the little bastard out and interrogate him with a twelve-volt car battery.

22

Hollywood Jungle

DAN MUST HAVE MADE UP HIS MIND ON THE FLIGHT, FOR WHEN HE ARRIVED in Los Angeles he called to tell me that he would be enrolling at UCLA. I was deeply relieved. For the time being at least, I wouldn't have to worry about him. Fortunately, Dan didn't have to worry about me either. I was hard at work on the film about ivory poaching that Geoff and Charlie were producing. I was surprised to learn that Harry Percy, the duke of Northumberland, was also involved as a producer.

I asked Charlie to tell me more about the duke and why he would want to be part of such an undertaking. He explained that as a young man, Harry had been ill with a mysterious condition that resisted all attempts to find a cure. He had spent so much time resting that he had seen just about every film ever produced. Movies had become his passion, and he wanted not only to invest in and help produce a film, but also to act in one. He had asked Charlie and Geoff to find a script with a message that could positively impact the world—and help him produce it.

Harry was a godson of the queen and one of only twenty-five dukes. The highest rank of British aristocracy, they include some of the largest landowners in the country. Harry spent half the year in one of his ancestral

homes, Alnwick Castle, a gloomy Norman stronghold complete with turrets, massive walls, and a dungeon in Northumberland, a bleak region in
northern England. The rest of the time he lived in another home, Syon
House, the grandest "stately home" near London. It had a colorful, if
somewhat disturbing, history. In 1547, King Henry VIII's coffin lay in
state in what was then Syon Abbey on its way to Windsor for burial.
During the night the coffin burst open, and in the morning dogs were
found licking up the king's remains.

On a dismal January afternoon in 1991, Charlie, Geoff, and I drove
to Syon to discuss the film. The traffic crawled along the dreary suburban streets of Chiswick and Brentford until, quite unexpectedly, we spotted a grand gateway, elaborately decorated with columns and crowned by
the Percy emblem, a fierce lion. Although it was the middle of winter, the
scene was absurdly pastoral, with acres of brilliant green grass and clusters of wet cows sheltering under dripping trees. At the end of a long
drive we drew up to the side of the austere house.

"Good grief," I muttered as we rang the bell and were greeted by a
dour housekeeper, straight out of central casting, who led us along dark
and icy corridors past kitchens and utility rooms that appeared to have
changed little in the past few centuries. Looming above us were life-size
paintings of Harry's glowering ancestors, appearing uncomfortable in
their stiff robes and funny-looking fur hats.

We were shown into architect Robert Adam's famous Green Drawing Room (circa 1765) and settled ourselves to await "His Grace," who
wandered in and sat down on a sofa opposite. Tall, plump, and extremely
pale, Harry pulled out a tapered cigarette holder and lit an unfiltered
cigarette with tobacco-stained hands. I watched in horror as the glowing
ash grew longer and longer, hanging for a painful moment until it
dropped on a pale-green silk sofa cushion, burning a black-rimmed hole.

"Oh dear, Mother will be furious," Harry said, depositing a linen
napkin over the evidence.

Though apparently in need of care when dealing with domestic matters, Harry was clear and focused about the goals of his new film company, Hotspur Productions. (His distant relative, the original Harry

Hotspur, was immortalized in Shakespeare's play *Richard III*.) He listened attentively as Geoff and Charlie began to set out their ideas for a movie that would create awareness of how ivory poachers massacred thousands of elephants each year. I took notes and contributed where I could. As executive producer, it would be Geoff's job to provide an acceptable script, hire a director, oversee location scouting, cast the actors, and supervise the actual shooting and editing of the footage. With the right distributor in place to guarantee the money, an investor would see all of his money back, and maybe even make a profit—although Geoff warned Harry that the film business is notoriously risky.

Three months later the duke agreed that Hotspur would partially fund the film and Creative Visions would coproduce it with him. Geoff and the duke would be executive producers, Charlie and I would act as associate producers, and Harry would have a role in the film. The duke seemed exuberant the day we signed the deal, perhaps because he was accompanied by Barbara Carrera, a strikingly beautiful Nicaraguan actress who had played Fatima Blush in the James Bond film *Never Say Never Again*.

Wearing a crimson silk top and flimsy pants, Barbara, who had just flown in from Beverly Hills, gritted her teeth as gale-force winds flowed through the open windows. My teeth chattered as we stood to clink champagne glasses and toast the successful completion of the negotiations. I could scarcely believe that in the space of a few short months, I had graduated from promoting industrial glass in a dismal London suburb to helping produce a feature film with the queen's godson!

Our first priority was to commission a suitable screenplay, and Geoff decided that we should fly to Hollywood to interview writers. I was thrilled, because it meant a chance to spend time with Dan. Throwing myself into my new role as a producer, I bought a pair of fake designer sunglasses, two classy silk dresses, and a pair of strappy high-heeled shoes, while Geoff hired a Rolls to take us to the airport. Sinking into the leather seat, I closed my eyes and tried to reconnect with the healing spirit within me that had gradually led me out of the depths of despair after I left Nairobi. It had been weeks since I'd had time to meditate, and now nothing came through—there seemed to be interference on the line. I soon gave up and read a book on Los Angeles. Geoff squeezed my hand reassuringly. Fortunately he was there as my mentor and teacher, so maybe it didn't matter if I could no longer hear the voice inside me.

After a twelve-hour flight, we neared Los Angeles, which lay shrouded in an ominous blanket of yellow smog. Flying in over "the Valley" gave me an idea of the urban sprawl that stretched across fifty miles of reclaimed desert. Although Geoff had visited L.A. often, this was my first visit since a trip to Disneyland when I was five. The guidebook informed us that more than eleven million people lived down there, fraught with every type of problem: racism, gangs, poverty, and too much affluence.

Known as the City of Angels, it was perhaps more famous as the City of Broken Dreams. Every year thousands of scripts are written, and at any one time there are more than seven hundred films awaiting distribution. Out of every two hundred films undertaken by the studios, only one actually appears on the screen. With statistics like that, I figured we would have been better off promoting Brite-Shield Glass, but Geoff was unperturbed.

"Someone has to be the one out of two hundred," he said, surveying the vast metropolis below us, "and it's going to be us."

As I tottered off the airplane in my high heels, it seemed that everyone around us was wearing Reeboks, a T-shirt, and Bermuda shorts. And a baseball cap, of course. Pale and overdressed, we looked like arrivals from an alien planet. Sailing into town in the bright red convertible Geoff had rented, I gaped at the six-lane freeway lined with dinosaur-like oil pumps, endless shopping malls, and garish strip joints. Los Angeles was everything I had expected it to be, only more so.

The next day, sporting new jeans, sneakers, T-shirts, and baseball caps, we were treated to a farce that only Hollywood could have staged, as one writer after another pitched their ideas for scripting our film. So it went, day after day for two weeks, each writer contriving a more far-fetched story than the last. Despairing, we returned to London and kept on looking, which meant commuting between my flat and a variety of hotels in L.A.

Several months passed before we finally found a script we liked. It was by screenwriter and director Stewart Raffill, a giant, silver-haired cowboy who had several box-office successes behind him. Well written and not too expensive to produce, *Lost in Africa* told the story of two young teenagers, a boy and a girl, who are kidnapped by a gang of poachers while on safari in Africa. Although they can't stand each other for much of the action, naturally they fall in love by the time they're rescued. The film seemed perfect: it even included a great role for Harry.

Our next task was to scout locations in Africa. "The best part of making films is this," Geoff decreed, beaming, as we set off for a cruise down a Zimbabwean river followed by a visit to a baby rhino preserve. After a week of luxury hotels, I was in heaven.

However, once we were back in London, reality set in. Every morning we awakened to a fresh set of seemingly insoluble problems, including battles with the bank, crises with the casting director, and disputes with the distributor. Working out of Geoff's mews house during the day, we returned to my place for the inevitable phone calls we had to make to the producer we had hired in California, an ordeal that often lasted until beyond midnight. Geoff virtually moved into my flat, which didn't please Mary Anne or Amy.

As our days grew more frantic, I began to realize that, however charming he was as a friend, and however diplomatic as a producer he may have been with others, he was quick to bellow at me when something went wrong. After years of living in Italy, where passions quickly flare and equally quickly fade, he was apt to forget what he had said in anger, while I, incurably sensitive, remained distressed for hours. Still, I was determined to make the most of the opportunity that had been given to me and did my best to be positive.

During the summer of 1991, Geoff and I decided to move to California for six weeks to oversee the run-up to production. We chose the Shangri-La, a funky Art Deco hotel on Ocean Avenue in Santa Monica only twenty minutes away from UCLA, where Dan was taking courses.

Sometimes he and I met to walk down to the ocean in the morning, passing scores of homeless people camped out on the narrow grass verge beyond the row of palm trees that rimmed Ocean Boulevard. I had often greeted the people sleeping on bundles of rags and tattered plastic bags as I passed them on my own, but I was delighted when, on our first walk together, Dan introduced me to several by name. Another time, after a homeless man wearing an imaginative outfit created entirely from black plastic bags stared at me too long, Dan teased him, saying, "Lay off her, Jack; she's my mum!"

One of our stays in Los Angeles coincided with Dan's twenty-first birthday, and we planned a surprise party for him, flying Amy in from London for it, hiding her behind a curtain in our hotel room. After she leaped out, Dan's glittering eyes showed how much his little sister meant to him. That night we offered him a job on the film, which we hoped would go into production the following spring.

The next day Dan drove Amy to Rodeo Drive, the glitziest shopping street in Beverly Hills, where he dumped two battered cardboard cartons filled with smelly Moroccan leather goods and silver jewelry onto the sidewalk outside the chic shops. Draping Amy with bracelets and belts, he cheerfully hawked the goods to a parade of curious tourists. As he was bargaining with a Japanese businessman, a young salesman dashed out from the nearby Gucci store. Worried that the salesman might be protesting this illegal operation, Dan explained that he was collecting for the next STA charity safari—to the Sahara Desert. When the man handed over twenty dollars, grabbed a belt, and disappeared inside, Dan laughed and pocketed the bill.

Dan also sold his wares on Venice Beach. Wearing a World War II fighter pilot's helmet, complete with hazy goggles, he befriended tourists and the colorful characters who worked the boardwalk. He even managed to charm two tough cops, who had demanded to see his nonexistent hawker's permit, into buying a handful of bracelets for themselves.

After Amy returned to London Dan focused on his classes, though I noticed that he usually managed to escape Los Angeles every weekend on a different exploit—a trip to Las Vegas, say, or a quick run down to the Mexican border town of Tijuana. As he had in Nairobi, he managed to make each one an exciting adventure—a mini-safari. These outings provided photos for his collages and material for essays he wrote for his English literature class.

My favorite of his writings was one in which he described a dream encounter with the great American essayist Ralph Waldo Emerson. After sharing a drink with Dan in a sleazy bar in South Central Los Angeles, Ralph, wearing a leather jacket emblazoned with "The Great American Scholar," takes Dan on a hair-raising ride on the back of his Harley-Davidson to the UCLA library. There the poet (now a creaky 186 years old) climbs onto a table to harangue the apathetic students.

"Listen up, bookworms," he shouts. "The one thing of value is the active soul—the soul, free sovereign, unencumbered. This every man is entitled to. This every man contains within himself; although in almost all men, obstructed, and as yet unborn."

Those words struck a chord in me. One day I hoped that I, too, could be an active soul—though just then I felt far too blocked and encumbered ever to be so free.

Dan and Amy flew home to Nairobi to spend Christmas with Mike, leaving me feeling depressed and homesick for Africa and for our family Christmases. Geoff and I returned on our own to London.

Over the holidays Geoff asked if he could move in with me whenever we were in London. We were already spending all our time together, he reasoned, and living under the same roof would save money. He promised that it would be only for a short time since we were due to start filming in Kenya in April. I wasn't pleased, and I knew Amy would be upset. On the other hand, money was tight, and it seemed unfair to ask Geoff to pay rent elsewhere if he could live more cheaply with us. Maybe that extra time together would give us a chance to work on a strategy to raise money to make a film out of my book, *An African Affair*. Hesitantly, I agreed and he moved in the next day.

After the Christmas break, Dan moved to Mount Vernon, Iowa, a small town close to my parents in Cedar Rapids, where he planned to attend Cornell College. With that institution's thirty-day sessions, he could sign up month by month until the film shoot began. He stayed with his cousin John Wellso, a Sotheby-trained antiques dealer who turned over a room in his house so that Dan could create a studio. Encouraged by John to design a large installation piece, Dan began assembling one from photocopies of collages that he painted and decorated with tiny drawings and slogans. I was pleased to know that he was again taking his art seriously.

Dan's letters to me from Iowa included vivid descriptions of slush and snow, his sadness at the death of Nana (his 106-year-old grandmother), and his admiration for a pretty red-haired girlfriend who, he said, reminded him of me. He confessed that his greatest joy was still being on safari:

Sometimes I feel self-indulgent, but it is available to me now and I love it . . . although it is a stage and there will be a time to settle down.

His tone changed as he outlined some of his goals for the future—in particular, being able to provide financially for the family he hoped to have one day, and to provide them with the opportunities he himself had experienced. It will always sadden me to read his final paragraph:

I don't know why I feel as if I am writing a suicide note. Maybe it's because I have never written down so much of what I'm actually thinking, and the frightening thing about doing that is that people can compare what you actually are doing or end up doing. If you can't live up to it, maybe that is committing 'ambition suicide.' Oh well, here they are: my cards on the table. Let's see where I am when I'm Nana's age. Will it have been a noble life?

Meanwhile, Geoff and I finalized our preparations for the shoot. We left for Kenya in mid-April and were met at the airport by Dan. Wearing an enormous grin and clutching a bouquet of flowers, he looked more like a potential suitor than our new third assistant director. It was two years since I had been in that country, and as I stepped into the intense African sunshine, I was flooded with memories of my old life. Immediately surrounded by aggressive taxi drivers who grabbed at our bags, I recalled the first time I had landed in Kenya, full of hopes and dreams.

There was no time for reflection as Dan swept us off to downtown Nairobi in Deziree. Her two expeditions across Africa had left her a wreck, and we had to shout to be heard above her rattles and roars. Dan had ripped off her roof and stripped away the doors, leaving only a skeleton that attracted the smiles of everyone we passed. The Cowboy Junkies blared from his boom box and we sang along, squinting as the wind whipped into our faces. I commented on the increase in traffic, which reflected the population increase from twenty-five to thirty million. Unemployment was rampant among young people, which had led to a massive rise in crime. Carjackings were common, and violent robberies an everyday fact of life.

I was anxious about seeing Mike again, but we agreed to meet for lunch, with Dan and Geoff too. Although Mike and I had been separated for more than three years, and he had been going out with other women, this was the first time he had seen me with another man. I felt uncomfortable during our brief and inevitably tense get-together. Mike appeared to find it equally difficult to deal with me. He rarely looked me in the eye, but smiled politely when Geoff tried to lighten the mood by teasing Dan about the ordeal that awaited him on the set as our "third AD."

Despite the grand title, the third AD has one of the worst jobs on a film, usually little more than a glorified "go-fer" (as in "go for" this or that). But Dan didn't mind and couldn't wait to get to our location in Shaba National Reserve, a remote and beautiful game park in northern Kenya. Our production coordinator had assured us that it was safe to shoot there, but I was still concerned, for it was a dangerous area crawling with *shifta*s, cattle-stealing thieves from across the Somali border, ready to rob anything of value. Most were armed with cheap AK-47s, acquired during the civil war now ravaging their country. For years the violence had been escalating there as ruthless warlords and their clans fought viciously for control.

The next day we flew to Shaba—the duke was with us by then too—and the minute we arrived, we doubled the guards around the lodge to ensure his and our safety.

Never having been on a film set before, I was overwhelmed by the intense pace and seemingly impossible demands on every member of the crew. Frantic by day, I looked forward to evening visits from Dan, who had quickly made himself indispensable on set. In his lowly position he was the last to bed and the first up, distributing the call sheets before dawn. As one of the few white people there who could speak fluent Swahili, he distinguished himself throughout the day as an interpreter with the locals, his wicked sense of humor often defusing potential crises.

Toward the end of our ten-day shoot, the director asked Dan to produce a herd of camels for a critical scene the following morning. He set off cheerfully in a Land Rover but grew increasingly alarmed when he failed to locate a single camel. As dusk approached, he finally found six mangy beasts and bargained at length with their shady-looking Somali herder, who promised to deliver them at daybreak. Not trusting him, Dan wrapped himself in a *kikoy* and slept with the smelly, spitting animals, which he triumphantly drove on to the location just in time for the shoot.

His camel feat further endeared him to the crew, though his popularity was sealed with his regular deliveries of the highest quality marijuana. Sold in the local market in bundles, like carrots, it cost a few cents a joint, which made for a happy crew.

Among the local actors there was a beautiful young woman, Neema, with dark, haunting eyes, olive skin, and long black hair. Like the model Iman, she was Somali, although she had grown up in Kenya. One evening Dan confided that he was very attracted to Neema, and in the next few weeks the two became deeply involved. In the past he had somehow managed to see several women at the same time without promising to be faithful to any of them. This time, though, that wouldn't work. Intelligent, determined, and temperamental, Neema demanded commitment, and Dan became obsessed by her tempestuous spirit. When I asked him about their relationship, he brushed aside my questions and I backed off, aware of how deeply he had fallen for her.

Many days I was tempted to get on a bus and hightail it back to Nairobi, for I felt exhausted by the challenges we faced. Geoff was growing increasingly short-tempered, not only on the film set, where his battles with the casting director, the location team, and the bank were endless, but also with me. Worn down by the constant pressure, I wasn't sure I wanted to be a film producer after all. After one exhausting day I was in tears, so Geoff sat me down for a hard talk.

"You said you wanted to learn how to communicate important ideas through film—well, this is what it's all about," he said crossly. "No one likes producers. You have to toughen up, Kathy, or you can go back to doing public relations. But if you want to touch millions of people, this is what it's all about. You can't cry and expect anyone to respect you."

Much as I hated to admit it, I knew he was right. Fortunately, the last few days of the shoot went smoothly and I was able to regain an upbeat attitude. Still, I was delighted when the footage was finally "in the can" and we could enjoy a big celebration with the crew and cast. Geoff promised that once we were finished editing the film, we would start working on *An African Affair*.

Once we were back in Nairobi, Dan and I set up a time to be together on our own. "I'm taking you to my favorite restaurant," he announced. Hurtling through the familiar streets in Deziree, I felt almost as I had so long ago, when I had been the one to lead the family to the newest restaurant, often in the most questionable part of town. But this time, Dan was in charge. Cranking up the volume on his boom box, we roared down seedy River Road, stopping before a hole-in-the-wall dive. Recognizing me, the owner beamed and quickly called for a round of Cokes and two orders of chicken tikka.

Watching Dan usher us to a table surrounded by white plastic chairs, I knew I wouldn't have felt happier dining at the Ritz. After we finished, he pushed away the plates and said that he wanted to let me know that he hoped to become a filmmaker after college. I told him I thought it was an excellent choice, because that career would incorporate his skills as a storyteller, along with his love of music and photography—and he could indulge his passion for travel. I added that I hoped one day we could make a film *together*, but he shook his head.

"Mum, I don't think the film business is good for you," he said. "It's time for you to forget about making deals and get creative—start writing. You have to find your own voice again."

I explained that I simply couldn't do anything on my own just yet. I would have to wait until the film was done. Geoff and I had successfully completed the most difficult and potentially hazardous part of the production, but there were months of editing ahead in Los Angeles, and we still had to tie up the tricky details of our distribution arrangements.

After we returned to London in July, Geoff took me out to dinner and we reflected on how far we had come professionally, and how many mountains we had climbed in Hollywood and Africa since our lunch two years before on the Rock of Gibraltar. We had manifested our creative vision. We were in high spirits that night: the prospects for our film were looking good, and we expected to be ready to sell it in Cannes the next May.

23

The Front Line

DAN'S SPIRITS WERE EQUALLY HIGH WHEN HE CALLED ME FROM NAIROBI IN June of 1992 to say that he was running a photographic business. Using his home darkroom, he was developing photos he had shot for magazine advertisements. In his spare time, he had convinced Neema to star in a short film that he hoped would help him get into UCLA's film school in September.

Soon after that call he received an invitation from the head of UNICEF to fly to in northern Kenya to photograph several refugee camps that were rapidly filling with people fleeing the catastrophic fighting in Somalia. He was so shaken by the misery he saw there that he wanted to use his work to draw more attention to the plight of the refugees.

Back in Nairobi, he met a young Reuters reporter, Aidan Hartley, who had grown up in Africa and was also interested in its regional politics. Having heard rumors of a possible famine in Somalia, Aidan invited Dan to join him to see what was happening there. Intrigued by the possibility of breaking an important story, Dan immediately accepted.

Somalia had been plagued by years of civil war that had destroyed the country's infrastructure, severely impeding both the production and the distribution of food. In January of 1991, the country's president, Siad Barre, had been driven out of the capital, Mogadishu, and had retreated into the countryside, leaving two warlords, "General" Mohamed Farrah Aidid and Ali Mahdi Mohamed, to battle for the ravaged city. Tens of thousands of people were known to have died of starvation due to the disruption of local farming and the theft of international food supplies by the corrupt warlords. It was suspected that the famine had begun to spread across the country.

On July 5, Aidan and Dan flew into Mogadishu. Founded by Italian colonialists, it had once been a legendary city of gleaming white buildings that graced the shores of the Indian Ocean, its boulevards lined with fine restaurants and shops, fancy hotels, and elegant apartments. Its harbor became a busy destination for luxury liners and cargo ships. Now the city lay in ruins, its buildings frequently the scene of violent fighting. In the doorways and along the roadside, Dan saw gray bundles, barely recognizable as human beings huddled together; militiamen armed with AK-47s, rocket launchers, and grenades patrolled the streets; and bullets or shrapnel had pockmarked nearly every wall. The humid coastal air reeked of refuse, death, and decay.

Aidan hired a car and two armed guards to accompany him, Dan, and Sam Kiley, a young reporter for the *Times* of London, into the ruined town. They stopped first at the city's historic Mogadishu Cathedral, where its bishop had been brutally murdered while offering Mass in 1989. Since then, the cathedral had been almost completely destroyed by insurgents.

Stepping over piles of rubble, Dan photographed the headless statues of Jesus, Mary, and the apostles. Vandals had stripped the sanctuary of everything valuable and had even exhumed the bishop's body to steal his ring and gold teeth. As the young journalists explored the ruins, a cluster of sullen Somali teenagers toting AK-47s and grenade launchers watched them. When Dan lifted his camera to shoot a picture of one bare-chested youth, a cigarette dangling from his lips, another raised his AK-47 and pointed it directly at Dan.

Dan kept his cool as he reached into his bag and pulled out his old man mask. Slipping it on, he broke into an impromptu dance. Completely disarmed, the young gunmen began laughing and one demanded to try on the mask himself—then allowed Dan to take his picture. Aidan was furious with Dan for provoking trouble and later stressed the importance of never attracting attention by taking risky photographs.

In a refugee center near the city of Baidoa, where the famine was thought to be at its worst, Dan and Aidan followed trucks that circled the town at dawn, picking up scores of bodies of people who had died overnight. Wrapped in colorful shrouds made from *kikoys*, the skeletal corpses were tossed into the backs of trucks like firewood. It was a horrifying initiation for Dan, who had never been able to stand the sight of blood, much less death. No longer speculating on the nature of mankind from a safe distance, he was now confronting its worst side face to face.

In a letter to my parents he wrote:

> To arrive in Mogadishu the first time is like falling into hell. The experience of seeing and photographing the horror of starvation and injuries has made me evaluate everyday life. The shattered bodies, the hundreds of walking skeletons, really left me changed in a way that I don't even begin to recognize myself.

He described how, as the haunting images began to emerge in his darkroom back in Nairobi, he was overwhelmed by the immensity of the tragedy and realized that his camera had acted as a barrier to his emotions while he was shooting the pictures. Only later, in the safety of his home, did he fully appreciate what he had brushed up against in person. One photo portrayed a cluster of half-naked, starving children lying on a bundle of rags, and another an emaciated infant with open but unseeing eyes being tended by his distraught mother. A third was of a famished little girl holding an empty bowl, surrounded by other starving youngsters.

When he offered these images to the *Nation*'s photo editor, the paper immediately printed several. To Dan's delight they were subsequently picked up by Reuters and relayed worldwide to magazines, newspapers, and television networks. He wrote proudly that Reuters paid 150 dollars each for the photos. "They were the highest paid shots in the history of the Nairobi office," he said. "But the value in experience was even greater."

The photographs of starving Somalis by Dan and other journalists who followed him had a profound effect on public opinion, much as Mo Amin's haunting images of the Ethiopian famine had triggered an influx of aid in 1984. In August of 1992, after pressure from people around the world, the United Nations launched Operation Provide Relief to bring in food supplies to Somalia.

After Reuters offered to buy his photos if he returned to Mogadishu, Dan accepted, even though it meant postponing his filmmaking course at UCLA. I questioned him about the decision but he responded, "What use is it to deconstruct the *Godfather* when I could do something to help people who are dying?" He also pointed out that all the famous journalists and war photographers were headed to Somalia, so for anyone who wanted to make a name, that was the place to be. As he had often done before, Dan convinced Mike and me that it was important to acquire hands-on experience about the world, reminding us of how much he had learned about politics, economics, and geography through raising money and delivering aid to the refugee camp in Malawi, not to mention the management techniques he had acquired when dealing with the disgruntled teen members of Team Deziree.

I admired Dan's commitment to follow his own path and hoped that now he would continue to fulfill his potential, not only for himself, but also for others. My parents had always encouraged him to get involved in community service, and he had observed Mike's deep involvement with the Rotary Club. He had also accompanied me as I interviewed extraordinary Kenyans who were tackling myriad humanitarian challenges. Without urging from Mike or me, he had put what he had learned into action, first by helping a single child, his friend Atieno, then Kipenget's family, and later the refugee camp in Malawi. Now he was trying to help an entire country. I couldn't have been more proud of Dan, and told him so.

I was equally pleased with Amy, who had been accepted at Lafayette College, a small liberal arts school in Easton, Pennsylvania. However, as the time for her departure approached, I wasn't sure how I could cope without my beloved daughter.

"Don't worry, Mumma," Amy said, "I'll be home for Christmas. It won't seem long at all." Like me, she was putting on a brave face. Although excited about her new life in America, she would be far away from Mike and her brother in Africa, and me in London. After so many adjustments, it was one more hurdle to overcome.

I flew with her to New York, and we rented a car for the drive to Easton. We chatted most of the way. However, as signs for the town began to appear, we became quieter, and I could feel a giant lump growing in my throat. We were both dabbing at our eyes when we turned in to the college's main gate. Red-nosed and shiny-faced, we arrived at her assigned dormitory, to be met by a cluster of young people dressed in shorts and oversized white T-shirts, which appeared to be the unofficial campus uniform. As we started hauling the bags and boxes into the red-brick building, Amy, in a gauzy shirt and long, flowing skirt, looked like Julie Andrews in *The Sound of Music*. Inside, we met her roommate, also named Amy, whose mother was stenciling decals around the room.

"We live close by," she said, beaming. "Your Amy's real welcome to come and visit us anytime." I was intensely jealous: I wanted the girls to come home and eat cookies in *my* house.

Later, we drove over to the Memorial Gymnasium, where we would say our goodbyes before Amy's freshman orientation. We clung to each other for a full minute, unable to say a word, before she gathered herself, opened the door, and walked off with a firm step. I drove away with all the confidence I could muster, but once out of her sight I pulled over and sobbed for a long time before I was able to begin the drive back to New York.

Dan's spirit and determination seemed to develop steadily, and he returned to Somalia often during the next few months. In the beginning, he was deeply moved by the challenges of the chaotic life in Mogadishu, but by the end of October, in a letter home, he sounded shell-shocked:

After my first trip to Somalia, the terror of being surrounded by violence and the many conflicts moved me to tears. But this was my first experience of war. Before Somalia, I had seen only two dead bodies in my life. I have now seen hundreds, tossed into ditches like sacks. The worst things I could not photograph.

One Sunday morning they brought in a pretty girl wrapped in colorful cloth. I saw that shrapnel had severed both her hands and feet. Someone had tossed a grenade in the market. She looked serene, like she was dead, but the nurse said she would survive. It made me think of the whole country. Somalia will survive, but what kind of life is it for a people who have been so wounded? I don't know how these experiences have changed me, but I feel different.

Although Dan said he had become accustomed to violence and shooting, he could not get used to the sight of people starving to death. To help him cope with such scenes, he began to chew *khat*, a bitter weed that offers a jittery, amphetamine-like high that cuts appetite and decreases the desire to sleep. Having seen some of my journalist colleagues turn to cocaine, marijuana, or alcohol, I was concerned and wrote him a letter, urging him not to get hooked. He wrote back, clearly annoyed that I would think he would do such a thing. My motherly concerns were irritating him, but it was hard to stop being anxious about his safety.

"Don't worry about me in war zones," he wrote. "It feels safer than in parts of Los Angeles, and in Somalia I never go anywhere without two armed guards with AK-47 automatic rifles." And that was supposed to *reassure* me?

I was even more anxious when I heard that he had bought a Beretta and was learning to shoot. Mike calmed me, pointing out that Dan was streetwise and that other journalists often wanted to travel with him because he knew how to handle tricky situations. He reminded me of an article Dan had written for *Executive*, a Kenyan business magazine, in which he described a circumstance he had once encountered and never again wanted to face:

The hardest situation to deal with is a frenzied mob, because they cannot be reasoned with. I try to appeal to one or two of the most sympathetic and restrained-looking people with the most effective assault rifles but I have realized that no photograph is worth my life.

One night, the telephone rang in my London apartment after Geoff and I had gone to sleep. Turning on the light, I saw that it was well past midnight. I have always hated late-night calls: they usually mean something is wrong.

"Mum, it's me." Dan's voice sounded unusually weary. "I'm in Nairobi, but I'm leaving tomorrow to visit Neema in Norway. I hope to see you on my way back through London." I was unnerved when he added, "It's been a difficult time, and I need a woman to talk to."

I thought this trip to Norway extremely unwise and said so. After Dan had been unable to commit fully to her, Neema had naturally moved on. She was now dating a Norwegian, a decision that had devastated Dan. Now he wanted to see Neema again and, no doubt, hoped to win her back. Given his mental state, and the fact that Neema was living with another man, visiting her would only cause all of them more pain. But it wasn't up to me.

It was several days before he called me again—this time from a village in northern Norway. "It's all sorted out," Dan said, sounding exuberant. "Neema and I are off to Stockholm for a week. See you when I get back." There wasn't time to ask what had happened. He had already hung up.

Sure enough, about ten days later Dan called from his grandmother's house to say that he was in London and wanted to get together. Unfortunately, he had to leave for Kenya later that very afternoon and could spend only an hour with me on his way to the airport. Though disappointed to see him so briefly, I was glad of the chance to spend time with my son. Geoff, wanting to give us some privacy, tucked himself away in our bedroom to do some work.

Dan's eyes avoided mine as he strode through my door carrying two pizzas. Pale and haggard, he appeared shattered, and for the first time in his life smoked in front of me, lighting one cigarette after another as he told me about his time with Neema in Norway and Sweden.

Their days had been stormy, he said. She had begged him not to return to Somalia if there was any chance of their remaining together, but Dan had refused, saying he was committed to his job there. Their relationship, always tempestuous, collapsed under the strain, and Neema threw him out of their hotel room. After a passionate reunion they went to Sweden, fighting and reuniting until they were both exhausted. Once back in Oslo, Neema tossed him out again, saying she had decided to remain with her Norwegian boyfriend.

Dan was increasingly angry with all the questions I asked him and dismissed my suggestion that he give Neema some space. The pain in his eyes reminded me of my own when I was with Jeremy, careening from ecstasy to despair in just a few moments. Like me during that earlier time, Dan now seemed unhinged. In his case, the violence and death with which he'd lived in Somalia had compounded the effects of his wild and demanding love affair.

"You're lucky you've experienced such passion," I said. "Many people never know what it's like to live, and love, so intensely. Committing to love is a monumental undertaking, but there are no half measures—and you can never 'make' someone love you. You can only choose to leap and hope that they will leap with you."

His face hardened at my words, but I had to keep trying.

"It's better to have loved and lost," I said, thinking of how much I had learned from my abortive affair with Jeremy.

Sharply he cut in, "I'd rather have loved and won."

I reached across the table to touch his hand. "But who knows what winning is?" I asked. "Maybe you *have* won."

He turned away. Desperate to reconnect with him, I pressed on. "Life has risks, and so does love," I said. "The only way to know if someone is right for you is to take those risks, hard as they may be. You chose to take the leap with Neema, and now you know. Someone once said that hearts are meant to be broken—open. You mustn't fear an open heart, no matter how painful it may be."

He stared at me, his eyes anguished, and my heart ached for him. I wished I could do something to alleviate his pain but knew that he would have to deal with it on his own. If he were lucky, the dark night of his soul would lead to a rebirth and renewal of his spirit; for love, as I had discovered, is one of the greatest catalysts to growth. When we are in its grip, we find new depths and heights of emotion and expression within ourselves, but if we lose the one we love, we must try to love who we are and who we can become on our own—at least for a while.

"At least you're truly alive, Dan, living firsthand with all the joy and pain that an engaged life entails." He had such a faraway look in his eyes that I wasn't sure he understood, or even really heard, what I was saying.

Suddenly there was no more time. We rushed up to the roof to snap a few pictures before his departure. I took a photo of him with a bandana around his neck, with his hands jammed in his pockets, smiling his familiar lopsided smile. Then he took a picture of me.

I could hear the doorbell beneath us: it was the taxi, come to take Dan to the airport. I followed reluctantly as he dashed down the hall to say goodbye to Geoff.

"Good luck, old chap," Geoff said, pressing a book into Dan's hand, a biography of one of his great heroes, Federico Fellini. Opening the first page Dan read out a quotation Geoff had copied by the great filmmaker: "There is no ending, no beginning, only the infinite passion of life."

"Thanks, Geoff," Dan said, his voice strong. "I'll remember that. Now, please take care of my mother."

At the door, he crushed me in one of his bear hugs. "No matter how crazy you are, Mum, I love you."

"I love you too, Dan," I said, my throat constricting. He ran down the steps and I watched from the third-floor window as he climbed into the waiting taxi.

"See you at Christmas!" I cried, banging on the glass. He looked up for a moment, caught my eye, and waved goodbye.

24

News from Hell

AFTER DAN LEFT, TARA FITZGERALD DROPPED BY FOR TEA. SHE TOLD ME about a troubling evening she had spent with him a few days before, when he had first arrived in London. It was November 5, Guy Fawkes Day, and that evening there were fireworks, blazing bonfires, and the boom of rockets everywhere. As they walked through the streets, Dan jerked uncontrollably at the crackle and pop of the explosions and ducked for cover when a car backfired.

That night, back at her place, he sat up with her, sharing horrifying images he couldn't excise from his mind—the body of a naked young girl who looked almost exactly like Neema, being washed for burial, and a dead mother and child, killed by a single bullet, still clinging to one another on the floor of a hospital morgue.

After talking with Tara, I called Amy at Lafayette and told her that I wanted to spend Christmas in Nairobi with her, Dan, and Mike. I thought it might be healing for us all to be together. The excitement in her voice was palpable. When I hung up the phone, though, Geoff was clearly upset. "What about me?" he demanded. "What am *I* going to do over Christmas if you go to Nairobi?"

"I'm sorry, Geoff," I said, my heart sinking. "But this year I really want to spend the holidays with my children." He was adamant that I should remain with him, so we argued for days. Torn between his needs and those of the children, I finally backed down and agreed to remain with Geoff.

Amy passed through London briefly on her way to Africa for Christmas, excited that she would spend the holidays in Kenya with Dan and her father. A couple weeks later I received a letter from Dan that began: "Christmas without a mother was a bit of a flop."

As I read on—it was a lengthy letter—I heard again the betrayal he had felt when I left the family and Nairobi, and I sensed that Neema's decision to cut off her relationship with him felt like yet another betrayal. It seemed clear that Dan was dealing with unresolved issues between us. If he was to trust women again, I had to tell him the truth about what had happened and why I had chosen to leave.

Unable to talk face to face and unwilling to speak over a bad telephone line, I wrote him a letter. In it I described the chain of events that had led to my leaving Mike, beginning with our inability to communicate our needs to one another. I felt ashamed as I explained my increasingly desperate attempts to find intimacy with other men when Mike and I failed to connect in this way, but now that Dan was twenty-two, I felt he was old enough to understand, if not approve the motives for, my actions.

I knew how upset and concerned he had been about Mike after I left, and how much it had hurt him to see his father cry. I didn't excuse myself or justify my actions but tried to explain why I was grateful that Jeremy had forced me, after eighteen years of running, to face the person I had become, and to become honest with myself—true to myself—and others. Jeremy saved my life, I explained, by intervening in what could have been a form of reluctant suicide as I began to spin out of control and self-destruct. I concluded the letter:

Lately I know you have been upset with me. I realize that you were deeply depressed by Somalia and by Neema's rejection of you. I believe that your feelings of rejection began many years ago when I left home. Those old feelings were stirred up by Neema's actions and you felt all those old, betrayed feelings again, but even more powerfully. You are a man now, and you understand what Mike must have felt. But I would ask you to try to remember who I am and who I was in all of this, and why it was that I did what I did.

Believe me, dear Dan, in order to change what I had become, I had to leave, nearly die, to emerge as the person I am now. What has happened to you in the past few months has been a sort of death too. But when you survive the pain, you emerge stronger than ever, and filled with greater courage and wisdom.

I know that you're frightened of being betrayed by a woman. I can only say that communication is the key to understanding. It's a two-way street, but if you keep the doors open at all levels—emotionally, intellectually, and, very importantly, sexually—you are unlikely to lose the woman you love. However, without the constant nurturing that is the sign of a healthy relationship, people can move apart from one another and lose the love that originally bound them together.

I love you very much. I have been terribly upset by your withdrawal from me over the past few weeks, and hurt by your inability to communicate your feelings so that I could answer your unspoken questions and discuss your anxieties. But there will be time over the next fifty years.

I am deeply sorry for the hurt I caused you, Amy, and Dad. But I love you all. Always remember that. And I am proud of you.

Dan called me from Nairobi after receiving the letter. Our conversation was intense, as was his voice when he told me that he had always known more than I credited him with and described how difficult it had been for him to watch what I was doing without saying anything to me.

My face burned with shame as I realized what he was saying. Dan, a keen observer of all that happened around him, would, of course, have been aware of my actions, but he had carried on our family's tradition of not addressing difficult issues—or perhaps he didn't want to add to my sense of pain and remorse by speaking out.

I wanted to reply now, but bit my tongue. It was up to him to let me back in—or not. But in the end his voice was gentle when he said, "Thank you, Mum. I hate what you did, but you were courageous to do it. Now I understand."

I put down the phone and wept, but these were tears of joy.

In the middle of January 1993, Amy flew back to Lafayette for her finals, and Dan left Nairobi and returned to Somalia. After months of unofficial apprenticeship, he was now an official "stringer" for Reuters, and one of their youngest correspondents, with a monthly retainer of two thousand dollars. He moved into the Sahafi Hotel in Mogadishu, its name meaning "journalists' hotel," run by a local character, Mohamed Jirdah, who realized the lucrative potential offered by the hordes of foreign correspondents with healthy expense accounts and no place to stay. In a devastated city with no power supply, the Sahafi had its own generators to run air conditioners and charge the reporters' satellite transmitters. Dan reported that although the general populace was starving, the hotel's well-chilled dining room offered reasonable pastas, not to mention fresh lobster and prawns.

Since Dan's first trip to Somalia in the summer of 1992, the situation in the country had deteriorated badly, despite Operation Provide Relief, launched that August. United Nations personnel were finding it impossible to deliver food and supplies successfully. Relief consignments were often looted as soon as they were unloaded.

Alarmed by these raids and the worsening famine, President George Bush Sr. initiated Operation Restore Hope to introduce stability to the war-torn country. On December 9, 1992, U.S. Marines landed in Somalia, and Dan had returned briefly to record the event, along with scores of other journalists. The predawn arrival of the troops was an unnecessarily dramatic exercise that foreshadowed the disastrous events in the months to come. When the Marines splashed ashore in full camouflage uniforms with their guns cocked, they were confronted not by Somali gunmen but by the lights, microphones, and cameras of international news teams, including veteran correspondents Tom Brokaw and Dan Rather broadcasting live to their viewers at home. Dan later scathingly described the landing as a "first-rate media circus."

Although the country was awash in weapons, the newly arrived U.S. military heading the United Nations mission decided not to disarm the local militias. This was a decision that would ultimately condemn the UN mission to failure. Within weeks, the foreign troops found themselves facing well-equipped and belligerent Somali units, encouraged by General Aidid, whose goal was to hijack as many deliveries of foreign aid as possible. Soon women and children joined the attacks on the American troops, often concealing weapons beneath their clothing. In their attempts to keep the peace, Marines were reduced to frisking ten-year-olds for guns.

Buoyed by his success earlier that year in getting his photographs published, Dan returned often to Somalia, where he got tips from more experienced journalists, including the feisty young Donatella Lorch, then the East Africa bureau chief for the *New York Times*. She had taken dozens of trips inside Afghanistan, sometimes dressed as an Afghan woman in a long, flowing black *burka*, to meet with *mujahideen* guerrillas (Muslim anti-Soviet freedom fighters) during the Soviet occupation. Dan also learned from Corinne Dufka, a former social worker (now photographer) who had braved conflicts in El Salvador and Bosnia to bring relief to the victims, that he should rely on his instincts and listen to his inner voice if he ever felt things were too dangerous.

"You'll know when it's time to get out of a situation, Dan," she said, adding, "You'll hear a little voice inside you."

I was delighted to hear that our old friend, cameraman Mo Amin, had turned up in Mogadishu to help cover the conflict for Reuters. Two years before, he had been filming in Addis Ababa, the capital of Ethiopia, when a munitions dump exploded accidentally nearby. Tragically, his assistant was killed and Mo lost his left arm. Astonishingly, he was back to work within weeks, using a prosthetic arm he'd had designed specially to operate his cameras. Knowing that Mo would keep an eye on Dan, I somehow felt Dan was safer when his mentor was in town.

Dubbed "the mayor of Mogadishu" by local Somalis for his bonhomie and embracing personality, Dan became well known as he traveled around the war-torn capital, relating easily to everyone from Admiral Jonathan Howe, who arrived in March as a UN envoy to oversee the transition from American forces to UN protective troops, to the thieves in the notorious Bakara market and the Somali children, who followed him down the streets as if he were the Pied Piper. Years later, Aidan Hartley laughingly said that Dan resembled the "fixer" in *Catch-22*, seemingly able to perform miracles in the midst of chaos. Unlike most other foreigners, he genuinely liked the Somalis and admired their warrior spirit. The locals appreciated him in turn as a "son of Africa."

But popularity wasn't enough to ensure safety in that volatile environment. In January there was a chilling item on the six o'clock BBC news about twenty-six-year-old Sean Devereux, a British teacher who ran the UNICEF office in the Somali town of Kismayo, who had been shot in the back. A photograph of this handsome young man, only four years older than Dan, standing in the bright sunshine appeared on the screen; he looked a lot like my son, with the same bright and eager expression on his face. A moment later his mother was interviewed. Calm and serene, she spoke without anger about the death of her idealistic son. "We were blessed to have him," she said. I turned off the television and sat in the darkened room. I couldn't bear to see any more.

As the situation worsened, Dan bought additional guns, although he didn't carry them when he was working as a photojournalist. He wouldn't tell me the details but confessed that bodyguards had saved him three times from being killed by snipers, a common threat in the everyday life of "Mog," as the city was known. In the same article that talked about the dangers of a frenzied mob, Dan described his fascination with, and revulsion for, this dangerous city. "Once one has been to these challenging, terrible places, one is always strangely drawn back to them because there's nothing that can compare to seeing the raw reality of the basic human need for survival. It disgusts and inspires."

I worried about Dan's mental health, particularly after he poured out his feelings on the telephone to me about a moment when he and a group of other reporters had watched helplessly from the roof of their hotel as a prostitute was stoned to death by a mob in the street for fraternizing with Pakistani soldiers serving with the UN. During another call, his voice broke when he described how he had given a dollar to a little boy to buy a Coke. When the boy came back with the change, Dan told him to keep it. The next day he learned to his horror that older boys had beaten the child to death for the coins. Dan was clearly concerned himself about what these experiences might be doing to his psyche, and I urged him to find someone with whom he could share his feelings.

In February, Dan printed thousands of copies of his Somalia photographs and sold them as postcards to U.S. soldiers, aid workers, and journalists with cash to spend in a country where there was nothing to buy. He also distributed hundreds of stickers printed with Cobra helicopters—a common sight in the skies over Mogadishu—and T-shirts printed with his designs. By April he had also published a paperbound book, *Somalia*, which included dozens of his photographs documenting the tragic destruction of the country, as well as his description of the world community's efforts to restore sanity. By May he had grown frustrated with the increasing violence and wrote that he didn't like "bang bang." I tried to lift his spirits by repeating how proud I was—and he should be—of his role in communicating such a fundamental human story to the world. In one letter I expressed my concerns about his safety and reflected on some of the challenges he might face when he returned from Somalia:

> It must be difficult to view the world with the same perspective as you had before, knowing that the problems of ordinary people are still important to them, though they seem nothing compared to the horrors you have seen. You have had to become hardened in many ways, I am sure. Surviving must mean a thickening of your skin and a more cavalier attitude to death and dying. I wonder how you will be in a place where people have their full quota of arms and legs, and the crack of a car backfiring doesn't signal danger.

He wrote back that I should "relax," that he was safe and "wouldn't die." He said that he had taken up weight lifting, using a broomstick draped with bags of sand, and enclosed pictures of his newly developed muscles and manly goatee. He added that he was going to bed early and reading everything he could lay his hands on—from Franz Kafka and Thomas Mann to John Grisham and T. S. Eliot.

He told me that he was sharing a room with a Reuters cameraman, Mohammed Shaffi, who, like his cousin, Mo Amin, was a Kenyan of Pakistani origin. Handsome and well built, with a well-groomed black mustache and an open smile, Shaffi seemed to know everyone and was generous with his advice to newcomers. This father of four children soon became a second father to him. Dan also spent time with Aidan Hartley, the Reuters correspondent who had first introduced him to Somalia, and a freelance cameraman named Carlos Mavroleon. An old Etonian and son of a Greek shipping magnate, he was known for his gutsy determination to show the news in his home country, as well his fearlessness while under fire.

Dan also talked about his budding friendships with Scott Peterson, an intense young photographer who worked for the *Christian Science Monitor;* Anthony Macharia, Shaffi's enthusiastic young Kenyan assistant; and Hansi Krauss, a talented young German photographer who worked for the Associated Press. Over the preceding months he had also grown close to another Reuters photographer, gentle and soft-spoken Hos Maina. The two men had occasionally overlapped in Mogadishu as well as Nairobi. I had known Hos for years: as a young rookie, he had often accompanied me on assignments for the *Nation.* Now in his late thirties, with a wife and three children, he had proved to be a particularly courageous chronicler, despite injuries sustained in a car crash.

However upbeat Dan tried to be on the phone and in his letters, Geoff and I watched television every night for information on Somalia, and every night it seemed increasingly like news from hell.

25

Summer Hopes

IN MAY OF 1993 I WAS LOOKING FORWARD TO AN EXCITING EVENT—MY
twenty-fifth Wellesley reunion. After being an expatriate for most of my
life, I was eager to renew contact with my friends and classmates from so
long ago. Naturally, I was anxious about how I would survive two days
with all those superstars: Secretary of State Madeleine Albright, First
Lady Hillary Clinton, and ABC newscaster Diane Sawyer were just a
few of Wellesley's distinguished alumnae, who included international
lawyers, bankers, politicians, and writers. I worried about what I should
wear and wished I could afford a face-lift.

I flew to Boston on my own. Geoff said he would meet me in New York
after my reunion. On arrival at Boston's Logan Airport, I crawled into a
cab for the trip to Wellesley and explained that I was attending my first-
ever reunion. "Are you nervous?" the cabbie asked. "Terrified," I answered.

In fact, my feelings were more complex. There was a large part of me
that was ashamed of my past, and I felt reluctant to face my more successful friends, or those who had led simpler lives and had perhaps hurt
fewer people along the way. But over the next two days, as my old class-

mates and I reconnected, it became clear that nearly everyone had faced major challenges. Many had survived painful divorces; some had never made it down the aisle; others had lost children to drugs or alcohol. The majority confessed to having gone through at least one devastating crisis that had left them emotionally or spiritually crushed. However, nearly everyone I spoke to said they had emerged from the experience as a stronger, wiser individual with a clearer perspective on life.

As my old friends and I carried on our conversations through cocktails and dinner, into the dorm rooms and bathrooms, I learned how these survivors had managed to overcome their major challenges to become the successful, loving, and effective people they were. It was truly eye-opening.

Thinking about all this as I lay in bed the last night, I had an idea for a book about how women deal with triumphs and setbacks as they seek to define themselves and to find purpose and fulfillment in their lives. I would call it *Women of Vision*. Over breakfast, I described the concept to an old friend who worked in a publishing house, and she liked the idea and took it one step farther: she suggested an exhibition by the world's greatest female photographers and a television series about women who had overcome huge obstacles to follow their dreams.

"Get the proposal to me as soon as you can," my friend said as we hugged goodbye. "We'll make this happen."

I left Wellesley feeling rejuvenated. My spirits were still soaring when I met up with Geoff in New York. He liked the book idea too and helped me create a list of extraordinary women to profile. Through a friend at the Vatican, he called Mother Teresa in Calcutta and enlisted her support and blessing for the project. Later that day, as he and I walked down Fifth Avenue, arm in arm, I felt invigorated by the prospect of tackling such an exciting project. We passed a newsstand, and Geoff stopped to leaf through a copy of *Newsweek*.

"My God, Kathy, look at this!" He pointed to the center spread, a photograph of a burning tank on a ravaged field captioned "Cry Uncle." Just above the tank, a gun helicopter hovered ominously. The byline read, "Dan Eldon, Reuters."

Geoff grabbed *Time* magazine and pointed excitedly to another shot of the same helicopter, this time flying low over several Somalis, who seemed to be running away in terror. Dan's byline appeared prominently on the edge of that photo as well. The front page of the *International Herald Tribune* featured a horrific shot of injured bodies lying on slabs in a makeshift hospital. Dan again. We raced through newspapers and magazines from around the world, helped by the newspaper vendor, who piled them on the counter, seemingly as pleased as we were to see Dan's name.

The photos were brilliant. But it was obvious that my son was closer to danger than I had imagined. All his talk about bodyguards protecting him seemed like so much bravado.

I stopped at the next phone booth and asked the operator for Reuters' telephone number in New York. I could barely hear over the traffic but somehow managed to get patched on from New York to Washington, then to the photographic desk in London. A cheerful Cockney voice greeted me at the other end.

"Excuse me," I shouted into the phone, "but I'm Dan Eldon's mother. Would you please tell him how proud I am of him that his pictures are appearing everywhere?" I knew he'd be embarrassed, but there was no direct way to reach Dan, and I had to get this message to him somehow. "Also, could you please tell him to be very careful?" I added, realizing how silly I must have sounded to a hardened journalist.

"You sound like my mum," chuckled the man on the desk. "She always worried about me when I was out in the field. Of course we'll get the message to him. He's still in Mog, and he's doing well."

Back at the hotel, I called Mike to share the good news. I also asked how he felt about Dan being in Somalia.

"Naturally I get worried about him," Mike said, his voice sounding calm. "But Dan can take care of himself. He'll be fine."

I nodded for my own benefit, wanting to believe him. "If you do speak to him, please tell him to take great care," I said, my throat tightening.

"He's coming out for a few days at the end of the month, Kathy. You can talk to him then."

I also called Amy, who sounded more upbeat than ever. Her previous semester had gone well, and she had decided on her major: international relations. I thought that was a terrific choice and told her so. Now, after a party celebrating her nineteenth birthday, she was on her way to Mexico City with her friend Christine, where the pair would learn Spanish while working as interns at a publishing firm. It sounded like the perfect summer.

Geoff and I flew back to London for the month of June. On the 26th, just before we were going to return to Los Angeles for further work on our film, Mike's mother, Gaby, threw a birthday party for me in her garden. It was a spectacular summer day. The grass was newly mowed, and the roses were full and fragrant in the summer air. The gathering included Valerie Leakey, who was in town along with ten-year-old Tiana, her pixie-like third child. Dark-haired and mischievous, Tiana led me away from the picnic table and the two of us practiced turning cartwheels in the grass. Then I lay on my back and balanced her with my legs in the air. "Fly!" I urged her, and Tiana flung her arms skyward. She collapsed, giggling, in my arms. The only thing that would have made the day even better was to have Dan and Amy there too.

Just as I was thinking that, the telephone rang. Gaby called to me, "It's Dan, to wish you a happy birthday!"

Back in Nairobi for a four-day rest, he sounded jubilant, delighted by the center spread in *Newsweek* and the exposure his photographs were getting around the world. He teased me about my call to Reuters, saying that it was hard to look like a seasoned foreign correspondent when his mother was telling everyone how worried she was about him. Despite his protests, though, I knew he was pleased that I had called.

After he talked a bit about his work, I described my idea for *Women of Vision*.

"Fantastic!" he said, and I could imagine his eyebrows rising as they always did when he was excited about something. "It's about bloody time you did something creative instead of making deals all the time, Mum. I'm so happy you're going to write again." He went on to tell me that he and Soiya Gecaga, now his girlfriend, were planning a safari together during her upcoming university break. He spoke about her in a tone I hadn't heard before, suggestive of a new willingness to commit to a relationship.

I was concerned, though, when he said, "There's just too much in my head right now, and I don't know where to put it all. It's not the pictures I take that cause the problem—it's the ones I *can't*." When I asked him what he wanted to do after Somalia, he mentioned covering the war in the Sudan for Reuters or possibly heading to Bosnia. I urged him instead to make good his promise to enroll in UCLA film school.

Then I begged him to be careful, pointing out how close he had been to the burning tank. Like Mike, he responded calmly. "I won't die, Mum," he said firmly, dismissing my concern. "My bodyguards look after me very well."

I knew there had been more close calls than he had revealed. "Don't you think it's time to get out?" I urged.

There was a long silence. "Mum, please don't ask me to leave," he said, with an intensity that made me realize how deeply he felt. "My job isn't done. It's an important story, and I have to stay. It won't be much longer." He said that he had recently told his bureau chief in Nairobi, Jonathan Clayton, that he wanted to leave Somalia permanently and that Jonathan had asked him to stay on for a few more weeks until a replacement could be found. I wondered if Dan's request had been prompted by the "little voice inside" that Corinne Dufka had described.

I could hear how conflicted he was about this, yet how badly he wanted my support. I was silent for a moment, recalling how he had defended my decision to leave the family and Kenya, even though he hated what I was doing. He had even said I was courageous to follow my heart. Now it was only fair that I back his decision to stay on a little longer in Somalia, even though I desperately wanted him to leave.

"Okay," I said. "No matter what, I'm proud of you, Dan. You're leading the life of your choice, and you're very brave."

The phone went dead. Then it rang again and I picked it up, relieved he had called back.

"Mum," he shouted over the crackling line, "I love you. It's been too long and we need to talk properly. I'm sending you a ticket to Nairobi."

"No," I retorted, "I'm sending you a ticket to London!" Flooded with our old warmth again, we both laughed. "I love you too, Dan." I hung up then, delighted that it would be only a month or two until we were together again.

There were several calls waiting for Geoff from Charlie Mayhew when we got back to Los Angeles and checked into the Shangri-La at the beginning of July. The news was good. Columbia Pictures would distribute our film internationally, which meant the duke would recoup his investment. We could all breathe again.

Over the next few days Geoff and I settled back into what had become our routine. In the morning, after my walk on the beach below the hotel, I stopped at a little kiosk on Ocean Avenue to pick up copies of international newspapers for news of Somalia. Things were dire. The Americans had pinpointed the warlord General Aidid as the principal villain in the deteriorating situation, but he eluded them. UN envoy Howe, in true Wild West style, had issued posters offering money to anyone providing information leading to his capture. It seemed odd that Howe's troops couldn't find him, for Donatella Lorch had managed to interview Aidid with no difficulty. But the combined intelligence of the CIA and international covert agencies couldn't seem to track him down.

Seated on her folding chair next to the newsstand, Debbie, the manager, always told me if Dan had a photo published that day. On Tuesday morning, July 11, she looked grim as she handed me a paper. "Dan's not in today," she said, "but I'm afraid the news from Mogadishu isn't good. The Americans are going after Aidid in a big way."

"Oh no," I said, feeling a wave of anxiety sweep through me. Sinking down beside her on a canvas chair, I gazed through a fringe of brilliant green palm fronds at the Pacific Ocean with its early-morning haze hanging low over the water.

"Do you worry much about your son being over there?" Debbie asked.

"I try not to," I said. "Dan grew up in Africa, and other journalists seem to feel safe when they travel with him." I tried to convince myself that I believed what I was saying, but it was no good. "I worry about him all the time," I confessed, with a catch in my voice.

Folding a paper under my arm I strolled along the sidewalk to the hotel, greeting the young Pakistani receptionist on my way upstairs. As always, Kamal looked neat in his pressed white shirt and black trousers. This time he stopped me, a look of concern furrowing his forehead.

"Any news?" he asked anxiously. All the staff followed Dan's story.

"I'm hoping things will change for the better in Mogadishu. Right now, it seems like no one is really in control," I said, wishing I could be more optimistic. At least no journalists had yet been hurt in Somalia.

Later that day, Geoff and I celebrated the completion of our film with a leisurely lunch in Beverly Hills. The sun was hot on our heads as we strolled along Rodeo Drive afterward and peered in the shop windows, smiling at the sight of tourists snapping pictures of the elegant displays. As we returned to the hotel, I was happy to know that everything would be changing soon. Dan would be out of Somalia, and I'd get to worry about him less and see him more. I couldn't wait.

New Dawn

THE ONE THING IN THE WORLD, OF VALUE,
    IS THE ACTIVE SOUL.
THIS EVERY MAN IS ENTITLED TO; THIS EVERY
    MAN CONTAINS WITHIN HIM, ALTHOUGH,
IN ALMOST ALL MEN, OBSTRUCTED,
    AND AS YET, UNBORN.

—RALPH WALDO EMERSON

26

July 12th

THE NIGHT AIR WAS HEAVY AND THE STREET BELOW OUR HOTEL ECHOED with the raucous voices of Sunday night moviegoers heading back to their cars from the Third Street Promenade. Tossing and turning, I couldn't seem to relax. Finally, after hours of staring at the ceiling in the heat, I peeled off the sheets and dropped into a fitful sleep troubled by disturbing dreams.

The phone rang. I opened one eye. Only seven o'clock. It had to be the producer calling from London; nobody in L.A. would be up yet. Groaning, I pulled the pillow over my head as Geoff fumbled for the receiver.

"Yes?" he barked. Dimly, as though from very far away, I could hear his words. "Oh my God, no!"

I threw off the pillow and knelt on the bed, watching him. His face was red and contorted. "Oh no," he repeated, over and over.

"It's Dan, isn't it?" I said.

He nodded. A wail escaped me in a tone I didn't recognize. It was the sound of my heart breaking.

Geoff put down the phone and tried to hold me, but I pushed him away. No one could have held me then, for I was beyond comfort. There are no words to describe the anger that engulfed me at that moment—a rage against God, against life, against anyone or anything that would hurt Dan, kill my son, who existed only for good.

"Who called?" I demanded. Maybe there'd been a mistake.

"Mike didn't know where you were, so he gave Reuters your sister Carolyn's number. It was your brother-in-law who phoned here."

"Tell me exactly what he said."

Geoff spoke slowly. "The caller from Reuters told him that Dan was killed together with three other journalists in Mogadishu."

"Why would anyone kill journalists?" It didn't make sense. "And how do they even know Dan was there?" I asked.

Dan's body had been recovered, Geoff said. The room blurred before me. I slid to the floor. Throwing back my head I howled like an animal, clawing at my face and hair. I have no idea how long I was in that state— perhaps five minutes, maybe ten—but then a curious thing happened. My rational brain started functioning again, as out of nowhere I remembered seeing the mother of Sean Devereux, the young aid worker murdered in Somalia a few months before, on television just after the death of her son. Calm and composed, she spoke about forgiveness, about healing. How could she have been so peaceful and loving?

I was at the opposite end of the spectrum, as angry as I'd ever been— mainly at myself. Then I grew silent, listening to a voice inside me. "Everything in your life has changed and you need to be prepared. Your hair is dirty. You must wash it."

I felt angry with myself that I could have such mundane thoughts at such a momentous time. Then reality hit me again and I doubled over, my belly gripped with a horrible pain. If I hadn't left Mike, Dan would have gone straight from ISK to college and would never have ended up in Somalia. If I hadn't been a journalist, maybe he wouldn't have followed that path. If I had flown to see him when he asked me to in our recent phone call, he would have been in Nairobi, not in Mogadishu. I had taught him the message of Delphi—to be true to himself, no matter what. He had stayed in the line of fire when he could have left. I was to blame for his death. I would weep over that for the rest of my life.

Geoff again tried to hold me but angrily I shrugged him off.

"Please God, I don't understand," I cried, wishing I were more religious and could comprehend how God could have let this terrible thing happen.

The telephone rang again. I held my breath. Surely Reuters was calling to say they'd gotten it wrong: Dan was okay. I picked up the receiver.

"Hi Kathy," said a cheerful voice. It was the one person I really knew in Los Angeles, Barbara Carrera, the duke of Northumberland's old girlfriend. "I wondered if you and Geoff would like to have breakfast with me." Barbara, who never got up before noon, was calling at seven in the morning!

"Barbara, the most terrible thing has happened," I said, the words tumbling out of me as I told her about Dan.

"I'll be right there." The phone went dead. Barbara lived at least forty-five minutes away in Bel Air.

I fumbled my way into the bathroom and stuck my head under the faucet. As the cold water hit, I was stunned back into the reality of the moment, aware of my warring thoughts. Logic versus emotion, belief versus denial. There *had* to be a mistake. But there wasn't. Dan was dead.

I poured shampoo over my hair and scraped my scalp with my fingernails, wanting to make my head hurt so much that I wouldn't feel the pain in my heart. I could hear the telephone ringing in the other room. When I stepped out, Geoff told me that Reuters had called with more details about what had happened. Apparently that morning UN helicopters had bombed the Abdi Villa, where it was thought that the warlord General Aidid was meeting with his followers. After the attack, a few of the survivors had raced to the Sahafi Hotel and begged the photographers and journalists to come with them and cover what had happened. When a small convoy of correspondents arrived at the bomb site, Dan and the other photographers began to shoot pictures of the dead and wounded. Without warning, there was a shift in the mood of the people: suddenly enraged by the atrocity, they struck at the journalists. There was a great cry, and the crowd became a mob. As Dan, Hansi Krauss, Anthony Macharia, Mo Shaffi, and Hos Maina started to run, they were chased by screaming men and women who hurled stones at them and beat them with pipes and sticks. So far only Dan's body had been recovered. There could be no mistake. Mo Shaffi was the only survivor from that group. Thank God for that, I thought, recalling the gentle cameraman whom Dan called his second father.

It was insane, I thought. Dan and his colleagues were only trying to help. Why would anyone want to kill them?

Imagining the scene, I wondered what the mob had done to Dan's body. I didn't want to think about it, but I couldn't help myself. Then I shuddered. Dan's body had been found, but where, where was his soul?

The doorbell rang. It had been just ten minutes since Barbara had called but here she was, her slender arms wide open to embrace me.

"I'm sorry," she said, "but he's all right now. You know he's all right." As she repeated the words over and over again, she stroked my hair, my face, my arms, holding me as a mother would hold an injured child.

"How did you get here so quickly?" I asked, confused by her prompt arrival. "And how did you know to call in the first place, at that early hour?"

Still holding me tightly, she explained that she hadn't been able to fall asleep that night. At three in the morning she had given up and had driven from her home in Bel Air to Santa Monica, where she sat in a temple for four hours, chanting a prayer to ease the passage into the afterlife of a friend who had recently died of AIDS.

"Suddenly, at seven, I had an overpowering urge to call you," she said. No one calls anyone at that hour in Los Angeles, but somehow, in the middle of her meditation, Barbara had felt that she must make contact. Now, rocking me, she began to recite a Hindu prayer for the dead, pausing between the lines to tell me what they meant.

"Dan is safe now," she assured me. "He has gone where he is meant to be. He is with God."

My rational self fought this. If there is a God, how could he let my child die? But my hurting self begged for more and I began to relax in her arms.

"Dan is with light now," she said. "Dan *is* light now. You are not to worry; he is safe. He has done his job on earth and has gone home to God. Do not be sad, because he is happy."

It seemed a miracle that Barbara was there, telling me exactly what I most needed to hear. Who had told her to come?

She left soon afterward. I looked at the clock. It was only eight thirty, but it seemed that a lifetime had passed since the phone call. I was suddenly, horribly aware that I had to call Amy, who was in Mexico with her friend Christine. The thought sickened me. I couldn't imagine her living without Dan; he was not just her brother but also her closest friend, her mentor—her tease.

With my call, her future would change forever. One moment she had a brother, but after we spoke she would be an only child. I wanted to put off the moment, allow her another minute, another hour, another day of peace, but I realized I had to call quickly. I didn't want her to find out what had happened from anyone else—or, worse yet, from the news. I closed my eyes and breathed deeply; there were no right words to destroy her life. I dialed.

She answered, excited to hear from me. She had stories to share about her flat, her new job . . . but I cut in. Speaking quickly, my words tumbled into the phone.

"Amy, my darling, this is the call I never wanted to make."

There was silence on the line as I paused, knowing I was doing it all wrong but not knowing how to do it right. I dragged the words out, one at a time. Once said, they couldn't be taken back.

"Dan has been killed in Somalia," I said slowly.

I heard an intake of breath, then a muffled, "No, Mumma, no—no!" Amy had dropped the phone, but I could hear her anguished moans. I yearned to hold her, to comfort her, to tell her that it was going to be all right. But that would be a lie. Heart racing, I held on, desperate to speak to her.

Christine picked up the phone.

"What happened?" she demanded.

I relayed all the information I had. "Please take care of Amy," I begged. "Pack everything and put her on the first plane to Los Angeles."

I sat on the floor by the phone. Everything hurt—my head, my stomach, my heart. Without Barbara's soothing presence at the outset, I don't know how I could have survived the excruciating pain. I had lost Dan, the magical adventurer. My son, the Pied Piper who helped others find their way in life. He was so young. Surely, of all the people in the world, God could have spared him.

"God!" I cried. "Why?" The question hung in the air.

I couldn't, wouldn't, let Geoff comfort me. Anger welled up in me again, turning to fury, then uncontrolled rage as I stamped around the room, hitting the walls, tearing up papers, throwing books, beating on the furniture, ripping at the curtains. I thought of Dan's body, limp on the dusty ground, and screamed, "You fool! Why did you have to go and help those people?" I stopped, blinded by my tears and ashamed of my words and actions. Huddled on the floor, I broke down all over again.

When the phone next rang, Geoff answered it. It was the Associated Press, wanting to talk to me. I took the receiver, struggling for breath. As I did, I closed my eyes, picturing Dan's soul taking off and flying so high that nothing, nobody could ever touch or hurt him again. I could see his spirit soaring and swooping, blithely free and alive, soaring toward a greater, all-encompassing light. But then a reporter's impersonal voice began to ask me questions. I could hear her fingers tapping the computer keys as I answered them.

"How old was your son?"

"Dan is twenty-two—I mean, *was* twenty-two." In a single instant, he had become the past tense.

"What college did he attend?" Her relentless questions continued. I hardly knew what I was saying. Finally, she seemed to have finished.

"Do you have anything more to tell me?" she asked. I could feel her fingers hovering over the keyboard.

"Dan could have been a diplomat or a politician. Journalism and photography were just part of his journey." I stopped, my voice breaking. Then, taking a deep breath, I continued. "He inspired other people."

Her tone became gentle. "Please go on," she prompted.

"He was a bright light that shone for a very short time," I said, then told her about Dan's STA safari to the refugee camp, the wells they had bought and the blankets they had donated for the children. I explained how he had helped Kipenget and her family, about Atieno's heart operation, about his book on Somalia and how much he had cared about the Somalis. "He saw the goodness and potential in others," I said. "He tried to help people help themselves."

When her fingers stopped, her voice softened even more. "I am so very sorry," she said quietly. For a brief moment, I knew that her head and her heart had found each other and that she shared my pain.

A television crew turned up shortly afterward, escorted into my room by Kamal, the front desk manager. He carried a little glass vase with three pink carnations.

"Thank you," I said, taking the flowers. He couldn't look at me. I squeezed his shoulder as he hurried from the room, eyes glistening.

The burly cameraman, dressed in a Budweiser T-shirt, khaki shorts, and dirty tennis shoes, adjusted the curtains, while the reporter, a suave African American in a designer suit, organized his notes. I ran a brush through my tangled hair and tried to cover my swollen eyes with make-up, before the cameraman pinned a tiny microphone on my collar. I realized that, for them too, Dan Eldon was just another story and they were in a hurry to make their deadline.

"Tell me, how do you feel?" the reporter asked, adjusting his tie. The question grated: should I say how I *really* felt—that I wanted to die? As I began to tell them about Dan and how he had affected people, the cameraman sat on the edge of the bed and looked at me through new eyes. He was no longer witnessing just another assignment; this had become *more* than just another deadline to be met.

"I have a son. He's only eight." He couldn't look at me. "I can't imagine losing my child."

When they left, the tears resumed, and I couldn't stop crying. I hated the Somalis for killing my son. There was no way I could ever forgive them for what they had done. Now I would never rock Dan's children in my lap, nor share the joy of his marriage. He would not protect me in my old age, nor nurture his little sister as she became a woman.

The phone rang again, and it was Mike, apologizing for the time it had taken for him to contact me. He explained that he had been at a meeting when someone from Reuters called to say that four journalists had been killed in Mogadishu. Mike had had to endure several agonizing hours before they called back to confirm that Dan was among those who had died. As he described his efforts to organize the return of Dan's body to Nairobi, his voice broke and there was a long pause before he continued. We said goodbye quickly, both aware that there was much left unsaid.

Throughout that long and terrible day, Geoff and I sat by the telephone as people called from England, Kenya—all over the world. Gaby called, and nearly all the members of my family. My father was so distressed he couldn't speak for three days. It was only later that he managed to rationalize Dan's death, explaining, "A man can live long but not live well. We were blessed to know such a good young person for twenty-two years."

It felt strange to be receiving calls about Dan's death when the reality of what had happened hadn't really sunk in. Often it seemed that neither the caller nor I knew what to say, and many times I ended up consoling friends who were trying to make *me* feel better. Although I may have seemed strong, I was numb, unable to feel anything. Now I know that my calm demeanor was due not to any inner strength but to the sense of shock that typically engulfs survivors following a sudden death. Indeed, after my initial hysterical outburst, I was relatively calm for the next week—detached even, as though viewing myself, and others, from a distant vantage point while I dealt with what had to be done.

Mike and I spoke several times that first day, working out travel arrangements and planning the memorial. He said people were flying to Nairobi from as far away as Hong Kong, America, France, England, and other African countries. They needed time to get there. We agreed to hold the ceremony in five days, on Saturday. But it wouldn't be a *funeral*: we would call it a Celebration of Life. We wanted a joyful gathering to commemorate the life of our son, who had led such an extraordinary, if brief, existence. Our conversations were short and to the point. We discussed what to do with Dan's body when it arrived from Mogadishu. We didn't talk about how we felt. If we had tried to, we couldn't have spoken at all.

Suddenly it was four o'clock and Geoff and I were late to pick up Amy at the airport. As we drove the familiar route, everything appeared strange, as though I were a foreigner seeing it all for the first time. The sun was shining, children were playing, and homeless folks on the beach were hustling money as they had always done. People were strolling down the street, laughing and talking as though nothing had happened. They didn't know about Dan.

Although we had driven to the airport many times, we sped miles past the sprawling complex and had to turn back for another try. As we pulled up at the international arrivals curb, we saw Amy, shrouded in a borrowed black jacket that was too large for her, waiting outside the terminal. She didn't see me even when I got out of the car and stood right in front of her, so I put my arms around her. Motionless, we sank down onto the pavement and clung to each other without speaking.

When she was little, I could soothe her with a song when she was distressed, give her medicine for a stomachache, or offer a Band-Aid for a wound, but this time I was helpless. There was nothing I could do to take away her suffering. I lay my head on hers and we rocked, oblivious to the sideways glances of the people around us.

In the car I tried to be brave for her. "It's all right, my darling," I said, describing what Barbara had said. "He's safe."

Her eyes glittered as she turned to me. "I want to believe that," she said fiercely. "I can't bear the idea of Dan being scared or hurting."

"He's where he's meant to be," I said, wishing I believed it.

As I held Amy, she began to cry softly, and I realized that for both of us, nothing would ever be the same again.

27

Dancing on the Earth

AS AMY AND I WERE LANDING AT HEATHROW, EN ROUTE TO KENYA, A FLIGHT attendant with tears brimming in her eyes handed me a copy of the *New York Times* with a front-page story by Donatella Lorch about the stoning of the four journalists. We had told her why we were flying to London, and during the flight she had discovered the article.

We were horrified to read that at least seventy-three Somalis had been killed in the attack, with another two hundred injured. No wonder the survivors had been so enraged. As painful as it was to read about the attack, I was moved to see that a huge photo of Dan surrounded by smiling Somali children accompanied the article. The photo had been taken by a friend of his in Baidoa, six months after Dan had photographed the starving children there, images that had been among the first to alert the world to the terrible famine raging in Somalia.

Valerie Leakey picked us up at the airport. She and her daughters, Lara, Kyela, and Tiana, had been staying in Geoff's and my flat for a few weeks' holiday. Kyela and Tiana had been dispatched to friends' homes, while eighteen-year-old Lara, Amy's good friend, manned the phones, together with Mary Anne's daughter Petra. Mary Anne flew in a few hours later, having talked her way onto the next plane to London from America the moment she heard the news. She wanted to accompany Amy and me to Kenya, but she was still a banned person. Her latest request for amnesty from the president had been turned down only a few weeks before.

"Don't think," Valerie commanded, as I started to worry about money and contacting people. "We have everything under control." Amy and I let the day flow over us, answering endless calls and greeting visitors.

Friends brought us copies of international newspapers, and we were touched to see that the photo of Dan that had appeared in the *Times* of London had also made the front pages of many other papers around the world. Geoff called from L.A. to say that the *Los Angeles Times* had run a story about Dan under the headline "A Bright Light." We also heard that Granada Television's *World in Action* team was already leaving for Nairobi to cover the story.

Just before we were to leave for the airport to fly to Nairobi, the fax machine rang. I flattened the curled paper and read passages from the *Tibetan Book of the Dead*, sent by Joanne Sawicki, an Australian television producer and dear friend. One line jumped out at me: "To see through the eyes of the mountain eagle, to look down on a landscape in which the boundaries we imagined existed between life and death shade into each other and dissolve."

Another fax quoted the physicist David Bohm's description of reality as an "unbroken wholeness in flowing movement. . . . [W]hat we, in our ignorance, call 'life' and what we, in our ignorance, call 'death' are merely different aspects of that wholeness and that movement."

By the time we boarded the flight to Nairobi, Amy and I were exhausted. I sank into a troubled sleep, waking up frequently. Each time, before I was completely conscious, there were a few moments of peace before I remembered what had happened. Then I felt nauseated as the horrible reality enveloped me yet again. I yearned to rest, but my mind was hyper-alert, obsessively processing the scene described in every newspaper—a crowd of enraged survivors turning on the journalists, Dan trying to climb on the Reuters vehicle as the truck pulled away, leaving him to confront the angry mob.

Mike met us at the Nairobi Airport on Thursday morning. There were new flecks of gray in his hair, and he seemed thinner than when I had last seen him. He was tense as he maneuvered us through the formalities and we drove through the slow-moving rush-hour traffic to his house, with Amy seated between us. During the painful years after I had left home, Dan had been the one person who had been able to make him laugh and feel there was hope for the future. Now we avoided each other's eyes.

The bodies of Dan and his three colleagues were being returned to Nairobi today. Those of his colleagues had been left at the mercy of angry Somalis for two days before it was safe to retrieve them. Dan's, stripped and badly beaten, had been picked up by a UN helicopter almost immediately. I shut my eyes to get rid of the image, but it wouldn't go away.

On the veranda of Mike's house, Mike's new cook, Obadiah, met us: "*Pole sana, Memsahib*," he said, bowing slightly. "I am very sorry."

Mike's foster son, Peter Lekarian, stepped forward and buried his head on my shoulder. I clung to him with both arms.

"Mama, I am so sad," he whispered. Unselfconsciously the young man rubbed away tears and handed me a letter, which I tucked away to read later.

From the corner of my eye, I caught sight of a familiar figure standing behind the others. It was William, whom Mike had reluctantly dismissed a year before when he was unable to get over his addiction to *chang'a*, the home-brewed liquor that can destroy a man's body and spirit. Now thinner and looking much older, he shook my hand, as always averting his eyes from mine as a mark of respect. He had been Dan's second father, and Dan had been William's white child. I knew that ever since William had left Mike's home, Dan had helped support him with money and clothes and had taken him out for occasional meals. Neither of us could speak. When he turned to leave, a moan escaped him that tore at my heart.

That night I was to sleep in the downstairs guest room, surrounded by my old furniture, brass ornaments, paintings, and wall hangings and by the familiar faces of my dearest friends in the world. I veered between wanting to take in every detail possible, and wanting all traces of my previous life to disappear so that there would be no painful reminders of my past.

Since my arrival early in the day, I hadn't mustered the courage to set foot in Dan's room. Finally, late that afternoon, I climbed the steps past the collection of his photographs, collages, and sketches that Mike had proudly hung on the wall leading upstairs. I studied each one closely, taking in images of beautiful girls juxtaposed against pictures of starving children and smoldering tanks.

One drawing stopped me in my tracks. It was of a man, his eyes wide open in fear, arms outstretched, falling to the ground as a mob wielded sticks, stones, and spears while attacking him. Crushed beneath their feet were the bodies of three other men. I turned the picture over and saw the words "Murder of the Messenger" and a date, 1988. Five years before.

I slumped against the wall, steadying myself as I tried to comprehend what I was seeing. Why had Dan drawn this scene? Did he have a premonition that he was going to be killed by a mob? Or was this just another strange coincidence?

I was trembling as I replaced the picture and slowly continued along the passage to his room. Then I pushed the door open.

Dust-speckled sunshine streamed in through the windows, illuminating the jumble in "the Depot," as Dan called his room, a place where things were "stored" on their way to some other place. Dozens of T-shirts and copies of his Somalia book were piled in a heap on the floor, ready for sale. A collection of Moroccan belts lay tangled in a cardboard box.

Several fat journals were stacked on an old tin trunk. I opened the top one. Unlike his other journals, which I knew included collages, whimsical drawings, and fanciful images, this final book, half-filled with photographs from Somalia, was stark and simple—nothing but photographs stuck on pages. Like his life, it was unfinished, the images standing as mute, powerful reminders of a life that had ended too soon.

I blinked back tears as I spotted pictures of our family scattered amidst the darkroom equipment that rose in a mound next to Masai headdresses and Moroccan swords. It was hard to look at the walls lined with artifacts from his many safaris and the dusty shelves stuffed with every kind of book. By the age of twenty-two, Dan had already accumulated a lifetime of memories.

I sat at his desk, the surface piled high with works in progress: a revision of his book on Somalia, carefully drawn designs for new shirts, an open journal with a few postcards glued to a page, illustrations for a new book, scraps of colorful Japanese paper, and faded bank notes from Zanzibar. There were brushes, pens, and inkpots, along with Elmer's glue and a beer mug filled with felt-tip markers. I ran my fingers across his treasures, recalling his excitement when I gave him his first black-bound artist's book.

Memories of Dan flooded through me: as a round three-year-old in a blue smock, oblivious to all around him as he swirled paint onto wet paper; as a youth, dubbed Lesharo, Laughing One, by his Masai mother, striding effortlessly across the bush with his friends. In Deziree, boom box blaring, as he roared through the streets of Nairobi. I buried my face in my hands. I didn't want to remember anymore.

It was at that moment that I first heard what seemed like Dan's voice inside me. "Everything's fine, Mum," he said gently. "I'm safe. Don't worry." Straining to hear more, I had to smile as words from Dan's beloved Bob Marley song flickered through my mind. "No woman, no cry, everything's gonna be all right . . ."

"Okay, okay," I whispered, wondering what had just happened. Then I was distracted by the sound of voices downstairs. Taking the stack of journals with me to share, I pulled myself together and went down to welcome the latest visitors, remembering that in Kenya, when something terrible occurs everyone comes to help. A continuous stream of friends turned up, bringing food or flowers to express their sympathy, love, and support. As I had learned long ago, death in Africa is a part of life, discussed without self-consciousness.

"It's God's will," said Pinki, a beautiful Indian woman whose husband had died a few months earlier. She reached for my hand.

"You will find the strength to be brave," promised Evelyn Mungai, a dignified Kenyan businesswoman who had been left with two small children when she was widowed many years before.

The courage of both these women filled me with great admiration. Their suffering imbued them with compassion and an appreciation of life that enabled them to help others face their own sorrow.

Nani Croze arrived, carrying an enormous bunch of flowers. Her eyes were red and swollen as she explained that Lengai was taking his final exams and wouldn't be able to make it to the service.

At one point Mike pulled me into the hallway. He had received word that Dan's body had reached Nairobi, and we had to make a decision. We agreed that instead of burying Dan's body, we would cremate him, for neither of us could bear the idea of his body contained in a box. We would scatter his ashes in his favorite place, where he had always hoped to make a home: on the wind-blown slopes of the Ngong Hills.

I disappeared into my room for a bit, desperate for an excuse to be alone. Weeping quietly, I sank down onto the bed and prayed for an injection of energy to get me through the rest of the long day. My head began vibrating and shivers went up my spine as I heard a voice inside me say, "You have everything you need within you to get through this time. Go in peace, with the knowledge that you are not alone."

At least, through this horrible tragedy, I was reconnecting with a deeper part of me I had ignored for months, even years. "Your life is beginning anew," the voice continued. "You have been preparing for this responsibility. Do not be afraid."

Too tired to even wonder who was speaking, I felt strangely comforted and drifted off. When I woke up an hour or so later and shifted on the bed, I heard Peter Lekarian's letter crinkle in my pocket. I unfolded the several pages of blue paper that described his friendship with Dan. The letter ended on this sobering note:

My brother saw the suffering of the Somali people and he made his mind up to show the world what was happening there. It is a mission no cowards would ever try. In every liberation there should be a sacrifice—of a blameless white ram, full of life and joy. The world is Somalia and needs redemption. Dan was a messenger and a messenger is never killed.

I believe that Dan is alive and lives with us. His love and joy
stay with us. My brother, he is light, he is wind, he is joy, he is love,
and he is peace.

Peter's words made me think about the drawing I had seen in the
upstairs hallway. Was it possible that Dan *was* a messenger? And if so,
what was his message? My mind raced. Could the death of one person
really contribute to the redemption or liberation of others? Could Dan's
spirit be alive? If so, could I talk to him? The questions wouldn't stop.

I tucked the letter away and went upstairs.

The rest of the day passed in a whirl as I wandered from room to
room in the rambling house, greeting the people who arrived with a
constant flow of offerings. In the kitchen, Obadiah and William prepared food for the little army of volunteers helping us. A committee was
meeting in the living room, planning Saturday's service, and two of
Dan's friends were tackling a pile of newspapers, clipping the articles
that told of the murder of the journalists.

That night I collapsed into bed but lay awake, haunted by images that
wouldn't go away. In my mind I saw dead Somalis laid out in neat rows,
then Dan running from a crowd beating him and tearing the clothes
from his bruised and bleeding body. He called to me, but when I tried to
reach out to him he disappeared. Whenever I rewound the tape in my
head, the nightmare started again, like repeated snatches from a horror
film. The birds began to sing as dawn broke, and I finally drifted off to
sleep.

Friday brought an influx of friends and family from Europe and America.
Amy's childhood companion, almond-eyed Marilyn Kelly, was there,
and Dan's beautiful girlfriend, Soiya, who had already booked a ticket to
Kenya in anticipation of joining Dan on safari after he left Somalia.
Guillaume, Dan's French photographer buddy, had to sleep on a balcony
under a mosquito net, and Darra, an old friend from Ireland, shared my
downstairs room. When nine of Dan's ten cousins arrived from the

States, the packed house felt as welcoming and alive as our home had always been in the past.

New York Times bureau chief Donatella Lorch turned up that day, and stopped by every day for the next week, exuding so much love and life that I could see why Dan had felt so warmly toward her. She described her last night with him and the few remaining journalists in Mogadishu, together on the candlelit roof of the Sahafi Hotel. Dan had managed to find a bootleg copy of the film *Pretty Woman* and a bottle of Scotch. The group dwindled as candles began to gutter in the early hours of morning, and someone played Edith Piaf's haunting song *"Je ne regrette rien,"* one of his favorites.

Before that gathering broke up, Donatella was unexpectedly summoned to the airport—there was one spare seat on a plane flying at dawn, and she had to leave immediately. Dan hugged her as they said goodbye. He told her not to be anxious, adding lightly, "Tomorrow we'll go dancing in Nairobi." Had she stayed, she probably would have died the next day too.

That evening, after dinner, I excused myself and went to bed early, aching for sleep. As I lay with my eyes open, fighting the disturbing images that continued to play in my mind, I felt shivers up and down my spine. Suddenly my head jerked back and my tongue probed the roof of my mouth. Then I heard a low, guttural voice speaking through me. Strange as this may sound, I knew it was Dan, who gave me instructions in a tortured voice that sounded almost annoyed by the fact that he couldn't sit me down, hand me a pen, and talk as we both doodled.

"Go to my room and get my journal," he demanded.

"I'm going," I mumbled. I pushed open Dan's door and fumbled for the light, revealing a room now piled high with the sleeping bags, mattresses, and suitcases of the many visitors Mike was putting up in his house.

I wasn't sure what journal Dan had in mind. Making my way through the clutter, I stood in front of the bookshelves. We had searched them once already and found several journals, which we had taken downstairs and put with the few I had taken down to share, so I felt sure there weren't any more.

Still, I ran my fingers along the dusty paperbacks, old comic books, a life of Churchill, Shakespeare's sonnets, a manual on photographic airbrushing, and three empty journals I had recently bought for him. Then, poking around the back of a shelf, I felt something tall and slim—a child's scrapbook that Dan had covered with zebra-striped wrapping paper. It was his first journal, started when he was seven. I laughed out loud. Apparently he didn't want us to miss a thing.

I returned to bed and placed the little book on the table beside me. I needed evidence to convince me, and others, that what had just happened was not a figment of my imagination. Or was it?

Just then there was a knock at the door. It was Mary Anne's daughter Tara, who had been staying at the house for the past five months. She and Dan, already true friends, had grown even closer, and at the end of his last visit home she had driven him to the airport. As he had done with so many people, Dan had seen in her a beauty and potential not yet fully developed. Through him, she had begun to believe in herself. I hugged her. She looked pale and exhausted, and I knew she had barely stopped crying for three days.

"I have to tell you something," she said, sitting on my bed. "I think Dan knew he was going to die."

"What do you mean?" I asked. I told her that Reuters had already investigated the whole thing and had come to the conclusion that Dan's murder wasn't planned. He and his colleagues were just terribly unlucky.

"I don't mean that," she said, struggling to find the right words. "I mean, he *knew*. A part of him knew." She explained that she and Dan had spent much of his last week in Nairobi together. He had hardly slept. He seemed to want to tie up everything and visited lots of his old friends, including some he'd had arguments with. And he took Tara to see her old house, the one Mary Anne had had to leave when she was deported from Kenya so suddenly.

"Also, he sorted through all his things," she said. "He gave away books, and clothes, and—"

I interrupted her. "What do you think was going on?"

"I don't know," she said. "But he talked about death all the time. He even told me he wanted to be buried in Deziree, like a Viking warrior in his boat!" We both had to laugh, despite ourselves. She described how the last night they had danced at the Carnivore until three and had talked until five in the morning. She had awakened him at six thirty because they had to go to the airport.

"I crawled into bed with him," she said shyly, "and we held each other for a long time without saying anything." I nodded, understanding— after the years she and Dan had spent living in and out of my flat, they were like sister and brother.

"Then later, before he went through the departure gate," she said, "we just clung to each other. I said, 'Please come back.' I had never said that before." Overcome, Tara wrapped her arms around me. I rocked her as we cried together.

Much to our amazement, Mary Anne herself arrived on Saturday morning. She had called a well-placed official in the ministry of foreign affairs and explained why, as my best friend, she needed to be at Dan's funeral despite her status as *persona non grata*. That official, an old friend of both of ours, quickly agreed that she could come for three weeks and immediately organized the visa.

The same morning, various Reuters people flew in from London, led by Mark Wood, their scholarly looking editor-in-chief. The team, wearing dark suits, ties, and somber expressions, arrived at Mike's house with the only survivor of the July 12 tragedy, Mohammed Shaffi, who appeared so battered he could hardly walk. Still in deep shock, his voice was low and his eyes downcast as he described being shot repeatedly and beaten by the mob. I had to lean forward to hear him as he told us how, just as they were about to kill him, he begged them, as fellow Muslims, to spare his life.

To his surprise, they dumped him, half-dead, in front of the American hospital. Ironically, it took the intervention of a journalist who happened to recognize him to get him admitted. Shaffi broke down in tears when he told us that he had loved Dan as a son. I said that I knew Dan had called him *babuji*, which means "little father" in Urdu. Now the sole survivor of the tragedy, Shaffi was suffering from complex and painful emotions. On the one hand, the father of four was relieved to be alive; but, at the same time, he felt intense guilt. As I hugged him, his shoulders began to quiver. Then, overcome by wracking sobs, he had to be led from the room.

A little later, Mo Amin, Dan's hero and role model since he had been a small boy, came in. He seemed to have shrunk since I had last seen him. His dark hair was speckled with gray and thinning on top, and his prosthetic arm hung by his side. He told us that it was he who had identified his four dead colleagues and accompanied their body bags from Mogadishu to Nairobi. Standing stiffly in the middle of the living room, he had difficulty speaking.

"Kathy," he said, his voice sounding weary, "you and Mike can be so proud of Dan. He never grew cynical; he was always smiling and filled with life. While most people his age were still wondering what to do, Dan had become a legend." I was proud to hear his words and knew how much they would have meant to Dan. It was Mo, after all, who had first encouraged him to become a photographer. It was hard to equate the vibrant young cameraman I had met so long ago with this exhausted man who had nearly lost his life over and over again to tell stories that he felt the world needed to hear.

Saturday morning was cold and overcast. We had asked Kipenget to let us hold the service of celebration on her land at the edge of the Great Rift Valley on the Ngong Hills. She received permission for this from the local chiefs, who also agreed that we could scatter Dan's ashes on sacred Masai land close by her hut. We had no idea how many people to expect and were worried about how cold they would be, seated on the grass in the cool weather.

The service was going to be filmed by Reuters and Granada Television's *World in Action* team, who were making a documentary on the death of the journalists. Mike and I agreed that we would both speak, but I didn't have a clue what I should say; I simply hoped for inspiration. In the meantime Mike was frantically busy trying to organize food, hire a choir, create programs, find loudspeakers, and make the parking arrangements.

There was another pressing problem too, and I could hear him on the phone to Dan's mechanic. "I *must* have Deziree back here by one o'clock. Make sure she can get to the service under her own power!" Dan's Land Rover was now a decrepit twenty-one-year-old, and he had spent enormous sums of money to keep her on the road. She had broken down again recently, but now she had to be at the service. She was, after all, Dan's second favorite woman—after Amy.

A few minutes later, Mike and I ran into each other in the hallway. So far there had been almost no time to be alone or discuss how we felt about Dan's death. We had always had a hard time communicating about the deeper aspects of life, and this was no exception. Despite that, I felt closer to Mike than ever before, lovingly reunited in a way neither of us could have imagined. The pain of the past seemed now to have been forgotten, lost in a far greater sorrow. Mike looked solemn as he pulled me into Dan's room and shut the door. His hands, with the long sensitive fingers I remembered so well, enclosed mine. He cleared his throat and paused for a moment, apparently trying to compose himself.

"Dan is being cremated right now," he said.

I cringed at the thought. Neither of us could bear being present for it, nor had I chosen to view his body when it was in the mortuary. I preferred to remember Dan as he looked before the mob had taken its revenge. I looked at my watch. Eleven o'clock. It was going on at the Hindu temple, Mike said, which had agreed to arrange the cremation since the Nairobi municipal crematorium had no gas that week. I hadn't wanted to know the time or place in advance, and even now I tried to deny the reality that our son's body was lying on a bed of fire, flames devouring his flesh, his hair, his bones. Our beloved Daniel, conceived on Christmas Eve. I pounded my fists on Mike's chest and felt a sob, then another, as he, too, fought for control.

"I'm so terribly sorry," I said, finally speaking the thought that had been tormenting me. "It's my fault Dan died."

Mike drew back to stare at me curiously.

"If I hadn't been a journalist, he wouldn't have wanted to do this job," I cried. "If I hadn't left home, he would have gone straight to college." As I fought to catch my breath, Mike stopped me.

"Don't ever say that again, Kathy. Dan lived exactly as he wanted to live. It's not your fault."

Shaking my head, I began to tremble once again as I imagined the flames.

When next I looked outside, it was no longer overcast: the sun shone brightly for the first time in weeks, and clouds billowed in the intense blue sky. Although Mike was a nonpracticing Jew and I, a fallen Methodist, we had asked Father Tom, a Jesuit priest we knew and liked, to officiate at the ceremony because we respected his ecumenical, expansive attitude toward life. Dan's existence wasn't about separations or denominations; it was about shattering barriers and finding ways to bring people together. After all, he had been cremated in a Hindu temple, the makeshift altar would be decorated with his ancient Muslim prayer sticks, a Jewish friend would be reading a Hebrew blessing, and a "born-again" African gospel choir would sing hymns.

I heard Mike call that it was time to go. I hurried into Dan's room and rummaged through his closet, looking for a jacket to wear. I found one that I was used to seeing him in and put it on, as much for comfort as for warmth. As I stuffed a handful of tissues into the pocket, I felt something bend under my fingers. Pulling it out, I gasped when I saw that it was a picture of me, smiling as I leaned against a mantelpiece. Dan had told me once that he had this very picture pinned up on his wall in the Sahafi Hotel and showed it to all his friends. Swallowing hard, I stuck the picture back inside the pocket and pulled the jacket tightly around me, like a hug.

Outside there was a roar in the front drive. Deziree had arrived, trailing clouds of black smoke. Everyone gathered around her, as though we were viewing Dan's body. I could still read the words "Fight the Power" in the center of the steering wheel in yellow paint. No one spoke for a long time.

"We'll meet you there," Mike said to Deziree's driver. "It's time to go."

I wasn't conscious of anything outside the car during the drive to the Ngong Hills—aware only of the driver, silent in the front, and the three of us on the backseat, holding hands, a family for the first time in five years, gathered for the saddest celebration we would ever attend.

A few minutes before two o'clock, we reached the crest of the ridge overlooking the expanse of the Great Rift Valley. As always, the magnificence of the view took my breath away. I remembered the first time I had been here with Dan, then about fourteen.

The car bumped across the parched grass toward the open space chosen for the ceremony, a natural amphitheater. Several hundred people were already sitting on the slope that ran gently down from the rounded knobs of the Ngong Hills. Below them stood the improvised altar against the magnificent backdrop of the Great Rift Valley, which lay dotted with spiky green acacia trees as far as the eye could see. Dan's cousins and closest friends unrolled long paper banners on the ground leading to the altar—banners covered with newspaper clippings, messages, flowers, and drawings.

I had realized earlier that I had to find meaning in Dan's death if I was to survive it. Or maybe I had to *make* it meaningful. Now, seeing Mark Wood stepping forward to greet me, it occurred to me that he might be able to help.

"Mr. Wood," I said, trying to come up with an idea that he would approve. "Please, we have to do something with this tragedy, transform it from the horror it is into something positive. Could we create an exhibition in memory of the journalists—and perhaps a book to go along with it—to remind people of the sacrifices made by those who try to tell important stories in conflict zones?"

He looked startled by my impassioned plea but was gracious in his response. "I'll do everything I can to help," he said gravely, shaking my hand. "You have my word."

I did not know it then, but with that promise Mark had given me the key to my recovery.

Father Tom led us to canvas safari chairs at one side of the altar. Amy sat between Mike and me, with Gaby and Mike's sister, Ruth, nearby, as the choir, on the other side of the altar, began to sing. Swaying in rhythm, they belted out a rollicking hymn of celebration, while the growing crowd continued to take their places on the hill, some settling on cushions or blankets and shading themselves with umbrellas. The scene was a sea of color: the bright red *shuka*s of the Masai warriors contrasting with the dark suits of the executives; the flowery dresses of the women, with the khaki safari outfits of many Kenyans.

The altar was covered with a printed African cloth held down by stones. A framed photo of Dan, smiling broadly, stood next to his Viking helmet, added at the insistence of his cousin John. There were pots of wildflowers, and two of Dan's ancient Muslim prayer sticks were propped up in front.

Father Tom, in a simple white surplice, began to speak with a strong Irish accent, and I leaned forward to make sure I caught every word. He spread his arms wide as though embracing the Great Rift Valley.

"It was in this very place that we first knew you as God," he prayed. "The earth plates moved, and out of that confusion, you brought us this." He turned and raised his arms toward the sky, the clouds, the hills, and then all of us.

"Like the earth plates, our hearts have moved today. Let us open them to the same creative fire that set a flame alight in the spirit of Dan Eldon. May love wrap around us all." His final words were carefully chosen: "Let us pray for peace in our hearts today and let us bring peace to the world." I added a silent prayer to his.

As he finished, a herd of goats drifted across the grass behind him, pursued by one of Kipenget's barefoot grandchildren, wearing only a small piece of scarlet cloth around his slim body.

There were many tears that day as Dan's brave journalist colleagues struggled to find words to describe their friend. We laughed at their descriptions of his infectious, loony sense of humor and his wonderful

spirit, which seemed to have touched the hearts of everyone he met. Ir-
reverent, endlessly creative, energetic, and joyful, Dan had inspired
them to believe in themselves, to follow their hearts, to find their purpose, and, above all, to be truly alive.

A beautiful young woman from a British newspaper told how, on a
long and frightening day stranded on a remote airstrip in Somalia, Dan
had sung her a song to bolster her spirits. He said that he had learned it
from his mother as a small boy, after he was too afraid to jump into a
river. I smiled when she quoted it:

Make believe you're brave and the trick will take you far;
you may be as brave as you make believe you are!

"Never show fear," he had cautioned her. "It's not cool."

Mo Amin spoke next. He had already been to the other three colleagues' funerals; this was the fourth. He moved slowly, as though in
pain, and propped his prosthetic arm on the podium. He sounded tired
when he began: "To achieve double-page spreads in *Time*, *Newsweek*, and
Der Stern, and hundreds of other magazines and papers, is a lifetime
ambition for any news photographer. Dan did it at twenty-two. It was his
eye, and brain, and hand that captured forever the anguish of a nation;
his pictures of Somalia are what millions who were not there carry
around in their minds. Dan's pictures stood out among the best."

Then Mo recited a poem by Sir Walter Scott, which, he said, was as
good an explanation as any for those who make their living on the edge,
who commute to wars and disasters and record the humanity and inhumanity they find there:

Sound, sound the clarion,
Fill the fife,
To all the sensual world proclaim,
One crowded hour of glorious life
Is worth an age without a name!

Mike rose to speak next. With flashes of humor he told how, only a month earlier, after he had punctured his ribs in a car crash, Dan had visited him in the hospital. Every day, he had dressed in a different disguise, once appearing as an U.S. Army major, saluting his way past the security guard.

Before Mike had finished, I spotted Deziree's silhouette coming over the horizon. But something wasn't right: instead of coming under her own steam, a beat-up truck was towing her. I had to smile. Only Dan had been able to manage his temperamental lady. Mike paused as she was ceremoniously maneuvered into a position of honor. Above the driver's seat the wooden eye of the *dhow* still offered protection for the owner who would never sit there again.

Then it was my turn. My mouth was dry when I walked up to the microphone, confronted by faces from all over the world, a mélange of colors and races, religions and creeds. I fingered the photo I had found in Dan's pocket and let the words flow through me. I looked at Mike when I said how important it is to heal torn relationships, to forgive, and to let go of anger and bitterness, for we never know how long we have on this earth to say we love each other.

As I spoke, I noticed many people looking up. Following their gaze, I saw a lone hawk circling above us, dipping and diving, soaring on invisible currents, lifting our spirits with him as he flew higher and higher into the clear blue sky.

I concluded my contribution by recalling lines from the Cat Stevens song that Dan had given me when I was feeling desperate after leaving my home in Africa: "You're only dancing on this earth for a short while." I explained that he had wanted me to start living again and had used the music to remind me of the preciousness of each moment we have. "If Dan were here he would say, 'You must dance your *own* dance. You choose the music for your dance. Dance it loudly, dance it proudly, dance it with incredible spirit, creativity, and joy—and most of all, dance your dance with love!'"

Trembling and dry-mouthed, I sat down, grateful when Mike put his hand on my shoulder to calm me.

The sun was setting as Amy stood to read a letter from Lengai. Head held high, she read his words with strength and confidence:

Dan was my best and closest friend. When we were young it was I who persuaded him up higher rock faces and bigger trees, but later it was he who showed me how to get everything possible from life. Dan had such fierce life energy. Everything he did was with total commitment. Every moment he lived completely.

Laughter was our strongest weapon and most potent medicine. We lived and laughed lifetimes' worth. Now Dan is with me always and our laughter will never stop.

Amy remained standing for a moment without speaking, then quietly said, "*Kwaheri ya kuonana*, Dan . . . goodbye until we meet again."

Stepping back from the altar, she lit the first of ten torches and handed it to Soiya, who thrust it into a tall pyramid of dry wood, saying, "We light this fire in commemoration of the sparks Dan lit in others." Nine other torches joined hers, and the pyre blazed upward. Behind it, the horizon seemed to be on fire too, rippling in the waves of the rising heat, while near us, Deziree shimmered like a mirage.

The choir stood, blue robes swaying as they belted out the song "Let there be peace on earth, and let it begin with me." Many people were crying, not just for Dan but for a world gone wrong. Minutes later, a little plane swooped out of the clouds and flew straight over the blazing bonfire, waggling its wings before it disappeared into the setting sun—a fitting salute to a son of Africa, my son.

The next day, just before sunset, Mike, Amy, and I, together with Dan's cousins, returned to scatter Dan's ashes. It was the moment I had been dreading most. This would be our final farewell.

There were slashes of scarlet and purple in the sky as the sun, a golden fireball, sank toward the horizon. A gnarled acacia tree showed us the way to the site of yesterday's pyre, now a heap of white ashes bounded by a circle by smooth stones within a larger ring of tree stumps. As the sky darkened, Dan's cousins made a new fire and tossed sticks into the growing flames.

I sat on a rock with one arm around Amy, trying not to look at the swirled-glass vase resting on one of the stones, specially blown by Lengai's brother, Anselm, for Dan's ashes.

The cousins had brought along Dan's boom box and put on "*Je ne regrette rien*." I hated hearing it, for I regretted so much. Father Tom, now dressed in a windbreaker, jeans, and sneakers, arrived to preside over the sad little gathering, and we all traded stories about Dan until the sun finally set.

To the accompaniment of Bach's *Magnificat*, Father Tom gave his final blessing. As he did so, a gust of wind, blowing up from the depths of the valley, stirred the dwindling fire into life. I wanted to stay forever in this faraway place with Dan.

After the flames had died down, my niece Amy opened the glass jar containing Dan's ashes and gently scattered them into the circle of stones. "I love you, Dan," she whispered. Mike and I hugged her, grateful for her willingness to do what we couldn't. It was very dark and cold when we finally picked our way across the dry grass back to the cars.

The memory of the lone acacia tree standing there, bent and twisted by the wind, starkly silhouetted against the night sky, burned itself into my mind. When I think of it, I am reminded of the poem by Mary Elizabeth Frye that we handed out at Dan's celebration:

Do not stand at my grave and weep
I am not there, I do not sleep.
I am in a thousand winds that blow
I am the softly falling snow.
I am in the morning hush,
I am in the graceful rush
Of beautiful birds in circling flight.
I am the star shine of the night.
Do not stand at my grave and cry,
I am not there. I did not die.

When we finally returned home that night, I collapsed into bed, desperate to sleep. I had promised the next day to write an article about Dan for the *Daily Telegraph* and knew I would need my wits about me. Having written nothing for publication in five years, and being too tired and distraught to think straight, I had originally wanted to turn down the request, but Mike urged me to create a piece that would reflect our son's life and spirit. Now, with the challenge looming ahead of me, I couldn't relax. I finally downed several sleeping pills in the hope that I could get a decent night's sleep, mentally apologizing to Dan, who had always disapproved of taking medicine. The pills had no effect; I tossed until nearly five o'clock before dropping off.

Two hours later, I woke up, my head whirling. I sat down to confront the challenge of composing fifteen hundred words but didn't know where to start. I closed my eyes and prayed for inspiration. I needed help; I just couldn't do this by myself.

When my fingers touched the keyboard, they flew spontaneously over it, as though possessed by a powerful energy. One hour later, five pages were full, though when I read them through I didn't recognize the words as mine. I faxed the text to the newspaper, then collapsed on the floor by the computer, where I slept for several hours.

The *Daily Telegraph* called me from London the following day to say that they had run the piece exactly as I had sent it, minus a few typos, in nineteen newspapers around the world. Almost immediately I began to receive letters from people who said they had been inspired by Dan's vibrant spirit and vision as depicted in that article. I have never felt that I was its author, though I can't explain who was.

28

The Snakebark Tree

FROM THE MOMENT I ARRIVED IN LONDON A WEEK LATER, MY MIND PLAYED tricks on me: I saw Dan everywhere—darting off trains and buses, mingling in crowds, jumping into cars, disappearing around corners. When I looked closely, the young men who had caught my eye barely resembled him, but I resented them all, unable to understand why they should be alive when Dan was dead. His death had robbed not only him of his future, but me as well—his future as he had seen it and as I had imagined it for him. I mourned his possibilities: the wonderful, terrible, joyous, agonizing, adventurous, disastrous, exuberant, growing years that lay ahead for him—and for me.

If the phone rang, I absurdly hoped it was Dan calling. When it wasn't, I wanted to escape, to sleep, to dream him alive again. It was too painful to see pictures of him, so I hid all his photos and could barely look at his abandoned Land Cruiser, Big Blue, still parked outside my apartment building.

One day, turning onto a busy road I had used a hundred times before, I lost concentration for a moment when my mind slipped to Somalia, imagining the screaming mob as it engulfed Dan's body. I heard a loud hoot and watched, as though in a dream, the face of a horrified man in a blue sedan as he crashed into my car. I know I shouldn't have been driving at all, a fact confirmed a few days later when I collided with the entrance barrier of a parking lot, waking up only as the attendant shouted at me, obviously convinced I was either drunk or a "nut case."

Over a month after Dan's death, as I was trying to answer some of the many condolence letters, I received the unexpected phone call from Debbie Gaiger that I mentioned in the prologue. After Debbie described her visit to the psychic Mollie Martin, I went to see Mollie myself. Although she frightened me with the long list of tasks Dan apparently wanted me to do, I was deeply moved by her comment that Dan's life and death wouldn't be in vain and that he had a lot more good to do.

Mollie said that although Dan was physically apart from me, he could still see me and was close by. That seemed possible: there had been several times when I felt as though I could hear his voice in my head, and once I felt a light brush across my shoulder. I'd also had a few vivid dreams when it seemed as though he were alive again, but I had dismissed everything as figments of my imagination.

Mollie also said I would be writing a book, speaking, traveling, producing a film about Dan, but that seemed far-fetched. It was proving hard for me to get out of bed in the morning, much less fulfill his purpose—or mine, for that matter.

Certainly that extraordinary conversation with Mollie gave me a lot to think about, but I was disturbed about something else too: I was finding it increasingly challenging to be with Geoff. Earlier that year, when he had objected to my flying to London to join Dan and Amy in Nairobi for Christmas, I had caved in, not wanting to stir things up between us, but nonetheless I resented him for it. Now, since Dan's death, I felt even angrier with him. Nothing he did was right: if he tried to comfort me, I wanted to be alone, but when he needed solitude, I demanded his company. I just couldn't stop being irritable and impatient with him. He was frustrated by my behavior and became more aggressive toward me, an attitude that led to even more frustration for both of us, along with a sense of alienation and loneliness that made me, and him, sad.

In late August Geoff and I had to return to Los Angeles, where a reshoot of several scenes from our film was about to begin. I hated leaving London, where I felt supported by friends and family who cared about me and had known Dan. In California, Geoff and I would be on our own.

About the same time, my closest confidante, Amy, had to return to college. On my way to California, she and I drove from New York to Easton, just as we had a year before. When we turned into the Lafayette gates, I cast a sideways glance at her. "It's okay, Mumma," she said, catching my eye. "You mustn't worry. I'll be fine."

But she was pale and drawn when she got out of the car. Her friend Christine, who had packed Amy's bags down in Mexico and put her on the plane on July 12, hurried down the dorm steps to greet her. A few young women quickly surrounded the pair, but others hung back. I knew how awkward they must feel. I remembered feeling strange myself when confronted with someone who had suffered a recent loss, not realizing then that an embrace and a simple "I'm so sorry" is all that's needed. I was learning that being a good listener is the best gift you can give to someone who is grieving.

I hugged Amy goodbye, and then she and her friends, laden with Amy's bags, headed up the steps of the dormitory. At the top, Amy turned back for a quick wave before disappearing inside. With an effort, I gathered myself for the drive back to New York. On the one hand, I hated leaving Amy alone and unprotected, grappling with her feelings of abject grief. At the same time, I would have liked to go off to school myself, to forge a clear, new path, far from the intense emotions clustered around me, now that I no longer had to be brave for my daughter.

Back in Los Angeles, I knew I had to concentrate, for Mark Wood had been true to his word and was arranging an exhibition and book of photographs taken by Dan and his colleagues. He was also planning a memorial service for them at St. Bride's, known as the journalists' church, on Fleet Street. But as much as I wanted to help, I was finding it increasingly difficult to function.

So far, shock and the need to put on a brave face for Amy had insulated me from the worst pain of Dan's death, but as the numbness wore off, I spiraled into a bundle of raw nerves. I lost eight pounds, my stomach ached all the time, and, like an invalid, I could eat only soft food. Far from my closest friends, and finding it difficult to communicate with Geoff, I felt isolated and alone. I recalled the state of despair I had experienced after leaving Mike, but this was far worse. I had no attention span and could barely understand what people were saying. I wanted to die. In fact, much of me felt as though I already had.

Only the thought of Amy without a mother kept me alive. Aside from her, I had nothing to live for. Before Dan's death, my life had begun to become an exciting adventure again and I had made the decision to write a book about women who had been through hell. Now I was one of those women—and I wasn't sure that I could ever find my way back.

I didn't know how to stop replaying Dan's death in my head, until I remembered the game he and I would play when he was little. "Draw how you feel," I would say. Later, when it was I who couldn't express my pain, he would hand me a pen. One afternoon I rummaged around in his old briefcase and pulled out a handful of felt-tip markers. Tearing a fresh page from a pad of art paper, I began sketching the angry figures that circled around my son just before his death.

As I drew, I was jolted into another dimension. From a vantage point high above a city of white buildings glistening beneath a clear blue sky, I watched my son get to his feet and begin to run. I could hear the thud of his feet pounding along the cratered street. His face was flushed, glistening with perspiration, and I could feel his terror as the crowd screamed at his heels. There were people he knew in the mob, people with whom he should have been safe, but even these familiar faces were distorted with rage. The veins on his neck rose as he ran, arms pumping, legs straining. His breathing became my breathing, labored and harsh, as he struggled to stay ahead of the crowd.

I reeled as rocks slammed into his back and sharp poles prodded his flesh, then heard myself cry out as Dan fell to his knees. I watched him appeal to the enraged people around him, trying to make them understand he had only come to help. If he could make them laugh, as he had done so often before, they might let him go. But as he had once written, a frenzied mob cannot be reasoned with. It has no mind, no soul, no logic, no compassion. Then there was another rock, more blows to his head, his shoulders, his legs. His knees gave way and, arms outstretched, he collapsed facedown in the dust.

Sobbing uncontrollably by this point, I drew a comet with a golden tail heading into the sky. Like a hawk soaring toward open sky, Dan was free at last, heading home.

I chose a thick black pen to draw a cluster of grieving women covering their faces in an age-old expression of despair, and then sketched myself in red ink, hunched over in mourning.

For a while after that I felt better, almost able to deal with the roller coaster of pain, but all too soon I was despairing again.

Both Geoff and I found the atmosphere of Los Angeles unsettling. With the film about ivory poaching completed, we were pursuing other, long-deferred projects, but our dreams were shattering around us. One proposed project collapsed the night before the financing was confirmed, and another film deal dissolved when the head of the studio was fired three days after accepting one of our scripts for production.

Every morning, Geoff woke up at five o'clock drenched in a cold sweat. He half-suspected I might return to Mike in Kenya and sought to isolate me from anyone who might get too close to me. Naturally volatile, his moods now veered from great gentleness to fury. Although I was grateful to him for teaching me so much about how to make films, I felt suffocated and wanted to leave. I was too sad and frightened to do anything about the situation, however.

Living like nomads at the Shangri-La didn't foster a sense of harmony. Drug addicts and homeless people camped out nearby, gang shootings erupted a few miles away from us in Venice, and we watched helplessly as the residents of nearby Malibu endured terrible rains, then mudslides, that sent their homes slipping into the sea. There was a constant, ominous sense of anxiety in the air.

Late one Saturday night, a nightmare awakened me. I was running down endless roads, into dead ends, breathless with terror. My heart was racing from the dream when in real life I heard a man crying for help on the street below. Hurrying to the window, I saw a shadowy figure kicking someone lying on the sidewalk.

"Stop!" I screamed. "Stop or I'm calling the police!" Hearing the shouts continue, I cried, "I'm coming to get you myself!"

"Are you crazy, Kathy?" Geoff muttered from the bed. "Shut the window and come back to bed."

For a moment, the attacker stopped and looked up. I could see his victim roll over.

"I'm coming down—now!"

The attacker dashed into the shadows of a nearby building. His injured victim stood unsteadily and shuffled down the street.

"That guy knows exactly where you live," Geoff said. "He could come back one night and do the same to you."

"One person could have saved Dan's life," I said bitterly, staring at the empty street below. "Just one person who cared."

We were having lunch in the hotel a few days later when we noticed a billowing black cloud rolling out over the ocean, blotting out the sun and transforming the bright afternoon to dusk. My eyes followed the cloud back to the hills of Malibu, where I spotted a flickering, crimson crest of flames. The whole area was on fire! Geoff turned on the television and we watched, horrified, as it raced over the tinder-dry hills.

The wildfire raged all night, impossible to confine despite the efforts of hundreds of firefighters battling it with helicopters and trucks. My heart ached for all those who saw their homes and all their possessions disappear in the flames.

In the morning, I went for a walk on the beach. It was almost deserted, except for the usual contingent of homeless people sheltered under the palm trees. The thinning smoke drifted around us, depositing a layer of fine soot and cinder. One man, dressed in a ragged T-shirt and jeans slimy with dirt, gestured for me to join him on the sand. I scrunched down next to him. He was probably in his forties, but his sun-darkened, worn face made him appear much older. Solemnly, he offered me a cigarette.

"No, thanks," I said, wishing I had something to offer in return. We talked about the fire and then he told me why he had become homeless. A few years back, his wife and three daughters had been killed when a drunk driver hit their car.

"I went crazy for a while, even tried to kill the guy." The man's eyes looked beyond me as he buried his cigarette butt in the sand. "I didn't quite manage to pull it off, and they arrested me for attempted murder. After they let me out, I started to drink, and . . ." His voice trailed off. It was obvious he had done his best to die. I understood exactly how he felt.

"Did you ever forgive the man who killed your children?" I asked. Although I had spoken about forgiveness at the celebration of life, I was talking then about relationships with people we love, not referring to the Somalis who had stoned Dan and his friends to death. I could never forgive them for what they had done.

"In the end, yes," he said. "The prison chaplain said that I had to let go of my rage or it would kill me—or I would kill someone else."

"How long did it take?"

As his eyes stared into the distance, I sifted through the sand with my fingers, wondering where he was.

"I'm still working on it," he said slowly, focusing on me as though seeing me for the first time.

After a time he spoke again. "I feel as if this fire has a message for me. You can't give up. You've got to keep trying, move on." I nodded as he continued. "I'm going to start over now. From this minute," he said, with a new light gleaming in his eyes.

"I know you can make it," I said, willing him to succeed.

Impulsively, I ran inside the hotel to grab a few T-shirts and a twenty-dollar bill. Back down on the beach I searched for the man everywhere. He had vanished. I tried every bundle of rags on the sand, then tore back up the steps to the strip of grass above and poked through the makeshift shelters to find the man who wanted to start a new life. I described him to everyone, but no one had seen where he had gone. I was ready to give up when I spotted him crossing Ocean Avenue. I ran to intercept him.

"Excuse me," I called out, trying to catch my breath.

He seemed stronger somehow, standing taller and straighter than before. "You gave me courage back there on the beach," he said, thrusting out his hand to shake mine. "I want to thank you for that."

"You made me feel stronger too. Please take these," I replied, passing the shirts to him.

"You don't have to do that," he protested.

"No, please," I said. "It would mean so much to me." I stuffed the cash into one hand.

He looked at me, his battered face breaking into a slow smile. "What's your name?"

"Kathy," I answered, extending my hand to shake his. "What's yours?"

"My name is Daniel."

My throat tightened and I stood motionless for a moment before asking, "Did you know that your name means 'beloved of God'?"

His rough hand enclosed mine. "I hope it's true. God bless you, Kathy—I'm starting over."

I never saw him again, so I don't know whether he was able to make a go of his life. But he helped me want to make a new start on mine. Meeting Daniel on the beach gave me a new beginning. With the devastation of the fire came purification, clearing the way for new seeds to sprout again.

We had flown back to London with Amy in mid-September, about a month and a half before the Malibu fire, for the memorial service at St. Bride's Church to celebrate the lives of Dan and his colleagues Hos, Anthony, and Hansi. St. Bride's, designed in the seventeenth century by England's greatest architect, Christopher Wren, is set in a quiet courtyard just off Fleet Street. For centuries it has served as the spiritual home of printers, overworked reporters, hacks who need a break, war correspondents home on leave, industry barons, and lowly runners. It's also the place where everyone who is anyone in the newspaper business has his memorial service.

Geoff and I decided to visit St. Bride's the day before the service. A cab deposited us near the narrow passage that led to the church, and we made our way through to the peaceful courtyard past a young tree that guarded the entrance. The sideways thrust of its tangled branches reminded me of the acacia tree standing guard near where Dan's ashes were scattered. I loved this little English tree, which wore a curious bark almost like a snakeskin, although it seemed out of place in the courtyard, surrounded by neat flowerbeds and perfectly trimmed magnolia trees.

Feeling wobbly, as though I were on board a heaving ship, I made my way into the sanctuary and down the side aisle toward a simple altar on which stood framed photographs of Dan and his three colleagues. A fat white candle flickered in front of each. Below, on the front of the altar, was a gold inscription: "And the word was made flesh and dwells among us." Dan's face was pale and glowing against the dark faces of smiling Somali children. I turned away, the image blurring before my eyes.

Geoff and I made our way to the back of the church and knocked on the door of Canon Oates, the rector. I wanted to meet the man who was shaping an event designed to create awareness of the dangers faced by war correspondents.

Canon Oates, who was in his office and glad to talk with us, explained that the memorial service was challenging to produce, as it had to be acceptable to all the religious sensibilities involved, including the fundamentalist Christian mothers of Kenyans Hos Maina and Anthony Macharia, the German Protestant mother of Hansi Krauss, Dan's Jewish grandmother and relatives, and my American Methodist family. At least he didn't have to worry about me: I believed that God is an intelligent force common to all the world's great religions.

"The service will be ecumenical, to say the least," Canon Oates promised. "We're expecting a large crowd," he added. "Everyone in this community was deeply moved by the tragedy. For them, it's 'There, but for the grace of God, go I.'"

The next morning Mike, Amy, and I hurried through spitting rain into the churchyard, as leaves from the little tree with the strange bark blew across our path. St. Bride's was so packed that ushers had to bring in more chairs for the latecomers. We sat together in the choir with the families of Hos and Anthony, the women in pretty flowered dresses and hats, the men and young brothers wearing new suits and solemn expressions. Opposite, Hansi's family was seated with a German delegation. Geoff, my father, Mike's mother and sister, and many of Dan's friends and mine were in the congregation, a mélange of races and cultures. Also in attendance were representatives of the British Foreign Office and the prime minister's staff, as well as a number of foreign diplomats and directors of various newspapers and broadcasting companies.

When Amy rose to speak, there was a deep silence. With her hair flowing halfway to her waist, she strode to the altar and paused for a moment to gather herself. I knew how nervous she was, but she lifted her head and explained that she was representing not only herself, but also the brothers and sisters of all the journalists killed.

I held my breath as her voice faltered. Then I breathed a sigh of relief as she continued, more forcefully this time: "Our four brothers were doing their best to show the people of the world what was happening in one tortured corner of Africa, and it is very difficult for us to understand why they were killed.

"We brothers and sisters have learned a difficult lesson. We thought we had a lifetime to tell each other how much we loved each other and how proud we were. But we didn't, and now I know that it's important to tell people how we feel, to make sure if our spirits fly out tomorrow, that we have resolved everything we possibly can in this life."

I squeezed Mike's hand and felt his fingers enclose mine in a gesture I recalled from long ago.

"My brother taught me that an individual *can* make a difference. You don't have to go to Somalia to make things better in this world. I would ask you, together with me, to make a new beginning—to pick up from where Anthony, Hos, Hansi, and Dan left off, to continue our journeys through life as they did, living with determination and compassion, with perseverance and kindness, and always with laughter and love."

As Amy rejoined Mike and me, our hands still tightly clasped together, I felt that she had begun a journey of transformation, turning her grief into a new purpose, one that I hoped would guide her life from then on. It made me proud to watch my warrior daughter—I was perhaps even a little surprised too, for it was always Dan who had been the noisy leader, with his "little sister" a quiet presence, bringing up the rear.

The St. Bride's choir sang the *African Sanctus*, swaying, drumming, and clapping with all the verve of an African choir, injecting so much life into the church that Christopher Wren might have sat up in his grave and sung along. As the lyrical notes of the music rose higher and higher, the sun burst through the windows, pouring light and warmth onto the congregation below. A dove appeared at one window, fluttering its wings to remain in place.

When the service was over, Mike led me out of the church. We sat for a moment beneath the little tree and he handed me a poem. Written with his whimsical sense of humor, it depicted Dan drawing his ethereal journals and organizing multicolored angels in heavenly pursuits. The last lines unlocked the tears I had struggled so hard to contain:

Whatever way
you spend your endless time
I wish you well, my son.
Live as fully now as you did
when you were here with us.

That evening we attended the opening of *Images of Conflict*, a powerful exhibition of sixty-four photographs taken by Dan and his colleagues during their time in Somalia—photos that had been reproduced in a book of the same name. Incredulous at the sight of the hundreds of people who had crowded into the gallery for the private viewing, I was even more amazed when Mark told me that the exhibit was already slated to travel to ten other countries. I wished I could have told Dan. He would have been so pleased.

29

The Message

THE MOMENTARY SENSE OF JOY I FELT AT THE SUCCESS OF THE *IMAGES OF Conflict* exhibit, and the sense of new beginning I felt after talking to Daniel, the homeless man, after the Malibu fire, quickly dissipated. Later that fall I was once again enveloped in a shroud of grief. I was even more depressed when a letter from Amy testified to her disintegration. She wrote of being imprisoned by pain and unable to tear out the "roots" of her sadness. Even so, she saw every night as a victory, for she had managed the impossible—making it through another day.

One evening she called with a note of desperation in her voice. "I can't do it anymore, Mumma. I can't go on without Dan. I don't want to live." I agreed with her: it would have been so much easier to leave behind forever the searing pain that engulfed me. But I knew I had to be brave for Amy.

Ultimately, the gift of grieving is the peace we feel when we finally accept the loss, realizing that although we may never get *over* it, we have at least gotten *through* it.

Despite my attempt to comfort her, I wasn't sure that I would ever be at peace again. The waves of grief and guilt that engulfed me came more frequently and lasted longer, and instead of getting better, I was barely hanging on to my sanity. Amy and I spoke often, trying to shore each other up. When she was down, I tried to be strong. When I was collapsing, she gave me a reason to continue. One day, unable to concentrate on her studies, she called in tears.

"Try to find someone to hug," I urged, remembering how good it had been for me to care about the homeless man on the beach. It seemed paltry advice to alleviate such profound sadness, but after our conversation, Amy signed up as a volunteer in a children's cancer ward and spent several afternoons a week playing with children who were as much in need of comfort as she was. Their parents' grief was something she understood and could share, while the love the children gave back gave her strength.

In one late-night call, she talked about how a critically ill six-year-old had asked her about death. "You know how a seagull sometimes soars off into the sky, leaving the flock behind," she had said gently. "Dying is like that. Even though we can't see the bird anymore, we know it's still flying,"

I so wanted to believe that was true, but I remained skeptical about the idea that Dan's spirit could still be alive. Then once again, out of the blue, something happened that made me think it just might be possible.

I was back in London for a few weeks when the telephone rang. "Mrs. Eldon?" the voice asked, sounding anxious. "It's Kwame Wiesel and I've got something I have to tell you." Kwame, one of Dan and Amy's friends from ISK, was now a musician and writer living in London.

Kwame said that for the past few years he had been paying annual visits to a medium named Brenda Lawrence to stay in touch with a dead uncle whose wisdom he valued. However, a few days ago, when he'd walked into her dining room, something peculiar had happened. Instead of connecting Kwame with his old relative, Brenda had described an enthusiastic, handsome, funny young man whose sense of humor kept her in giggles. It seemed obvious that the spirit knew Kwame very well, because he teased him about his latest girlfriend.

Over the course of the conversation, Kwame became convinced that the young man was Dan. Even the language was characteristic of his old friend, who kept referring to him as "man." After the third, "Hey, man, what's happening?" the medium laughingly told the spirit to "stop manning me!"

Kwame said he felt compelled to call me because Dan had wanted him to relay a message. "Tell my mother to stop taking those pills," he had said through Brenda. Kwame sounded embarrassed now as he asked whether that instruction meant anything to me.

It did. I explained that since Dan's death I had resorted to taking sleeping pills to combat my insomnia. Every time I downed one, I mentally apologized to him, aware of his aversion to medication.

"I'm so sorry, Mrs. Eldon," Kwame said. "I didn't want to upset you, but he was adamant about my getting in touch with you."

I hastened to reassure Kwame that he hadn't offended me and that I would stop taking the sleeping pills.

"I'll send you a tape of the session," he promised. "You'll see that I hardly said anything. Dan did all the talking."

Although incredulous at first, after I listened to the often-humorous conversation between "Dan," as relayed by the medium, and Kwame—a conversation that included information Brenda Lawrence could not possibly have known—I decided to book an interview with her. I gave a false name, as I had with Mollie Martin, just in case she had read any newspaper articles about Dan's death. Driving to her home in the London suburb of Richmond, I felt butterflies in my stomach, aware that I was setting myself up for major disappointment if Dan didn't come through.

Mrs. Lawrence, a comfortable woman in her midforties, disarmed me with her warmth as she ushered me into a cozy dining room and invited me to sit down at a round table covered with an embroidered white cloth.

"Would you like a cup of tea, dear?" she asked, and I nodded, determined not to say anything that would offer clues about myself. Brenda returned with a tea tray and placed it on the table next to a vintage tape recorder. "Do you want this taped?" she asked. I nodded again and pulled out my notepad to make doubly sure I didn't miss anything. She didn't waste any time on small talk.

"There's a young man trying awfully hard to get to you," she said. "He's jumping around so much that I think I'll let him settle down first." I could hardly breathe, barely daring to hope that it was Dan. "But there's someone else," she added.

I was disappointed when she began to describe the second man waiting to speak to me. She said he appeared to be in his midseventies and had suffered from a "wasting condition" but had died of a heart attack. Broad-shouldered and on the heavy side, he had a Mediterranean complexion, though he had become thin and sallow due to the illness. She said he was strong-willed and determined and had continued working until nearly the end of his life.

"He seems to be family of some kind, and he's sending you love." At first uncertain, I realized she was describing Mike's father, Bruno, a determined Romanian, who, though normally tanned and fit, had grown so frail while battling lung cancer that he'd had to give up a long career as a management consultant. A heart attack had been the cause of his death.

"Thank you, Bruno," I said, touched that he had turned up, though I hoped he would move aside and let the other, younger spirit come through. Brenda peered at the space above my shoulder. I followed her glance, but saw nothing. I recalled my encounter with the medium Rosemary Brown, when she had described spirits in my living room, an idea that had frightened me at the time. But now I wanted nothing more than to see one particular spirit: Dan.

"Yes, love, it's all right, darling," she said encouragingly. I looked around me, wishing I could make out the features of the person she was speaking with. She leaned over and confided, "He's gorgeous—a tall, handsome young man." She smiled and nodded, apparently listening to a conversation only she could hear. "He's saying, 'Mum, Mum,' so I guess it must be your son." Stifling a gasp, I reached for the tissues.

"He says his death was sudden." Brenda's next words poured out so quickly it was hard to write them down. "It wasn't an accident. Whatever happened was unexpected and unjust. He describes it as a 'travesty.'" Her hand touched the back of her head. "I feel dizzy and it hurts—just here. I think he must have died from a head wound." I couldn't say if she was right or wrong, because no one had told us the specific cause of Dan's death.

"He wants me to tell you that his passing was very quick. It was as though he was totally removed from the experience. One minute he was here; the next minute he was gone."

Brenda held up her hand, as though trying to slow down the flow of words in her head.

"Hold on, love," she requested. "We have plenty of time." She cocked her head to one side, listening again, then continued. "Your son seems to be describing a woman. He says she is wild and beautiful and he's sad that he isn't with her anymore. He says she's under cover somewhere, almost as if she were lying in state." I had no idea what she was talking about. As far as I knew, Dan didn't have any girlfriends who had died. I shook my head.

She looked at me quizzically. "He says that she needs her gear box stripped, her engine parts soaked in oil, and her transmission completely overhauled."

I burst out laughing as I remembered that his wild and beautiful Deziree, the ancient Land Rover, was propped up on blocks under a shelter in Lengai's family compound. "I understand," I said, but it was clear that she didn't.

Brenda focused for a moment and then said, "Now he's showing me lots of books. He's stuck pictures into them and wants you to make one book from them. Does this make sense?" I nodded. Dan wanted me to use the journals to create a book.

"You should use the proceeds from the book for a charity you're setting up in your son's name," Brenda said. "It should benefit children." This too made sense. We had just started a bank account for a Dan Eldon Memorial Fund and were using the money we had raised to refit his more recent Land Cruiser, Big Blue, still standing in front of my London flat, to give to a children's orphanage in Croatia.

"Now he's talking about seeing his photos on display." I thought about *Images of Conflict*. Could he have been there with me when the show opened? "He's happy about that but says that now you must inspire forgiveness and tolerance in all that you do. Man's inhumanity to his fellow man is due to ignorance, not intent, he says. Children must be taught not to hate."

That upset me, because as much as I wanted to share that message for Dan, I still couldn't forgive the Somalis for what they had done—and wasn't sure I ever would. I didn't say what I was thinking, afraid that my negativity might put a damper on the one-sided conversation.

"Do you have any questions?" Brenda asked.

"How is he? What's he doing?" I asked, crumpling the tissue in my hand. There was a pause and I worried that she might have lost him, but then she continued with a smile. "He says he's learning how to make things happen."

Although it was a general comment, applicable to anyone, I pictured Dan hawking T-shirts to the angels and hustling postcards to the saints.

Suddenly serious, she said, "You have tremendous work ahead of you that will be profound in its nature. There will be more exhibitions; you'll be speaking to large groups, writing a book, and making a film about your son."

I had heard some of that from Mollie Martin, but it still seemed highly unlikely. Aside from the article about Dan for the *Daily Telegraph*, I had barely written for publication since leaving Kenya five years before; and aside from saying a few words at his memorial service, I hadn't given a speech in years. She was way off track on this one. Still, I felt overwhelmed by the possibility that she might be right.

"How can I do all this?" I asked, as I had asked Mollie Martin, unable to imagine how I could ever fulfill Dan's requests.

"Your son says that he and his 'Team Spirit' will be helping you," said Brenda, beaming. His silly pun made me smile too.

Serious again, she asked, "Does the name Gaga, no—Gugu—make any sense to you?"

I shook my head, uncertain what she was talking about. Then I laughed out loud and explained that Dan's beloved Uncle Sergiu, or Gugu for short, had died a few years earlier.

"I also see United Nations flags around you and your daughter," Brenda continued.

Completely bewildered, I shook my head. "I doubt it." I had last visited the UN when I was ten and couldn't imagine what would ever take me back to New York. "Just keep it in mind," she said.

"One more thing," Brenda added as she shook my hand at the door. "Your son is sending you love and reminding you that he is always with you."

"Where is he?" I asked, looking around, again wishing I could catch a glimpse of him.

"Right there," she said, pointing to a spot just left of my head. "Like an angel on your shoulder."

Despite my reservations, I drove home whistling. Later I played the tape for Geoff, who agreed that I had said nothing that would have given Brenda Lawrence any clues about Dan's life—or details of his death. However far-fetched the idea might be, after two remarkable experiences—first through Mollie, then through Brenda—it was getting harder and harder to deny his continuing presence. Even the skeptical journalist in me had to admit that there was something going on that defied logical explanation. Mollie and Brenda—and Dan—had given me convincing grounds for believing that life doesn't end with death. In fact, the end seemed to be a brand-new beginning. But the beginning of what?

30

Images of Conflict

THE *IMAGES OF CONFLICT* EXHIBITION WAS PROVING TO BE A GREAT SUCCESS in various venues and was now on its way to Kenya. There was no time to think about Dan's other requests before I had to fly to its opening in Nairobi in November 1993.

Kenya's President Daniel arap Moi launched the event at the Gallery Watatu. Surrounded by a dozen burly bodyguards, the president toured the exhibition and honored the four dead journalists in a speech that asked people to understand the sacrifices made by correspondents in the name of truth. There was a certain irony in his words, as Kenya didn't have the best record when it came to press freedom.

Next, Mike announced the founding of a new center, the DEPOT— the Dan Eldon Place of Tomorrow—located on an old farm in Limuru, about twenty miles from Nairobi. Named after Dan's eternally messy room, which he called his "depot," the center Mike had spearheaded was backed by the Rotary Club. Mike described it as a kind of "Outward Bound on the savanna," designed to encourage creativity and offer leadership training, especially to youth.

Once the show was declared officially open, more than six hundred people, the largest number to attend an opening in the history of the gallery, flowed through the room, viewing Dan's Masai headdresses and spears, his collection of journals, his maps, and even his battered old chair. Many of the artifacts from his bedroom had been moved into the series of spacious rooms, along with sixty framed prints, photographs, and collages. His books, postcards, and posters were on sale, as well as T-shirts, *kikoy*s, pants, bags, and hats decorated with motifs from his art. Standing in a corner of the gallery, I studied the rapt faces surveying Dan's images and imagined how delighted he would have been to be there too. Then it occurred to me that, if I were to believe my conversation with Brenda, he probably *was* there—an idea that delighted me.

Wandering through the room, I tried to take in the scope of Dan's myriad images—most new to me, to my surprise. I stopped in front of a large framed black-and-white photo, apparently shot by Dan while perched high in a scraggly tree. He had aimed his camera straight down at a cluster of half-naked, smiling African children, their hands outstretched toward him, trying to catch a soccer ball that hung in the middle of the frame. I realized that Dan must have retrieved a ball stuck in the branches of the tree, then tossed it down, managing, in one split second, to capture the anticipation and joy on the kids' faces as they tried to catch it.

That frozen moment stopped me in my tracks. I was Dan's mother and should have known him better than anyone, but seeing those new images reflecting moments that I hadn't shared or, in many instances, even known existed, brought him to life in a brand-new way. It was unexpected, unsettling, but ultimately exciting to learn so much about Dan through his work. Most intriguing for me was his unique way of exposing people on camera, revealing them for who and what they were— good, or otherwise. His keen photographer's eye made words unnecessary. The pictures said it all.

In that crowded gallery, surrounded by so many people, I had yet another epiphany. Standing in front of Dan's searing images from Somalia, I realized that he had gone through his dark night of the soul and had come out the other side. His passion for expression, for the revelation of hidden truths, had become his life's purpose. In that respect he was luckier than the many people who never figure out who they are or what they are all about. Despite his youth, Dan had listened and understood the message of Delphi, "Know thyself," and had died being true to himself. Perhaps that's all any of us can hope for.

Although at the exhibit I found myself embraced by scores of old friends and strangers, of all races and religions, and was swept along by a spirit of love and acceptance, outside in the streets Kenya had changed radically. In the few years since I had left the country, the population had swelled to nearly thirty million. Jobs were impossible to find, and unemployment was rampant among young people, which had led to a huge rise in crime. Carjackings were common and violent robberies an everyday fact of life. Thanks to the influx of Somali refugees, anyone could buy an AK-47 for ten dollars on the street.

Still, as challenging as the current situation was, I was glad to be back in Kenya, though it felt strange revisiting a place where marriages were still in a constant state of flux. There were new pairings everywhere among the Kenyans I knew, a continuous game of marital musical chairs. Many of the women were alone, their husbands having left them.

On my last day, I visited Valerie Leakey, now living on her own with her three daughters, Philip having moved on to another woman. I recalled how lost I had been without Mike in the early days and wondered how she was handling the separation.

On my way to the Leakey's house, I nearly got lost looking for the narrow dirt track off the main road that used to wind through plains dotted with wildlife. Although still unpaved, it had turned into a busy thoroughfare lined with tin-roofed houses and crude buildings made of concrete blocks. *Matatus* careened past, and so did trucks packed with chickens and kids, the derelict vehicles billowing black smoke as they labored up the hills.

I had to talk my way past Valerie's guard, who reluctantly opened the rickety gate leading to her house. I recalled the first time I had visited their mud house, dimly lit with light flickering from hurricane lamps that hummed in their tiny living room. Over the years, their simple dwelling had evolved into a double-storied, respectable stone house with electricity and a water pump, though the lights still ran on a generator fueled with gas carried from town in cylinders. The water was the color of the river that still ran through the gorge below.

Valerie and I sat on the terrace overlooking the place where Lara's *ayah* Wanjiru had confronted an angry lion with her broom. She seemed as strong as ever, though a bit sad when she pointed out the site of that long-ago New Year's Eve party, now a jungle of twisted tree trunks overgrown with rough brush and roots. As we recalled that evening and all the adventures we had shared as young wives and mothers, I felt a sense of nostalgia, realizing how much I missed my old life in Africa. Suddenly, I wanted to go back in time, to leap over the years and be thirty again; innocent, filled with hope and promise, married to Mike with two little children, yearning for peace, harmony, openness, and friendship in my marriage. If only I could try my life all over again and see if I could do a better job, hurt fewer people along the way, including myself.

Tiana appeared at the door and I hugged her, recalling the last time we had seen each other: in London, on my birthday, when she "flew" with my help. It seemed a lifetime ago. We sat together, sharing homemade cake while Valerie shared the news, telling stories of death and disaster that she listed as though ingredients in a recipe. "Life must go on," she said with a shrug when I asked her how she coped with so much tragedy.

There was a quick movement and a tiny dik-dik dashed for cover in the dense bush across the gorge. Above us, dots in the clear blue sky, a pair of hawks circled. The air smelled like honey and cut grass. Kenya still was paradise, if you didn't look too closely.

"What about you, Kathy?" Valerie said, turning her glance to me. "We need you here. Why don't you come back and live with people who care about you?"

Since leaving Kenya, I had often wondered why I continued to reject the place that had welcomed me so warmly. But I knew in my heart that there was something I had to do in and with my life, and I couldn't do it here.

Later, as I headed back across the plains, spirals of dust swirled into a dense cloud behind my borrowed car. Rattling over the rutted track, I was aware of how soft I had become, removed from the elemental challenges of life lived on the edge; now I was bubble-wrapped, safety-capped, insured, preserved, insulated, and cushioned from anything that might cause me harm. Maybe at least after this visit I could be more courageous as I tried to transform Dan's death into something that could give extra meaning to life wherever I lived.

As I rattled down the potholed road back to Nairobi, I thought about how hard it had been to say goodbye to Valerie and my other friends here and, above all, how difficult it would be to leave Mike. When we'd been together over the past week, we had enjoyed each other more than we had since we were courting. I laughed at his jokes and he at mine. Every morning, I went up from the downstairs guest room and joined him for breakfast on his bed—formerly our bed—sharing toast and tea on dishes I had chosen as a young bride, served on a battered metal tray we had received as a wedding present in what seemed like another lifetime. Surrounded by my old belongings, it felt completely natural to be together with Mike. We weren't pushing each other away in blame or anger, or sitting in frozen silence. The pressure was off. And therefore, almost miraculously, we had found the friendship, the peace, I'd always hoped for.

But now it was too late, for this would be the last time we would ever spend this kind of time together. Mike was seriously involved with Evelyn Mungai, the Kenyan businesswoman who had offered me such supportive reassurance after Dan's death. A dedicated entrepreneur and humanitarian, she had much in common with Mike, who had brought her into his Rotary Club as the first woman member. As I thought about them together, I felt a wave of nostalgia for the couple Mike and I once were and wondered if perhaps there was still a chance for us to be together if their relationship didn't work out.

The day I was to leave Kenya, I spent a long time in Dan's room. Though many of his belongings were now at the DEPOT, Masai shields still lined the walls and his bookshelves were still filled with dusty books and treasures. It looked as though he had dashed out of the room on an errand and would return at any moment, and I thought I could feel his lingering presence. I stroked the plaster mask of his face that Nani had made when he was sixteen years old, and sat at the desk where he had created his journals. His view was the tops of trees, and the startling expanse of sky I loved so much.

"Are you here, Dan?" I whispered, listening hard inside. "I'm scared. I don't know what's coming next." There was silence and I thought he must have moved on, but then a tune came into my mind, and I hummed the closing bars of the song I had taught the children from *The King and I:*

Make believe you're brave and the trick will take you far;
you may be as brave as you make believe you are!

Yapping as he always had, Murdoch, Dan's Jack Russell, bounded into the room. Scruffy and frayed around the edges, he was much the worse for wear after too many battles with the big bully dogs in the neighborhood. Dan always said Murdoch hadn't figured out he was a dog. "He thinks he's a buffalo," he would say, laughing, pointing out that Murdoch hadn't come to terms with the fact he was barely more than a foot long and weighed fourteen pounds soaking wet. Murdoch sniffed Dan's old shoes and looked up expectantly. I patted his head. "Come on, boy, it's time to go."

I said goodbye to the staff lined up by the car to wish me farewell. I missed William, but without Dan to help him out he had returned to his *shamba* in western Kenya. Mike opened the car door for me and I slid onto the seat, fighting back the emotion that threatened to overwhelm me. I waved as he got behind the wheel and we pulled out of the drive, narrowly missing Murdoch, who ran along beside, barking wildly.

At the airport, Mike and I held each other for a long time. As we pulled apart, he said, "I love you."

"I love you too," I whispered back, unable to see him properly through my tears.

When I got back to L.A., Amy told me that she had decided to take a semester off from Lafayette and was planning to move to New York City, where she would work as a waitress while trying to figure out what to do next.

Meanwhile, I was determined to tackle the task of fulfilling Dan's request to use his death as a form of inspiration. I didn't have a clue how to start, but the answer came in a most unexpected way, when I called to thank his journalist friend Donatella Lorch for the powerful piece she had written about Dan and his friends in the *New York Times Magazine* a month or so after their death. Donatella said she thought that her mother, Maristella, who headed the Italian Academy for Advanced Studies in America at Columbia University, might be able to help me. As Maristella and I spoke on the phone, we discovered that we shared a desire to raise awareness of the dangers faced by foreign correspondents in war-torn countries. Stories and pictures from these countries appear routinely in our morning papers or on the news, but how they get there is anyone's guess.

Together, we two mothers hatched an idea: an international symposium we called "War and Peace in Somalia: The Role of the Media, an International Perspective." We planned it for February 1994 in the rotunda of Columbia's Low Memorial Library, an imposing gray neoclassical building at the center of the university campus. Gathering my courage, I called broadcaster Dan Rather, who promised to give the keynote address. Once he was on board, a dazzling roster of high-powered leaders and eminent journalists agreed to speak as well—among them former UN undersecretary Brian Urquhart, president and CEO of the Associated Press Lou Boccardi, and Reuters editor-in-chief Mark Wood. Several hundred people were invited to the two-day symposium, which would be covered by major media outlets.

On the day before the conference, my parents took the last flight out of snowbound Cedar Rapids, Mike arrived from Kenya, and his mother ignored a new hip replacement to make it from London. Maristella had asked me to speak, a daunting prospect considering the eminent crowd. The night before the event, I locked myself away in my hotel room, breathing a sigh of relief as my fingers began to fly over the typewriter keys, turning out a three-page speech in record time. Once again, I didn't recognize the words as mine, causing me to wonder about the nature of inspiration. Was it possible that I was channeling thoughts from somewhere, or was I tapping into a higher wisdom within myself?

The next morning dawned crisp and cold, with a dusting of new snow over a blanket of dirty slush. I entered the great rotunda with a sense of awe, watching as the seats filled with students, academics, diplomats, journalists, and media industry leaders from around the world, aware for the first time that out of a great tragedy had come a new opportunity: a chance to create new understanding among people who could use media to help shape a better world.

In his opening address, Dan Rather implored the audience to be aware of the individuals who risk their lives every day to bring us the truth. His message was repeated in various ways throughout the morning, as foreign correspondents and their bosses communicated the importance of media in shaping international policy. My turn to speak came at lunchtime. Battling a pounding headache, I barely glanced at my notes, praying that the right words would flow through me. As if listening to someone else, I heard myself begin, "My son was devastated by what he saw and had to shut down his heart to do his job. None of us can read the paper or watch television with our hearts wide open. The pain would be too great."

I scanned the upturned faces of the journalists and editors as I begged them to reconnect their heads and hearts and use the media to stir, stimulate, inspire, and galvanize people into action to help create a more peaceful world. Paraphrasing the words of St. Francis of Assisi, I said, "Where there is violence, let us make a move toward gentleness; where there is anger, let us begin to forgive; where there is chaos, let us find harmony; and where there is hatred, let us learn to love."

That day I spoke not as a journalist but as a mother on behalf of all mothers. When I finished, there was a long silence and I could see many handkerchiefs in use. I was aware that somehow the words I had spoken had touched the hearts of those present. But when the audience stood to applaud, I knew it wasn't for me. I was merely a conduit for information and inspiration from somewhere else—or so it seemed to me. Still, it was a moment of transcendence and a foreshadowing of what could lie ahead, if I only had the strength to take that challenging path.

The *Images of Conflict* exhibition was on display in the university rotunda and I watched silently, my heart overflowing with pride, as students filed by framed enlargements of photos by Dan and his fellow journalists. In a section featuring Dan's collages, I saw images of his adventurous safaris, young women he had loved, the horrors of fighting and famine, his *joie de vivre*, even his dire quotation from Plato, "Only the dead have seen the end of war." It seemed that nothing had changed in the last two thousand years.

A shot of a newly arrived young American soldier touching fingers with a delighted Somali child stood in stark contrast to one of a haggard Marine standing guard before the ugly cavity in a stone wall that had been blasted by a mortar shell. Oddly, the cavity resembled a human face—its mouth open in an anguished cry. Only one photo raised a smile from viewers. In Dan's last published image, taken on the beach in Mogadishu the day before he was killed, a pair of blond female Marines wearing miniscule bikinis lie on brightly colored towels beside their neatly stacked rifles.

Just before I left the exhibit that day, a young man pulled me aside. "I've been looking for a new path in my life," he said, his eyes shining. "Your son inspired me and has pointed out the direction I'll take in the future. Thank you."

I was able to help the Associated Press and Reuters organize a second seminar a few months later when news anchor Tom Brokaw agreed to open a similar conference at Duke University. There a spokesperson for the United Nations announced that the organization was changing its regulations: from that week on, its helicopters would be insured to transport non-UN personnel, including journalists. Had the rule been in force a year earlier, Dan and his colleagues could have been saved by the helicopter hovering over them during the attack. It was a bittersweet gift.

Over the next few years, thanks to increased awareness about the dangers faced by frontline journalists, additional changes were made: freelance photographers and writers were finally able to obtain life insurance when working in conflict zones, and news-agency bureau chiefs stopped pooh-poohing the idea of post-traumatic stress disorder in photographers and correspondents who covered wars, famine, and other horrifying situations. Still, the biggest challenge remains to this day: how to inspire ordinary people to care about what they read in the news or view on television and respond in ways that can change our world for the better.

31

The Journey Is the Destination

SOON AFTER THE CONFERENCE AT DUKE, AMY CALLED TO SAY SHE HAD MADE a monumental decision. I assumed she had chosen a new college to attend in the autumn.

"No," she replied laughingly. "I cut my hair!"

I listened as she described how she'd sat in front of a stylist as he surveyed the locks that flowed halfway down her back.

"Take it all off," she'd said. Gripping his scissors, he'd fixed her with a penetrating stare. "Someone left you, didn't he, darling?"

"Yes," she'd said decisively. "And now it's time to move on."

I knew she was right, but a new haircut wasn't going to solve my problems.

The difficulties between Geoff and me had grown worse, and our constant bickering had eroded the foundations of our relationship. The death of a child can threaten even the most secure bond, and ours had never been that stable. Alone in America, where our work kept us, without a circle of friends or family, we felt like two corks tossed about on a stormy sea. Something had to change.

The two of us talked about it endlessly, trying to find a way to keep what we had that was precious, while letting go of the noxious parts. One thing we agreed on is that we had to find a place to live in Los Angeles—no more of this "camping out" at a hotel—if I was ever to realize my new dream of making a film about what Dan had once called his "mission on earth." Geoff and I decided to visualize the ideal home. Together we wrote down every detail: a light-filled apartment in a low-rise complex surrounded by shrubs and trees above Sunset Boulevard, where the air is cleaner and the views are more expansive.

"I'd love a swimming pool," Geoff said, "and a Jacuzzi." I protested that our wish list was getting out of hand.

"You always tell me miracles happen," he replied. "So let's give it a try." I added to our list a swimming pool set among beds of flowers and, at the last minute, a Jacuzzi. Then I called an agent with details of our vision.

"It's unlikely you'll get anything like that at the price you have in mind," the agent said, "but I'll give it try."

After days of seeing cramped, dark apartments in our price range, we agreed to rent a modest apartment off Melrose Boulevard. Then, on the day that we were due to sign the lease, the agent called.

"I've got something that just came on the market. It's a bit out of your price range, but have a look anyway." He gave me an address on a quiet street half a block above Sunset Boulevard, in West Hollywood.

Stepping through a wrought-iron gate, Geoff and I entered what seemed like another world. Pots of crimson geraniums and yellow daisies surrounded an immaculate swimming pool, brilliant purple bougainvillea tumbled through the slats of a latticework enclosure, and tall palm trees rustled against the sky. In the distance I could see the blossoms of a jacaranda tree just like those we'd had in Kenya, and the scent of gardenias wafted through the air. The unit for rent was on the upper floor of the two-unit Sunset Plaza building, more like a house than a condominium. Inside, huge windows offered a spectacular view stretching across Los Angeles to the ocean. And yes, there was even a bubbling Jacuzzi. The price was over our limit, but the owner agreed to a rent we could afford and we moved in the next day.

We loved it. But despite that improvement in our living arrangement, Geoff and I were still battling all the time. A few weeks after we settled into the new place, we reluctantly concluded that sometimes the kindest thing you can do for a person you care about, and are living with but are constantly fighting, is to let him or her go. He made plans to return to my flat in London, while I would remain in Los Angeles. That way we would be able to work together and visit each other but continue our relationship more harmoniously.

We returned to London so I could pack, comforted by the thought that at least we each had a home of our own. Our final days together were sad, but with the tough decision already made, we were gentle. We were determined to avoid blame, and I remained grateful to Geoff, who had taught me to communicate important issues and ideas through the medium of film.

I was folding the last few clothes into my suitcase when Amy called to tell me that she had made another big decision. She would go back to college and had sent in applications to Boston and Columbia Universities. I could barely contain my delight. That good feeling was still warming me when a knock came at my door: my taxi was waiting outside.

I rushed into the bathroom for one last look at the dancing women on the wall, still whirling and twirling in their circle of love. Impulsively, I pulled the sun god off his nail and stuck him into my bag. I would need his company in Los Angeles. As I did so, I could almost hear Amy's voice: "New beginning number six-four-three-nine!"

When I arrived back at the Sunset Plaza, I unpacked my bags and pulled out my brass sun god. I felt a familiar shiver down the back of my neck as I polished it with my sleeve, marveling at how much life it had seen in the years since Mike and I had picked it up in the old flea market in Sri Lanka. As it began to gleam, I listened within, trying to hear the wisdom that had guided me during the terrible days after I had left Kenya, and again after Dan's death. It had been months since I had meditated, but I breathed deeply and heard these words:

Realize that you are standing on the shore of your future existence. When the time is right—and you are not to determine that time—a great wave will crash upon it and the swell will take you out to sea, sweeping everything along in its wake. It is then that you will begin your true job on this planet.

Although retaining a healthy skepticism about the nature of these communications, I listened closely.

Amy arrived in Los Angeles for a nice long visit before heading back to college. Slimmer than before, and more confident with her stylish new bob, she was clearly excited about the future, though we were both painfully aware that the first anniversary of Dan's death was just one month away.

"We've got to make it special, Mumma," Amy said. I agreed but couldn't imagine what we could do. Then she had an idea.

"I know, we'll declare July 12th "International 'Do it, Dammit' Day!" she announced triumphantly. Reaching for her colored pens, she started to make a flyer, decorating the margins of her paper with a beaming sun god and dancing angels, complete with halos. One angel, in shorts and carrying a pitchfork, looked remarkably like Dan. She added the following text:

JULY 12TH

July 12th is nearly upon us. But before you roll over and sleep through the day, think what mischief Dan would have made! Join us for:

"DO IT, DAMMIT" DAY!

Please select from the following:

Hug a Land Rover
Start a journal
Apply a well-toned, naked body to your skin
Make a grump laugh
Do something you've always been afraid to do
Blast Tosca, reggae, or Piaf
Take someone you love on a picnic

We sent off more than a hundred letters around the world, laughing—and crying—as we licked the stamps. We were beginning to heal but were discovering that scar tissue takes a long time to cover open wounds. I was slowly beginning to accept Dan's death, and sometimes hours would go by when I didn't think about my son. However, the idea of forgetting him, even for such a brief time, felt like a total betrayal. Worse still, it seemed that my vivid memories of our life together were beginning to blur; his characteristic gestures and outrageous wit were not as clear as they had been, and the stories I loved to tell were fading from my memory. I couldn't remember certain incidents we had shared, moments that I'd always thought were indelibly etched in my mind. Nevertheless, after I stopped continuously recalling Dan's life—and death—a stream of new ideas and thoughts started to flow through me, smoothing and dulling the nightmarish recollections that had haunted me for so long.

It seemed that my brain was reorganizing itself, quietly, inexorably, moving me from total despair toward gentle acceptance. However, I was reluctant to completely give up the familiar, if now less searing, pain that lurked at the fringes of my soul.

Amy was going through a similar process, and a few months after the anniversary of Dan's death called me in tears. "Mumma, I'm forgetting so much about Dan," she said, horrified. "I'm scared I won't remember anything soon."

She read me a few lines from her journal that expressed exactly how I felt too:

> I wish I had taken time to memorize Dan. It's like when I try to remember a poem word for word but then I forget entire stanzas and maybe even pages.

Desperately seeking something that might comfort her, I happened to catch sight of the dream catcher hanging over my bed. Created by a Native American craftsperson to "capture" bad dreams, the little bent-wood hoop, decorated with feathers and beads, triggered something in my mind.

"I know," I said, making it up as I went along. "You can create an Angel Catcher."

"What's that?" She sounded skeptical.

"It's a book that you can fill with pictures, stories, letters, poems—whatever will remind you of your brother," I said. "It will help you express your feelings and remember details about him. You can have it forever. One day," I added hopefully, "you can show it to your children when they ask about their uncle Dan." She promised to try.

Whenever we talked about our memories of Dan, the image of him working on the vibrant pages of his journal was apt to surface in our minds. Since his death we had located seventeen of his black-bound books, filled with his pictures, photographs, drawings, and collages, and those were all now with me. I had found three hidden away in my London apartment, we had discovered eleven in Nairobi, and my aunt in Northridge, California, had called to say she had just uncovered three boxes that Dan had left in her garage during his UCLA days. Hoping to discover more in them than journals, I had driven there immediately and located the packing boxes with some trepidation, uncertain what might be buried there.

In the first I found nothing but a pile of rank-smelling leather belts, the last of the bric-a-brac that Geoff and I had smuggled into the United States after Dan's Moroccan adventure. The next held only art supplies, including dried-up paints, inkpots, and brushes. The last box was hardest to open, but when I slit the tape and opened the flaps, I discovered what I had been hoping for: three bulging black journals carefully wrapped in colorful *kikoy*s. Strangely, instead of feeling triumphant, I felt like an intruder, trespassing on private territory, and closed the boxes quickly before loading them into the car.

When I arrived back home, I braced myself to go through the books. I had looked at quite a few with Dan over the years, but I was often in too much of a hurry to fully concentrate on what he was showing me. If his death had taught me one thing, it was to be present in the moment, and I knew now that this was the moment to fulfill his request to share with others the experiences he'd recorded in his journals. I spent hours leafing through the pages, savoring the words and images, the humor and life that flowed through them.

Throughout each book, Dan asked questions in his distinctive handwriting, including one that both delighted and haunted me: *What's the difference between exploring and being lost?* And what may have been his ultimate answer: *The journey is the destination.* I also loved a vibrant double-paged spread of an African savanna decorated with feathers, alongside paper cutouts of buffaloes, a cheetah, and, incongruously, a Buddhist monk. Watched by a grinning red sun god, a tiny stick-figure like those I had sent him cartwheels across the horizon, a reminder of how I imagined Dan to be—eternally, joyously, defying gravity.

After studying every page, I cradled one journal close to me, as I would have held the grandchild I would never have from him. I tried to be comforted by a quotation that Dan had copied on three different pages in a single journal: *Death is a horizon, and a horizon is just the limit of one's vision.*

Inspired by Brenda's request, relayed from Dan, I wrote a proposal for a book based on his journals—a book that I hoped would inspire other young people to follow their dreams. Stuffing four volumes into a carry-on case, I flew to New York to discuss the project with various publishing companies.

"Beautiful," the first editor commented, thumbing through the pages of one of them. "But if the artist is dead, how could we promote the book?" Closing it, she turned to me with a frown. "I'm afraid it isn't for us," she said, "but we'll keep the proposal on file in case something changes."

I got the same response wherever I went. The work was good, but a collection of images created by a dead twenty-two-year-old wasn't commercially viable. Sadly, I hid the journals away in my bedroom closet. It was far too painful to have them in sight.

Money was tight. My share of what Geoff and I had earned making *Lost in Africa* was gone, and I had nothing to pay the rent. One morning, realizing that I must have been crazy to leave the love and security Geoff had provided, I stood in front of a picture of Dan on the bureau in my bedroom.

"I'm so mad at you!" I cried, growing even more distraught when I thought about never again seeing Dan's crooked grin. Memories flooded over me—Dan, arms open wide, standing with a bunch of flowers, waiting for me, or dragging me along on his latest adventure. I longed to sit beside him, talking until midnight or leafing with him through his latest journal. As much as I wanted to believe that his spirit might still be around, it wasn't enough. I wanted him to be physically there—to be flesh-and-blood *real*. Suddenly, feeling very vulnerable and alone, not to mention foolish, I whispered, "Who's going to look after me when I'm old? Why did you have to leave me? *I need you!*"

It sounds too absurd to be true, but just then—as if Dan had heard me and intervened—the telephone rang and a male voice announced himself as Robert Coles, the editor of *DoubleTake* magazine. He had seen Dan's work at the traveling exhibition at Duke University, he said, and wanted to feature five pages of his journals in the next issue of his photographic magazine.

"We'll be paying the usual stipend," he said, quoting a figure that would pay the rent for the next three months. As I put down the phone, I heard a noise in the living room and hurried in to see what had caused it. I looked around but spotted nothing until my eyes caught sight of my sun god, which had fallen off the wall. When I went to hang it up again, I noticed that both the hook and the wire were perfectly intact. What, I wondered, had made it jump off the wall? As I hung it up again, it smiled its cryptic smile. And I smiled back.

The five-page feature came out in November, strategically placed at the very end of the magazine. The journal pages seemed to glow next to my words describing Dan's brief life.

A few days later I received a call from Annie Barrows, an editor with Chronicle Books in San Francisco, who said she had seen my article and wanted to view the journals. The next weekend she flew down to meet me and turned out to be a feisty young woman Dan would have appreciated.

After we had been through the journals carefully together, she outlined her idea for a selection of pages representing Dan's changing interests over the years. Chronicle quickly gave the project the go-ahead. During the next few months, Annie returned several times to L.A. to work on the book, which we decided to call *The Journey Is the Destination*. From the seventeen hundred journal pages, she selected over two hundred to reproduce in full color. Boldly, she decided to let Dan's images speak for themselves; there would be no captions, and the only text would be an introduction in which I would tell the story of his short life.

Annie confessed that several times she had awakened in the middle of the night feeling as though Dan had been watching over her shoulder and wanted to say something to her. More than once, she had changed the order of the images or added another page as a result. When I didn't hear from her for a while in mid-September, I assumed she was busy preparing for her baby, due in mid-October. It was many weeks later that I discovered her daughter had been born four weeks early, on September 18—coincidentally, Dan's birthday.

The Journey Is the Destination was published in October of 1997. It was reviewed widely, including in *Time* magazine, the *New Yorker*, and *USA Today*, as well as in scores of other papers and magazines around the world. Perhaps the review that touched me most was the one that ran in the *Washington Post*, which described the book as "a talismanic journal of an artist's youth." The reviewer added, "For young people who doubt that a life grander than MTV and the mall can be achieved in this age, Eldon's journals prove otherwise."

Although the book contains few words, it continues to ignite the spirit of people who want more than simply to survive their lives. Since its publication, Dan's book has sold more than one hundred thousand copies worldwide, and I have received hundreds of calls, letters, and e-mails from people thanking me for the inspiration it has provided them. Oprah Winfrey helped spread Dan's message to millions of people around the world, not once but three times on her show.

One of the most startling calls was from a young woman who introduced herself as Mei-Ling Hsu, a reporter from the *Beijing Youth News*, a paper with a readership of over two and a half million people. She was working on an article about Dan and wanted some further information. Her next words startled me. "We consider Dan to be a hero of the Chinese people," she said.

"Dan would never consider himself to be a hero," I protested, knowing how much he would have hated that description. "He was just an ordinary young man who saw the world in an extraordinary way."

She disagreed. "No," she said emphatically, "during his life, he tried to bring people together, to break down the barriers that separate us from one another. He saw the best in those he met and encouraged them to live not only for themselves, but for others as well. That's why I believe he is a hero."

Mei-Ling sent me her article a few weeks later: a two-page spread with several pictures. There was a note attached: "He changed my life. Thank you."

32

Dying to Tell the Story

AT CHRISTMAS, AMY WAS BARELY IN THE DOOR WHEN SHE REACHED INTO her backpack and pulled out a black-bound book.

"It's my Angel Catcher," she said proudly. As together we turned the pages of her journal, she pointed out the quotations, drawings, photographs, and stories about Dan that she had included. Every entry brought back a world of memories, reminding me of who he was—and who he remains in the minds of those who love him.

Among Amy's comments were descriptions of her feelings after Dan had been killed. One in particular touched me:

> I discovered how few things seemed really important in life. Petty arguments, parking tickets, and lousy boyfriends didn't matter so much to me anymore. I decided that love and honesty were far more important and that I would try to resolve all problems with those I loved, so if I died suddenly I wouldn't have any regrets.

Amy showed her Angel Catcher to friends, both hers and mine, who had also suffered the loss of someone dear to them. We discovered that many people wanted to use the concept to create their own book. At first we simply photocopied the pages, but we couldn't keep up with the demand; so eventually we submitted the concept of a guided journal to Chronicle Books, which accepted it. *Angel Catcher: A Journal of Loss and Remembrance* encourages mourners to deal with their feelings by expressing them through art, poetry or essay writing, and other creative outlets they might invent on their own. It also suggested that readers celebrate and commemorate the life of someone who has passed on by planting a tree, starting a garden, or helping a child in need.

After completing the journal, Amy and I realized yet again that humans can't rush through the grieving process. Each phase must be endured; every feeling experienced. It's foolish to deny our anger or pain or seek to avoid them by keeping busy all the time or by traveling. We need to grieve a husband, wife, or best friend whose life brought meaning to our own, or a pet whose love kept us company. Over time we will find new focus for our lives, new people and activities to fill the emptiness we feel, but there are no shortcuts to grieving, and no way out— only through.

As I have discovered, the more imaginatively we delve into our sadness, the greater our capacity for joy will be when we eventually emerge from our tunnel of darkness. For humans are capable of rising above their sorrow to regenerate and expand. We can even learn to dance again—and one day, perhaps, even to fly.

I moved another step closer to recovery when the Freedom Forum, a nonpartisan foundation advocating free press and speech, asked me to speak at the dedication of a memorial to dead journalists at the Newseum, a museum of journalism in Arlington, Virginia (later relocated to the nation's capital). First Lady Hillary Clinton was to be the guest of honor.

The temperature was hovering around 113 degrees when Amy and I arrived at the memorial, located outside the Newseum. My throat tightened at the sight of the magnificent glass tribute, nearly two stories high, etched with the names of over one thousand journalists who had died in the past hundred years while covering the news. I found Dan's name near those of Hansi, Hos, and Anthony. Amy and I stood for moment, all too aware of the three blank glass panels awaiting future names.

I was nervous as I searched for my seat and relieved when I was intercepted by Canon Oates, the vicar of St. Bride's Church, who had flown to Washington for the occasion.

"You'll be fine," he said, kissing me on both cheeks. "Just relax and let the words flow."

It was easy for him, I thought, with God on his side. Meanwhile, my hair was plastered to my head with perspiration. One of the ushers led Amy and me down the aisle to our assigned seats, and we sank down with relief.

We jumped up again almost immediately as the First Lady and her entourage swept into the enclosure and headed straight for the row of vacant seats in front of us. Elegant in an ice-green suit, with her signature pearls around her neck, Mrs. Clinton shook hands with me and I sat down, my heart racing. After a series of introductory comments, the First Lady stood to give her speech, eloquently commenting on the role of journalists in peace and war. I was impressed with her fluency and ease in front of a tough audience of journalists and was disappointed when she and her bodyguards left before my speech. People were fanning themselves with their programs, and one woman had to be helped away, overcome by the heat.

"Give me a breeze when I speak, Dan," I muttered under my breath. "Otherwise nobody will be able to concentrate." But nothing stirred. It was finally my turn. Amy touched my hand reassuringly as I moved past her to the podium. I had to smile as a waft of wind teased my hair. Then I suppressed a chuckle when a current of air nearly blew my notes off the stand. As I concluded my speech, I referred to a quotation by Ralph Waldo Emerson that Dan had included in a paper when he was a freshman in college. It embodied what he had once called his "mission on earth":

The one thing in the world of value is the active soul—free, sovereign, unencumbered. This every man is entitled to, this every man contains within him, though in almost all men, it is obstructed and, as yet, unborn.

My hair was blowing in a stiff breeze as I concluded, "Let our souls be reborn today, dedicated above all to the communication of inspiration, and of truth."

When I finished, a bagpiper, his face glistening with sweat, saluted the dead journalists with the sorrowful tones of "Amazing Grace" as many in the audience wept for those who had sacrificed their lives to tell the truth.

Later I sent a copy of my speech to Mrs. Clinton. I knew she would never have the time to read it, but I wanted her to have it anyway. To my amazement, two years later, I received a handwritten note from the White House:

Dear Kathy Eldon,

I have thought often of your son Dan in the last months, as I have traveled around New York talking with people, particularly young college-age and twenty-somethings. The "Active Soul" keeps me going, as I know it does you. The challenge is to convey effectively the work of that active soul both in individual lives and in society amidst the clutter of our times, so that all of us—but especially the young (in age and heart) know we have work to do to inspire peace in and among us.

Please give my greetings to your daughter Amy and know that you are both welcome in the White House—or wherever we may be!

Blessings and best wishes,
Hillary

I was thrilled when Amy called to say that she had been accepted at both Columbia and Boston Universities. She chose BU's College of Communications and would begin classes after the holidays. "I want to make films after I graduate," she explained. Knowing how unhappy she had been about her brief experience making *Lost in Africa*, I was surprised and told her so.

"Not silly feature films, Mum. I want to make documentaries that tell important stories." She hoped to work on a documentary about frontline journalists who put their lives at risk to tell stories. She wanted to know why such people do what they do, but even more important, she hoped to explore the effect of their work on them. She hoped it might help her understand what drove Dan to become a war photographer, and what might have happened to him had he lived. Disappointed when she got only a B on the proposal when she submitted it as a class assignment, she perked up when a friend of hers managed to get it to Pat Mitchell, the president of documentary films at Turner Broadcasting System, which also operated CNN.

Amy and I had a great meeting in Los Angeles with Pat, who soon called us, saying she loved the project but had to get Ted Turner's approval before she could give the "green light." She asked me to a gala dinner the following week, where I could try to convince him. Nerves rattled, I hung up. A neighbor loaned me a chic outfit, earrings, and a fancy purse for the event, and I turned up, trying to appear as though I did this sort of thing all the time. But when I met Ted's wife, Jane Fonda, she took one look at my glassy eyes and said, "You look awfully nervous."

I blurted out why I was there and was relieved when Jane offered to convince her husband of the merits of the project. Apparently it worked, because we got word the next day that TBS would fund the film.

Pat Mitchell and her head of production, Jacoba Atlas, brought in award-winning producer Kyra Thompson to write a treatment for a documentary we called *Dying to Tell the Story*, which would profile six frontline journalists, all of whom had regularly faced death to get their stories. We were amazed when Kyra suggested that we weave Dan's story throughout the film, along with those of the six top-tier journalists. Amy and I bubbled with ideas, facts, and figures. As we got further into the project, we discovered dozens of worrying statistics about the risks journalists encounter. Since 1990, the numbers of journalists killed while doing their job had risen steeply: in 1993, the year Dan and his colleagues perished, fifty-six others had died, with many more harassed, tortured, or imprisoned. The number had grown since then. I was distressed to read the statistics, but Amy found it even more emotionally challenging. She put her concerns in a letter to her father:

> I believe man is good, but when people become infected with hatred, killing becomes a disease. Why do we keep ignoring evil? Probably because it's too painful to confront. But if we close our hearts, we keep repeating the mistakes of the past. Just when I think we are all basically wicked, I read writings from the Dalai Lama, Gandhi, and Martin Luther King Jr. that challenge me to shake myself awake from apathy and helplessness to keep the flame of hope alive.

Jacoba Atlas was impressed by Amy's passion and asked her—then barely twenty-two and without any on-camera experience—to present the documentary. As soon as she graduated, she moved to Los Angeles, where my cramped apartment became the office for our fledgling company, Creative Visions. Amy slept on the sofa in the second bedroom, which doubled as our production office, jammed with books, photographs, and tapes.

As we moved closer to our start date, I grew anxious. The shoot was going to be long and complex, with locations in England, Israel, and South Africa—and now that Dan's story was to be included, we would visit Nairobi and Mogadishu as well. These would be the two most ambitious and potentially dangerous sequences, especially if we were to film the Abdi Villa, where Dan and his colleagues had been killed.

I had to evaluate the risks for our team very carefully, and I lay awake many nights worrying about my daughter, for she would be interviewing war-toughened correspondents and talking on-camera at the site where Dan had been killed. I didn't want her to be overwhelmed by the experience, but she told me she could handle it. Like her brother before her, she was on a mission and wouldn't be diverted. "I need to see the place where Dan became a man," Amy said. "We can't stop now."

My principal concern was that Somalia was still a disaster zone, even more dangerous than it had been when Dan died. In 1993, the presence of UN peacekeeping forces in Somalia had meant there was some semblance of order. Now, with a devastated economy and no government, constitution, or police, the country was no more than a battleground fought over by rival warlords. One was General Mohamed Aidid's son, Hussein Mohamed Aidid, who controlled only one sector of southern Somalia but whom the Somali National Alliance had declared president of the entire country. Two others had divided the rest of Mogadishu between them. Hussein Aidid was the undisputed overlord of the area around the Abdi Villa, where Dan and his friends were killed. We would have to obtain his permission if we wanted to get in, film the interviews, and get out safely. To fly in without his okay would be beyond foolish.

After we had taken every precaution, I was nonetheless worried about the safety of Amy and our crew. When I asked my eighty-nine-year-old father for guidance, he said we should go if it was safe, enthusiastically adding, "The only difference between success and failure is determination and follow-through."

But still I wasn't convinced. Finally, I decided to call Brenda Lawrence. It had been several years since we had spoken, and I wondered if she would still be able to communicate with Dan.

"Dan is saying he is very proud of his 'little sister,'" she said over the phone. "She has come a long way in the past few years. And so have you," Brenda added. "He loves you so much, and is very proud of you."

I desperately wanted to believe that, but her words could apply to just about anyone. However, what she said next made me sit up and listen. Although I had told her nothing about our new project, she relayed that Dan said he knew I was "worried about the place where you're going." He assured her, Brenda said, "It will be all right, as long as you get in and out in one day."

That left me with a hard choice to make. We had planned to spend a night at the Sahafi Hotel, because the crew needed two full days in Mogadishu to get the footage. To reduce the time would make their job extremely difficult. After much deliberation, I decided that we would not take the risk and, feeling rather foolish, canceled the hotel booking.

On the second of September, 1997, Amy and I flew to London with Kyra Thompson. Our plan was to shoot four interviews there before continuing on to South Africa, and finally to Kenya and Somalia. There was a strange atmosphere in London, since just two days earlier Princess Diana had died in an automobile crash in Paris trying to elude a pack of paparazzi. All I could think about was the long journey that lay ahead for her children as they struggled with the sudden loss of their beloved mother. I kept my eye on Amy, aware of how tired and vulnerable she appeared after the long flight from Los Angeles.

The next day she was too exhausted and nervous to eat breakfast. I tried to appear confident as I watched her sip a cup of tea while poring over a sheaf of notes, memorizing the questions she had prepared for each of her subjects. She and the film crew took the Underground to shoot her first interview in a Covent Garden pub, and I went by taxi to meet them.

For her first interview, Amy had chosen Carlos Mavroleon, the free-lance cameraman who had known Dan in Somalia. Carlos represented the "bang-bang" school of reporters, an apparently reckless breed that faces death as coolly as if ice water ran in their veins. He talked about how hard it was to maintain a relationship while taking on dangerous assignments that put "the utter evil and the supreme good side by side." After years of that life, he was planning to switch to the safer career of filming documentaries. Regrettably, he would die before that happened, while pursuing a story about terrorist training camps run by someone few of us knew about then—a man named Osama bin Laden. Carlos's last words to Amy chilled me. "Be bloody careful," he warned. "Somalia is a nightmare. I was held up at gunpoint three times in one day on my last trip three weeks ago."

Amy was most anxious about her second interview, which was with her greatest heroine, CNN correspondent Christiane Amanpour. Clear, cool, and often brusque on air, she was gentle with Amy, and her eyes glistened when she said that Dan had been doing exactly what he wanted to do—and that he had died for a purpose. Amy listened intently. I knew how much she wanted to believe it, but I could see she wasn't yet convinced.

Amy's last two interviews in London were with veteran war photographer Don McCullin, who had clearly been traumatized by all that he had seen, and puckish BBC correspondent Martin Bell, famous for his spotless white suits. He showed Amy his matching white flak jacket and explained how embarrassed he had been when he was felled by stray mortar shards while covering a story in Bosnia. He was upset that he was immediately evacuated and received excellent medical care in England, while locals, most wounded far more seriously, were lucky to receive any assistance at all.

In South Africa, Amy interviewed Peter Magubane, one of the most courageous photographers during the years of apartheid. He had been imprisoned by the Nationalist Afrikaner government for his pictures of brutality against innocent civilians and had spent more than five hundred days in solitary confinement, often tortured. Amy paled when Peter described the grotesque death of his son, who had been shot and whose body was then hacked with machetes by a mob. Peter said the atrocity had turned him into a "wounded tiger," even more determined to search out and report the worst stories of injustice. As a result, his house had been burned to the ground—and with it, all his negatives.

"Have you forgiven the people who hurt you and your family?" she asked.

"In my profession, if you don't forgive, you can't portray your subjects properly."

Amy asked him to explain what he meant. "It doesn't mean that I have pardoned those people, or excused them, but as we have discovered through the Peace and Reconciliation process, forgiveness is the path to freedom. It's not for the other person; it's for yourself." I listened to his words carefully, knowing they carried an important message for me.

Our final stop was Kenya. After nearly four hours of flying, my stomach was churning as the plane began its descent into Nairobi's Kenyatta Airport. I was returning to the country I loved beyond measure, but a land fraught with painful memories. I could never forget that my son's ashes were intermingled with its red soil.

Once in the arrivals lounge, I began scanning the crowd. I had to stop myself: I was looking for Dan, who always met me with a big bunch of flowers on my arrival in Nairobi. But of course he wasn't there, nor was Mike, who had left word at our hotel that Amy and I should join him for dinner.

That evening, we found Mike relaxed but animated as he described his new job overseeing six successful companies. He spoke with great pride about his greatest love, the DEPOT, which housed a collection of Dan's art and artifacts and offered leadership-training courses for Kenyans, rich and poor. In the years since Dan's death, nearly ten thousand people had already flowed through the center.

At one point Amy excused herself, leaving us alone at the table. I felt myself flush at his gaze.

"I'm afraid I've got lots of new lines in my face," I said, turning away.

"Each one is hard-earned," he said, tracing the furrows in my forehead with his finger. "It's what gives your face character and makes you beautiful."

Mike's tenderness seemed to revive a part of me that had been shut down for years, and we began to talk about what had gone wrong in our marriage. We agreed that neither of us had known how to communicate, so instead of confronting our problems together, we had chosen to ignore them and distract ourselves in a swirl of activities. We never took enough time to be alone together and appreciate one another until it was too late.

After the waiter finished pouring our coffee, Mike leaned forward, and I could see that he wanted to say something but wasn't quite sure how to begin. Gently he broke the news that he and Evelyn were getting married. I fought to control the emotions welling within me, a strange mélange of sadness, longing, resentment—but ultimately relief. I realized why the evening had felt so comfortable: it was because Mike was happy. No longer feeling hurt or abandoned, he could face me with quiet contentment. Now it was I who was hurting. As we talked, I knew that Evelyn was the perfect wife for him, and I was happy for them both.

When Amy rejoined us, her face betrayed a complicated mixture of feelings. Mike had told her the news already, and she had been worried about how I would react. But when I got up from the table at the end of the meal, I had no desire to hold on to, restrain, or possess Mike. At last I was finally able to release him. I could move on and so could he. We had torn down the walls between us and could transform our relationship with what the Greeks termed *agape*—an openhearted, compassionate love that nourishes, uplifts, sustains, and forgives.

Still, later that night, after we had turned out the light and Amy had fallen asleep, I let myself cry. I had to grieve for all that I had left behind, though I knew I would need all the strength I could muster for what lay ahead.

Early the next morning I had to secure our authority to enter Somalia and confirm that Hussein Aidid was still willing to allow our interviews in Mogadishu. The key to all this was in the hands of his so-called ambassador in Nairobi, whose headquarters were in a block of flats next to Chester House, which still housed the Press Center where I had worked with Mary Anne. My stomach tensed as my taxi pulled up in front of the building, now dilapidated, with paint peeling off its walls.

I couldn't resist looking inside the Press Center, where I spotted the familiar bronze plate engraved with the names of the journalists and companies who had offices there. The name *Mohamed Amin* leaped out at me, along with a host of memories. Three years after Dan's death, Mo had been killed too—standing in the aisle of a hijacked plane, negotiating with armed men, when the plane ran out of fuel and crashed into the sea. I recalled Mo's sparkling eyes and inquisitive spirit. My friend had been only fifty-three at his death, but it was—literally—two lifetimes since he had let the seven-year-old Dan peer through the lens of his camera. I recalled the phrase proudly displayed in his office: "I'll sleep when I'm dead." But I couldn't imagine that Mo's active soul—or Dan's—would ever rest.

Next door, I took the decrepit elevator up to the ambassador's apartment on the fourth floor and made my way down a long corridor that smelled of rotting plants and cooked cabbage, clenching and unclenching my hands. What if the "ambassador" said no to our request? I would never find out what had really happened to Dan. The man simply *had* to agree. Offering up a silent plea to whoever might be listening, I took a deep breath and knocked on his door.

A slight Somali in his fifties, wearing a pinstriped suit and carrying a silver-topped fly whisk, greeted me with a solemn bow and ushered me to the sofa. Going straight to the point, I formally asked him for permission to fly into Mogadishu for a day to interview his president and any willing witnesses to the death of Dan and his colleagues.

"I will speak with our esteemed president," he said, standing up to dismiss me. "You will have a reply tomorrow." My heart sank. I had been hoping for an instant answer.

Nevertheless, after a nail-biting day, we learned that Aidid had agreed we could come, provided we hired his "security" team, apparently a euphemism for a bunch of AK-47-bearing thugs. That meant another two thousand dollars in the budget, but there was no turning down the offer.

That night I lay awake for hours, full of doubts about my decision to fly to Mogadishu. I finally dropped off just before the alarm sounded at the ungodly hour of four o'clock. Amy and I dressed quickly and hurried downstairs.

33

The Story

IT WAS EERILY SILENT AS WE STOOD WAITING FOR THE REST OF THE TEAM in the cool night air, savoring the time before dawn when even the birds and insects are quiet. Mohammed Shaffi, sole survivor of the July 12 tragedy, joined us under the street lamp outside the Nairobi hotel wearing a khaki vest stuffed with camera equipment, lenses, and film. Our cameraman and Victoria Waldock, who was producing this segment, arrived next, followed by Guillaume Bonn, a friend of Dan's who was serving as the stills photographer. Quietly, we reviewed the security arrangements and concluded that we would be safe. Still, when the minibus arrived to take us to the airport for our chartered flight to Somalia, I was shivering, more in apprehension of the day ahead than from the chill.

Our pilot, Captain Mohammed, a Kenyan Somali with the aquiline features and olive complexion of his countrymen, met us at the hangar. Hustling us into the aircraft, he explained that we would fly to the "K-50" airfield fifty kilometers outside Mogadishu—farther from the center of town than other options, but safer because it was in Aidid's sector.

As our plane droned toward the border, the sky was bright with stars, the earth below a shadowy blur. Each of us was silent, lost in our own thoughts. I dozed fitfully. Many Somalis must have known we were coming, and a film crew would be an easy target for kidnappers hungry for publicity or ransom money. This was our last chance to turn back.

Still, I had a more personal anxiety that I hadn't mentioned to Amy: I wasn't sure how I would react to the Somalis I'd meet in Mogadishu. After four years, I was still angry when I thought about the attack. In the last analysis, it was Somalis who had murdered Dan and his friends. Would I be able to deal with them? Could I ever forgive them? I couldn't imagine being like Gandhi, who once said, "If you want to see the brave, look to those who can forgive. If you want to see the heroic, look to those who can love in return for hatred." True forgiveness was still beyond me.

The sun rose abruptly as we neared the border. The sky was streaked with purple for a moment, then faded to reveal a misty green ribbon of land stretching toward the Indian Ocean. Within a half hour the little plane began its descent. Amy tapped me on the shoulder, pointing to a perfect rainbow that hung over the horizon. Brenda had once said that we should view rainbows as reminders of our connection to the spirit world—rather like bridges to another dimension. I opted to interpret this one as a positive omen.

The captain swooped low over the airstrip to check that no animals had strayed onto it, then circled to land near a heavily damaged building that looked as if it had been used for target practice. He shut down the engine and we gathered our bags. Shaffi pushed open the door, and I felt a rush of hot, humid air.

As I exited the plane, I gasped at the sight of our official security team: twenty armed men, each cradling an AK-47 in his arms. They stood in a semicircle around the plane, some dressed in faded army fatigues too large for their slender frames, others wearing colorful T-shirts and the ankle-length wrap of striped fabric traditionally favored by Somali men. A few had combat boots, but the majority stood in old flip-flops. One in particular caught my eye. Skinny, barefoot, and draped in a camouflage shirt over baggy trousers, he couldn't have been older than twelve. He didn't look like a mascot, however, because his gun was the same size as everyone else's. I thought about Dan and how he had so quickly befriended

Somalis like these young men, most barely out of their teens. Yet when I smiled tentatively at them, no one smiled back.

Despite the intense heat and humidity, Amy and I were wearing long skirts and long sleeves, in deference to the Muslim dress code, and we now pulled scarves around our heads to act as veils.

"Don't show fear," Shaffi muttered under his breath. "Just act like this is something you do every day." But it wasn't. We were in Somalia, one of the most dangerous countries in the world, and we had only eleven hours to accomplish what should take two full days.

We followed Captain Mohammed into a concrete shell, stripped of window frames, doors, and light fittings—anything that could be removed. A guard sat slumped in a broken chair outside an inner room, his fingers resting lightly on his AK-47.

An "immigration official" stepped out to meet us. Shaffi and the captain disappeared with him into the office to deal with the paperwork—a polite term for executing the bribes to get us into the country. Swatting flies, the rest of us spoke quietly, afraid of being overheard. A tray of hot tea and glasses arrived, and we sipped the sweet liquid, grateful for something to do. Sweat dripping down my face, I felt increasingly nervous, aware that we were losing precious time we couldn't spare.

I ran over the schedule in my mind. We had to get into town, at least an hour away, film Dan's room in the Sahafi Hotel, talk to Hussein Aidid, interview Shaffi at the Abdi Villa about the last fatal scene of Dan's life, and return to the airfield by six. With no landing lights on the airstrip, we couldn't take off after dark; and whatever happened, we couldn't risk being stranded there for the night. My desperate calculations were interrupted when Caption Mohammed and Shaffi reappeared.

Shaffi looked relieved. "Come on, let's go," he said. "They're keeping our passports, but there's nothing we can do about it right now."

Outside, two Land Rovers awaited us. A bizarrely painted vehicle pulled up in front of them and I recognized from Dan's photographs that it was a "technical"—a four-wheel-drive vehicle or flatbed truck converted to carry a bazooka or machine gun.

Amy was in the first Land Rover with the camera crew, while I followed behind her in the second, trailed closely by a second technical. I watched in horror as Amy's car swayed violently from side to side, careening along the narrow, unpaved road. Suddenly, another technical came speeding toward us. At the very last possible moment, the oncoming vehicle, bristling with gunmen, veered to the side. Both our Land Rovers ended up straddling the shoulder. The one I was in shuddered to a stop and refused to start again. Our gunmen leaped off the technicals and surrounded us, nervously fingering their weapons.

"Quick!" Shaffi cried, throwing open the door. "Get in the other car." My heart was racing as we jammed into the backseat of Amy's Land Rover and set off again, leaving the second car behind. During the hour it took to reach Mogadishu, we passed only a few other vehicles, all technicals piled high with crates and boxes, furniture, and sullen young Somalis cradling AK-47s. Most seemed very young, and I reminded Amy that Dan had once said, "For schoolkids, guns are more fun than mathematics."

At first, the buildings we saw in the distance looked like normal apartment blocks, but as we drew closer, I realized that virtually all had sustained severe damage. The walls of the once grand Italianate villas and office buildings were pocked with bullet holes or damaged by heavy artillery. Shaffi explained that the infrastructure of the city, including its entire electricity and water supply, had broken down. Three million people had died during the fighting over the past few years, and survivors were living in the debris. Men with sticklike limbs squatted on boxes or upturned buckets, watching our convoy go by with curious stares, while women, their slender frames wrapped in billowing dresses and veils, talked animatedly as they cooked over open fires.

We finally lurched to a halt at a gate set in a high white wall that surrounded the Sahafi Hotel. After the stifling heat and humidity outside, we were grateful for the welcoming cool of the lobby. A man came from behind the desk, introducing himself as the manager, Mohamed Jirdah. I had heard many stories about the affable businessman who had converted his establishment into a haven for journalists.

"I am so sorry for what happened to your son," he said in heavily accented English. "Dan Eldon was my very good friend." Mohamed said that he had been devastated when he heard what had happened to Dan, for he had grown close to him during his extended stay at his hotel. He opened the guest book and pointed to a scrawl that he said was Dan's "signature." I showed it to Amy, who giggled. It said, "Napoleon Bonaparte."

Mohamed reached under the desk and pulled out a stack of the *Somalia* books Dan had published, as well as a box containing a collection of the Cobra helicopter stickers and T-shirts that Dan had made and sold. One of his most popular shirt designs was a circle around an AK-47 machine gun with a line through it, along with the slogan, "Thank you for not looting." I recalled how amused he had been to report that the first batch of two hundred shirts had been stolen from the storehouse.

Mohamed beckoned to two Somalis in their midtwenties, wearing neatly ironed cotton shirts over striped *kikoys*. As soon as I heard their names, Ali and Abdi, I knew that they had been Dan's bodyguards. This was one of the moments I had been dreading, for they were the ones who had driven away and left my son to die at the hands of the mob. On the other hand, I desperately wanted to hear their stories. Disarmed when Ali stepped forward and hugged me, I found myself hugging him back.

"Dan was my friend," he murmured, his eyes suddenly moist. "I wish that I had saved his life. I am so sorry for what happened." I nodded as he explained that the enraged crowd had swarmed around their vehicle and would have murdered them too, if they had stayed. Hearing his story, I found myself patting Ali's arm to reassure him. It was obvious that he and Abdi had been devastated by the death of the young man for whom they had risked their lives on many previous occasions.

"Everyone loved Dan," Abdi said with huge grin. "Especially the kids." He said that Dan would often take food into the refugee camp next to the hotel, and he loved to amuse the camp children with his masks and silly antics. Unlike the older, more seasoned foreign reporters who had endured wars elsewhere, Dan was new to war and had grown up among Africans. That's why he remained sensitive to its horrors, and especially to the plight of the young refugees.

"Thank you for being my brother's friend," Amy said, hugging them before our whole team followed Shaffi up the stairs to the second floor. Light filtered in through sculptured openings as Shaffi led us down the corridor to room 242, where I could see one of Dan's faded and peeling Cobra stickers still on the door. Shaffi pushed it open.

"This was Dan's room."

I hesitated for a moment before stepping slowly over the threshold, as though I were intruding. I had often tried to imagine the place where my son had spent so many weeks during what had to be one of the most challenging and traumatic times of his life. Now I felt like a trespasser. I stood still for a moment, taking in the cool, dark room. Shutters covered the windows, and flowered spreads lay neatly folded at the foot of the beds. I surveyed the bare beige walls, trying to imagine them plastered with Dan's drawings and photographs. Suddenly overcome, I sat down on the bed and closed my eyes. I wanted to feel his spirit close to me, but the room felt empty. He was gone.

Swallowing hard, I stood up, then opened the bathroom door, recalling a photo of him huddled by the toilet with a flashlight, developing his photographs. I wondered how he had felt as he gathered his equipment for the last time and hurried out the door.

"We have to get going," whispered Victoria, as though speaking in a church. Reluctantly, I left the room and trailed behind Allan, who filmed Amy and Shaffi as they climbed the steps to the roof, where the journalists used to gather to escape the heat and humidity of their rooms, talking and smoking together.

It was now midday and my eyes teared from the glare of the sun as I stepped out. Heat waves rose from the concrete below, pockmarked with craters. When my eyes finally adjusted to the brilliant light, I realized that we were surrounded by at least ten armed guards. This new group was Mohamed Jirdah's hotel security. Taller and more heavily built than our official bodyguards, they wore mirrored sunglasses, high-laced boots, pale-green khaki fatigues, and bandoliers of bullets across their chests as they scanned nearby roofs and the street below. No one smiled.

Shaffi led Amy to the edge of the roof, trying to locate the remains of the Abdi Villa. He spoke quickly, describing how Dan and Hos (who had arrived that morning to replace Dan) and the other journalists watched U.S. Cobra helicopters circling in the sky like angry hornets, descending one at a time to pound the house, surrounded by billowing clouds of black smoke. I stood behind Allan Palmer, his camera rolling, and tried to imagine how Dan must have felt, watching from the rooftop as the scene unfolded before him.

Shaffi said he had been drinking tea with a Pakistani commander at the UN command center when the attack began. Rushing back to the hotel, he set up his camera on the roof, where a number of journalists had already gathered, and began filming the villa, only a five-minute drive away. Everyone agreed that it was too dangerous to get to the scene while the gunships were firing. Soon after the forty-five-minute attack ended, however, members of General Aidid's armed guard arrived at the hotel and asked the reporters to follow them to the site to record what had happened. Dan and his colleagues knew several of the Somalis, who guaranteed their safety.

But why did he take the risk? What was so important that he would venture out of the safety of the hotel compound? He knew that no picture was worth his life, and it was clear that the mood in the streets was ugly and the situation terribly dangerous. Minutes before, Dan had bandaged the head of Scott Peterson, a young photographer from the *Christian Science Monitor*, who had already been to the villa. He had tried to shoot some pictures of the carnage, only to be beaten by the survivors. Dan had even called Reuters in London to tell them he wasn't going, a decision they had encouraged. What made him change his mind? Why was the story so important that he would stay on an extra day even though Hos had already arrived to replace him?

Shaffi explained that after confirming their security, Dan, Shaffi, Anthony, and Hos piled into the Reuters vehicle. Another vehicle, carrying

German photographer Hansi Krauss of the Associated Press, followed behind them, and finally a third car with an Italian team. On the drive across town, Dan told Shaffi that he was worried and asked him if it was wise to be in the first car of journalists. Shaffi agreed and the driver slowed down, but none of the other trucks passed them; in fact, the Italians turned back. Dan had half-jokingly said to Shaffi, "*Babuji*, you stand next to me when we get there. My white skin is going to save you today."

When Shaffi asked him what he meant, Dan said that American helicopters wouldn't shoot if they saw a white man taking photographs. Shaffi agreed, feeling that the risk of being killed by mistake by the U.S. troops was greater than any threat from the Somalis.

As he told the story, Shaffi grew agitated, and Amy rested her hand on his arm to calm him. We knew how tortured he was as the sole survivor of that terrible day. He had spent months in London, suffering from the effects of post-traumatic stress, and now we were asking him to tell the story that he had tried to forget. Worried for his mental state, I was relieved when Victoria stopped him. It was time to hurry to our appointment with Hussein Aidid, she reminded us.

Our Land Rover drove at top speed to Aidid's compound, which extended over several city blocks. A noisy crowd pressed around us once we had passed through the gates and parked, their faces peering curiously at these foreigners being pushed toward the building by a posse of heavily armed men.

Upstairs, in a large room lined with broken white tiles, a stone-faced guard instructed us to wait for the president, who was "in a meeting." Rows of white plastic chairs stood along the side walls, and a faded Somali flag with gold tassels hung limply from a pole.

After what seemed like an interminable wait, there was a great flurry as a cluster of men carrying machine guns burst into the room. Behind them appeared a small, rather plump man in a dark suit. It was President Hussein Aidid, looking more like a suburban accountant than a warlord. Like his twelve siblings, he had been educated in the United States. He lived outside Los Angeles until 1996, when his father, the infamous warlord Mohamed Farrah Aidid, was killed in Somalia. Then Hussein, a public works employee who had served as a reservist U.S. Marine, left Southern California and returned to Somalia, where he was declared president.

We stood up to greet him. After shaking our hands, as if going through a receiving line, he motioned us to one end of a long wooden table, settling himself at the other. Soft-spoken, he formally welcomed us to Somalia with an incongruous American accent. With preliminaries over, Amy asked her first question as Allan filmed the proceedings.

"Mr. President, what do you miss about America?"

Thinking for a moment, Aidid answered wistfully, "Swing dancing."

I tried not to laugh out loud. The idea that a warlord should miss swing dancing astounded me. But Aidid went on to say that he was also nostalgic for Big Macs, Starbucks coffee, and California beaches. Then, perhaps aware that this was a rare opportunity to make his case to a worldwide audience, he turned to me. "I want to apologize to you for the loss of your son," he said solemnly. "But really, both the Somalis who died on that day and the journalists were all victims of United Nations troops under the control of the American military."

I nodded politely, although his statement didn't make any sense to me. After he and Amy had spoken for a while, he introduced us to a young woman, Fatima, a delicate beauty with fine features and sculpted lips who was standing by the door. She pulled her veil close around her head with one hand as she extended the other in the soft handshake favored by most African women. In heavily accented English, Fatima explained that she was Aidid's cousin, and not only had she lost her brother and father in the July 12 attack, but she had been wounded herself. I suppressed a gasp when she tossed back her veil and guided my fingers over several lumps and ragged scars hidden beneath her hair. She told us there were still fragments of shrapnel in her head.

"That's terrible," I said, shuddering, aware of how much she and so many innocent Somalis must have suffered both physically and emotionally, both before the attack and since.

She nodded proudly, then pulled up her veil and turned away.

"Fatima will escort you to the Abdi Villa," Aidid said, rising from the table to indicate that the interview was over. We stood to attention as his bodyguards closed around him and marched him out the door.

A surge of adrenaline shot through me on our journey to the Abdi Villa, and I prayed for strength to handle what I was about to see. I was soothed by Fatima's soft voice as she told us about the morning of the American attack on the villa. A group of General Aidid's supporters had called a meeting, she said, to discuss a response to a peace initiative from Admiral Howe. Religious and clan leaders, professors from the university, and elders of the community had gathered for it. Many, weary of the violence and bloodshed, were opposed to Aidid's policies and wanted him to end the fighting. Among them were businessmen eager to begin the potentially lucrative task of rebuilding Mogadishu. The one important person who was absent was Aidid himself.

Leaving their shoes outside the door, the men arranged themselves around a large upstairs room. The chairs were reserved for the religious representatives and clan elders, the most senior of whom was ninety years old, while younger men sat on woven mats on the floor. As the group began to discuss the options available to them, women and young girls hurried up and down the stairs with trays of tea and cakes while children played in the courtyard outside.

Fatima was interrupted when our convoy came to a sudden stop in front of a once-impressive stone wall, now crumbling and overgrown with weeds and long grass. We had finally arrived at the villa.

Although I had rehearsed this moment for years, I still dreaded actually seeing what I had visualized here. I felt Victoria's eyes on me. "You okay?" she asked. I nodded. I was far more concerned about Amy, who was pale and tense.

"Hurry, hurry," our guards shouted as they herded us out of the Land Rover. As Amy stepped down, she nearly tripped over her long skirt. The youngest gunman reached out to stop her fall. I watched his eyes soften as she thanked him before she pulled her veil across her face and followed Shaffi into the ruined shell of the villa.

Originally white, the walls of the spacious three-story building had been blackened by smoke from the fire that raged after the mortar attack. Most of the roof and facade had been blown away by the bombing, leaving it like a derelict dollhouse, rooms filled with piles of debris. I stood without moving as I took in the scene, trying to feel Dan's spirit in this terrible place, but I sensed nothing but the stares of the guards following my every move.

Allan began filming Fatima as she explained to Amy that she had been downstairs preparing tea with the other women when suddenly, without warning, she heard the throbbing roar of an American helicopter gunship overhead, then another. The first deafening explosion was followed quickly by seventeen more hits as the forty-pound projectiles slammed into the building, bringing down the roof, penetrating the thick walls, and bringing down the staircase. She described hearing the screams of survivors pinned under fallen beams or trapped in burning wreckage. Although bleeding from cuts to her head, she tried to run upstairs to help, but the structural damage made it impossible.

She had then darted into the courtyard, from which she saw U.S. military sharpshooters in gunships firing down on any wounded who were crawling from the blazing villa. Minutes later, Marines dropped down on ropes and stormed the building, deliberately shooting at any survivors, then photographing the faces of the dead, apparently to confirm if General Aidid was among the casualties.

As soon as the helicopters began to withdraw, frantic Somalis rushed in to rescue the wounded and dying, loading them into wheelbarrows, passenger cars, or pickups to take them to the hospital. Fatima's face was ashen as she described the carnage, and I felt nauseated, imagining her pain, not only from her own wounds, but at seeing her friends and relatives dying in the rubble. I reached for her hand and held it.

Shaffi then told his story, taking up the narrative an hour or so after the attack. When the convoy of journalists approached the burning villa, helicopters were still circling over the compound, where hundreds of people had gathered and were helping with the frantic rescue attempts.

"The crowd went quiet when we arrived," he said, "and they watched as I began filming with Anthony next to me and Hos over there." Shaffi spoke quickly, gesturing with both hands as he relayed the images imprinted on his mind.

"Then Hansi moved in beside me, and Dan stood here," he said, pointing nearby. "People were bringing out bodies from the house. It was really shocking. I filmed one dead person whose bloody body was badly broken in the attack. There was a second in the other pickup inside the compound, and then a third was carried out of the house in a carpet and shown to us. We filmed four bodies in all."

The horrors he had witnessed were etched on his face, as they must have been on mine as I listened to the details of the story I had longed to hear. I had seen the grisly footage and knew that many more people had been killed or wounded, but now I wanted him to stop, to rewind, to hit PAUSE forever, to save me from the truth about the last moments of my son's life.

Shaffi had kept his camera running for three or four minutes, he said, before moving toward the house. Horrific as it was outside, they knew it would be far worse within, where people had been crushed by falling masonry.

"We had taken only a few steps when one of the men rescuing the wounded picked up a stone and threw it at us," Shaffi said, pointing toward a spot near the gate. "Then a few people from the crowd attacked, throwing rocks and pushing us, shouting, 'These foreigners are to blame.'"

After that, someone else grabbed a pipe, and before Shaffi knew what was happening, people were screaming and attacking the reporters from all directions with iron bars, stones, sticks—anything they could lay their hands on.

"'We're not American,' I cried, but it didn't do any good. We weren't Somali. Then Dan turned to me and said, '*Babuji*, let's get out of here!' I took the camera off my shoulder and said, 'Run, Dan.'"

Shaffi was silent for a moment, collecting himself. Then he explained how the stricken survivors, who had been desperately searching the ruins for their loved ones and friends, suddenly turned into a murderous mob, bent on vengeance, blood for blood. Hos Maina, who had a paralyzed hand and difficulty moving quickly, was easily caught and brutally beaten to death. I clasped Fatima's hand harder as Shaffi then described how the mob ripped off Hansi Krauss's bulletproof vest as he ran, stoned him, and finally peppered his body with bullets. Anthony Macharia, barely twenty-one, was faster than the others and had almost made it back to the Sahafi Hotel when a woman stepped from an alley and struck at his head with a long knife. Anthony fell and was immediately overwhelmed.

Meanwhile, Shaffi had climbed onto the back of a pickup truck he thought belonged to Reuters, but it was the wrong one, and he found himself standing on a pile of bloody corpses. He jumped off and started running until he, too, was thrown to the ground and beaten. Somehow he managed to get up again and run, but stopped when confronted by a man aiming an AK-47 at him. He was shot two or three times but managed to keep going. He begged the driver of a passing vehicle to open the door and let him in, and the man complied. Shaffi thought he was safe until one of the passengers tried to strangle him. "Do you know what the fucking Americans have done here?" the man screamed.

Shaffi pleaded with them to spare his life, saying that he, like them, was Muslim. Finally they relented and dumped him, half-dead, in front of the U.S. military hospital. Ironically, because he wasn't American, the hospital refused to treat him until a fellow journalist recognized him and demanded that he be admitted.

I drew a deep breath. Shaffi had described the deaths of three of his friends. There was one more. I swayed slightly, feeling as though the ground were moving. Amy's eyes caught mine, and I nodded slightly to reassure her. Shaffi was watching us.

"Go on," I said. I had to know the truth.

At first Dan had been luckier than the others. When the angry survivors closed around him in the courtyard he had looked for the Reuters vehicle, but its driver, frightened by the swelling mob, had already pulled outside the gates. Dan ran after it and was trying to climb on board when it sped away. Above him, adding to the noise and confusion, was the throbbing roar of a UN Blackhawk helicopter circling the site to monitor events. The pilot spotted the young white man running from the mob and radioed back to base, asking permission to pick him up. There was a long pause, and then he was told to wait until his superiors could determine whether all American troops had made it out.

Shedding his heavy flak jacket, Dan ran down the street toward the hotel, eluding most of his pursuers until he rounded a corner and was ambushed by another enraged group. Falling to his knees, he tried to reason with his attackers, as he always had been able to do as a boy, attempting to defuse anger by reason, fast talk, or a joke. But there was no time, and as he had always said, it's impossible to reason with an angry mob. Someone smashed a stone against the back of his head, there was the slash of a machete across his neck—and Dan was gone.

My body recoiled as Shaffi reached the horrifying end of his story.

Shortly after Dan's death, Keith Richburg of the *Washington Post* had interviewed the UN helicopter pilot, who was angry that his request to pick up Dan had been refused. Unwilling to disobey orders, he circled above Dan as he ran, hoping to frighten off the mob. Fifteen minutes after the Somalis had killed Dan, he dropped down, without permission, to pick up his naked body, spread-eagled in the dusty street. The official autopsy report recorded multiple bruises and wounds on his body, open cuts on his face, and stab wounds to his stomach. The stated cause of his death, a blow to the top of his skull, was exactly what Brenda Lawrence had said in our first conversation.

As I contemplated Dan's last moments, Shaffi's face crumpled and he turned away, unable to speak.

Fatima took over again. Picking her way through the ruins, foul with animal feces, she struggled to find words for her own feelings. "Why did the American soldiers kill those innocent people at the meeting?" she asked, shaking her head.

Shaffi echoed her anger. "I have to blame them for what they did," he said, his voice cracking. "Maybe my life was spared to tell the world what really happened."

"Well, thank goodness you were saved," Amy said, wiping away a tear; and when Allan turned off the camera a few minutes later, I embraced Shaffi. He was silent, though his heaving shoulders said it all.

Wandering off from the group, but still under the watchful eye of several guards, I tried to imagine the scene, hearing the murmur of women's voices, the clatter of dishes, and the happy cries of children suddenly shattered by the din of the helicopters and the crescendo of the bombardment. If I had been a Somali woman and my child had been killed that day, perhaps I, too, would have wanted to retaliate.

Only now did the tragic double irony of what had happened come home to me. The UN bombing of the Abdi Villa, executed by US troops, had wiped out the core of the only Somali peace faction that wanted to stop the fighting and start rebuilding the country. No wonder the Somalis hated Americans so much. The survivors had lost their sons, fathers, brothers, mothers, and daughters in the brutal attack. When the group of foreign journalists came to record what had happened, the rescuers thought they were more soldiers sent by their American attackers to film the dead. In seeking revenge, the mob killed the people who could have told the real story of what happened that day.

Lost in these reflections, from somewhere far away I could hear Fatima's voice calling, shrill and urgent, "Come, come, come!"

"Mum, we must go! Now!" Amy's voice penetrated my reverie, and I hurried down the steps into the harsh sunshine. She and the rest of the team were already halfway across the courtyard. "You've got to hurry, Kathy; it's getting dangerous!" Allan urged from the back of the group.

Outside the gate, twenty or thirty people, mostly women, clustered around our vehicles, their long dresses a bright patchwork against the green grass. Their faces were contorted with rage as they shouted and shook their fists at the gunmen on the technicals and banged the sides of our Land Rover. I wondered who among them might have helped kill my son and his friends. As I hurried toward our vehicle, I could see Amy's pale face within, pressed against the window. One of our guards pushed me in beside her and slammed the door.

"Mumma," Amy cried, clutching my arm. "I was so worried about you. Never do that to me again."

With a screech of tires, we tore off.

During the race back to town to drop Fatima off at Aidid's headquarters, I felt dazed. When we arrived, I wrapped my arms around Fatima and felt her body tremble as I hugged her.

"I'm sorry," I whispered, feeling my heart open as I held on to her for another moment before she opened the door and stepped down, pulling her scarf up to shield her face.

I was lost in my thoughts and Amy was withdrawn as we sped through the streets toward the outskirts of the ruined city, watching the people eyeing us. Suddenly, the Land Rover swerved and I slammed hard against Amy. Jarred back into reality, I prayed we wouldn't have a flat tire or a breakdown. We had to get to the airport, and quickly.

Keith Richburg later described the Abdi Villa bombing as "the UN's first officially authorized assassination": according to UN sources, the forces under Admiral Howe's command thought Aidid was in the villa when they attacked the building. Later, Howe admitted that his information had been faulty, but his spokespeople claimed that only a dozen people had died in the attack. However, the Red Cross estimated that between fifty-four and eighty-five were killed, including men, women, and children, with up to two hundred injured. The day after the incident, the legal adviser for the UN Justice Division in Somalia resigned, having submitted a memo in which she stated that some UN states would regard the attack as "nothing less than murder committed in the name of the United Nations." Admiral Howe promised an inquiry, but nothing was ever made public.

The sun was already sinking low over the horizon when we arrived at the airfield. Our phalanx of *khat*-chewing guards, guns firmly in hand, quickly surrounded the plane, which looked very vulnerable on the deserted strip.

Once on the plane, Shaffi still looked worried. "We don't have our passports back yet," he muttered, not even trying to reassure me. He stood at the top of the steps and translated for us while Captain Mohammed engaged in a noisy negotiation with the leader of the guards. "They won't give them to us unless we hand over another two thousand dollars."

It dawned on me that our guards were no longer protecting us but were holding us for ransom. After more anxious minutes, our captain appeared at the door and handed Shaffi a fat manila envelope.

"Buckle up," he commanded.

"What happened?" Allan asked.

"I paid," the captain answered. "Now just hope we can take off."

As we rumbled down the runway, I realized that I finally understood what Dan had meant by those words he had written about his encounter with the buffalo: "I knew the buffalo might kill me, but later, with the sight and smell of it behind me, I felt as though a lifelong veil had been lifted from my senses."

The sky was a wash of pastel colors as the captain revved the engine and bounced down the runway, gathering speed. I held my breath as we passed the knot of guards staring at us. Amy waved at the youngest gunman, who lifted his hand to wave back, then dropped it quickly, as though afraid the others might see. Still, he seemed to stand up straighter, and there was a trace of a smile on his face. I remembered a phrase of Dan's, relayed through Brenda—"Man's inhumanity to man is mostly due to ignorance, not intent"—and recalled his belief that the only way to create peace in the world is to teach children not to hate and give them a reason to have hope for their future.

While the plane raced to the end of the runway, Amy nudged me. "Look over there, Mumma." I followed her finger. A rainbow had appeared on the horizon yet again, but this one was upside down, lit up like a smile in the sky.

As the plane rose, there was a spontaneous cheer in the cabin and I breathed a sigh of relief, knowing we were safely on our way. Feeling strangely peaceful after the longest day of my life, I settled back in my seat. The noise of the engine grew quieter as we soared into the African night.

34

Forgiveness

THE NEXT MORNING WE HAD ONE FINAL SHOOT, OUT ON THE NGONG HILLS, near the circle of stones where Dan's ashes had been scattered.

Amy went ahead with the crew while I followed with Lengai Croze, who had agreed to drive me out to the location. At twenty-six, he was a man now, strikingly handsome, with the same strands of hair stubbornly hanging over one eye. I hadn't seen him since before Dan died, and he hugged me for a long time without speaking. Then, proudly, he led me out to Deziree. But she wasn't herself anymore. Gone were the buffalo horns, the eye of the *dhow*, and the graffiti on the windshield. Her scratched and peeling paint was now a discreet shade of ivory, her windows and doors replaced, and her canvas seats neatly upholstered.

She looked beautiful. However, I wasn't sure whether Dan would have approved of his wild woman being transformed into a respectable matron. When Lengai turned the key, she sputtered and died, but at the second try coughed and roared to life—beneath the cosmetic changes, her unpredictable old self.

I couldn't resist asking Lengai if we could stop to take a picture of our first house with its large lawn, arching jacarandas, and climbing bougainvillea that blazed up the garage walls to the roof. I especially wanted to see the tree house again.

"I'm afraid you're in for a shock," he said regretfully, stopping the car outside our old gate. A sullen guard wearing a tattered T-shirt and dirty jeans pulled open the metal barrier to let us through. Inside, the bougainvillea still hung over the garage, scarlet and purple, but the structure itself tilted at an alarming angle. Our lawn was now a used-car lot, jammed with rusting hulks. The jacarandas were dying and the house was a wreck, with many of its windows cracked and roof tiles broken. When we walked around to the back, there was no trace of the tree house; the branch that had once proudly supported it was bent almost to the ground. There was no suggestion of William's clothesline, or of the family who had lived here so long ago.

"Kathy?" Lengai looked concerned.

"I'm okay," I said. Hurrying back to the car, I couldn't wait to leave.

As Deziree ground up the long, steep gradient to Kipenget's *boma* on the edge of the Great Rift Valley, I reflected on the deeper meaning of Dan's phrase, "The journey is the destination." A family, like a tree, takes root, puts out leaves, flowers, and fruits, reaches for the sky, and then withers. Each of these stages is as much of a true destination as all the others. The tree house, along with William's line, had indeed vanished, but nothing could destroy the reality of our years here together. The link among us, however stretched and strained, remained unbroken.

At the top of the escarpment overlooking the Great Rift Valley, we stopped to gaze at the clouds flouncing their way across the sky. The sound of sheep bleating and the cries of children echoed across the vast bowl, its sweeping green contours punctuated by the glint of many new tin roofs and curls of smoke. Despite them, for me the view remained the most magnificent sight on earth.

"I understand why Dan couldn't leave Africa," I said. "Why he had to go back and try to make it better."

"It's addictive," Lengai agreed, turning back onto the main road. "Gets under your skin like chiggers. You scratch and it gets worse."

When we reached Kipenget's, a new fence of wooden poles enclosed a patch planted with raggedy rows of maize and greens, and her wooden hut appeared more dilapidated than ever. She strode up the narrow path toward me, a smile creasing her face even as tears welled in her eyes.

Looking beyond her I could see that Amy and the crew had arrived before us. Kipenget's grandchildren were clustered around Allan, who was setting up his camera. Lengai handed Deziree's keys to Amy, since she would drive the car in the next sequence. Amy had always hated struggling with the Land Rover's tricky clutch, so I held my breath as I watched the vehicle lurch forward, stall, then creep ahead again. Suddenly it veered off into the tall grass. It was a minute before I realized that Amy was weaving giant figure eights. Deziree was dancing in her hands.

By the time Allan had finished shooting, the sky was a swirling mass of coral, burgundy, and gray. A low murmur rose from the cattle being herded back to their *boma*s, and I could smell wood smoke drifting over the dry grass. Kipenget's grandchildren watched while Amy walked down the narrow pathway to the stones enclosing the patch of earth that held all that remained of Dan's body. She looked achingly vulnerable as she stood there, her arms folded tight across her body, her long dress blowing in a sudden breeze. I remembered a couple of lines of the poem by Mary Elizabeth Frye that was read out at the celebration of life:

Do not stand at my grave and cry,
I am not there. I did not die.

It was hard *not* to cry. But this time I wasn't grieving for Dan. I was mourning the long and painful time it was taking Amy to find peace after his death. Yet, even as I watched her in the golden light of sunset, I could see that something had happened to her: she looked different. Now twenty-two, the same age Dan had been when he was killed, she stood straight and tall, and her dark eyes glowed. With a sense of fierce pride, I realized that a torch had been passed. Amy was taking over where Dan had left off. No longer in his shadow, she herself was becoming a beacon of light.

The next day, on the flight back to London, I caught a glimpse of my reflection in the window and smiled. Now, with our film in the can and our team safe, I finally felt I had achieved something worthwhile. I knew how proud Dan would have been of Amy and, I hoped, of me too.

One of the first calls I received in Los Angeles was from Mike. "Thank God you didn't spend that night in Mogadishu," he said. "The day after you filmed in the Sahafi Hotel, the owner was kidnapped. He's been released now, but if you'd been there, you, Amy, and your crew would probably have been kidnapped too."

Sadly, there has been no end to the wreckage and destitution in Mogadishu since then, either for Somalis or for foreign journalists and aid workers. Now Somalia is one of the deadliest nations for journalists. It's hard to imagine what could bring peace to such a devastated country.

It took five months to edit the film, interweaving old video clips of Dan with Amy's interviews and the material we had shot in Africa. One of Amy's jobs was to review hundreds of hours of war footage. She grew increasingly disturbed by endless images of violence, blood, and despair she was witnessing until she discovered a reflection by Winston Churchill that seemed to make her feel better: "We shall draw from the heart of suffering itself the means of inspiration and survival."

She described her own emergence from the horror of Dan's death in an article about her brother in a Boston University publication:

> Over time, I found that pain visited less frequently and when sorrow washed through me, it wasn't as deep or intense as it had once been. When I felt happy it was bliss, because I had known the extremes of sadness. My worst nightmare had become a reality, and I survived—reborn through my grief, profoundly aware of how precious life really is.

Once our film, *Dying to Tell the Story*, was delivered, we waited on tenterhooks for the verdict on our efforts. We were floored to learn that the first screening would be in New York—at the United Nations.

At five o'clock on November 10, 1997, Amy and I had just finished dressing for the UN event, sponsored by the Overseas Press Club of America. When the front desk called to say that Mr. Mohammed Shaffi was waiting for us downstairs, we hurried out of the room and into the elevator. I surveyed Amy, standing beside me in a silver-blue tunic and narrow silk pants with a soft scarf draped over one shoulder. She appeared radiant and calm, although she said she felt more nervous than the morning we flew into Somalia. She peered at me closely, licked her finger, and rubbed a speck of mascara from my cheek.

We were both laughing as the elevator doors opened and we spotted Shaffi, handsome in a dark suit and tie, standing in the center of the lobby. Smiling broadly, he enveloped us in a double bear hug. Amy asked about his family, and he confessed that he had seen little of them, for his job always seemed more important. However, he said he was proud that the work he had done in Africa had saved lives and added, "Now I have the rest of my life to make up with my children."

He handed his camera to a passing stranger and asked the man to take a picture of the three of us together before he was escorted to his car. That photo was to become a precious memento, for two years later, at age forty-nine, gentle Shaffi died of a massive heart attack while on assignment in Jerusalem, leaving behind his wife and four children. His death, like that of Carlos Mavroleon, shattered Amy and me, because we had come to love him like a brother.

Outside the hotel, the doorman saluted as he hailed a cab. Amy and I piled in, talking excitedly about the evening ahead. When the driver turned to ask where we were going, I drew a sharp breath and stared at his proud, finely sculpted nose, his skin the color of bronze silk, and his dark, hooded eyes. Seeing my reaction, Amy gave our destination. She and I exchanged glances. Of the thousands of cabbies in New York, ours was clearly Somali.

"Where are you from?" I asked, knowing the answer. He told us his name was Ebrahim and that he was from Mogadishu.

"What a coincidence," Amy murmured.

I told our driver about Dan's love of Somalis and what had happened to him. Ebrahim listened carefully, and when we stopped at a traffic light he turned and told me, in his heavy Somali accent, that his family, too, had suffered losses in the fighting.

"I know all about your son and the journalists who died with him," he said gravely. Startled, I wondered what he thought of the incident but wasn't sure I wanted to know. When we arrived, he spoke again, choosing his words carefully.

"Your son and the journalists should not have been killed," he said. "It was a terrible mistake. The people of Mogadishu are ashamed of what happened." He paused, as though uncertain whether to continue, then looked me in the eye. "On behalf of all Somalis, I ask your forgiveness."

From somewhere inside me, I remembered what Dan's Masai brother, Peter Lekarian, had written in his letter to me: "The world is Somalia and needs redemption." In that instant I realized that if the world is to change, it is we, as Gandhi once said, who must change first.

"Thank you, Ebrahim," I answered simply. "I hate what the Somalis did, but I understand why they did it. I have forgiven the Somali people." I had no idea that these words would come out of my mouth, but the moment I had spoken them I knew they were true, and to be able to say them was a blessing.

When I tried to give Ebrahim money for the fare, he waved his hand. "Friends don't pay in this cab," he said, shooing us away.

Amy and I joined the stream of people flowing toward the scores of flags fluttering in the brisk November wind beneath the soaring facade of the United Nations. Pausing for a moment, I recalled Brenda Lawrence's prediction that Amy and I would one day stand here together. We strode inside and entered the vast hall, filled with an audience of eight hundred diplomats, journalists, and heads of media organizations from around the world. When they had settled in their seats and the lights had been dimmed, I braced myself to introduce the film, a story that Dan and so many of his brave colleagues had died to tell.

35

Wings

AMY AND I WERE THRILLED WHEN *DYING TO TELL THE STORY* WON SEVERAL important awards, was nominated for an Emmy, and was broadcast by CNN to over 120 countries. Years later, the film is still shown in schools and universities around the world. Tragically, however, frontline correspondents are even more endangered than ever—stalked, harassed, tortured, or killed for simply doing their job.

After our adventures making the film and our delight at its commercial success, Amy and I were determined to put our experience to good use. We returned to my Sunset Plaza apartment in Los Angeles, where she camped out in my second bedroom, which also served as my office. Over the next few months, we planned a series of documentaries for CNN about countries in the midst of change—troubled nations moving from war to peace, chaos to harmony. It took months, but we finally scraped enough money together to shoot a pilot in Lebanon, then recovering from decades of civil war. To our intense disappointment, after weeks of editing the project was turned down.

As our bills mounted and our confidence slumped—and with it my creative visions of producing films, books, and exhibitions that would inspire positive action in the world—I grew increasingly anxious about the tremendous odds we faced as we tried to create media that "mattered."

Then I remembered Teddy Roosevelt's precept: "Do what you can with what you have where you are." I had been told that one day I would write a book. Well, I had my letters, journals, tapes, and photos around me, and it would cost nothing to sit down at my computer and start it. But as I began to explore my life in Kenya and consider how I might present it, I started to have qualms about sharing embarrassing, even shameful, details about my past—details that it would be necessary to reveal if I wanted to write a truthful book about my life.

I felt just as nervous about expressing my belief that the evidence of metaphysical communication through psychics such as Rosemary Brown and Sylvia Browne deserved serious scientific study, and even more sensitive about revealing my conviction that Dan's spirit had survived his sudden death. Nothing else could explain to me the communications through Mollie Martin or Brenda Lawrence, or the extraordinary consequences of those communications. Still, what would professional, hard-bitten journalists make of my conviction? It was all very unnerving, and I wasn't sure what to do next.

One night, while confiding my anxieties to my journal, I felt a twitch in my hand and watched my fingers write the words "love," "power," and "energy" in a neat script that didn't resemble my own. Heart thumping, I recalled the moment on the shores of Lake Turkana when the same mysterious words had first appeared in my journal. I never did figure out what they meant back then, and they certainly didn't make any more sense now. I watched curiously as the pen, gripped in my fingers, continued to move across the page, writing a string of admonitions: "You have all you need to accomplish your mission on earth"; "Trust, for we are with you at all times—never apart, not for a minute"; and finally, "Things are unfolding as they should."

Ridiculous, I thought crossly, slamming the book shut. I needed more than reassuring words. If my "Team Spirit," as Dan, through Brenda

Lawrence, had once described the invisible supporters that supposedly surrounded me existed, then they needed to offer evidence of their existence before I would go public with my story.

Just as I was grappling with this dilemma, I bumped into an old acquaintance, Alan Neuman, a television producer, who had done some serious research into paranormal phenomena. I told him my problem, and he immediately offered to help me.

"Come with me," he said, "and listen to a lecture being given by my friend J. C. Elliott, a senior NASA physicist who was awarded the highest civilian medal of honor our country gives for his contribution to the safe return to earth of the endangered Apollo 13 crew." Eager to be distracted, I readily agreed.

Jerry C. Elliott, who preferred to be called J. C., was a ruggedly handsome man with a full head of black hair and an air of calm authority. He began his speech to the crowded hall by describing his upbringing as a half-Scottish, half–Native American child in a small Oklahoma town. Known as Little Bear by his grandfather's people, he learned from them about the healing qualities of plants, the ways of the spirit, and how to communicate with his dead ancestors, he also learned to communicate telepathically with friends and relatives over great distances. When he was forty, the elders of his tribe bestowed their highest honor by renaming him High Eagle to reflect his spiritual awareness and his willingness to share what he had learned with others.

J. C. described how, in his other life as a NASA engineer, he worked in the realm of logic, focused solely on scientifically provable hypotheses. At first, he saw little scope for connecting his divergent worlds. But over time he had come to accept that there was much more to reality than he could see or measure. Sometimes he had to operate beyond the bounds of rational thinking and simply let go, surrendering to a force he couldn't see or define, but knew existed.

He went on to speak about the concept of individual freedom, asserting that "to be free is to break the bonds of whatever possesses you. Growth can occur only when the bonds are broken. A spirit, once escaped from the bonds of the earth, can soar like an eagle. Eagles fly higher than other creatures and can see the full expanse of the earth, the unity of life, and the oneness of God and creation."

I felt the hair on the back of my neck rise as J. C. continued, emphasizing the need for each individual to connect with the essence of God, whether conceived of as the Great Spirit, Higher Consciousness, the Source, Energy, Light, or what he called the Force. As I listened to his words, I felt as if he were directing a challenge at me, one I could resist or seize. I wondered whether, if I completely gave myself to this Force and liberated myself from my old patterns of behavior, it would allow me to fulfill my purpose, wholly, authentically, fearlessly—and with integrity.

After the lecture Allan introduced me to J. C. as a documentary filmmaker and journalist with a special interest in learning more about the intersection of physics and metaphysics. At the end of our conversation, J. C. invited me to visit NASA headquarters to enable me to research an article on the subject. I took him up on his offer immediately, and we set a date.

A few weeks later I flew to Houston and took a taxi to the Lyndon B. Johnson Space Center, which looked like the sprawling campus of a well-endowed university, except for the huge Saturn V rocket that lay on the ground outside the gate.

J. C. spent the day demonstrating some of the sophisticated technology developed by NASA. I felt that he understood the real reason for my visit: my desire to understand how he reconciled his training as a scientist with his spiritual beliefs. There was no time to discuss this during our packed day, but at the end of it he offered to drive me to the airport.

I climbed into his truck and J. C. turned his key in the ignition. Looking straight ahead, he said, "I've been watching you all day, and I know a lot about you."

"Like what?" There was more than a hint of challenge in my voice.

He pulled into traffic. "You, my friend, have been perching for a long time. Now you're ready to fly."

"How did you know that?" I asked. I never normally talked about my dreams about birds to anyone.

"An eagle knows a hawk," he said. "And this hawk is ready to soar." We drove in silence for a few minutes as I tried to absorb what he had said. Then J. C. pulled to the side of the road and stopped the car beside a bank of brightly colored spring wildflowers.

"I want to tell you a story," he said. "Once, a long time ago, there was an eagle that spent his days flapping his wings, flying long and far as he surveyed his kingdom below. It was very tiring and he would grow weary, returning often to his perch to rest. Each time it took longer to build energy for the next flight.

"One day, after battling with the wind, he grew too tired to fly. He was terrified, knowing that he would sink to his death like a stone. At the last moment, with all energy gone, he stretched his wings as far as they would spread, held them in position, and waited to fall. To his surprise, instead of plunging to the earth he continued flying—but this flight was different, for he was riding the wind effortlessly, sailing like a ship on a buoyant sea.

"The eagle was exhilarated by this new ability. After resting for a moment on the wind, he flapped again and rose even further. From this elevated height his view was longer and his vision wider. Once again, though, he grew tired and stretched his wings as far as he could, hoping to cushion his fall. And again the wind caught him—but this time he rose higher and higher on a current of air that took him above the clouds, soaring toward the sun."

"What do you mean?" I asked.

"I'm saying that the flight of the eagle is like our quest for greater energy and a wider view of creation. We spend our lives flapping our wings, thinking we have to *make* things happen if we are to move ahead. When you stop flapping—battling life—and have enough faith, God, Energy, the Great Spirit, whatever you want to call it, takes over. It is then that you learn to soar, to ride the Force as an eagle rides the winds."

I loved that image, so different from my old recurring nightmare of a bird smashing against an invisible barrier and plummeting to its bloody death. Then it occurred to me that whenever I had been totally committed to something that I knew was part of my purpose—whether working on one of Dan's projects, Amy's, or my own—I seemed to receive the resources and support I required exactly when I needed them.

As I was turning the idea over in my head, J. C. pulled the truck back onto the road. Five minutes later we were at the airport. After a quick hug, he drove off and I headed for my gate.

Once in the air, I closed my eyes, picturing an eagle soaring toward the sun. Far below, in my imagination, a hawk flapped its wings like crazy but couldn't seem to take flight.

J. C. and I spoke a few times during the next few weeks as I worked on an article about my visit to NASA. One evening he called me outside of working hours. "How are you, Hawk?"

"Things could be better," I said, still facing seemingly insurmountable challenges on every front and no closer to finding proof of the existence of life in another dimension.

"Are you ready to stop perching and write that book?" he asked.

"Are you kidding?" I had to smile. "I'm still clinging to the branch for dear life."

"I've written something for you," he said. "May I fax it?"

I turned on the machine and tore off the first page as it came through.

Flow

Flow occurs when all elements, all things
act in synchronicity
with natural rhythms.
To be in tune with each thing
that comes into one's awareness
is to be in the flow.

There had been little synchronicity and certainly no flow in my life of late. I wondered why. I read on:

Obstacles to flow are
mere disruptions

which only serve
to test the strength
of the flow.

If that was true, then perhaps all the obstacles I faced were just tests.

All things occur
when they are ready
and it is time.

After one or two further exchanges, another fax emerged from my
machine:

It is time . . .
time to lift the wings and soar,
time to be free.

I knew he was right. I had to be courageous enough to tell my story
truthfully—no matter what the consequences might be. Roughly sketching an outline, I sat down at my computer and closed my eyes. Then I felt
a familiar shiver run down my back, and my fingers began to move over
the keys.

36

Love Catcher

A CURIOUS THING HAPPENED THE DAY THAT I FINALLY COMMITTED MYSELF to writing the book. The telephone didn't stop ringing—and everyone I spoke with seemed to have a new project for me. It was as if once I had committed myself to be true—and truthful—no matter what, the genius, power, and magic that Goethe had once described began to flow. There was a deluge of work, and I realized that a great tide of energy was sweeping me forward toward a variety of new goals. I remembered clearly the words that had come to me one day during meditation at the Sunset Plaza: "When that time comes, you will begin your true job on this planet." The timing certainly wasn't mine. I wished that the right time had arrived years ago, but I guess I hadn't been ready before.

It was difficult to write my book, however, for Amy and I had begun producing *Global Tribe*, a series for PBS hosted by Amy about courageous grassroots change-makers in South Africa, the Philippines, and Mexico.

There was something else too. Determined to fulfill another of Dan's original messages, relayed through Mollie and Brenda, Amy and I decided to launch a foundation, linked to our ongoing production enterprise, to celebrate and support creative activists like Dan. Soon our

Creative Visions Foundation, based in my home office, was flooded with requests for guidance from young filmmakers, journalists, dancers, actors, and artists using media and the arts to tell important stories.

Jessica Mayberry, a recent graduate of Oxford University in England, was among the first to ask for help. She wanted to teach Indian villagers how to use video to share stories about the challenges they faced: child marriages, abusive husbands, and injustice in their communities. We helped her hatch "Video Volunteers," which brought young filmmakers like Jessica to India to teach villagers, often illiterate, the skills needed to become community videographers.

Over the next few years, Jessica would transform her idea into the world's largest, most diverse network of community producers—former slum dwellers working as teachers, students, rickshaw drivers, and diamond polishers—who were trained as journalists, videographers, and activists to expose underreported stories and right the wrongs of poverty, injustice, and inequality.

Although delighted to be helping creative activists and developing our own projects, working with Amy in our small apartment in West Hollywood led to major tensions between us. As we discovered, it's not easy for mothers and adult daughters to work together, much less live in close proximity. When Amy was entertaining late, I couldn't go to sleep at my normal hour, and if I felt like writing all night, she was forced to sleep with eyeshades and a pillow over her head. Amy had no privacy, nor did I, and we had our share of arguments. However, if she stomped out the door in a temper, she would always crack it open again just enough to bellow, "I love you!" in case I keeled over and died when she was out. We had both learned an important lesson from Dan's sudden death: never leave an issue unresolved with those you love.

Fortunately, the apartment downstairs became free, and Amy moved in with a roommate. After she left, I covered the walls with Dan's prints, photographs, and collages. I also taped more thoughts and inspirational sayings onto the refrigerator—among them, Dan's now-tattered admonition by Winston Churchill to "never, never, never ever give in," which had never seemed more relevant.

The increased space between Amy and me helped our relationship, but I found it difficult not to act like a mother in business meetings—my shins were permanently bruised from her less-than-gentle kicks administered beneath the table when I treated her as a daughter instead of as a colleague. She certainly deserved respect, for she was the canny observer in meetings, intuitive and wise, while I tended to be the enthusiastic cheerleader who had to be hauled back to earth by my ankles when I got too excited.

Living apart also made it possible for me to consider dating again. After the pain of leaving Mike and then Jeremy, and the challenging relationship I'd experienced with Geoff, I had avoided relationships for fear of causing more pain—to myself or someone else. When I mentioned my feelings to Amy, she confessed that having lost Dan, she was afraid of ever loving anyone again, terrified of the pain that comes from loving then losing. As we talked, I realized that I was also afraid of losing *myself* if I loved again. Perhaps the only way to maintain my equilibrium was to remain single.

Still, ever hopeful, Amy persuaded me to join an online dating agency. After an entire year, only a few males had bothered to respond to my profile—apparently they were the only men in Hollywood willing to go out with a woman who confessed to being over forty.

"Why can't I find a decent man?" I asked Amy over dinner one night. Just then, I was struck by an epiphany. She and I had written *Angel Catcher: A Journal of Loss and Remembrance* to help us heal from the deep grief we felt after Dan's death. Now we could put together a new journal to help me, maybe even us, find true love.

"Definitely crazy, Mum," she muttered. "What can you say about healthy relationships? All I've seen you experience is pain and loss, jealousy and obsessions, breakups and makeups—so what could you possibly tell people about finding the right partner?"

I saw her point. "But that's exactly why you should help me write the book," I said.

The next day I began researching various aspects of love. When Amy saw that I was serious, she helped me outline a journal that might enable us—and hopefully others—to discard our old scripts and patterns and create new ones to attract happy, healthy relationships. It took two years, but by the time *Love Catcher: Inviting Love into Your Life* was published, I felt like an expert on how *other people* had found, and kept, great relationships. However, despite all I had learned, my own love life remained as frustrating as ever. Something was blocking me from finding the kind of man I longed for.

I decided to follow the advice of a workaholic film editor with whom I had been close and who was acutely aware of my internal struggles. He handed me the telephone number of a therapist. "Go see her," he begged, "so you don't go on hurting men—or yourself—anymore."

A week later, I turned up at an ivy-covered house near the Getty Museum where I met Joanne, an elegantly dressed woman in her fifties who greeted me with a firm handshake and a look that made it clear that there would be no messing with her. I explained my challenges and asked her to help me remove the obstacles that might be standing in the way of becoming the person I wanted to be—one who could love, and be loved by, a good man. After a few sessions she reminded me of a very important life principle: In order to be loved, you have to feel that you *deserve* love. In other words, to receive love, you have to be able to give love—not only to your partner, but also to yourself. That seemed like a tall order, for there were aspects of me that I still didn't *like* about myself, much less love.

Joanne also pointed out that, in her words, "we attract at our own level." As I thought about recent relationships, I saw her point: life had indeed provided a mirror. When I was sad, unfocused, and dishonest, Jeremy had responded in kind to my unsettled, negative, self-destructive energy. With Geoff I had never had a fully committed relationship. Now I wanted an integrated, evolved, positive individual to share a life that balanced work, family, and spiritual growth. Unfortunately, Joanne said that meant I had to *be* that person. Despite the fact that I had long ago merged the "two Kathys," whose divergent goals had caused me so many problems, it seemed that I had a long way to go before I became truly whole.

With Joanne as my guide, I set off on a journey to understand what might be standing in the way between me and love. My initial optimism waned as the weeks and months went by. Despite the light that Joanne helped shed on many aspects of my life, after a year in therapy there was still a shadow inside me so dark that even the brightest beams didn't penetrate it. Unwilling to spend more time or money to locate the key to that darkened room, I was ready to give up, but Joanne wouldn't let me. "We're not stopping until you dissolve this block," she said firmly.

She looked at me with a penetrating gaze. "Tell me, Kathy," she said, "why do you think you can't have what you really want?" I sat in silence. I didn't really want to know, or even consider, the answer—perhaps the truth would be too painful to bear.

Leaning toward me, my sophisticated therapist in her affluent Los Angeles home offered much the same advice the gentle nun had given me in a shabby Nairobi shopping center: "Be peaceful, Kathy," she said. I could hear the echo of Sister Leone's voice when she added, "Inside, you know all the answers."

I nodded, knowing she was right—but was I courageous enough to go there? I wanted to bolt from the room when she said, "Close your eyes. Just breathe."

Subduing the urge to flee, I followed her instructions. As I breathed deeply, I acknowledged that in truth I *did* know the answer to her question—and had all along. It was guilt that had kept me from feeling worthy of receiving the success and love I desired.

My mind flashed back to my wild days in Africa. Although I had tried to move on, I still felt ashamed about my past. There was something else too, even more distressing. Despite Mike's protests to the contrary, I still felt in some way to blame for Dan's death. After all, I had encouraged him to become a photojournalist, unwittingly launching him on a journey that had led to his murder on that dusty road in Mogadishu.

I struggled to put into words the thoughts that had long been buried in the deepest recesses of my mind. Joanne sat without speaking until I was finally quiet.

"Is that it?" she asked, sounding almost disappointed. "From the way you began to speak about yourself I thought there was much more to come." I shook my head.

"Now I have a few more questions," she said, peering at me with her characteristic no-nonsense look. "You forgave the Somalis who killed your son?"

I nodded. It had taken a long time, but finally I had gotten there.

"You have forgiven Mike?"

"Yes, of course." As he had said, if we both had been able to do it over again, we would have behaved differently.

"Has he forgiven you?"

I nodded again, grateful that we were now good friends.

"How about Jeremy?" she probed.

"He did the best he could," I answered. I would always love the tormented man who had set me on my path of self-discovery.

She stared into my eyes. "What about Dan?"

I looked up, unsure what she meant. He hadn't *tried* to die. Then I realized how angry I had been with him for leaving me. I still was. It was irrational, of course, but she was right. I had to forgive my child for dying.

Eyes brimming, I nodded.

"Now you have one more person to deal with," she said, tilting her head to one side as though coaching a very slow child.

Again, at first I didn't comprehend what she meant. Then the understanding swept over me.

"You have to say it, Kathy," Joanne pressed, folding her arms in front of her. "Tell me."

It took a long time, but I finally managed to form the words she demanded to hear. "I forgive . . . me."

Later that night, it seemed that a skylight had opened onto my soul, dispelling the remaining pool of darkness within me. Finally I understood that every action—each deed, word, or choice—not only affects us as individuals, but also has an impact on many others through the endless network of our relationships. Sometimes, to save ourselves, we make decisions that hurt those we love, praying that over time the wounds will heal and that we will be forgiven—and that we can forgive those who have caused us pain. As a result, a heart may be broken many times before it cracks open enough for the spirit to free itself and finally become what Emerson once described as an unencumbered, unobstructed, "active soul."

With that revelation, I prayed that my soul could finally be free, unburdened of the guilt that had confined me for so long—ready, willing, and perhaps even able to search out and find my mate.

I decided to employ the principles of creative visualization that had worked so well for me when I first moved back to London—this time to materialize the perfect man. I pulled out a notepad and began listing the qualities in a man that were important to me. Most of all, I yearned for a kind person with a warm, open heart who loved his family but was at ease wherever he found himself. Tall would be good. And ideally my ideal mate would be a bit unpredictable—after all, neither of us would want to get bored.

As the list grew longer, I decided that I was really tired of lentils and beans; a comfortable lifestyle wouldn't hurt—so I added that too. Two houses would be fun, I thought, letting my imagination run wild. When I showed my requirements to Amy, she made me add that the man must be of a "suitable age."

"One more thing, Mum," she said with a knowing smile. "Anyone who ends up with you needs a great sense of humor if he's going to survive." I appreciated that particular vote of confidence!

As a coda to my visualization, I wrote a note to the man I hoped would one day share my life:

We have so much to do—you and I.
A lifetime of being apart to catch up on,
A universe of experiences to share.
A cosmos of adventures awaits us
When the time is right . . .

"Oh, and one *more* thing," Amy said. "You need to run your choices past me because, let's face it, your judgment is questionable."

I wasn't at all sure about my prospects. At my age it would be a miracle if I found someone who could meet even a few of my expectations. It took some months, but one day Amy mentioned in passing that she talked about my quest for the ideal partner with Rick, an old friend of mine who lived in Malibu. And not long afterward Rick phoned me to say that he thought his next-door neighbor might be the right answer. Michael Bedner headed the world's leading hospitality design firm with thirteen offices around the world. Fun, charming, intelligent, and generous to a fault—so Rick said—it seemed his only drawbacks were that he traveled much of the time and, since his divorce twenty years before, he avoided commitment. He sounded too good to be true, but I agreed that I should meet him after Amy Googled his name and discovered that he had been on a committee with UN Secretary-General Kofi Annan, which earned her approval.

Rick, still acting as go-between, told me to meet Michael on a bench in front of a restaurant in Santa Monica Airport. Dressed in my best suit and high heels, I felt like a nervous seventh-grader as I awaited his arrival. When the appointed hour went by and he hadn't shown up, I was about to leave. Then I caught sight of a tall man with a mane of white hair and a neatly trimmed Hemingway beard hurrying toward me. Wearing pressed khaki shorts, a striped shirt, a suede jacket, and loafers, he enveloped me in a hug that took my breath away. When he drew back, I was instantly attracted to the mischievous hazel eyes that sparkled at me from behind tortoise-rimmed glasses.

Over drinks, we found that we were both from the Midwest and had separated from our spouses in the same year. He had two sons, Misha and Ilja, who were almost exactly the same ages as Dan and Amy, and he was quick to tell me that his parents were the kindest, most generous people he had ever met. Both had had very limited education: his father was the son of a miner, and his mother had left school at fifteen to support her family by working in a box factory. She had died when Michael was only nine.

Knowing that he was an architect and designer, I told him about Dan's offer to build me a hut at the end of his garden to "tend his goats." Michael chuckled as he promised to construct a straw-bale house wherever

I pleased—with no responsibility for looking after domestic animals. As we parted, I nodded enthusiastically when he asked if he could call me. Then I stewed for three weeks before I heard from him again. When he finally called he explained that he had circled the globe on a business trip in the meantime.

Our second dinner was even more fun, but Michael disappeared soon afterward on another long journey—although he did send a bunch of flowers through his secretary.

When he called again, I decided to invite him to my place. Annoyed about his disappearing acts, I served him our usual fare—a bowl of lentils and rice—with a beer from the back of the fridge. He seemed genuinely enthusiastic about my mushy stew. Later that night, when we ended up in my bedroom, he laughed out loud as he tried to maneuver his way around the cartons of books that took up most of the space around my bed. Mortified, I wanted to disappear under the covers, but he drew me to him, and within a few moments I had forgotten everything except how wonderful it felt to be held. That night, with his arm wrapped around me, I slept better than I had in years.

When Michael arrived the following week to take me to dinner, I opened the door to find him clutching a screwdriver and surrounded by a mound of boxes. "We have a job to do," he announced as he began hauling boxes up my steps. During the next three hours he assembled and filled six bookshelves. "So much for the minefield," he muttered as he placed the last book on a shelf. "I feared for my life." And then we went out to eat.

Several weeks later Michael called from Abu Dhabi with an invitation to spend the following weekend at his Malibu home, which turned out to be one in a compound of several houses perched on the shore of the Pacific Ocean. Hand in hand, trailed by Michael's little dog Sammy, a rescued Jack Russell, we wandered the beach together for hours, marveling at pelicans diving for fish, a pod of feeding dolphins, and a seal we named Sid. It was hard to go our separate ways Sunday evening.

Captivated by Michael's magnetic presence and irrepressible spirit, I couldn't wait to return to Malibu, but by Wednesday he had vanished again on another business trip. After much soul-searching, I decided he was too unpredictable, even for me.

I had almost managed to forget him when he reappeared. This time he allowed me a little more deeply into his heart, or so I felt—but then he departed on yet another trip. Perhaps it was just as well, for had I seen any more of him, I might have found myself starting to fall in love, and suddenly the idea of losing my independence and merging my life with someone else's was so daunting I wanted to run for cover. It was one thing to desire a partner but quite another to commit to a flesh-and-blood man with a family history as complex as mine, imbued with similar hopes and dreams, and possessing equally confusing memories of old relationships. Faced with the prospect of loving—and then possibly losing—him, I began to falter.

Then, as so often happens, life intervened. One day talk-show host Rosie O'Donnell called me after receiving no fewer than three copies of *The Journey Is the Destination* for her fortieth birthday. She said she had found Dan's work an inspiration, not only for her own painting but also in her personal life at a time when she needed it. As a thank-you, she invited me on a cruise for her family and friends on a ship she had chartered—and said I could bring anyone I wished.

Curious to see what his reaction would be, I asked Michael to join me. I was delighted when he accepted. I hoped we would have time to talk during the voyage, but I barely saw him, for he was as popular as the Pied Piper, constantly trailed by a pack of laughing children hoping to be tickled, tossed in the air, or dragged along the deck by one foot. Watching him with kids, many who were being ignored by their own grandparents, made me like him even more. Every youngster seemed to treat him like their uncle; and every adult, like their best friend.

After we returned from the cruise, Michael invited me to spend another weekend at the Malibu house and suggested that I bring Amy along. Although I didn't say anything to her, I had recently met Michael's neighbor Jon Turteltaub, who was renting Michael's second house, a two-story Cape Cod next door. Handsome, intelligent, and genuinely hilarious, Jon was a film director who seemed like a good match for Amy.

There was just one small problem, as I discovered when I took Amy over to meet him: he was dating another woman.

To my delight, several months later Jon was unattached. Amy, now tanned and radiant after a visit to Costa Rica, was bubbling with excitement as she joined me for a walk on the beach. Suddenly her words trailed off and I saw that she had spotted Jon, standing on the balcony of the house next door, talking with a friend. He waved us up, and within minutes he and Amy were bantering like old pals. Later that day he came over to Michael's, trailed by his dog Archie, a 150-pound Leonberger, on their way to Children's Hospital, where they were volunteers. The next morning Amy dropped by his place with a pan of homemade apple crumble. Then he turned up at Michael's home with Girl Scout cookies.

Theirs became an old-fashioned courtship, more Iowa than California, and within a year they were engaged; six months after that they were married on a ranch in Malibu, complete with African drummers and a rented giraffe. It was only much later that Jon confessed that he never really liked apple crumble.

Within another year Amy was pregnant. When she asked her doctor for the baby's due date it was—when else?—September 18, Dan's birthday. In fact, Jack Eldon was born a day late, a week after the gentle passing of my ninety-nine-year-old father, who had only recently put away his tennis racket. My mother joined her husband of seventy-four years soon afterward, departing with the same spirit of love and dignity that had graced her long life.

37

Soaring

OVER THE NEXT YEAR, MICHAEL TOOK ME ON A NUMBER OF EXCITING TRIPS around the world to visit his offices in Hong Kong, Singapore, New Delhi, and Dubai. I decided to invite him to Kenya, for he had never been to Africa and was intrigued by the idea of going on safari. After spending a few days in Nairobi, we headed into the bush for some time alone together. Stripped of our cell phones and e-mail, and far from the stresses and excesses of our ordinary lives, we were finally able to relax as we straddled our spitting camels, trekked through desert thornbushes, and sipped sundowners beside a crackling fire. We found we were able to peel away the protective layers behind which each of us had sheltered since the trauma of separation and divorce. Finally, we could communicate more freely, deeply, intimately.

On our final night in Kenya we stayed in a simple stone enclosure at the edge of a deep ravine. The wind echoed across the hills and a lantern cast flickering shadows on the walls as we discussed how difficult it was to contemplate a new, committed relationship at our age. I admitted that despite what I had discovered about myself, I was still nervous about starting over again, knowing how painful loss could be if things went wrong.

"Yes, it's one of the things they don't tell you when you're young," Michael said. "People rarely mention that if you fall in love it may end one day, and he or she will be gone. And they certainly *never* tell you that if that happens, there's always the chance to dive in once more.

"But if you don't take the risk," he concluded with a wry smile, "you'll never again experience the joy that's possible between two people who truly love each other."

The way he said it, and the look he gave me, made me realize that one day Michael's home might become mine, which was still a daunting thought. But then I remembered a remark I had once passed on to Dan: "An open heart is the goal; it is not to be feared." Fear—that was one of the things I wanted to put behind me. It was time to love again.

Much later, after the noises of the African night had died down and the air was cool, I opened my journal and began to write. As my flashlight beam began to flicker, there was just enough light to add these words:

All is as it should be—life unfolding perfectly, rhythmically, and endlessly, teaching me who I am and can be. I am grateful.

On the plane back for a stopover in London, flying over northern Kenya in the darkness, I no longer felt the painful *mal d'Afrique* that had haunted my departures ever since leaving the country in 1988. I was finally at peace. Africa didn't seem like home anymore—though neither did the United States nor England. I realized that my true home was someplace I'd never thought to look—deep inside myself.

As I reflected on my long, often tortuous homecoming, I became aware that although I had to travel thousands of miles to Africa to first lose, then find, then ultimately be true to that self, there is an unexplored continent within each of us waiting to be discovered—a place of joy and sorrow, of darkness and light, with limitless potential, challenging every aspect of our being. To respond to its call is to embark on a voyage that will leave us forever transformed, for it is during this safari of the soul that we confront who we are and who we can become. Cocooned in my seat, and lulled by the drone of the engines, I drifted off to sleep, won-

dering if, after a lifetime of asking questions, I had finally, without noticing it, lived my way into at least some of the answers.

After a week in London, Michael and I returned to Malibu, and soon
afterward he invited me for a walk. He said he wanted to introduce me to
his favorite palm tree—one that stood, tall and proud, a hundred yards
up the beach from his house. Seated on the sand beneath it, he explained
that during one of Malibu's worst fires, flying sparks had ignited its bark
and it had begun to smolder. Michael, one of his sons, and their friend
Dan had created a chain of hoses, then placed a tall ladder against the
palm and sprayed its trunk until they managed to extinguish the fire. As
he spoke, I realized that he was describing the same fire that Geoff and I
had witnessed from our hotel back in 1993, soon after Dan's death. I told
Michael about the homeless man named Daniel who had given me the
courage to start over again. "I'm awfully glad you didn't give up," he said,
reaching into his pocket and pulling out a small box.

Suddenly, he took my hand in his.

"Will you marry me?" he asked, slipping onto my finger a ring with
a multifaceted circle of diamonds. We hurried up to Amy and Jon's home
to share our news, but they greeted us at the door holding a bottle of
champagne and four glasses. Apparently Amy had spotted us from their
veranda and had somehow suspected that Michael was about to propose.
Jon had filmed us, realizing that Amy's suspicions were true when he
captured the glint of my ring with his telephoto lens.

Six months later, on June 21st—the summer solstice—a troupe of
African drummers and singers prepared the way for our barefoot wedding party, including seventeen flower-bedecked children ringing tiny
bells; Michael and his sons, wearing tuxedo shorts; Amy, carrying nine-
month-old Jack; my new daughters-in-laws Sangini and Jamie; and,
bringing up the rear, our ring-bearers, Archie and Sammy. With Kenyan
and California flags flapping above us, and surfers gliding by on foam-
tipped waves, we said our vows before several hundred joyous friends,
relatives—and my "Team Spirit."

After our guests left, I settled into the heart of my extraordinary life
and tackled my memoir in earnest. It took a long time, because I was

constantly interrupted by Jack—and his baby brother, Daniel, born on Easter Sunday 2010.

As I finish my story, I am deeply grateful that Amy and Jon's children, now six and three, still live next door to Michael and me, enabling us all to go on adventurous safaris, heading down the beach "as far as the eye can see" in search of miniature buffaloes that might have got caught in the tide pools or pink giraffes tangled in the kelp.

The other day I wandered along the beach at sunset and in the half-light saw two youngsters running across the sand. My heart fell still as I watched. Shouting, they leaped into the air over and over, tumbling on top of each other, turning cartwheels before picking themselves up to tussle again. Following behind, their parents, dark silhouettes against the crimson-streaked sky, shouted encouragement. I stared, alone with my memories.

The scene blurred, and suddenly I was on the shores of the Indian Ocean, gold-rimmed and smooth, as the sun, a giant crimson orb, slowly sank beneath the horizon. The sand was still hot under my feet as Dan dashed ahead, his voice shrill against the lapping of the waves. Amy struggled to keep up as he climbed a low wall that bounded the beach.

At the top he reached down to pull his little sister up next to him and they stood on the edge, arms rising.

"Fly!" I cried.

My mind shifted and I was back, standing on the shore of the Pacific Ocean again. What if I had never gone to Africa? What would have happened had I stayed forever in our safe British suburb cloistered behind net curtains, living a sensible, secondhand life? What would Dan be doing now? Would I still be the lost, hungry woman hiding behind a smile?

I'll never know, nor do I need to. But three decades on, what my heart now understands about the power of the human spirit and its ability to love, heal, and transform everything—including the meaning of death—lightens my sorrow and intensifies my joy in life and living.

Turning back toward our house that evening, I felt my pace quicken and I glimpsed a cluster of seagulls, barely visible in the fading light, nestled on the sand. As I neared them they scattered, skimming away low over the restless waves. The birds' sudden flight triggered another memory, this one from my week in London with Michael.

On our last day he'd had work to do, so I had set off on my own by bus. The city had never been more beautiful. There were daffodils, irises, and tulips in the parks. Spring had arrived and the sun glinted from church spires, twinkled on the tips of the towers of Parliament, and warmed the tourists who meandered across the park lawns toward Westminster Abbey. It was the half-term holiday and children were everywhere, their bright jackets like candy wrappers against the gray sidewalks.

"St. Bride's," I said to the conductor, and jumped off when he pulled the bell. It had been many months since I had spoken with Dan, either through Brenda or by hearing his voice inside my head, and I wanted to feel close to him again. Ducking against the wind, I walked through to the churchyard. Spiky purple flowers bloomed in the water-darkened soil that lined the paving stones, while buds sprouted on the little tree with the snakeskin bark whose branches now jutted every which way toward the sky.

Once inside the sanctuary, I found the book inscribed with the names of all the journalists who had died, much like soldiers, in action—Hos, Anthony, Hansi, Mo Amin, Carlos Mavroleon, and countless others. One name leaped out at me, the letters crisply etched in perfect calligraphy on handmade paper:

> Dan Eldon
> Photographer, humanitarian, and adventurer
> Killed while on assignment with Reuters
> July 12, 1993
> "Safari as a Way of Life"

Without a gravestone, this was his only epitaph—and I'm sure he would have liked it that way. Before leaving, I lit four candles for Dan and his friends. Even after so many years, the sight of his picture and all the names in the book sent a sharp pain through my heart.

Brushing away tears, I headed for the silver footbridge over the Thames to the Tate Modern Gallery. There I spotted a young man leaning against the railings, a guitar beside him on the pavement, a bright knit cap barely containing his tangled dreadlocks. Studying me, he picked up his guitar and began to sing softly. When I got close enough to hear the words, I stood still and buried my head in my hands.

The singer stopped suddenly. He was clearly worried about me, but I shook my head to reassure him. "Thank you," I said, dropping a five-pound note into his guitar case.

He smiled and launched into his song again, this time louder. Tossing my inhibitions to the wind, I joined in, belting out the words for everyone to hear. "No woman, no cry, everything's gonna be all right . . ."

Heading on across the river, I paused for a moment on this "Sword of Light," as the bridge is called, an elegant reminder of hope in the twenty-first century.

Below, a cluster of gulls caught my attention as they fluttered wildly, gathering momentum to rise above the swirling winds. I watched two more take off together; one joined the flock while the other found an upward draft and wheeled away, soaring high, wings outstretched against the clear blue sky. I saw it rise, flying fast toward the sun, ascending higher and higher until I turned away, blinded by the dazzling light.

Acknowledgments

Writing this book has been like threading my way through a challenging maze. After groping through it, I realized just how many people have helped shape me, have influenced the way I behave, and have accepted who I have become. When I reached the end of the writing, I was still not quite out of the maze and needed the loving support of generous friends, old and new, until *In the Heart of Life* was actually published.

Sadly, it is impossible to thank everyone who played an important role in my life and in writing my story. All those who have done the most for me and meant the most to me play their parts on these pages, and I would ask them to accept the book as an expression of my gratitude to them. But there are some who do not appear in it who have given me invaluable help in getting my life's journey onto paper, and those I thank here.

I am deeply grateful to Sylvia Browne, who introduced me to Nancy Hancock, executive editor at HarperOne, who became my multitalented, infinitely patient, and deeply perceptive editor; her thoughtful notes were essential in shaping this book.

My parents, Russell and Louise Knapp, planted the seeds of adventure that grew into my lifelong quest for adventure and purpose and my desire to record what happened along the way. My son Dan and his "Team Spirit" have been my constant inspirations as I have tried to share a story that I hope will not only inspire readers, but also empower them to believe they can do far more than simply survive their lives. My daughter, Amy, was an invaluable critic, graciously tolerating my annoy-ing requests for comments on the "latest draft," and Mike Eldon kindly gave his blessings to a book that celebrates the enduring power of love across time and multiple dimensions.

Thanks to a dedicated crew around the world, I received helpful notes on storytelling and much-needed encouragement to keep writing—even when I never wanted to see this manuscript again. There are far more crew members than I can include here, but special thanks to Jacoba Atlas, Carol Beckwith, Clarissa Bernhardt, Joey Borgogna, Marissa Charles, Alicia Dougherty, Alison Fast, Angela Fisher, Mary Anne Fitzgerald, Jessica Lapham, Leslie Levin, Lori Levin, Eva and Yoel Haller, Claire Humphry, Larry Kirshbaum, Tim Lapage, Brenda Lawrence, Amy St. Onge, Steve Polivka, Penny Rhodes, Bonnie Solow, Meg Thompson, Julie Woodward, and my outstanding Creative Visions team. I am espe-cially grateful to Donald Paul, the teacher who appeared when I was "ready," if blissfully unaware of all that would follow.

This book would not exist without Adrian House, my mentor, edito-rial adviser, and dear friend. From the day I showed him my first manu-script, he has been unrelentingly supportive as I have tried to weave together a readable story about a messy, sprawling life strewn across six continents. Adrian's wife, Perella, provided a nourishing kitchen and safe haven where I had the time and peace not only to recall, but also to ex-press in writing, some of the extraordinary experiences that have shaped my life.

I am beyond grateful to John Campbell, who has been my wonderful warrior agent, nurturing this project with humor, skill, and total dedica-tion.

My final thanks are to Michael, who fuels me with his generous, cou-rageous, and loving spirit. Without his love, I would not have had a joy-ous destination to an endlessly challenging, but never boring, journey that has revealed extraordinary secrets of death—and life—beyond my wildest imaginings.

Credits

Grateful acknowledgment is given to the following photographers for the use of their work in this publication's photo insert: © Kathy Eldon: p. 10 *(top)*; the photographs on pp. 1–4, 13 *(top)*, and 14 *(middle and bottom)* appear courtesy of the Kathy Eldon archives. © Dan Eldon: pp. 5 *(top)*, 8, 10-11 *(Murder of the Messenger)*, and 11 *(top)*; the photographs on pp. 6 *(bottom)*, and 7 *(top and bottom)* appear courtesy of the Dan Eldon estate. © Chris Helcermananas-Benge: pp. 5 *(bottom)* and 6 *(top)*. © Yannis Bechrakis: p. 9. © Ruth Eldon Harper: p. 12. © Alan Palmer: p. 13 *(bottom)*. © Josh Feldman: p. 14 *(top)*. © Amy Eldon: p. 15 *(top)*. © Christian Calderon: p. 16.